Stephen Leacock

his remarkable life

Stephen Leacock
his remarkable life

Albert Moritz
& Theresa Moritz

Fitzhenry & Whiteside

Fitzhenry & Whiteside Limited
195 Allstate Parkway
Markham, Ontario L3R 4T8

In the United States:
121 Harvard Avenue, Suite 2
Allston, Massachusetts 02134

www.fitzhenry.ca   godwit@fitzhenry.ca

Fitzhenry & Whiteside acknowledges with thanks the Canada Council for the Arts, the Government of Canada through its Book Publishing Industry Development Program, and the Ontario Arts Council for their support of our publishing program.

National Library of Canada Cataloguing in Publication Data
Moritz, A.F
    Stephen Leacock: his remarkable life
Rev. Ed. Of Leacock, a biography.
Includes bibliographical references and index.
Hardcover : ISBN 1-55041-600-6
Paperback : ISBN 1-55041-737-1
1. Leacock, Stephen, 1869-1944. 2. Authors, Canadian (English) - 20th century - Biography. 3. Humorists, Canadian - Biography. I. Moritz, Theresa II. Title. III Title: Leacock: a biography.

PS8523.E15Z93 2002 PR9199.3L367Z78 2002

U.S. Cataloguing-in-Publication Data
Moritz, Theresa Anne, 1948-
    Stephen Leacock : his remarkable life / Theresa Moritz & Albert Moritz.
Rev. Ed. Of: Leacock, a biography / Moritz: Toronto: Stoddard, 1985. [400] .; ill.: cm
Includes bibliographical references and index.
Hardcover : ISBN 1-55041-600-6
Paperback : ISBN 1-55041-737-1
1. Leacock, Stephen, 1869-1944. 2. Humorists, Canadian - 20th century - Biography. 3. Authors, Canadian - 20th century - Biography. 4. College teachers - Canada - Biography. I. Moritz, A.F. (Albert Frank). II. Title. 818/.5209 B 21 CIP PR9199.3.L367.M67 2002

Design by Karen Petherick, Markham, Ontario
Front cover image courtesy of: Notman Photographic Archives, McCord Museum of Canadian History, Montreal;
Back cover image courtesy of: National Archives of Canada C-31930;
Flap image courtesy of: National Archives of Canada C-31967.
Printed and bound in Canada

To Jean Belden and Mary Elizabeth Moritz,
and to the memory of
Professor Louis H. Belden

Contents

Introduction

Have you heard this one? A bored Brit travelling in North America on business picks up a cheaply printed book at a Montreal train station newsstand and decides he's found the world's next big thing. The punchline? He has.

It was 1910. The Brit was publisher John Lane, whose firm The Bodley Head was mourning the death of its premiere North American talent, Mark Twain. Lane had paused in Montreal hoping to add to his collection of engravings and stumbled on *Literary Lapses*, a slender locally printed volume of humorous sketches. Lane never said what exactly caught him, but it may have been the first words of the first piece: "When I go into a bank I get rattled. The clerks rattle me; the wickets rattle me; the sight of the money rattles me; everything rattles me. The moment I cross the threshold of a bank and attempt to transact business there, I become an irresponsible idiot."

It was "My Financial Career." This poignant self-revelation of a man faced down by capitalist institutions and reduced to keeping his fortune in a sock has been part of popular culture for more than a century, from its first periodical appearance in 1895, through edition after edition of *Literary Lapses*, continuously in print since 1910, in many literary anthologies, and in the form of an animated short by Canada's National Film Board.

The author of this little classic and Lane's next big thing in transatlantic humour was Stephen Butler Leacock. Already forty when Lane discovered his self-published book, Leacock exploited the opportunity with ferocity, quickly establishing himself as a humorist of both genius and consistency; despite dizzying changes in the world he wrote about, and despite the perturbing, shifting waters of popular taste, he remained an acknowledged master of the art until his death in 1944. Each book that appeared, and there were many, was scrutinized for signs of advance or retreat from the standard he had set with *Literary Lapses* and the masterworks that followed it in rapid succession — *Nonsense Novels* (1911), *Sunshine Sketches of a Little Town* (1912) and *Arcadian Adventures with the Idle Rich* (1914). He had become a name.

The renovation of humour that Leacock accomplished would have been enough in itself to make his last thirty-four years a remarkable life for a man. But in an entirely different sphere, Leacock was already a name in 1910. It was against the advice of friends zealous to preserve his prestige and thriving career as economist and political pundit that he decided to put together the little book John Lane came across. His position as professor of political economy at McGill University in Montreal, where he had been hired even before completing his doctorate under Thorstein Veblen at the University of Chicago, had encouraged him to remedy the lack of a sound university textbook in the field with a book of his own. *Elements of Political Science* (1906) remained in wide circulation for the rest of his career; in fact, it was his largest single source of writing income, more lucrative than any of his humour bestsellers. He was known also as an expert and a popular lecturer on political and economic issues. In 1907 his standing won him the plum of a world lecture tour on behalf of the Cecil Rhodes Trust; he spoke on the future of the British Empire to audiences in the home country and its major colonies, stirring controversy wherever he went with his insistence that reform was necessary to make the Empire the globe's dominant political institution in the coming century.

This was the man Lane telegraphed to ask for permission to print a commercial edition of *Literary Lapses*. As remarkable as either career was the way in which Leacock proceeded to move back and forth for the rest of his life between the role of academic savant and the new identity Lane had opened to him, that of popular author accorded the same sort of celebrity-watching attention that was being lavished in those days on the still-new popular icons, movie stars.

When in 1921, after more than a decade of steadily mounting popularity, Leacock made an extensive tour of Great Britain as a humorous
lecturer, he found his steps dogged by the press and the populace, just
as were those of Charles Chaplin, Mary Pickford and Douglas
Fairbanks. In fact, both Chaplin and Hollywood's royal couple were
in England at the moment of Leacock's tour, and he found that he
was as popular as they were, and as much a focus of newspaper
attention. It was a fact that he treated with irony but used with brio.

However, such trips had to be fit in around his classroom
schedule at McGill: he never considered giving up his careers as an
educator and as an economist, seeking influence on national and
world leaders, in order to devote himself entirely to literature. As a
writer, too, he found that world events repeatedly directed the course
of his thought and work away from popular entertainments. Even
what he wrote for the popular audience refused to be confined to the
category of humour: histories, travel literature, biographies, philosophical explorations of the art of humour, autobiography — he
produced all of them, lectured in all these fields, and drew up plans
for more.

Most of this production occurs after the watershed year of 1910.
Equally fascinating, though, is the trajectory of Leacock's early years,
in which he prepared himself for the several professions in which he
won distinction. Born in England and only one generation away from
wealth and social position on both sides of his family, he was
condemned to join the tide of sanctimoniously cast-off grandchildren
of the British Empire. His father, Peter, was one of those suspect
offspring whom their parents scattered on the winds to the colonies,
so that they would not divide or otherwise devastate the accumulated
wealth at home. As harsh as was the treatment of Leacock's father by
his grandfather, sending him out ill-prepared to backwoods Ontario,
it echoed in Leacock's own actions when, at seventeen just out of
high school and the eldest son at home, he drove the now alcoholic
and abusive Peter to the rail head near the family's failing bush farm

and threatened him with violence if he ever returned.

That Leacock refused to be buried by the troubles that piled on him in his early years was not uniquely his accomplishment. He had a loving, determined mother; he had a tutor who encouraged him to take pride in his studies; there were tiny remittances on behalf of his education from the same relatives who had marshalled the original banishment to Canada; there was even a scapegrace uncle who, like a guardian angel, intervened to save him from a dead-end job so that he could finish university. Above all, perhaps, there was the tradition of learning and accomplishment he fell in love with from his earliest student days, a tradition that promised him rewards for excellence.

If there is a single theme that runs through all his experiences and all his writing, it is the theme of Anglo-American tradition: valuing it, criticizing and renovating it, democratizing it, and recognizing that it was inextricably involved in the language into which he had been born. Most centrally and radically, this theme became the project of creating Canada: a new version of English values, purified and modernized by means of an American-style sense of freedom and critical curiosity, synthesized in a way to remove the faults of each, and exemplified in a new type of personality, as represented by Stephen Leacock. Leacock was secretive about his personal and interpersonal life, the realms where unconscious psychology and psychological development are best manifested. But he left a voluminous and distinct record of what may be called his conscious psychology, because it was to this that he devoted his efforts, constructing a new man according to a new model that would dominate the childhood terrors and injustices to which he had been subjected. In himself he prophesied a world in which neither the closed English caste system nor the brutality of American competitive individualism would destroy the ideal he saw: full access to the fruits of civilization and freedom for anyone who made himself intellectually capable to treat civilization critically and creatively.

Leacock violated the most familiar model of the New World self-made man by maintaining that self-realization was not only breaking with the past but also acknowledging one's debt to it. Again and again, he struck out boldly in favour of the new, but always with an eye to preserving all that was valuable. This mixture of reverence for tradition with determined reform was evident especially in his approach to what he considered the most important among his various careers, education. In his own studies, he encompassed both the traditional rhetorical focus on language arts and the modern discipline of economics, and as an educator he worked for modernized and more realistic learning which yet based itself on the preservation of humane values. This same blending was evident in his politics, whose core principle was that Anglo-American traditions required immediate reform so that each person would have worthy fulfilling work at a level of remuneration that permitted a dignified life. It was a demand he never ceased to make, even as he campaigned for the maintenance of the British Empire in the belief that, if reformed, it was the best vehicle available to carry its members into the future. It was a demand evident in his devotion to Canada, which he saw as the potential beneficiary of the lessons a student of history might gain from studying both the accomplishments and the errors of its two closest relations, Great Britain and the United States. It was evident, perhaps most clearly of all, in his life, as he voraciously reached out for each new thing — in his studies, in his writing, in his lecturing, in his personal relationships with family and friends — while striving simultaneously to hold on to every cherished thing he loved.

The unity of Leacock's conscious personality is clear enough, but it is complex and in it he purposely set himself to overcome the separation of forces that are usually looked at as incompatible opposites. This is why it is common for those who write of him to emphasize not the harmonization of disparate elements but instead their incongruous juxtaposition. How could he be both economist and humorist? How could he be Canadian and yet aim his humour at both Brits and Yanks, as if he were one of them, and succeed? And there are other supposed incongruities that are mentioned over and over in characterizations of Leacock's life and work. How could he be brilliantly funny, and so insistent that the best humour is kindly, while on certain subjects, such as the rights of women and the human dignity of non-British subjects of the Empire, he determinedly failed to see the error in what he chose to conserve? How could he maintain that artistic quality matters and then allow himself for whatever reason — money, lack of time, pride, carelessness — to dilute the canon of his work with a certain amount of chaff? And didn't he sometimes err when he tried to blend a light treatment with a serious subject? And was not the philosopher of kindliness in fact squelching the ironic savagery that could sometimes be glimpsed under the polished surface of his prose, thus preventing the emergence of what the world perhaps needed, a great satirist in the tradition of Johnson, Swift and Dryden?

These difficult questions require other answers than simply an appeal to Leacock's struggle to retain tradition while reforming it. They lead into the psychology of a young man who felt entitled to belong and yet felt denied full belonging, who burned with genius and was dismayed to find the world didn't always welcome genius, who loved the learning that set him free but stopped short of the vision that freedom properly interpreted and distributed would require him sacrificing some things he was bent on preserving, who aspired to build a better world with the ennobling tool of humour but could not forebear wielding his great gift as a weapon. It takes us, with caution and under the guidance of Leacock himself, into the mystery of human laughter, which binds up in itself our darkest qualities, our fears, our competitiveness, our cowardice, our aggression, along with hope, generosity, and the most brilliant sallies of intellect.

Leacock's universality is due to the ideals and aspirations he conceived and the problems and failures he equally expressed. It is probable that humour is loved primarily as a relaxation, a release of tensions, a soothing of abrasions, but this means that humour to be great and relevant must contain and express, however covertly, those same irritations. Leacock's success in capturing the stresses of the world of his time, as well as eternal human stresses, caused him in his heyday to be considered — as he still should be considered — the next great American humorist after Mark Twain, and at the same time the first great British humorist of the twentieth century, and an innovator in both traditions. Although with Leacock his Canadian identity was a conscious, deeply-felt choice, even an invention, and although it may be tempting to suppose that it was his uniquely Canadian perspective that produced his humour, he offered his work to the entire English-speaking world and in fact to the world beyond. He was indeed that *rara avis*, a universal humorist, whose stream ran deep and pure when it was not muddied by the prejudicial exclusions he could succumb to.

We are indebted to all those who before us have cared enough for him to tell the story of his life; the notes to the text will give the specifics of our debt. Here we will only, paraphrasing Robert Benchley's praise of Leacock, say that we enjoyed their work so much that we have written everything they ever wrote: our book brings together all important and verifiable published facts on Leacock narrated and attested in various books, essays and articles. One recent work of scholarship deserves special note. Carl Spadoni's massive critical bibliography of Leacock's writings has enabled us to make significant corrections and additions to the account of his publishing career, and other aspects of his life, as compared with that found in our first assay at Leacock biography, *Stephen Leacock: A Biography*, published by Stoddart Publishers in 1985. Our narrative also makes full use of the two most important collections of Leacock's papers, those housed at the Stephen Leacock Memorial Home in Orillia, Ontario and the Redpath Library of McGill University, and of some smaller collections.

Finally, our thanks go to our editors at Fitzhenry & Whiteside, Richard Dionne and Evan Jones.

My Victorian Boyhood

According to a family history, the Leacock line's wealth and position, such as these were in the 1860s, sprang from an ancestor who had shipped out from England many years before as a cabin boy and had made a fortune in the wine trade, managing vineyards and exporting wine back to England. Although this wine business continued to flourish in Madeira as late as Stephen Leacock's lifetime, and he had cousins on the island, his own branch of the family's active involvement had ended long before his birth, when his great-grandfather John retired to take up the life of a country gentleman on the Isle of Wight, establishing there his estate, Oak Hill.[1] In nineteenth-century English society, Leacock's family was not landed gentry, having been at Oak Hill a bare three generations by the 1860s, but it was nevertheless an important and established part of the community; Leacock himself was never to share in the benefits and delights of this status.

A determining presence in Leacock's life was his grandfather, John's son, Thomas Murdock Leacock, the inheritor of Oak Hill and family autocrat in the days of the humorist's childhood. Although it appears he was permitted to visit this grandfather only once, Leacock devoted a considerable portion of his writings on his English childhood to Thomas, locating in him the motive force behind his own family's compulsion to make a living by hard farming and away from England. As Leacock portrayed him, Thomas was a man content to live in leisure and provide for his children nothing besides a push in the direction of working to support themselves. Leacock pointed out that his father in youth, his grandfather, and his great-grandfather John after having left business all had lived off accumulated wealth: "nobody in the family did any work (any real work) for three generations, after which, in my generation, we were all broke and had to start work, and work in the low down sense where you work by the hour..."[2] By the time he came along, the inheritance had been exhausted. Leacock's comments imply that he saw Thomas, who never had to support himself and never contributed anything to the family wealth, as the key actor in this decadence.

Leacock's father, Walter Peter, born on 15 January 1848, was a younger son of Thomas and enjoyed the pleasant upbringing filled with leisure activities and socializing that belonged to a scion of well-to-do Isle of Wight landowners.[3] Among Peter's social set from childhood was Agnes Butler, his future wife, who was a frequent summer visitor to the island that had been her mother's home. Yet when their romance began in 1866, Agnes being then twenty-two and Peter seventeen, she must have seemed to him almost a new acquaintance, for she had not been to the Isle of Wight in several years. During that time he had not only passed from childhood into adolescence, but was contemplating what he must have thought a premature and violent immersion in adulthood, his father having determined him for a life abroad. Thomas Murdock Leacock had already directed his two oldest sons, John and Charles, to careers as officers in the Royal Navy. He planned to send Peter, who had shown no distinction in education and no special ambition, overseas to farm.[4]

The young woman who, in that Isle of Wight summer of 1866,

encountered the boy faced with this difficult prospect was herself at a crossroads, that which for a daughter of the Victorian upper middle class led either to marriage or to spinsterhood. Agnes Emma Butler was born on 8 January 1844, the youngest child of the Reverend Stephen Butler (Leacock's eponym) and Caroline Linton Palmer.[5] Each of Agnes's parents had been married and widowed and each had several children by the earlier union; a half-brother of Agnes's received a Victoria Cross for heroic service in the Indian Mutiny of 1857. The Reverend Stephen Butler was a Hampshire man who held the living of Soberton, where Agnes was born. However, he and Caroline Palmer had been married on the Isle of Wight, in the bride's home parish. There Caroline and her family had been friends of young Peter Leacock's paternal grandmother, at the time Mrs. Young due to remarriage after being widowed; the Youngs had a home, Westridge, not far from Thomas Murdock Leacock's Oak Hill.

By the age of eleven Agnes was an orphan, her mother having died when she was only five and her father six years later. Those six years seem to have been difficult ones for the Reverend Stephen Butler, a distinguished clergyman who by that time held the living of Holy Trinity Church in Southampton. After his wife's death he suffered nervous attacks and generally failing health, and was at least once carried from his pulpit in the throes of what seems to have been an epileptic seizure. Thickening the atmosphere of misfortune, Agnes had an early childhood fall and a resulting concussion that affected her health throughout her life. Balancing such adversities, she was well cared for and educated by attentive relations on both sides of her family. On her mother's side, she was the niece of three distinguished university educators: Herbert Bradley, dean of Merton College, Oxford University; Granville Bradley, headmaster at Marlborough; and Andrew Bradley, classics master at Liverpool College. Through her father's mother, Agnes was descended from British diplomat Sir Henry Lushington, father of Tennyson's brother-in-law Edmund Law Lushington. Her father's family, the Butlers, had been established for

Agnes Leacock (née Butler), Stephen Leacock's mother, photographed about 1855, twelve years before her marriage to Walter Peter Leacock.
Courtesy National Archives of Canada C-31913.

more than one hundred fifty years in their home, Bury Lodge, at Hambledon Downs, Hampshire.

Despite the loss of her parents, Agnes remembered her childhood as a happy time. She lived with the family of an uncle, the Reverend Thomas Butler, first at a cottage near Bury Lodge and later, following the death of her grandfather Butler, at the Lodge itself. Educated at private boarding schools and at a fashionable London finishing school, she became an accomplished young woman whose active life included church work and watercolour painting. In short, her background and upbringing were the conventional ones that, in the nineteenth century, produced the polished wife of a gentleman. By the age of twenty-two she was facing her destiny, to succeed or fail in finding a marriage at her social status.

The few details now known of the courtship of Agnes Butler and Peter Leacock come from an account of her early life that Agnes wrote much later, in Canada, at the request of her children.[6] According to this, another of her uncles, the Reverend Charles Butler, took her to the Isle of Wight in the summer of 1866. She related that Peter, who was fond of sailing, would come in the evenings in his own boat to Seaview, where she and her Uncle Charles were staying. She would slip out to meet him and would go out on the water in Peter's blue boat. The couple spent the days together at Oak Hill and went to visit Peter's relations, the Youngs, at Westridge. Their liaison continued into the following season. Agnes's sister, Kate, was visiting in England briefly from her home in Calcutta, and Agnes spent much of the fall with her at Portsmouth, where Peter came frequently to visit her. In mid-December Agnes took a trip to London to visit other family members for Christmas. Peter followed soon after and they were married clandestinely. Agnes wrote:

> I can never think of it without sorrow and shame for deceiving my kind good uncles. It was Uncle Charles I was staying with — he went to the station and took

my return ticket to Waterloo Bridge for me little thinking I was going to meet Peter and be married to him. They had nothing against his character, but he was not quite eighteen and a Roman Catholic and going to the Colonies. They had not then decided where.

She herself would turn twenty-three in seven days.

Agnes and Peter were married on 1 January 1867 in a ceremony attended only by two witnesses and the officiating minister, the Reverend J.L. Macdonald, at All Saints Church near Paddington Station in London. Their engagement was kept secret from both families until after the wedding had taken place. It seems likely that the cloaked romance included a sexual liaison that resulted in pregnancy; the couple's first son was born only seven months after the wedding.[7] Certainly a reason for haste, this might well also explain the couple's dissimulation: Agnes must have feared the reprehension of a highly respectable, church-connected family in which she held an orphaned and dependent position, while Peter, if he was not motivated simply by a blundering momentum, may have hoped for easier terms from his own father, given that he was now a family man. Thomas Murdock Leacock, however, had once and for all destined his son for the life of a South African farmer.[8]

After the wedding, the couple took rooms in Burand Street, Russell Square; their colonial destination having been chosen for them, they bought tickets for Natal. In the period before embarkation the Butler family refused to allow any visits from Peter, and not only because of the secret marriage. The staunch Anglican churchmen of the family had been disappointed in the Leacocks years before when Peter's mother had converted to Roman Catholicism and had caused all her children to be baptized in that religion. Prior to this event, the families had been close enough that Agnes's father had been the godfather of Peter's brother, Charles, in his original, Anglican baptism.

Although there is no sign that Peter actively practised the Roman Catholic religion, his conversion nevertheless was a barrier for Agnes's relations. Thus, Agnes and Peter began life together with a baby on the way, the ill will of both their families, and the ironic gift of a far-off farm that seemed meant to get them out of the way. There was also a bit of capital that Agnes brought. A formal marriage settlement, written after the wedding, reveals that she came to the marriage with four thousand pounds' worth of investments that had been made for her by her family and from which she drew a small income.[9]

In March 1867 Agnes and Peter took ship on the S.S. *Burton Hatter* for their first venture as colonial farmers. They were both good sailors and enjoyed the trip until the final week, which was spent in sight of the Bluff of Natal in repeated, fruitless attempts to land. The farm that had been purchased for them, near Pietermauritzburg, was a developed property. "Those were the days of sailing ships, of infinite distances and long farewells," wrote Leacock of his parents' adventure. "They went 'up country' to Maritzburg in oxcarts and then out beyond it to settle." A land agent was there upon their arrival to show them around the comfortable house and farm buildings, facilities for raising livestock, and one hundred fifty acres given over to the growing of corn. It was, Leacock wrote, "long before the days of diamonds and gold created the South Africa of sorrows,"[10] the time when discoveries of precious metals and gems were to make South Africa a goal of late-nineteenth-century economic adventurers. In 1867 the country was known in England as a place admirably suited to lucrative farming. Early in the century the British government had conducted studies of the relative merits of southern Africa and Canada as destinations for emigrants, and had decided entirely in favour of Africa because of the milder, more familiar climate and the country's more settled way of life.

Agnes's autobiographical narrative for her children gives an account of the young couple's journey to Pietermauritzburg and the further thirty-mile trek to the farm. She recalled it as a genteel expe-

7

Leacock's grandfather, Thomas Murdock Leacock.
Courtesy National Archives of Canada C-22899.

dition, an exercise in civilized dabbling at "roughing it." She travelled with an Irish maid, and her retriever ran alongside the party and harried the bearers transporting the family's heavy luggage. The English community they found at their African farm was reminiscent of home, even to the extent of being embroiled in a dispute over Anglican church matters, precipitated by the famous John William Colenso, mathematician and Bishop of Natal, who was questioning the literal interpretation of the Old Testament (his "mild aspersions on the Pentateuch," Leacock wrote, "opened the way, like a water leak in a dam, to heresies that swept away the literal interpretation of Scripture"), and vigorously insisting Christian moral principles be applied to the problem of race relations in South Africa. The gracious community, the mid-Victorian atmosphere of lusty public debate over questions of history, theology and social ethics, all this familiarity seemed a promising beginning. But when economic hardship resulted from the destruction of the first crop by locusts, the couple quickly decided that the farm was untenable. They returned home at once, Agnes complaining of the discomforts of the climate. The one tangible thing they carried back from the trip was their first son, Thomas James, born on 14 July 1867.[11]

During the next eight years, Agnes and Peter were reduced to a lower social and economic level than they had known prior to their wedding, or than they had apparently expected to maintain in Africa. They were poor and adrift upon their reappearance in England, and their fortunes persistently sank. They were not welcome to their families, and they spent no more carefree summers devoted wholly to boating and other leisure pursuits on the Isle of Wight or in Hampshire country seats. Instead, they moved often and to ever smaller homes. Leacock later pointed out that, of the six children his mother brought with her to Canada in 1876, only two had been born in the same place.[12]

Although the African farm failed, Thomas Murdock Leacock persisted in directing Peter towards an overseas farming career; he made it clear that this was the only future he would help to finance. There is evidence that Peter sought, at least fitfully, some occupation that would permit him to remain and prosper in England. In 1869, on Stephen's birth certificate, he listed his occupation as "asphalt contractor," a line of work which, to whatever extent he pursued it, did not render him independent of his father.[13] His principal occupation at this time was to study farming in fulfillment of his father's demand that he should prepare himself for another trip abroad. It seems likely, then, that Thomas attributed the South African retreat to his son's softness and incompetence, and was in no mood to do anything but demand better performance. For Agnes, the early years of married life represented a dismaying change from her childhood and adolescence as the niece and ward of a cultured, prosperous clergyman. In reduced circumstances she followed her husband to a series of small towns including Swanmore (Hampshire), Shoreham-by-Sea (Sussex) and Porchester, near Plymouth and famous as the birthplace of Charles Dickens. Her work as a mother increased almost every year. After Thomas James, the son born in Africa, there followed Arthur Murdock (born 29, 1868) and then, at Swanmore, Hampshire, a village on England's quiet southern coast, her third child and third son, Stephen.[14]

Stephen Butler Leacock was born on 30 December 1869,[15] just two days before his parents' third wedding anniversary, in the middle year of Queen Victoria's reign, and was baptized on 23 January 1870[16] at the Anglican church of Saint Barnabas, which stands on a hill near the cathedral city of Winchester. Grace Pierpoint, a friend of Agnes from her London finishing school, was Stephen's godmother. Swanmore was only a brief station in the wandering existence of the family during Leacock's first six years. Located about eighteen kilometres south of Winchester, it has grown considerably since the Leacocks lived there, but the cottage in which Stephen was born, in a second-story bedroom under thatched eaves, is still standing near the centre of town, with a historical marker to memorialize the writer's birth.[17] In 1869 the building was three centuries old, according to its present owners; although far from luxurious, it was a comfortable and respectable accommodation for the small family, not by any means the tenement the Leacocks would inhabit in Porchester during the period immediately before their emigration to Canada. When writing late in life of his childhood, Leacock commented that Porchester, his family's later residence, and not Swanmore, was the site of his only clear English memories, for he could recollect incidents and scenes from only his last two years in the country. The Swanmore home appears not to have occupied an important place in the minds of any of his family, for it is seldom referred to. In fact, for much of his life Leacock incorrectly believed his birthplace had been not Swanmore, Hampshire, but the village of Swanmore near Ryde on the Isle of Wight, where his paternal grandfather and great-grandmother had their homes.

Agnes found herself unwelcome to her husband's family and ostracized by most of her own. However, it seems likely that she and Peter lived in Swanmore and then in Porchester because this enabled them to be close to Butlers who were still sympathetic and from whom the young family received, through Agnes, more assistance than from Thomas Murdock Leacock. From Swanmore she was permitted to visit Bury Lodge, but had to do so alone, without her husband or children. The Reverend Charles Butler was one family member who did not cut her off; he apparently remained on cordial terms with her. As for Porchester, even though Leacock later wrote sarcastically that "we were placed in Porchester so that we couldn't get to the Isle of Wight too often,"[18] it may have been chosen because Agnes's uncle Charles was serving there during the mid-1870s; Leacock recalled hearing him preach and visiting with him in the town.

Porchester was where the Leacocks waited for Peter to bring them to America. In 1874 Peter was sent by his father to a new farm, in Kansas, "because at that time," wrote Leacock, "the railway only

Leacock photographed at Ryde on the Isle of Wight, probably in 1875.
Courtesy National Archives of Canada C-31959.

got that far."[19] There he was supposed to prepare the property for his family, which by then included Charles John Gladstone (Charlie), born 6 December 1871, and a first daughter, Agnes Arabella (Missie), born 15 March 1873. While Peter was away in the United States, presumably readying the house and perhaps seeing to the planting of a first crop, the five-year-old Stephen wrote him to announce the birth of another new baby, Edward Peter (Teddy), on 6 January 1875:

Porchester
Ja

My dear Dadda
I thank you for the book. Jim has a young Xtmas [sic]
tree We have got a new Baby he was born on the 6th
We very often go in to Fareham

Your affec son
Stephen [20]

Soon after, Peter returned with the news that the farm in Kansas had been destroyed by grasshoppers. With very little delay, his father sent him out again, this time to Ontario. In his autobiographical writings Leacock referred scornfully to his grandfather's determination to settle his children away from the Isle of Wight: "I gather that he wanted the Island for himself and didn't want his sons to come crowding on to it. That's why they were sent out across the world wherever it was farthest."[21] For many generations past, throughout the centuries of England's substantial empire, the provision for younger sons in wealthy families had often taken the form, for gifted and troublesome children alike, of the purchase of land in the colonies, in the hope that money would buy more abroad and provide a better future than was available in the mother country. Hence, Thomas was but emulating the long-established conduct of higher orders than his own in English society. He was later to provide, if this is the word, in much the same way for another younger son, E.P., memorialized by Stephen Leacock in his late essay "My Remarkable Uncle."[22]

After the Natal debacle, Thomas lifted his interdict at least once, the only Oak Hill visit Leacock remembers in his reminiscences. On this occasion he made the future humorist a present of a fragment of wood from the American frigate *Chesapeake*, captured by the British *Shannon* in a famous War of 1812 naval battle off Boston Harbor. This became a possession Leacock treasured throughout his life, developing a hobby-obsession over the later fate of the *Chesapeake*, whose timbers he made a point of researching to their eventual destinations. He traced many of the best beams to a corn mill in Wickham, near Porchester, and found the mill still operating when in 1921 he made a triumphal platform speaking tour of Great Britain. In his last years he was seeking a magazine to publish an essay he had written on the subject, and he reused much of the material in the first chapter of his never-completed autobiography. But the visit on which he received this gift was also the single trip to his grandfather's home that he records. The wood fragment may have been given to young Stephen only in celebration of the fact that his parents were about to leave England for good. Leacock was isolated from the large extended families that existed on both the maternal and paternal sides; in writing of a 1921 visit to Bury Lodge, he revealed that there had been for him only one fleeting childhood visit to Hambledon Downs and his mother's family seat: "We went down into Hambledown village and to the 'pub,' where I had all that peculiar gratification that goes with 'the return of the native.' There were several old men round and it was astonishing what they could remember over a pint of beer and still more over a quart.... I didn't mention that I had been there only once before, for ten minutes, as a child of six."[23]

Leacock's fondest reminiscences of England were of the town of Porchester, opposite Plymouth. He lived there for two years, until the

The Leacock family photographed on the Isle of Wight, about 1870.
From left: Thomas Murdock Leacock, Edward Philip ("E.P.") Leacock,
Walter Peter Leacock, Stephen's older brothers Jim and Dick, and
Agnes holding Stephen.
Courtesy National Archives of Canada C-31928.

spring following his sixth birthday, when his family departed for Canada, and had his earliest few months of formal education at a Porchester private school that his two older brothers also attended. The only lesson he remembered from it was his first instruction in geography, the teacher holding up a map and leading the children in a chorus, "The top of the map is always the north, the bottom south, the right-hand east, the left-hand west!" He was tempted to ask whether the top might be the north only because the teacher held it that way, but feared the ruler. What he gratefully remembered about Porchester and the Portsmouth area was, first, the depth of English history that it held in its buildings and associations, and second, the typical if somewhat fairytale-like Englishness, redolent of Gilbert-and-Sullivan fantasy, that he recalled in it.

Porchester was named for Porchester Castle (the word "Porchester" meaning "port castle") and in Leacock's day was a tiny settlement on the west shore of Portsmouth harbour. In the neighbourhood was Paul's Grove, where according to ancient and apocryphal legend Saint Paul had preached to the Britons. The castle itself, a huge turreted rectangle, was mainly of Norman construction but had been built upon an earlier Roman fortification. Inside its precincts the Normans had, in the twelfth century, erected the Priory Church of Saint Mary in the Close, restored after fire damage through the munificence of Queen Anne. This was the church of Stephen's "uncle" Charles (Agnes's uncle), where the family attended Sunday services. Stephen remembered Charles Butler's satisfaction that Porchester was unaffected by new religious movements, that no one there attended church revival meetings or suffered sudden conversions but got religion" gradually during "eighty years of drowsy Sundays."[24] When in adulthood he looked back to England, he could see in Porchester a legacy that was transmitted to him through the Victorian era but went much farther back: to the Napoleonic wars, the era of empire building and the rise of the Royal Navy, and beyond to the medieval, Norman, Roman and legendary pre-Roman history of the nation. Perhaps this is a source of the strong and poetic sense of history Leacock possessed.

In childhood Leacock had been well aware of the symbolic presence of Nelson's flagship *Victory*, which had been retired to Portsmouth harbour, but it was only later, probably, that he realized how close chance had placed him to Charles Dickens's birthplace, for he did not read his first Dickens book, *The Pickwick Papers*, until he was living in Canada. His Porchester school stood on a rise that looked down on the street where Dickens had been born, in 1812, at 1 Mile End Terrace (today 393 Commercial Road, Portsea, the Dickens Museum), and to which the novelist had returned in 1838 while touring the Portsmouth area to research *Nicholas Nickleby* (1838-39). Dickens's death at fifty-eight had occurred the year after Leacock was born, and as a young boy Leacock did not know yet that he was living formative years in the very scenes that had also helped shape the writer whose work would become definitively important to him.

If the mature Leacock shared with Dickens the passionate belief that English tradition must be reformed to preserve, refine and democratize its advantages, it was in part because both writers spent in the Porchester locale some bittersweet early years that impressed them with a deep love of their heritage and a realization of how inse- cure their possession of it might be. Leacock, in addition, was acutely aware that he had been meant to be born, if the person who later became Stephen Leacock would have existed at all, in South Africa, and that his own way of being English was entirely due to what Canada had enabled him to make of himself. In 1921 he revisited the house his family had occupied in Porchester and to his adult eyes it was a poor place. He found pathos in the tiny hallway his mother had called a parlour and the cupboard she had "had the nerve" to term a breakfast room. "I felt hurt and humiliated coming out. I hadn't real- ized how used I had become to being well off, to living in comfort and having everything.... After that I had not heart to go on and see the castle. It might have turned out to be just nothing as beside, say, the Royal York Hotel in Toronto.... It is better not to go back to the place you came from. Leave your memory as it is. No reality will ever equal it."[25]

His mother, however, transmitted to him in Canada not humiliation at having been hounded from family and country but pride in ancestry and national origin. If Leacock continued to reflect on his English roots in these mid-Victorian years on the southern coast, this was largely due to the care with which Agnes protected and nourished them. She stamped him with the notion that he sprang from the union of two established English lines: "My family were Hampshire people on both sides, not of course the real thing going back to the Conquest, but not bad."[26] His whole career as man and writer expresses the polar impulses to valorize his English heritage and to mock it, his humour often springing, as perhaps all humour does, from a belittlement that depends on and obliquely honours what it tears down. His wry bitterness achieves some of its effect from the way that Leacock the sardonic, wounded outcast keeps fascinatedly hanging around the object of his potshots.

Leacock's written reminiscences of his English years are from late in life; basically autobiographical in character, they are dominated nonetheless by his instinct for highlighting incongruous details and embroidering upon certain facts. He does not provide anything like a detailed narrative. He himself could recall only a few scenes, feelings and events of his final two English years, and family tradition appears to have been scant, indicating that he received little communication from his father and that his mother's memories were carefully crafted to edify rather than convey bitter experiences in circumstantial detail. It is also true, though, that the inner life of Leacock the child is absent from his accounts of the period, including his major one, the early pages of his planned autobiography, the four completed chapters of which were posthumously published as *The Boy I Left Behind Me* (1946). For this book he drew upon an earlier

18

essay, "Migration in English Literature," which he had published in *My Remarkable Uncle* (1942); he also alluded to his years in England in the title essay of that volume, the story of his uncle E.P.'s experiences in Canada. All these works embody the inimitable persona of Leacock's late maturity and old age, blending antic humour with a sense of the tears of things, kindly mockery of human foibles and philosophical pardon with disquieting intimations of eternal futility. But they all exclude, almost studiously, any description of the perceptions, emotions, thoughts, and judgments of the boy of six. This boy, as he was in himself, is kept hidden as if to shield him, while the simple fact of his long ago existence becomes a vehicle for the probing wit and the mobile colourings of irony and melancholy that belong to Leacock's accomplished prose.

Leacock's assessment of his English childhood in *The Boy I Left Behind Me*, in so far as any clear opinion emerges from his string of anecdotes and jests, can only be termed cheerful in comparison with his family's actual situation. He places emphasis on the historic associations of his family's residences, in part because he could supply the deficiencies of memory from such material, but also to avoid a too-direct recounting of his early years. For example, in describing his parents' brief African episode, he gives most of his attention to Bishop Colenso, whose liberal theology had so enraged members of the southern African Anglican community that some of them had been refusing to have their children baptized by him. Leacock's oldest brother was one of the infants involved in this controversy. Similarly, in speaking of his mother's family seat, the Butler ancestral home, Bury Lodge, he mentioned only its close associations with the history of the game of cricket. His account of Porchester mixes scant memories, incidents from his 1921 return visit, and information that would be suitable for a tourist guidebook or history. Though Leacock's own empathetic sense of the past enriches his account of the street in which Dickens was born, Nelson's flagship swinging at anchor in the harbour and the ancient church where Charles Butler served, the most vivid pages describe scenes of his later visit, such as his attempt to evoke some reminiscences of Butler from a local nonagenarian: "'There was the meanest man that ever came to this village. He'd 'a stopped every poor man's beer, he would, if he'd had his way. Don't talk to me of the Reverend Charles Butler.' I decided not to."[27]

One of the most interesting features of Leacock's reminiscences is his changing interpretation of his father. In these works written in close succession during the last years of his life, he is increasingly ready to express blame toward his father for not accepting family responsibilities or dealing effectively with the conditions of his life. In 1912 in a brief autobiographical sketch written as an introduction to *Sunshine Sketches of a Little Town*, Leacock passed off the family's move to Canada in a joke: "My parents migrated to Canada in 1876, and I decided to go with them."[28] In writing of his uncle E.P., who drew his father into disastrous Canadian land speculations, he portrayed Peter as a simple man, well-intentioned but ill-suited for business and practical affairs. But *The Boy I Left Behind Me* cast doubt on Peter's willingness to do what was necessary to support his family. Leacock glanced skeptically at the locusts of Africa and the grasshoppers of Kansas and implied that he exonerated them from full responsibility in the failure of Peter's pre-Canadian farming ventures. Pointing with tactful reticence to a deeper problem, he characterized Peter's "study" of farming in Hampshire as a series of beer-drinking bouts with local agriculturalists; even at this, he says, his father was bested.

Leacock left Porchester in 1876 and was not to return to England, even on a short visit, for many years. The decision to come to Canada was made by or for his parents in the mid-1870s, almost immediately after Peter's return from Kansas. Thomas now bought his son a one-hundred acre farm in Ontario near Lake Simcoe, to which Peter went early in 1876, leaving Agnes to prepare the six children for a voyage across the Atlantic. Years later, Leacock remembered that his mother cried at the thought of leaving England; it is probable that she knew, despite her earlier retreat to England from Africa and her husband's from Kansas, there would be no coming back from Canada. Her journey with her children began in Liverpool on a ship of the Allan Line, the *Sarmatian*, a vessel that combined steam and sail and that so impressed the young Leacock that he carefully followed its subsequent career until it was broken up after the First World War.

For Stephen and the other five children, the departure was high adventure. When the *Sarmatian* sailed in May of 1876, the Canada that lay before them was in its ninth year since Confederation, which had united the colonies of New Brunswick, Nova Scotia and Canada (divided to form Ontario and Quebec) into the Dominion of Canada, a self-governing nation. In 1869, the year of Leacock's birth, the young country had met one of its first serious challenges: Louis Riel and the Métis (prairie-dwelling descendants of French and Aboriginal intermarriage) opposed westward expansion in the Red River Rebellion near the site of present-day Winnipeg. By 1876 Canada had grown to reach from sea to sea by adding to the original four provinces three new ones, Prince Edward Island, Manitoba and British Columbia, as well as the vast Northwest Territories. The first Dominion census (1871) counted 3,689,257 inhabitants, but immigration was increasing the number rapidly; by 1891 the population had grown to 4,833,239. Now the Leacocks were added to this flood of new entrants, the great majority of whom in those years came from Great Britain and provided the country's soldiers, lawyers, engineers, storekeepers, politicians, professionals, journalists, educators, shopkeepers, skilled workers and labourers. Leacock later wrote of the stirring sensation of the departure and of the sight of the receding cliffs of Dover. But his chief recollection was of his first glimpse of Canada, the Gaspé coast, and of the striking contrast its bright, rocky harshness made with the verdurous benignity of the English shore.

Leacock's father, Walter Peter Leacock, photographed at Sutton, Ontario, on 15 July, 1877.
Courtesy National Archives of Canada C-22898.

The Leacock family as it was at the farm in Egypt, Ontario.
Courtesy National Archives of Canada C-25716.

The Struggle to Make
Us Gentlemen

Agnes and the six children began their Canadian journey at Montreal, where the *Sarmatian* docked in May 1876; they transferred to a river steamer for the trip to Toronto and passed Kingston on a festive 24 May Victoria Day, not a holiday in England. Their destination was a backwoods farm south of Lake Simcoe, a large and beautiful body of water, a natural magnet and centre for settlement, which lies due north of Toronto. A train — "a funny train it seemed to us, all open and quite unlike the English carriages" — took them from Toronto to Newmarket, forty-five miles north and at that time the nearest railhead to the south shore of Lake Simcoe, another seventeen miles beyond. The Leacock farm lay on a rise of ground four miles south of the lake. The nearest sizable community was the south shore village of Sutton; the Leacocks' property was closest to the tiny settlement of Egypt in the Township of Georgina.

Peter, with a hired hand, met his family at the railway station and packed them and their belongings into two horse-drawn wagons to make the rough, hours-long trek to the farm over dirt tracks and on corduroy roads through cedar swamps. He told the children crowded on the bucking wagon that the narrow dirt road through empty fields was their road, and Egypt their village. Leacock records the feeling that they had left behind the quiet charms of a traditional English town overlooking one of the world's busiest harbours for a straggling village of taverns and one general store, which was the only relief from miles of swamp. The farm dismayed them further. "Our own farm with its buildings was, I will say, the damnedest place I ever saw," Leacock wrote. Even the modest home Agnes and the children had shared in Porchester made these new surroundings seem dismal and forbidding. Agnes said nothing at the time but she later told Stephen that her first sight of the home in which she expected to spend the rest of her life had broken her heart.[1]

Today the trip from Toronto to the farmstead can be accomplished in a pleasant drive of little more than an hour. Egypt is now only a crossroads, marked by a sign and one building dating from the turn of the century, a former one-room school that is now the Egypt Women's Institute. There is no Leacock shrine either at the village or at the farm; in fact, few but local people know where the family once lived. The site of Peter Leacock's hundred-acre farm is now the west half of Lot 6, Concession 4, in the Township of Georgina; it stretches north of Concession Road 4 about three hundred yards west of the road's intersection with York Regional Road 18, known locally as the "Egypt sideroad." A rough tractor trail leads north from Concession Road 4 to the northern boundary of the farm, which is situated on a rise that provides a panoramic view to the south of fertile farmlands dotted with houses and barns. Here at the end of the property furthest from the road stood the buildings. As in Africa, an established working farm, rather than an undeveloped tract of land, had been purchased for Peter, but it turned out to be a poor one, partly in Leacock's estimation due to the inconsistency of his father, who "alternated furious industry with bouts of idleness and drinking," and who knew little more about farming than his hired man, "Old Tommy," a Yorkshire native who "had tried a bush farm of his own and failed."

The farm house was of logs covered with clapboard. Leacock saw it this way: "Someone had built a cedar log-house and then covered it round with clap-board and then someone else had added three rooms stuck along the front with more clap-board, effectually keeping all the sunlight out. Even towards the sunset there were no windows, only the half-glass top of a side door." Shortly afterwards Peter enlarged it; his own addition was of frame lumber and lath and plaster, a form of construction even less intelligently adapted to the climate, and proved much colder than the rest of the building: "Everything froze when the thermometer did." After the family had left the farm but during Leacock's lifetime, the original portion of the house was removed, which came as a surprise to family members when they made a nostalgic pilgrimage to the site in the 1940s.[2] Other farm buildings included three log barns, two of them running east and west and the other running north and south between their western edges, so that the three buildings formed a U. The farm's facilities were completed by a large implement shed and outhouse with an attached smokehouse. None of the buildings is now standing on the site; the last of them, the house, burned down on 25 February 1960. The land is still under cultivation, but the owner lives some miles distant.

Peter and Tommy worked the farm, growing wheat and other grains. The cash crop was wheat, but during the depression that hit Ontario in the 1870s wheat rarely returned a profit and bankruptcies were common. Leacock remembered only one year in which the farm did not work at a loss. The property also included grazing land for cattle, a market garden and a yard for a few sheep, chickens and pigs. Leacock was up at 6 a.m. to tend the cows and other animals, and in the summer had special responsibility for the garden. The farm seemed to him "one big stink...the phew! of the stable — not so bad as the rest, the unspeakable cowshed, sunk in the dark below a barn, beyond all question of light or ventilation, like a medieval oubliette; the henhouse, never cleaned and looking like a guano deposit island off the coast of Chile, in which the hens lived if they could and froze dead if they couldn't..."[3]

On this property the family lived in virtual isolation. The nearest neighbour was almost a mile away, the roads were poor, and bad weather often made travel altogether impossible. The one important break in this solitude was the weekly trip to Saint George Church in Sutton, which the children contrived to make a pleasure excursion as well as a religious observance by meeting with friends to swim, boat or skate. Sutton was only four miles away but the trip took at least an hour by wagon, involving as it did many hills and stretches of difficult road. The boys were accustomed to walking behind the wagon to rest the horse on the inclines and to lighten the load on the declines. If conditions isolated the Leacocks, they were also separated from their neighbours by Agnes's determination to keep the children away from influences she considered deleterious. At risk, in particular, were their cultivated manners and accents. All of the nearby families but one were considered undesirable. The Leacock children were taken out of the local Georgina Township school, which was located on or near the site of the present Egypt Women's Institute, built as a school in 1900 to replace the one that the older Leacock children attended for a time, this first school having burned down in the 1890s.[4] Stephen had studied there for a little more than a year before Agnes became dissatisfied with it, in part because during the winter months the trip was often very difficult, but mostly because Agnes feared loss of habits of speech, behaviour and dress that the children retained from England. In the summers she would never allow them to participate in the local practice of going barefoot; it was "a question of caste and thistles,"[5] Leacock said. She succeeded at least partly in her efforts: Leacock maintained his British intonation throughout life.

The isolation of life on the farm, located in a "lost corner of Ontario,"[6] was perhaps the dominant impression Leacock carried away from his late childhood and early adolescence; his writings refer to it again and again. The railway did not reach Sutton until 1879, and he did not see a train for the three years between his first arrival in Canada and the gala opening of the Sutton station. Although

Canadian inventor Alexander Graham Bell had patented his telephone in the year that the Leacocks immigrated, and although Ontario was the scene for some pioneering firsts in telephone technology (the first long-distance call, for example, in 1878), home service was still years away. Besides letters, there were no means of communication except to meet and converse face to face. The population of the district was sparse and far-flung; to travel one of the monotonous farm roads at night was to pass through miles of darkness broken only by an occasional glimpse of a kerosene lamp from the window of a distant farm house. There was a silence, Leacock recalled, that no city dweller could imagine. "We lived in an isolation unknown, in these days of radio, anywhere in the world... There were no newspapers. Nobody came and went. There was nowhere to come and go. In the solitude of the dark winter nights the stillness was that of eternity."[7] The years from 1876 to 1882 were for him "a six-year unbroken sentence." He feared above all to discover that these conditions would for him be perpetual.

Edward Philip ("E.P.") Leacock as a Member of Legislative Assembly, Manitoba, 1878.

Courtesy National Archives of Canada C-31963.

Into this family solitude, in the fall of 1878, burst Peter's younger brother, Edward Philip, Leacock's "Remarkable Uncle." E.P., as he was called, was two years younger than Peter and was being provided for, much as Peter had been, with financing intended to settle him in the colonies. He was on his way to the Canadian west, drawn by tales of the fortune to be made in real estate in the rapidly opening province of Manitoba. A rail route across the United States to the Pacific Ocean was already completed, and John A. Macdonald, campaigning that fall to be returned as prime minister, was promising that soon there would be a Canadian railway from coast to coast. Immigrants were going to the prairies, and the hard times in Ontario drove many settlers off their failing or bankrupt farms in hopes of better fortune farther west. The children were in awe of their dashing bachelor uncle, fresh from a tour of the Mediterranean and bright with anecdotes of distinguished friends. E.P. remained at the farm long enough to become involved in the national election. He was conservative and an expert at barroom canvassing, where he used his name-dropping claims of acquaintance with English aristocrats, knights and military commanders to flatter local farmers and tradesmen into voting for the Macdonald Conservatives. Extending his efforts to the speaking platform in Toronto as well as in the Lake Simcoe district, E.P. stayed in Ontario long enough to see Macdonald returned to power and then moved west. He might have "stayed to reap the fruits," Leacock commented, but "Ontario at that day was too small a horizon" for E.P., who blithely proclaimed "that the star of the Empire glittered in the west..."[8] He wanted Peter to follow him.

From the beginning, life on the farm had not suited Stephen's father; accustomed as he had become to long, if pointless, trips in distant parts, he found the promise of quick wealth in the west far more attractive than the uncertain fortunes available to him in Egypt, Ontario, in those days of depression when "mortgages fell like snowflakes, and farmers were sold up, or sold out, or went 'to the States,' or faded humbly underground." It is difficult to date Peter's departure to join E.P. in Manitoba, but it probably came sometime in mid-1880 or in 1881; in *The Boy I Left Behind Me* Leacock acknowledged that he himself had been mistaken in earlier writings that stated Peter had left for the west with E.P. after the fall 1878 election. Peter was in Egypt early in 1880, for Maymee Douglas Leacock was born on 24 November 1880. Leacock's two older brothers, when they started classes at Toronto's Upper Canada College in November 1881, gave their father's profession as farmer, while Stephen's 1882 registration form listed Peter as a real-estate agent in Winnipeg. It seems that he could not have left Ontario before the late spring of 1880. At the other limit, it is known he arrived in Manitoba while the boom in real estate, which collapsed in 1882, was still underway.[9]

To finance his expedition Peter held "a sale of our farm," in Leacock's words, "with refreshments, old-time fashion, for the buyers," at which the "poor, lean cattle and the broken machines fetched less than the price of the whisky."[10] It is never made entirely clear by Leacock or in family records what this sale meant, but it was not a sale of the property itself. The farm continued to be worked by the Leacocks, for the boys had to labour summers in the fields, perhaps under the management of Agnes with the help of Old Tommy, or perhaps under an arrangement with a neighbour. The poor returns and steady losses the farm had produced for six years, and the sale of machinery and animals, indicate that in Peter's absence the family depended largely on gifts from England. When Peter set out, nine children remained behind with Agnes: the six she had brought from England, and George (born 1 March 1877), Caroline (born 16 August 1878) and Maymee. Peter left promising that soon the struggle to make ends meet would be ended by the fortune he would make in the west.[11]

With Peter absent, life for the family revolved primarily around the children. Agnes's love of her Victorian and English heritage manifested itself not only in the negative campaign to keep them from backwoods manners but in her determination to provide them with a good education. Stephen more than any other of his brothers and sisters took up from her this esteem for learning and also developed a measured and equivocal respect for the English tradition in which the particular form of education he received was rooted. After withdrawing the children from Georgina Township School, Agnes first tried to give them lessons herself. Excellently educated in her own right and armed with a trunkload of textbooks she had brought from England, she nevertheless found the job impossible. As Leacock explained, "it was no good, we wouldn't pay attention, we knew it was only mother."[12] With the practised eye of a long-time student and teacher, he laid some of the blame for her lack of success on the books she used. These included Slater's *Chronology*, Peter Parley's *Greece and Rome* and Bishop Colenso's *Arithmetic*, all of which reduced learning to rote responses to leading questions. He remembered with much greater approval his mother's fondness for literature; she introduced him very young to the novels of Walter Scott, Daniel Defoe, Charles Dickens and Mark Twain.[13] *The Pickwick Papers* was a particular favourite but, unlike Dickens, Mark Twain took some time to work his way into Leacock's two-man pantheon of the greatest modern writers, for *The Adventures of Tom Sawyer*, sent to the family soon after its 1876 publication in the United States, was not an immediate hit with him.

In her determination to keep the children out of the local school, Agnes appealed to Thomas Murdock Leacock, who provided money to hire a tutor. In Great Britain, private home education by a tutor as the preparation to high school or university was still common, and not only among titled, landed or wealthy classes; it was often a practice in the homes of poor but well-educated clergymen, for example. Such tutors were not unknown in Ontario, but they were much more frequent in the homes of well-to-do gentlefolk and established families than in farmhouses like the Leacocks'; a noteworthy example from the period is provided by Joseph Scriven, the author of the popular hymn, "What a Friend We Have in Jesus," who had worked for many years in the Rice Lake district, 50 miles east of Egypt, as tutor to the children of a retired naval officer, Captain Robert L. Pengelly. The hiring of a tutor was, both symbolically and practically, an assertion by Agnes of the rights and privileges she felt her children deserved by virtue of the class to which the Butlers and the Leacocks belonged.

In the Sutton area Agnes found her tutor in Harry Park, a university student unable to finish his studies because he had run out of money.[14] Establishing an orderly schoolroom in the Leacock house, Park organized a class of five children, including the four oldest boys — Jim, Arthur Murdock (Dick), Stephen and Charlie — and their oldest sister, Missie. Park saw that the best student of the group was Stephen, who returned the favour by memorializing the young teacher's instruction as the best he had ever received: due to Park, he was by the age of eleven an excellent speller and sound calculator in mathematics and possessed a solid preparation in literature, history and geography. Park ran his class with strict discipline, despite its location in a busy household; in fact, his watch overruled the claims of the kitchen clock. The theory of education that emphasized individual encouragement of the gifted rather than limited programs geared to the abilities of the average child, which Leacock preached all his life, had roots in his early success under excellent and very personalized tutelage. Leacock continued as Park's student for about three years, and for some time after the three eldest boys went on to Upper Canada College, Park remained a fixture in the Leacock home, teaching the younger children.

During this same period, Agnes made some other changes in the family routine; everything indicates that she was taking advantage of Peter's absence to shape life to a more gracious pattern, more to her liking, and discover advantages and pleasures even in the remote Simcoe region. Beginning in 1880, the family moved to the shore of Lake Simcoe during the summer months; at first their "summer cottage" was a tumbledown former rectory for which Agnes paid a yearly rent of eight dollars. This innovation immediately produced more society and a kindlier view of Ontario among the children, even though the older boys had to spend much of the summer working the farm while their father was away; along with his private formal education, Stephen continued the practical immersion in agriculturalism that gave him a thorough dislike of it. Yet now there was more in his life than isolation in the backwoods, dreary and burdensome labour, and the financial worries that were becoming greater and more apparent as the boys grew older. Leacock dated his love of the Lake Simcoe region from his late childhood, when he was able to travel more freely off the farm to join his brothers and sisters and their friends in Sutton and at the lakeshore in games, and especially activities on the water. Swimming, boating and skating drew him to the lake year-round. With his mother's successful determination to make trips away from the farm more frequent and less difficult-seeming, even the winter weather that had been a barrier to the children's freedom became a delight. It was Lake Simcoe itself that especially drew Leacock to feel himself throughout life an adopted son of the region. "Here the blue of the deeper water," he wrote, "rivals that of the Aegean; the sunlight flashes back in lighter colour from the sandbar on the shoals; the passing clouds of summer throw moving shadows as over a ripening field, and the mimic gales that play over the surface send curling caps of foam as white as ever broke under the bow of the Aegean galley."[15] The boys built rafts, which sometimes were caught in the changeable weather on the lake and had to be towed to shore. Leacock's writings often jibe at the troubles a novice has in sailing Lake Simcoe; he was a Simcoe hand, one who studied the lake throughout his life and made it a part of his personal history.

Just as Porchester had done in England, the Simcoe region gave him associations that became foundations of his life and values, in this case of his identity as a Canadian. He remembered a settler's grave hidden in an overgrown patch of bush on the Leacock farm; this was history, just as surely as a cathedral or monument of Europe represented history, and in adulthood he faulted his early teachers for not having conveyed it to their pupils. In *The Boy I Left Behind Me*, he recalled that only a few miles to the northwest of Egypt, between Lake Simcoe and Georgian Bay, lay the Huronia of the seventeenth century, the home of the Huron and a principal site for Jesuit missionary activity until in 1649 the Hurons' enemies, the Iroquois, forced the French to abandon the region and their historic mission town, Sainte-Marie-among-the-Hurons. From that time until after the Napoleonic Wars there had been virtually no European settlement in the area, although England had begun efforts to create a colony there before 1800 under the direction of Colonel John Graves Simcoe. In a manner of speaking, the farm at Egypt was only one generation away from the wilderness; Leacock remembered bonfires from the summer of his arrival that cleared out the last of the primeval cedars and oaks that had not fallen to the first wave of homesteading.

While his later writings never compromise his own rejection of the farm, he often celebrated the rural people he had known in this period, and judged that their way of life had in many ways been replaced by something worse in the agricultural communities he observed as an adult. The devotion of his tutor, Harry Park, to learning had flowered and perhaps was even intensified in its unpromising setting.[16] He remembered the Sutton village doctor of his childhood, Charles Noble, as not only healing the sick but supporting whole families in the aftermath of injury or death. Although he recognized the importance for him of the railway's coming to Sutton, which put Toronto only a single short trip away, he could still regret the resulting destruction of commercial boat traffic on Lake Simcoe. Trains effectively connected the area with the outside world but also eliminated a picturesque and charming mode of travel best suited to the needs of the small communities around the lake.

It was hindsight in which Leacock first glimpsed the Simcoe area kindly; he dated his realization of his appreciation for it from 1882, when he enrolled in Upper Canada College in Toronto, the city with which he would primarily identify himself for the next "seventeen years and a half, as a schoolboy (boarder or day), or as a student, or teacher, or both college student and teacher together."[17] In February 1882, just turned twelve, he began attending classes but barely had time to start missing home before illness forced his removal. After three or four days of "standing up, utterly homesick, and chorusing out declensions and conjugations...and living through clattering meals that I could hardly eat for homesickness," he came down with scarlatina, a mild form of scarlet fever.[18] His illness had passed off within a day, but he was kept in the school dispensary and after another day his mother arrived and took him back to the farm, where he spent approximately two months recuperating and studying Latin. He returned to Upper Canada College after Easter to find that his first bout with homesickness had inoculated him: "in less than no time it had all changed, all began to feel familiar and easy. The lessons were to me a mere nothing because they had shoved me a class down and I knew it all, and with that I began to make a few timid friendships, and to feel proud of walking with my friends down King St. all in college cricket caps..." The fact that Upper Canada College overpowered the desire to return home became for him one proof of its virtues: it had helped him both endure the first shock of separation from his family and set out on a path of independent effort.

The choice of Upper Canada College for the education of the Leacock boys was in some measure a matter of necessity.[19] It was the nearest secondary school to the farm and in 1881, when Stephen's two older brothers began there, Toronto was a single convenient train trip away from Sutton. It was also, in fact, one of only two prestigious high schools in the province, the other being the Anglican-founded Trinity College School, in Port Hope, which had recently graduated the poet Archibald Lampman and sent him on for higher studies to Toronto's Anglican college, Trinity, with which it was affiliated. But if conditions dictated Upper Canada College, it was also fortunately the case that in the 1880s the school had reached a tidemark of excellence and prestige. Founded as a private boys' school in 1829 by Sir

John Colborne, then lieutenant-governor of the Province of Upper Canada, it was associated with the University of Toronto, chartered in 1827 as an Anglican college but secularized in 1849. A training ground for university-bound young men, Upper Canada College had a reputation that admirably answered Agnes's ambition to bring up her sons as gentlemen, while its academic culture, perhaps without her knowing this, was free of most of the besetting ills of English "public" (i.e., private) schools, such as snobbery, reinforcement of social class divisions and privilege, corporal punishment, and the practices of hazing and fagging.[20]

The school stood on the north side of King Street, its grounds stretching east and west from Simcoe Street to John Street, and north to Adelaide Street. This large campus formed a pleasant green preserve near the wharves and warehouses along Toronto's lakefront, where the "new railways sliced off, as everywhere in Ontario, the shoreline, vilified with ash-heaps and refuse." The brick college buildings were in a heavy, severe style that Leacock compared to an asylum or penitentiary, although he approved heartily of their interior arrangements of dormitories, classrooms and study halls. He soon adapted to dormitory life; *The Boy I Left Behind Me* gives a detailed and affectionate account of the school's boarding house and its society, which he found one of the most rewarding aspects of high school, for it allowed him to share his entire day — sports, classes, studies and leisure — with his fellow students. For him, school life revolved around the camaraderie of the boarding students; day students, he noted, had to leave before sports activities began, in the late afternoon after classes were over: sports were a special delight to him, especially cricket, although he never excelled at it. In 1882 there were more than one hundred day students and approximately one hundred boarders. Boarding students were allowed off school grounds only on Saturdays and Sundays, except that daily passes were given to visit a tuck-shop, "The Taffy," at the northern border of the campus on Adelaide Street; there a boy's twenty-five or fifty cent weekly allowance seemed plenteous for "[o]ne could do oneself very well with five cents a trip — three cents for pop drunk out of the bottle and two cents for two doughnuts or cakes."[21] The students were all equally short of pocket money, which emphasized to him the school's relative freedom from class consciousness and divisions. He also remembered fondly that during his first school year the students attended lectures and debates given by University of Toronto students: a tame pleasure by later standards, perhaps, but for him at that time a most exciting event.

In the 1880s Toronto was a rapidly growing city whose business district stretched almost a mile up Yonge Street from the lakefront; tree-shaded residential districts were beginning to fill the rolling hills to the north. The westernmost major centre of a country in the midst of rapid, sometimes troubled development and western expansion, the city was then in what Leacock called "its final stage of comfortable and completed growth as a prominent centre of life and industry, intercourse and arts, before the coming of the electrical age brought the rapid transit and communication that was to turn it into something ten times greater; to foster suburban growth, bring great industries to the fringe of the city itself...and turn all such provincial towns into metropolitan centres."[22] The green, broad-avenued city of 60,000 was the site of increasing cultural activity, and visiting dignitaries such as Matthew Arnold found it quite different from the muddy, distressing town earlier visitors from abroad had reported on. There was increasing cultural activity in the city. But the cultural, literary, economic, and scientific life going on around the twelve-year-old Leacock was not yet, of course, well known to him, although it was the matrix for the growth to excellence of the school he attended and represented the destiny for which that school was preparing him, already abetted by his own eager efforts. He finished his first year with excellent grades, especially in Latin and English literature, and then he went home, as he would each summer of his five-year high school career, to work on the farm and spend periods at Sutton and Lake

Simcoe. There he must have received with mixed feelings his mother's unexpected decision that during the academic year 1883-84 she would rent a house in Toronto and he would have to attend school as a "day boy." This may have been intended in part as an economy measure, for all three of her older sons would now live with her. Then, too, Agnes herself was doubtless weary of farm life and rural isolation. Perhaps she was seriously considering the possibility of moving the family off the farm altogether, on the strength of Peter's speculations in the west or the hope of continued money from England. She took advantage of what Leacock recalled as a "casual legacy" from England, which he regretted that she had spent rather than invested; renting the farm to a neighbour, she left her younger children at Egypt in the care of Harry Park, moved to Toronto, and took a house on John Street, near the college.[23]

Family tradition recalled the John Street house as shared by Agnes and Peter, with the younger children also present. Leacock indicated in *The Boy I Left Behind Me* that the trip west had not kept his father or uncle away from Ontario entirely; he remembered seeing E.P. ushering around his business partners from Winnipeg. It was probably during this academic year of 1883-84 that the eldest Leacock son, Jim, dropped out of Upper Canada College to go west and work with E.P., and he may have made the trip to Manitoba with his father. On 28 June 1884, Stephen wrote to Peter in Winnipeg to give news of the family's summer holiday plans, including the droll narration, in which the humorist's tones are already evident, of a train trip to Sutton that had begun badly: "The little ones all started for the lake this afternoon; they went this morning, but they missed the train. Mother wants me to tell you that it was not the children's fault that they missed the morning train, as they were all up at half past four, in fact they hardly slept at all, and their trunk had been packed about a week before." Stephen also mentioned to Peter his mother's condition following the birth on 28 May 1884, at Toronto, of the tenth Leacock child, Rosamond Mary (Dot): "Mother was out in the yard for the first time yesterday and had the pleasure of beating me in a game of croquet."[24]

While Leacock flourished at Upper Canada College, his brother Jim, who had dropped out to work, was employed as an office assistant for E.P. The "remarkable uncle" had conferred a mythical Portuguese Dukedom on him, Leacock wrote, which enabled E.P. "to say to visitors in his big house…in a half whisper behind his hand, 'Strange to think that two deaths would make that boy a Portuguese Duke.' But Jim never knew which two Portuguese to kill." His brother Dick, who "couldn't learn anything by any known academic process,"[25] also dropped out, probably during the 1883-84 school year, and returned to the farm, then occupied only by Tommy, the hired man, and his wife; prompted by the call-to-arms surrounding the North West Rebellion of March-July 1885, Dick joined the North West Mounted Police and was soon assigned to the Regina barracks. Leacock's younger brother Charlie (born 6 December 1871) joined him at the school as a fellow "day-boy," the fact of his attendance as a day student as well as his birth date suggesting his enrollment probably occurred in the autumn of 1883.

Leacock continued to win high marks in all his subjects and immersed himself in student activities, as an upperclassman participating in the debating society, chairing the football club, and working during his final year, 1886-87, as an editor of the school newspaper, *The College Times*. On 7 April 1887 it carried the first signed article he ever published, "The Vision of Mirza (New Edition)." Its postscript has the rhythm of his humorous delivery:

> I have since made inquiries as to who my friend the genius was. I only succeeded, however, in finding that he is in the sixth form; but as there are so many geniuses in the sixth, the information has not enabled me to discover his identity. I have heard that a price of ten demerits has been set on his head.[26]

Besides providing academic education, sports, and activities such as debating and the newspaper, Upper Canada College was also supposed to be shaping him into a "gentleman" in the meaning of the term derived from the English caste system: this goal so important to Agnes was regarded by Stephen with more than skepticism. Impressed from childhood reading by the American principle that "all men are created equal," he could not help but notice that his mother was setting him a course that was intended to secure for him a social place of privilege based upon his supposed birthright of being a gentleman due to the class into which he had been born.[27] His survey of Ontario history in *The Boy I Left Behind Me* emphasized the efforts made by early provincial officials to transplant English class consciousness and mores to the Canadian backwoods. His uncle E.P. could touch a love of title and eminence in every farmer and tradesman, and his mother maintained strict discipline among her servants: the lowest maid was "as low and humble as even an English Earl could wish it." While mocking these transplanted manners, Leacock did not divorce himself altogether from the traditions he found among the conservative Anglo-Canadian residents of Ontario. He had benefited from his mother's convictions, but he refused to be regarded as someone who relied on being a "gentleman," born to claim things he had not worked to earn. He argued that the better life should be available to all, or to all whose merits and application could win it.

So when Leacock evaluated Upper Canada College in retrospect, he praised its remarkable freedom from the taint of class distinction (*The Boy I Left Behind Me*), yet castigated it for making even its half-hearted, ineffectual efforts to be "a school of gentlemen" ("The Struggle to make us Gentlemen" in *My Remarkable Uncle*). He recalled that when, as underclassmen, he and his friends first heard the phrase, they felt the impossibility of achieving such an exalted standard. Over the years, however, they began to absorb many doubtful examples of gentlemanliness from the school "old boys." Leacock's oblique but withering final judgment on the ideal comes in his version of an incident — perhaps embroidered — from his own experience. In order to complete a form, a teacher asked him for his father's occupation. He replied that his father did nothing, meaning that his father "was probably to be found along on King Street having a Tom-and-Jerry in the Dog and Duck, or at Clancey's but whether to call that his occupation was a nice question." Hearing that Peter did "nothing," the teacher promptly wrote down the occupation as "gentleman."[28]

Whatever hopes had accompanied Agnes's move to Toronto, the experiment ended before Leacock had graduated in 1887. His chronology in *The Boy I Left Behind Me* is often vague, but there he recalls the family's abandonment of the Toronto house and retreat to the farm as occurring in 1886, and lays the blame for it on Peter: "Then my father came back (broke) from the North-West in 1886 and this meant another move back from Toronto to the old farm, but I was not in it, being a boarder at Upper Canada College."[29] From this and his statement that he attended "as a boarder and as a day-boy and finally as a boarder again," it appears that despite the house on John Street Leacock may have gained the point of being boarded even before Agnes's departure from Toronto; it is just possible that he boarded only at the end of his first year and in the portion of his final year following the family's return to Egypt, but the impression he gives in his autobiography of his school days suggests a longer career than this as a resident student. Probably in 1886, then, Agnes and Peter and the younger Leacock children fell back on their dilapidated, nonpaying Egypt property, leaving Stephen and Charlie behind as Upper Canada College boarders.

In his last year at school (1886-87), Leacock reached the top of his class, winning all the individual subject prizes and the award for general proficiency. "For me," he recalled, "the old-fashioned system of going up and down, and trying to move up to the head of the class and stay there, proved altogether too congenial and attractive, and helped give a false bias to my education." In his first two years he had not taken academic competition seriously, and had learned easily and sincerely; not striving for a high ranking, he had still achieved outstanding results. "But from the third form on I got more and more drawn into study and overstudy, till presently I filled all my time outside of school as well as in. After the third form, by this continuous industry, I ranked first in everything except mathematics; and after the fourth form first in everything, by learning by heart in mathematics every possible thing that would let itself be learned by heart."[30] Remembering his mother's old textbooks on the farm, he lamented that he had placed the pursuit of top marks ahead of serious study, two endeavours which he never confused and never believed contributed to one another in a simple, direct way. In the summer of 1887 he graduated as head boy of Upper Canada College.

The Leacock farmhouse at Egypt, Ontario; the building is now gone.
Courtesy National Archives of Canada C-25716.

He had already taken his matriculation examinations for the University of Toronto and received excellent marks. His chosen future was to go on to university, with no specific course of study or career yet in view but only the desire to pursue education, in which he had proved able to distinguish himself and which had separated him for five sweet years from the day-to-day drudgery and bleak forecast of the farm. But even as he was choosing this course and taking pride in his honours, he realized that university might be out of his reach. The source of money available to him in the past was gone; his grandfather did not provide for education beyond high school. His older brothers had set a family pattern by going to work but were as yet unable even to help Agnes out of their small pay. And he could expect no help from his parents. In either 1885 or (as Leacock himself recalled it) 1886, when Peter returned to Ontario from Winnipeg, the collapse of the Manitoba land boom had left him bankrupt and discouraged. He and his family were virtually without funds, depending almost solely on the income, about eighty dollars per month, from the small investment Agnes had brought to the marriage, and drifting ever deeper into debt. Stephen's and Charlie's school expenses were safe, provided by Thomas Murdock Leacock for as long as they were enrolled, but Peter and Agnes had no choice but to stay with the younger children at the one place where they could live, the farm. Chafing at the unaccustomed restriction of life there after years in a boom town, Peter now took no pains to conceal his drinking from the children. He would not work the increasingly debt-ridden property.

Within a few months of Leacock's graduation there finally came a crisis that is most fully narrated by Elizabeth Kimball, daughter of Leacock's youngest sibling, Daisy (born September 1886). In *The Man in the Panama Hat*, her reminiscences of her famous uncle and the extended Leacock family, Kimball states that a moment came when Agnes had to carry Daisy out of the house to escape Peter who, in a drunken rage, had attempted to harm Agnes with a knife. Leacock rescued his mother and baby sister from the bitter cold, according to Kimball, and drove them to a neighbour's house, where they remained for several days, until he had succeeded in forcing his father to leave the farm. Other family members have placed Peter's final departure in the summer of 1887 (although a cold summer night is possible) and have agreed with Leacock's brief and reticent statement that his father simply decided to leave: "Things went worse than ever for my father on his return to the farm — a shadowed, tragic family life into which I need not enter.... The situation ended with my father leaving home again in 1887. No doubt he meant to come back, but he never did. I never saw him again." Whatever the precise timing of the departure, family traditions seem agreed that it included an incident in which Leacock, the oldest brother then at home, confronted his father at the Sutton railway station and threatened to kill him if he ever returned.[31]

He never did; Agnes afterwards always spoke of herself as "separated" from her husband. The family must have felt great relief that a growing threat of physical danger was removed, but at the same time the situation Peter left behind was grim. In the absence of Jim, Dick and his father, Leacock was "the head of the family at seventeen," a responsibility that potentially cancelled his hopes of university education. His older brothers could not afford to send money, and his mother lived on at the farm "because it was unsaleable" with a "bodyguard" of Tommy, the Yorkshireman hired hand whose wage, like the mortgage, was never paid, and his wife. Agnes's eighty dollars per month and a constant slide into debt provided for Leacock's eight younger brothers and sisters. It was Agnes and Stephen who now, like wife and husband, had to analyze the situation and decide what to do.[32]

Leacock upon his graduation from Upper Canada College in 1887.
Courtesy National Archives of Canada C-31965.

Education Eating up Life

From June 1887, when he graduated from Upper Canada College at the head of his class, until the autumn of 1899, when he entered the University of Chicago to study economics, Leacock lived the crucial years in which most young people search for the meaning and pattern of the world, establish a place in it, and develop a philosophy of life and an art of living. Unfortunately, this period between the ages of seventeen and twenty-nine is the least documented in Leacock's career; his struggles and decisions take place largely out of our sight. *The Boy I Left Behind Me* breaks off shortly after 1889, while the witness of external sources — reminiscences, press accounts and the like — does not begin in earnest until his 1901 arrival at McGill University, Montreal. To fill in the intervening years there are brief anecdotes by friends, and deductions that can be made from Leacock's writings of the time and from the considerable amount he later had to say about education and teaching.

For only one year between his high school graduation and his forced retirement from McGill was he free of teaching duties: the academic year 1887-88. Despite the upheaval caused by his father's departure, he enrolled in the University of Toronto in November 1887. The previous June he had taken the matriculation examinations and his scores had placed him among the university's ten highest-ranked applicants in all but one subject; on the strength of this performance he received a $100 scholarship. At that time, the cost of a year of study, he later calculated, was at least $300, including tuition and fees, books, and room and board. He had no substantial expectation of being able to complete his degree; family finances were stretched to the limit to pay for even one year. Yet he mentions no plan to attend part-time, a possibility he would have known from the example of Harry Park, and appears to have decided to take the chance that time might bring some means of support. If he and Agnes hoped that a successful year at university would evoke further funds from England, they were mistaken. A review of finances when the academic year ended in late spring 1888 showed there was no money with which to go on.

He did have a remarkable year, placing very high in all but one of his six subjects; the exception was mathematics, at which he was in the second rather than the first rank of students.[1] He was enrolled at University College, a non-denominational liberal-arts college among the University of Toronto's many religious-affiliated colleges, including Trinity (Anglican), Victoria (Presbyterian), St. Michael's (Roman Catholic) and Wycliffe (Methodist, where he roomed). Records are lost for student performance in 1887-88; all that can be said is that he completed freshman courses with very high marks. Comments in his writings indicate that his mathematical subject was algebra and his other five subjects were English literature, and Greek, Latin, French, and German; however, reference to an Italian teacher indicates that he also studied this language during the year. Due to his very high marks and the excellence of the Upper Canada College program he had accomplished so successfully, the university entitled him to enter the following year as a junior rather than a sophomore. He himself referred to this achievement as "taking two years in one," which he really did not do in the sense of performing a double class load.[2] But the effect was the same: the university credited him with two years. Despite this outstanding performance, no help came from England, and at home no help could be expected from his family. Jim was a courthouse clerk in Winnipeg and Dick belonged to the North-West Mounted Police; neither could as yet spare any money even for Agnes, who on her monthly income of perhaps eighty dollars had to support the eight children at home, ranging in age from infancy to sixteen.[3] Until Leacock was able to begin helping her, she got along by drifting further into debt. At eighteen, after brilliant successes at Upper Canada College and the University of Toronto, Leacock found that he could not continue, as his more well-to-do friends would, directly through university and into a profession. He would have to work first. He decided on high school teaching. In the late nineteenth century, Ontario elementary school teachers were trained at normal schools (teachers' colleges),[4] but a growing number of high schools in the province was creating the need for a program to qualify people without bachelor's degrees as high school instructors. Only a few years before Leacock entered the profession a procedure had been established at several Ontario high schools whereby students with some college qualifications could gain high school teaching certification by completing a thirteen-week program of studies in education, including student teaching, observation of classroom techniques and readings in education theory. In September 1888 Leacock was accepted as one of six men and women student teachers to begin a three-month preparation of this type at Strathroy Collegiate Institute in Strathroy, a small town near London, Ontario. The few months there were his first experience of an independent life. The year at the University of Toronto had been by comparison a close continuation of an established routine of travel between Sutton and Toronto; he had simply moved from an Upper Canada College dormitory to a Wycliffe College dormitory and, just as at Upper Canada College, had followed a demanding schedule emphasizing study of classical and modern languages. Strathroy marked a departure from this now familiar life; the trip there was the first railway journey Leacock made in Canada outside the familiar one between Sutton and Toronto. At Strathroy, with his belongings packed in a simple wicker suitcase, he made the acquaintance of boarding houses, lasting only one afternoon in his first. He stopped briefly in the room he had just taken, and wrote a note to his mother in which he complained of conditions in the establishment: "Dear Mother [he recalled the note as saying], I arrived at Strathroy all right, but the boarding house I am in looks a pretty rotten place, so I don't expect to stay long." He left this in the room and went down to the communal dinner, where the landlady soon appeared and told him that if he did not like her house he could leave: "so I was on the street again, less 25 cents, moving on to the next sign *Rooms with Board*," where he found the accommodations more or less identical. This was the beginning of his boarding-house experience, which "spread intermittently over many years and from which presently I found much food for reflection." He had no doubt that "the origin of those truths" (postulates such as "all Boarding-Houses are the same Boarding-House") contained in "Boarding-House Geometry," one of his earliest published humour pieces, reached back to Strathroy.[5]

The boarding houses were more troublesome to Leacock than were his pedagogical studies. After success in demanding academic programs, he was so comfortable in the new routine of observing and giving classes that it soon grew tedious; in retrospect, though, Leacock the veteran professor praised it because it had lasted only three months, while student teachers shortly after were required to devote a full year of their university education to practice teaching. The program qualified him as a teacher of English, French, German, Latin and Greek, and he was highly recommended by the Strathroy principal, James Wetherell, who administered the training. In his Strathroy period Leacock was most affected by an occasion when Wetherell called on him to take over a demonstration class in English that the principal had begun. Leacock, the high school humorist, continued the lecture in a voice and manner so exactly like Wetherell's that the students were delighted. "I am afraid I admire your brains more than your manners," Wetherell afterwards told him; he remembered the remark through the years and recorded it in his autobiography.

> The words cut me to the quick, I felt them to be so true and yet so completely without malice. For I had no real "nerve," no real "gall." It was the art of imitation that appealed to me. I had not realized how it might affect the person concerned. I learned with it my first lesson in the need for human kindliness as an element in humour.

Nor did the incident persist only in Leacock's memory. When he introduced himself many years later to a newly appointed principal of McGill University, General Sir Arthur Currie, Currie replied that he had been a scholar in 1888 at Strathroy Collegiate Institute, and remembered Leacock well as the student teacher who had so brilliantly mimicked Wetherell.[6]

The Strathroy program was arranged to coincide with the fall school term so that newly certified teachers could start to seek work in January. Leacock began his search with little to go on, although some jobs were advertised; he lost one of them, at Bishop Ridley College, to a future principal of the University of Toronto, H.J. Cody. But an old friend quickly came to his aid. In 1889 Harry Park was principal of Uxbridge High School and he offered a post there as language master at a salary of $700 per year. Leacock accepted immediately. Uxbridge, a town of fifteen hundred inhabitants with a new brick school building, was less than twenty miles from his family's farm; in comparison to Sutton, it was large but still quiet ("dull but unaware of it"). In June, with his contract for the coming fall signed, he went to spend the summer with his mother at Sutton, a then arduous eighteen-mile trip, setting a pattern for all the summers of his high school teaching career; for the next ten years he participated each summer in the busy social life of the cottage communities around lakes Simcoe and Couchiching. Lady Matilda Edgar, the mother of Leacock's friend Pelham Edgar, provides one glimpse of the summertime Leacock of 1889. In August, writing to Pelham from her summer place at Lake Simcoe, she mentions that a family member "drove over to Sutton to get supplies & took his dinner with Stephen Leacock who is camping out with his uncle at Jackson's Point. He says Stephen looks a different fellow, altogether strong and well set up. So the year away from study has done him good. He has been teaching at Uxbridge."[7] Jackson's Point, near the estate of the prominent Sibbald family, is opposite Georgina Island and is one of the main points on the south Lake Simcoe shore; the uncle in question is certainly E.P.

In fall 1889, shortly after classes at Uxbridge began, Leacock received an offer to teach in another rural community, Napanee, at $200 per year more. When he asked to be let out of his contract, the Uxbridge trustees refused. In *The Boy I Left Behind Me*, he states that their action was contrary to the general practice of the time; due to generally poor salaries and expectations, teachers were customarily permitted to follow any advancement that presented itself. He stayed but soon afterwards another opportunity arose, this time for no more money but at a better school: Upper Canada College. His alma mater offered him a position as a junior language master that would mean not only relatively prestigious employment but also the chance to continue his university studies in Toronto. When the trustees again refused him, he asked for a meeting at which, encouraged by the surprise of one trustee's support, he requested a week to find a replacement.

Many years later, in 1936, this incident came back alive when a former Uxbridge trustees wrote to Leacock in response to an article he had published in *Maclean's*, in which he had told his version. Former trustee F.N. Raines, by then an elderly lawyer in Vancouver, was incensed over Leacock's presentation: "I am one of the 'merry fellows' you mention as trustees of the High School who refused to let you go when you were a teacher under Dr. Park as principal," Raines introduced himself. He objected to Leacock's implication that the trustees had not let him go: they had done so when he received his Upper Canada College offer, but his previous, Napanee, offer had come in mid-term, when finding another teacher would have been too difficult for the school. He criticized Leacock for complaining of his yearly salary of $700 — Raines himself had taught one year at $350 during an earlier period. Leacock carefully wrote back to Raines, again giving his side of an event that still impressed him after the passage of forty-six years. He mentioned the Napanee offer and then recalled:

> Later I was offered a job at Upper Canada College and they let me go provided I would get a substitute which I did. I appealed to the men in person and they were going to refuse when Mr. Brittain said with great emphasis let the boy go you can't expect to keep a boy like that in Uxbridge. All my life I have appreciated the warmth and kindliness of what he said and that's why I remember it.

In 1943, when writing *The Boy I Left Behind Me*, he scrupulously pointed out that the salary of teachers in the 1880s and 1890s, when he himself had been of primary school age, had been $300 or $400.[8]

Leacock did not accomplish his departure entirely by his own efforts. His uncle, E.P., at this time in Toronto, helped him obtain a few days' delay in accepting the job offer from the principal of Upper Canada College, and "with the aid of teachers' lists and a flood of telegrams...he unearthed a teacher, a modern language teacher. It is true that his candidate when produced looked far from modern and short on language, indeed I believe the good old man was hauled out of retirement, but he filled the bill…" It is at this moment that Leacock's reminiscences in *The Boy I Left Behind Me* end with the words, "I was free."[9] Free in a comparative sense: free to work days at a job he increasingly disliked and to attend university in the evenings, while continuing regular monetary contributions to his family, which he had begun to make from Uxbridge and which added to the difficulty of his attempt to save money for his own future education. Nonetheless, he was back in Toronto and had gotten partway round the problem that had troubled him in Uxbridge — the possibility that he would not be able to earn enough in teaching to return to university. In fall 1889, he began teaching at Upper Canada College and simultaneously attending the University of Toronto as a third-year student.

Leacock's Upper Canada College superiors testified he was one of the best teachers the school ever had. Few of his students have left comments, but B.K. Sandwell, later a prominent literary man and one of Leacock's best friends, once recalled that although "he always had something good to say" he was not interested in teaching for its own sake but only to earn money for his education.[10] Leacock himself claimed to have had no difficulty either in following the prescribed procedures for language teaching or in maintaining classroom discipline. The secret, he said, was never to give the students a moment to doubt your authority: begin speaking at once, speak on the subject and command their attention. He counselled against attempting to engage students' affection through humour or sympathy, and maintained that good classroom order would inevitably follow from these principles as it had for him.

High school teaching, however seriously he took it, occupied his thoughts mainly as an occupation he was beginning to wish to escape, and his constant dispraise of it, then and later, sprang from this and not from finding himself to be a failure at it. He was busy

attempting to finish his bachelor of arts degree, which his job contra-
dictorily permitted and interfered with. During his first year at Upper
Canada College, he taught until three o'clock and then spent what
time he could in university classes. Class attendance was not then
compulsory at the university: this made it possible for him to enroll in
the requisite third-year program towards an honours degree in
modern languages even though his work frequently prevented him
from being at lectures; the honours degree also gave him more latitude to choose his courses than a regular pass degree would have
done. He put such emphasis on classics in his course selections that
many of his classmates assumed he was taking a degree in classical
rather than modern languages. At the end of the academic year he
again placed very high in all his subjects and won a special award for
studies in German.[11]

In addition to his teaching and studies, Leacock devoted himself
to caring for his family on the Egypt farm. He frequently conducted
sightseeing excursions to Toronto for the younger children and was
always home for the holidays. His youngest sister, Daisy, particularly
remembered him as the inspiration for Christmas celebrations:

> I don't remember Stephen being at the farm much in
> the summer, although he spent most of the holidays
> there. But in the winter, and especially at Christmas,
> I remember very clearly, he used to bring Dot and
> me wonderful toys "from town" (Toronto). He loved
> Christmas, and in later years he would have us hang
> up pillow slips instead of stockings. "Stockings aren't
> half big enough," he'd say. If the pillow slips were
> only half full we never noticed. It was the excitement,
> Christmas morning, of diving into them to see what
> we'd get. I do remember one Christmas at the farm.
> Dot was six and I was four. Stephen got Dot skates
> and after breakfast we went down to the pond. (Our

farm was inland, away from either Lake Simcoe or the Black River.) Stephen took a kitchen chair and had Dot push it about to learn how to skate, which she did in no time at all. Every Christmas we got new hand sleighs, and we would try them out as soon as we were dressed, and while we lived on the farm we would go sleigh-riding across the south fields which sloped away from the house.[12]

Daisy's reference to her age places this holiday in December 1890, during Leacock's second year at Upper Canada College and his senior year at the University of Toronto. Just turned twenty-one, he still had a fondness for childhood amusements; Daisy remembers that the boys, led by Stephen, borrowed the new sleds to assemble ice boats for skimming over frozen Lake Simcoe.

During his last year as a University of Toronto student, doubtless encouraged by the ease with which he had balanced his studies and teaching, Leacock began to be involved in extra-curricular activities, especially the university newspaper, *The Varsity*, and the debating society. He was co-editor of *The Varsity* for several months and was remembered in accounts of student dinners and dances as a good speaker. However, these additions to his schedule finally proved too demanding. He resigned his co-editorship early in 1891, and even found himself in the position of accepting help from his University of Toronto Italian teacher, who took over some of his Upper Canada College classes to allow him time to study for his final examinations. Even so, his performance on them was much below the standard of the previous year. The difficulties he was experiencing, and the ingenuity he used to overcome them, are suggested by the story of how he came to take a third-class mark in ethnology as one of his final grades. With his friend G. Howard Ferguson, a future premier of Ontario, Leacock was studying frantically for the upcoming examination in algebra, a subject in which both did poorly. Fortuitously,

Leacock came across a university regulation that entitled him to substitute, even at that late date, another subject. He struck upon the idea of taking the examination in ethnology, for he believed the subject would require only reading the textbook. Leacock and Ferguson made the substitution. A poor showing in ethnology based on instantly acquired knowledge came as a relief compared with the algebra mark they had expected.[13]

Graduation in the spring of 1891 was the end of Leacock's university career in Toronto. The sheltered social and intellectual oasis that the university provided for many of its students had not been available to him, but his degree brought him a promotion and salary increase at Upper Canada College. Soon he was also appointed a housemaster, in charge of a dormitory; this reduced his living expenses, provided an addition to his income and ended his running skirmish with boarding-house proprietors by giving him living quarters at the school. At the same time, he took on another responsibility of adulthood; the aging British trustees had asked to withdraw from the administration of Agnes's finances, and in spring 1892 Leacock became one of her three new, Canadian trustees; the others were G.M. Rae and Leacock's lifelong friend and lawyer, Goldwin Larratt Smith. Thus he now knew the concrete details of his family's economic situation. Agnes's assets were her marriage settlement, the cash and the stocks that had been given her in trust. These investments had generated the $80 per month on which the family had primarily relied in the 1880s; they had consisted originally of £700 of stock in the Great Indian Peninsular Railway, £1,773 in three per cent Consolidated Bank Annuities, and £1,173 in cash, but had been somewhat depleted by Agnes's occasional need to draw on the capital. Leacock's own improved finances enabled him, in 1892, to accomplish the long and deeply desired goal of moving his mother and the younger children to a better residence than the farm. His terse comment in *The Boy I Left Behind Me* bespeaks the businesslike, no-nonsense side of the young Leacock, impatient to inject practi-

This group portrait of the 1891 staff of the University of Toronto Varsity *includes Leacock, standing at far right and wearing his mortarboard.*
Courtesy National Archives of Canada C-31953.

cality and decisiveness into the chaotic family situation: "I at last got rid of the rotten old place on my mother's behalf simply by moving mother off it and letting it go to the devil, mortgages, creditors and all."[14] The Leacocks were apparently helped in this endeavour by the Sibbalds: a sign of the respect in which Leacock and Agnes were increasingly held.

But Leacock's demeanour at Upper Canada College belied these serious concerns and efforts, according to those who knew him at the time, such as Pelham Edgar, a former classmate from his Upper Canada College student years, who had returned to the school to teach English and as a married man lived in the married teachers' residence. Later an influential critic and historian of Canadian literature and a professor at Victoria College in the University of Toronto, he remembered the Leacock of this period as a man who seemed unambitious and unconcerned about the future. Many of the school's best faculty members were rising young scholars who went on to university posts in Canada and the United States — the ambition entertained by Edgar himself; although Leacock was professedly saving money to further his education, Edgar remembered him as someone whose talents could have been put to better use. On the surface at least, Leacock himself did not manifest this worry. By the summer of 1894 it seemed he was becoming positively frivolous. According to family tradition, at one point he dropped everything to pursue a young woman with whom he had fallen in love. Her mother took her to Colorado for a tuberculosis cure and he went in pursuit; refused permission to see her, he remained at the foot of the mountain where her sanatorium was located. When her mother finally relented, it was Leacock's turn to grow cold: the family hymn-sing to which he was invited sent him back to Toronto immediately.[15] Equally unsuccessful were some sentimental stories written soon after this episode; his first writings submitted for professional publication, they all were returned without encouragement from periodicals in New York.

About the same time, however, his natural genius for humour, which he must have long known he possessed, was receiving its first serious practice and polish, as he nurtured an ambition, perhaps quietly, to become a published author. Edgar remembered Leacock the high school language master as a great storyteller. He would call on Edgar and his wife at their quarters in the married teachers' residence, especially on Sundays after church, and entertain them with anecdotes. On such occasions he presented ideas that took form as some of his first published sketches, including "My Financial Career" and "Boarding House Geometry." He professed to have composed them in church during the sermons, which provided, he said, one of the quieter times during his week. With Edgar and perhaps other friends on the academic staff to serve as sounding board, in 1894 Leacock turned with a newly professional intent to the writing and publishing of humour; at this time, his record in the field consisted of eleven sketches and columns that appeared in the Upper Canada College *College Times* and the University of Toronto *Varsity* in 1887 and the four succeeding years. This activity had lapsed after the appearance of "Imogene: A Legend of the Days of Chivalry," a story which already looked forward to his *Nonsense Novels* (1911), in the *Varsity* during October 1891, half a year after he had left the university. Some of his time in the early 1890s must have been spent getting serious about being funny, for suddenly in 1894 he emerged as a polished writer with a new and unique style that bridged the divide between a satirical, analytical type of humour and a humour of exuberant creative nonsense and verbal play. On 19 May 1894 the New York magazine *Grip* published "ABC: or, The Human Element in Mathematics," a piece which has been reprinted steadily in more than a dozen anthologies, most recently in 1992, and is available electronically. This was followed by "That Ridiculous War in the East: Latest Account of the Naval Engagement at Yalu" (*Grip*, 6 October 1894), which neither Leacock nor others ever pulled from the periodical columns, and "An Outline of a New Pathology: Diseases of the Clothes;" this appeared in Toronto's *Saturday Night* in the 8

December 1894 issue and was successful enough to be reprinted in London and translated into German, making its last appearance in a 1925 reprint in the *Montreal Standard*, syndicated by the Metropolitan Newspaper Service, New York. His fall 1894 output also included three brief spoofs of the poets (including Wordsworth, "How Tennyson Killed the May Queen," and Longfellow) published weekly, 3 through 17 November, in *Saturday Night* and later collected in *Literary Lapses* (1910).[16]

Despite Edgar's testimony that Leacock seemed unconcerned that his talents might be going to waste at Upper Canada College, Edgar is also the source for the information that about 1894 Leacock began reading economics and political science in his spare time. Famous in later life as an early riser who used the pre-breakfast hours for his writing, Leacock now began to study his new subjects in the mornings before his Upper Canada College routine began; he liked to compare himself to John Stuart Mill, who spent hours studying before going to work in a trading-company office. To help his friend, Edgar introduced him to James Mavor, a professor of history at the University of Toronto and an expert in what were then the very new academic disciplines of economics and political science. But Mavor took a strong dislike to Leacock and declined to direct him. Nothing daunted, he pursued his self-directed studies, and was soon encouraged and helped by the arrival at Upper Canada College of a man with interests similar to his own. Edward (later Sir Edward) Peacock, two years his junior, joined the teaching staff in 1895; before Leacock had left the school in 1899, bound for the University of Chicago, his new friend had already written and published *Trusts, Combines and Monopolies* (1898). Peacock became as famous and influential a financier as Leacock was an economist and the two remained in close contact until Leacock's death. Peacock left Upper Canada College in 1902 to join the Dominion Securities Corporation, which moved him to London in 1907; there he rose to become a director of several companies in at least four different countries, among them the

Canadian Pacific Railway and the Bank of England. His presence at Upper Canada College during the late 1890s surely helped confirm Leacock's choice of economics and encourage his study of it.

All that Leacock was achieving seemed threatened in 1895 by a wholesale firing of academic staff members at Upper Canada College, which had been severely affected by losses in income following a 1891 reorganization of the University of Toronto; the university was now receiving from the Province of Ontario funds previously given to the high school. This financial crisis occasioned a search for new trustees and new resources, and led to much adverse criticism of the principal under whom the belt-tightening measure of radical downsizing was undertaken. A new principal, George (later Sir George) Parkin, was imported to Upper Canada College; he had been principal of the College School in Fredericton, New Brunswick, 1874-89, where his distinguished record included a role in the education and encouragement of two of Canada's earliest important writers, the poets Bliss Carman and Charles G.D. Roberts. Parkin rehired many of the fired Upper Canada College teachers, including Leacock; despite a certain reserve of character that made him stand back from some of the personal vividness and eccentricities of his language master, Parkin eventually proved a strong promoter of Leacock's gifts. The shakeup convinced Pelham Edgar that it was time to leave the college and begin the doctoral-degree program he had been planning, but Leacock remained, apparently absorbed in his private studies, family duties, and social pleasures.

One of his distinguishing behaviours, troublesome to Parkin, was a blithe flouting of the school's preferred attitudes toward religion. Already during the early 1890s Leacock had begun to express a strong independence from even a social adherence to religious practice. There is a story that one Sunday he offered to help another master, charged with taking the Methodist students to church, by taking them there himself rather than attending Anglican services: "You know it's all the same to me," he said. Later, the conscientious young master was shocked to find Leacock in his rooms: he explained that he had gathered the boys but then found that another master was actually planning to go to the Methodist service. So he passed the charge along and took the chance to miss church altogether. Parkin described in his diary a disturbing meeting he attended in the mid-1890s with several of his young faculty members; he found them uninterested in maintaining the school's traditional policy of mandatory church attendance. In private the principal doubted he should continue if his teachers did not share his Arnoldian conviction that religious faith and practice were the fundamental principles underlying the building of character the school attempted with its students. The diary does not mention Leacock by name, but his infractions and explicit irreverence in this regard are well documented. Parkin represented the tradition of a strict link between conservative moral traditions (which Leacock shared), on the one hand, and religious practice, on the other.[17] By rejecting the necessity of strict, or any, practice, while continuing to accept and promote the ethical principles associated with religious tradition, Leacock took on the stance of many of the great thinkers and writers of the century just then ending. His subsequent writings prove that he took the idea of "faith beyond the forms of faith" very seriously, but in his approach to freeing himself from those forms there was at this period of his life no earnestness à la George Eliot or Thomas Carlyle but a characteristic witty irreverence.

Meanwhile, his first efforts at the professional publication of humour were proving to be the gateway to impressive productivity. Over the next three years he continued energetically to write and publish new humour, unhindered by his own academic routine, heavy course of private study, busy social life and perhaps apocryphal romantic adventures, and apparently unfazed by the upheavals of 1895: the firings of college academic staff members, the advent of Parkin, his rehiring, and the departure of his friend Edgar. From 1895 through 1897 he brought out several humour pieces annually, most of them in New York periodicals. His career as a humorist is often considered to have begun in earnest on 11 April 1895 with the appearance of one of his most enduringly popular pieces, "My Financial Career," in the New York publication *Life* (not the modern magazine of this name or its immediate predecessor).

It was a period of great comic creativity, and humour considered as a separate genre of literature — a characteristic nineteenth-century innovation — had attained enormous popularity and increasing respect as a phenomenon with its own forms of expression and its own representative geniuses. Mark Twain's career flourished as Leacock grew up in the obscurity of the Lake Simcoe farming region, and continued until the year *Literary Lapses* was published. Twain had begun with short sketches, essays and stories, but his most telling work had been done in his novels, whereas Leacock was already proving to be best at brief, occasional compositions that combined invented and autobiographical elements, shifting agilely between fiction and nonfiction, truth and tall tale, self-revelation and masquerade. This was his own development of the form in which Mark Twain had achieved his early success, developing the humorous sketch into something more abrupt, nervous, and rangily colloquial than its predecessor in the gentle essays of Lamb and Hawthorne, an earlier manner that near century's end was still flourishing in such writers as Robert Louis Stevenson. In the quiet demesne of Upper Canada College, far from the seats of literary power, Leacock was preparing to become the chief continuator of the great nineteenth-century tradition of American humour and the man who helped to transform it into the modern form that was taken from his hands by the writers who rose to prominence in the decades following his own earliest popularity: Don Marquis, Franklin P. Adams, Dorothy Parker, Robert Benchley, S.J. Perlman, Christopher Morley, H. Allen Smith, James Thurber and others.

The American humour of the late eighteenth and early nineteenth centuries, based on character (and often dialect as well) presented in brief sketches or stories, sprang from Washington Irving and from the Major Jack Downing stories of Seba Smith that began to appear in the 1830s. This tradition received its major impetus before Mark Twain from a Canadian, the Nova Scotia judge Thomas Chandler Haliburton, who gained international fame with his stories of the shrewd Yankee clock peddler, Sam Slick, the first volume of which appeared in 1836. One of the early nineteenth century's most popular authors, Haliburton did at least as much as any other individual writer to establish humour, expressed primarily through sketches collected in volumes, as a separate and appreciated literary genre; he was a clear forerunner of Leacock also in the use of humour to promote the author's strong beliefs about social and political principles and issues. In the 1890s, American humorists of character and dialect included not only Mark Twain but Bret Harte, Artemus Ward and George Ade. However much he was attracted to American writers and features of American life and thought, Leacock was of course not an American but a Canadian; like his forerunner Haliburton, he was not only able but compelled to look both to the United States and to Great Britain. If his earliest sketches (such as "My Financial Career" and "Boarding-House Geometry") seemed quintessentially American in their presentation of contemporary vicissitudes through character, later essays combined American directness and demotic flavour with an urbanity and easy sense of culture that American writers seldom displayed, perhaps seldom sought. This is one of the factors that placed Leacock and keeps him among the very few great international humorists, able to cross the boundaries of taste not only between North America and Great Britain but between speakers of English and speakers of many other languages.

When his essays first began to appear in the mid-1890s, the New York periodicals that carried them were filled with the humorous work of Americans including Mark Twain, Bret Harte and O. Henry, and many London-based Englishmen, such as J.M. Barrie, the novelist George Gissing (*Diary of a Nobody*), and perhaps the most famous, then, of all living British humorists, Jerome K. Jerome, author of *Three Men in a Boat*. Jerome produced many magazine pieces later collected in volumes such as *Idle Thoughts of an Idle Fellow*, thus giving contemporary precedent to a method of publication that Leacock followed in all his humour books. In some respects Leacock resembles Jerome more than any other enduring humorist of the nineteenth century on either side of the Atlantic. Both write in a light, colloquial, generally nonacerbic vein, and both can present the ridiculous minutiae of daily life and popular culture in delightfully sharp detail. Both helped to father the modern humorous columnist who complains of changing fashions in food or transportation or social custom. Even their most elaborately expanded sketches can be traced to a starting point in the sort of ephemeral incongruity that is the province of the columnist. What distinguishes both Jerome and Leacock from many other humorists is the ability to see in such detail a reflection of the very nature of modern life and bring to the point a wide-ranging breadth and ingenuity of thought and expression.

If Leacock was seriously considering a career in popular literature, it was surely evident to him that his location in the cultural hinterlands was a barrier to success, although not necessarily an insuperable one. Most humorists of the time resided near the source of their income, that is, in London or New York. The uncertainty of a living from the sale of freelance pieces had turned many of the period's aspiring authors (Jerome is a good example) into staff writers and editors for popular magazines. For those who had to leave home and family to live in a literary centre, as Leacock would have had to do, the compensations were the chance of a livelihood and access to the writing community of the great cities. For example, Jerome's London friends included Arthur Conan Doyle, J.M. Barrie and Bret Harte, by century's end living out his life as a dandified Old West curiosity in the London literary milieu. In the New York — Boston area were such writers as Mark Twain and William Dean Howells, and a large number of popular magazines hungry for material, a powerful magnet to hopeful writers. Many Canadians felt the attraction of the literary centres, and some who left around the turn of the century became internationally popular authors. Examples are the novelist Sara Jeannette Duncan, who during Leacock's high school days had been a Toronto *Globe* columnist and had praised the writing he published in the *College Times*; and Sir Gilbert Parker, who wrote highly regarded historical novels about French Canada and served eighteen years in the British Parliament after settling in London in 1890 as a rising journalist. Bliss Carman, a native of Fredericton, worked for many years as an editor in New York, became one of the most popular "American" poets of the early twentieth century, and edited the first *Oxford Book of American Verse*. His first cousin Charles G.D. Roberts followed a similar path, as did the naturalist and popular author Ernest Thompson Seton; Roberts, a poet and fiction writer, and Seton are together credited with creating the animal story, a form that grew out of their Canadian experience but was presented to the world through their efforts in the New York literary marketplace.

However, Leacock would also have been aware that other Canadian writers had found their principal audiences in the United States and Great Britain without leaving home. The Ontario-born Presbyterian minister Charles Gordon wrote, under the pen name "Ralph Connor," a long series of highly popular and very moral tales of western adventure and expansion, which were much praised (as Leacock too would later be) by Theodore Roosevelt. In 1893 a world bestseller came from Nova Scotia-born novelist Margaret Marshall Saunders; she lived most of her life in Canada and her *Beautiful Joe* was based upon Canadian experiences but was set in the United States and achieved its greatest sales there. Leacock was one of those who did not move to New York or London to find better markets or to participate in literary life. His opportunities in Toronto were very limited. Apart from Edgar's appreciative listening, he was almost entirely without the support of a literary community.

He did possess a connection to New York's publishing world in the person of Peter McArthur, one of those Canadians who had radicated in the eastern metropolis to seek literary success. Later famous as a Canadian humorist called "the sage of Ekfrid," McArthur was a native of Ontario and a near contemporary of Leacock's; he attended the Strathroy teacher-preparation program the year before Leacock did, and was at the University of Toronto during one of Leacock's years there. In 1892, after working for Toronto newspapers, McArthur went to New York to try freelancing. He was working at *Life* when "My Financial Career" was accepted; more important, he was later an editor of *Truth*, another New York magazine, where contributions from Leacock began as soon as McArthur arrived in 1895 and ended the moment he left in 1897. During the 1895-97 period, Leacock placed twenty-five more pieces in New York; after "My Financial Career" appeared in *Life* on 11 April 1895, all of the remaining twenty-four were published by *Truth*, six in 1895, ten in 1896, and eight in 1897. This run began with the funny yet haunting and melancholy piece "An Experiment with Policeman Hogan" in the 29 June 1895 issue and included such classics as "The New Food" (28 December 1895), "The Awful Fate of Melpomenus Jones" (18 January 1896), "The Conjurer's Revenge" (8 February 1896), "Self-Made Men" (28 January 1897), and "Boarding-House Geometry" (15 April 1897). Leacock's last essay in *Truth* was "On Collecting Things" for the 14 August 1897 issue, after which his work did not appear again in an American popular magazine until 1913, when he began to publish in *American Magazine, Popular Magazine, Century, Collier's, Vanity Fair* and others.

Without McArthur's help, Leacock might have had much more initial difficulty publishing his work in New York in the 1890s; in fact, he might never have done so to the extent he did. For it seems likely that McArthur was not simply an eager receptor for contributions Leacock would have submitted to magazines in any case. Rather, the humorist and the editor formed a team, the connection stimulating Leacock to produce and the quality of Leacock's contributions adding to McArthur's success. As it was, Leacock became a regular contributor to at least one major magazine and so could be sure of a source of income and a prominent forum for his work. After McArthur left *Truth*, Leacock's comedic publication for the remaining years of the decade sank to four pieces. Three of these appeared in the *Canadian Magazine of Politics, Science, Art and Literature*, two in 1898 and the memorable "Hoodoo McFiggin's Christmas" in January 1899. Also in 1899 "Timothy's Homecoming" appeared in the *College Times*.

Most of these early pieces were collected in *Literary Lapses*, Leacock's first book of humour, which was not published until 1910. Was he in the 1890s considering a writing career, from which he was diverted to university teaching by the uncertainty of these earliest attempts? He was not prepared to emigrate to a publishing centre and journalism did not suit his idea of a worthy profession any more than did high school teaching. Factors other than fear of financial failure must have been uppermost in his choice of an academic career. His tastes and the education he had pursued marked him out for a level of participation in cultural and intellectual traditions beyond the ephemera of the popular press. His long-time service, willingly undertaken, to his mother and siblings, his acceptance of many of his mother's values, and his role as head of the family all spoke to him. Since he so disliked high school teaching, it may appear contradictory that he chose university teaching as a life's work, but he always directed his criticisms not against high school teaching itself but the general treatment and perception of teachers: the pay was too low and the acknowledgment from society too little, especially in view of education's importance. His own explanation, in *The Boy I Left Behind Me*, of why he took up and then abandoned high school teaching is that it was initially attractive because it gave a comparatively high starting salary, which he needed if he was to support himself, help his mother and pay his university costs. But as years passed, salary increases did not match the income available in other professions. Marriage too was a consideration: "Every career should look forward to marriage as a thing that can in due course and time be accepted with all that it brings in the way of children and a home, without the pinching and semi-poverty that reduces it to a status not good enough to rank with that of other professions. The trouble with our school-teaching in Canada is that up to now it does not offer these things."[18] Although he would eventually complain about university salaries too, a professorship would keep him in the field of education, which he deeply respected and was developing his own marked ideas about ways to modernize and improve, while providing many of the things he found lacking in high school teaching. He would be able to earn acceptance as an important voice in society, and speak to a much broader and more influential community on social and political issues. The emphasis that, later in life, he laid on the students who had gone forth from his classroom to be generals and statesmen suggests that, quite apart from his own ideas and writings, he intended to make an influential contribution to society through teaching itself. He wanted to teach, but not on a level at which it seemed his efforts went largely unappreciated.

Moreover, Leacock had begun to feel that his field, languages, for all its value, cut him off from the chance to be at the heart of modern changes in education and from the type of effect he wanted to exercise through his teaching. Along with philosophy and history, classical languages had formed the core of a liberal education for centuries. When language study was expanded to include modern languages, the methods of instruction followed the pattern established for Latin and Greek, emphasizing grammar and translation from literary and other texts. Leacock complained that he was never taught to speak French and was never expected to teach his students to speak it; throughout his life he wrote vigorously about the need, especially in a bilingual country such as Canada, to form a program of language teaching that would make acquired languages genuinely useful to the student. But his advanced and prophetic sense of the direction language teaching should take did not move him to work in the field as a reformer; language study, even if correctly conducted, was not what he wanted. He sought a subject that would enable him to feel a direct connection between his expertise and both his teaching and the contemporary world beyond the classroom and the campus.[19] So he had decided upon private studies of economics, in order to gain admission to a university that was a leader in the modern scientific study of this discipline so obviously central to the world at the turn of the twentieth century, with its bewildering, exhilarating profusion of developments in technology, transportation, communication, industrialism, corporatism, labour activism, political radicalism, and shifting international relations. He felt increasingly that the subjects he was teaching, the disciplines he had chosen as his own, were not relevant to the living problems and concerns of the day. Economics and political science were the booming "social sciences" of the time. Their appeal to him lay in their direct applicability to the running of a nation and the world, as well as to the teaching of those setting out for leadership.

In the meantime he maintained his high school-teaching routine and throughout the 1890s spent his vacations with his mother and younger siblings in the Lake Simcoe area. When Leacock moved them off the farm in 1892, Agnes and her younger children apparently resided in a large house called Rotherwood[20] that was part of the estate of the Sibbalds. The Sibbalds, who had grown close to the Leacocks and assisted them in several ways, were one of the region's principal pioneering families, having been led to Canada in the late 1830s by Mrs. Susan Sibbald. Rotherwood is now gone, but its site was not far east of St. George Church; the large area east of the church that comprised the Sibbald grounds is now Sibbald Point Provincial Park. In 1895 Agnes moved to Orillia, and later she lived with her younger daughters in Beaverton, on the east shore of the lake; this town remained the home of Carrie Leacock, Mrs. Jan Ulrichsen, who became the mother of Leacock's beloved niece and secretary of the 1930s, Barbara Ulrichsen. Afterwards, Agnes again lived on the Sibbald estate, in The Grange, a white stucco house that was still her home during the 1910s. These movements bespeak improved family fortunes that enabled Agnes to experiment in an attempt to find attractive living conditions. By the late 1890s new stocks and some new cash had enriched Agnes's trust as a result of bequests from the uncle who had so befriended her in England, the Rev. Charles Butler; the principal addition was approximately £3,000 in three and three-and-a-half per cent stocks.

That Agnes did not stay at Orillia or Beaverton evinces her preference for the south shore of Lake Simcoe, where the Sibbalds and other friends lived. In the 1890s she was not yet permanently settled there, but she was at last free of the worries of the farm. With her children growing up around her and more money coming to her from her older sons, she provided a household that was a relaxing change for Stephen during his summer months. Perhaps she had found little to recommend in the life of the Lake Simcoe area farmers in the 1870s, but in the 1890s she was living in a pleasant and leisurely manner reminiscent of her childhood days in Hampshire and on the Isle of Wight. Toronto businessmen were increasingly establishing summer homes for their families around Lake Simcoe, and Leacock was not only a part of his own family circle but a well-remembered member of the local summer-season sporting and social society, its tennis and cricket clubs, its cruises, dances and parties. He was an enthusiastic organizer of events: cricket matches, lake excursions, outings in his own small boat. Perhaps but for this diverting and flattering society, he would have left school teaching sooner.

Leacock as he was during his 1890s social summers can be glimpsed in stories that have been handed down from his local acquaintances and from a few intimate friends who continued to know him for many years. A friend from that period, Robert B. Pattison, throws much light on Leacock and the idyll that he and his family had made for themselves at Lake Simcoe and were to maintain and renew each year until age and death slowly brought it to an end in the 1930s. Pattison recalled that during the period when Agnes lived at Rotherwood, the Leacocks (presumably Stephen and one or more of his brothers) spent one or two summers at a nearby log house called The Parsonage and that E.P. was then living in a tent in the immediate area. Once when playing tennis at Rotherwood, Leacock interrupted his game with the score at thirty-forty to find a piece of paper: the answer to a geometry problem he was puzzling over had come to him during the game. Just before the match, he had been translating Virgil fluently and studying Greek and geometry simultaneously by reading Euclid in the original. The Parsonage held the many prize books the former Head Boy had won at Upper Canada College. At tennis, Leacock was skillful enough to give practice to his friend Maud Osborne, a noted Canadian champion in the sport. He helped organize and played in cricket matches pitting Lake Simcoe area teams and communities against each other.[21]

Other stories portray him as a good singer, an avid sailor and a careless dresser. A large number of them, including some by Pelham Edgar, disparage his sporting skills. Leacock's Upper Canada College colleague was a Lake Simcoe vacationer during these years: his father had a summer home there, and Edgar remembered many gatherings at which Leacock was present. In a memoir written at the time of Leacock's death, he mentioned that his friend, despite his professed enthusiasm for cricket, had not been a good player. He had not been on the school team (Edgar had). Edgar also remembered Leacock as not much of a sailor.[22] In later years, when Leacock was famous, stories multiplied about the Lake Simcoe fish that always succeeded in escaping the master teller of fish tales. In many instances, however, there are other accounts that directly contradict these and insist, especially in regard to sailing, on his skill. It bears remembering that Leacock was perhaps the leader of all those who would notice and later recall — perhaps even create out of whole cloth — the sorrowful limitations in his own performances as a sportsman. He laughed at himself, and in such a way as to make others join in and remember. Some of the stories about him seem almost as if he wrote them, as if

Beatrix Leacock: undated photograph, probably from before her marriage.

Courtesy National Archives of Canada C-33110.

they are self-deprecating sketches spoken by the voice we hear in his published work: Leacock was undoubtedly already creating the humorous personality and voice that he used on occasion in life as well as in his humorous writings and lectures. Another factor may also have contributed to the undoubted exaggerations of his sporting incompetence in some anecdotes from the period. For all his love of sport, he maintained an irreverent attitude towards the self-professed expert in this as in any activity, regarding such claims of proficiency as mostly complacency and self-delusion. This view, frequent in his writings and perhaps expressed just as pointedly in life, must have stung many of those who took pride in their cricket or boating prowess, especially since it came from a young wit who never ceased to compete with them and to mock the idea that a "star" merited any special respect or standing.

Above all, sailing and fishing were his sports, and much of his socializing took place around them. A ship breakfast he once gave on his boat, "Pilot," forecast many dinners he would later organize at his Old Brewery Bay home near Orillia: like them, it began in plans of elaborate formality but gradually, under the pressure of events, turned into an episode of good-natured foraging. The breakfast was to be at "seven sharp"; it got under way at eleven. The main course was announced as fresh-caught Lake Simcoe fish, but the fish did not comply. The guests decided to have bacon and eggs instead but had to settle for bread and butter, which Leacock had laid in "to be on the safe side." He did have milk, dubbed "cream," for the coffee, but there was no coffee. The canard that Leacock was a poor sailor may have originated in the fact that he was, at times, a foolhardy one, carried away by high spirits and humour. He once decided to shinny up the mast of his small boat, but when he was half way up his weight capsized the vessel, spilling himself and his passengers into the lake. This was not the only such mischance he caused. In fact, he developed a habitual joke for these occasions: while he floundered in the water, he would shout out, "And the last thing seen of the unfortunate sailors, they were clinging desperately to the torn rigging." On the other hand, when occasion called for it, he exhibited both skill and daring on the often dangerous waters of Lake Simcoe. One night a strong storm stranded his yachting party on a small island near Georgina Island. He himself sailed to shore and back to the island, through violent wind and waves and in the dark, to bring food and blankets.

At Lake Simcoe, during the summer of 1898 or 1899, Leacock met his future wife, Beatrix Hamilton, at a tennis outing on the estate of her grandmother, which was near Orillia. Beatrix's mother, Mrs. Robert Hamilton, was the sister of one of Toronto's richest men, the eccentric millionaire Sir Henry Pellatt. It was Pellatt who built the largest castle in North America, Casa Loma, among the most extravagant of all the white elephants raised by pre-Depression dreams; it remains today, looming on a bluff over downtown Toronto, one of the city's best-known landmarks and tourist attractions. Through Beatrix's grandfather, the first Henry Pellatt, father of Sir Henry, the entire family had good financial expectations, although the son's extravagance would later gut the estate that had been built up through banking and stock investments. Beatrix lived the comfortable, leisured life of a daughter of well-to-do North Americans of the period; her father, Robert Hamilton, was an investment broker and a colonel in an army regiment. After his earlier, perhaps apocryphal pursuit of the hymn-singing sanatorium patient, Leacock seems to have chosen the sort of girl Victorian mothers are supposed to have hoped their sons would choose: someone well-known to local society and of good family and comfortable means. Beatrix was, however, somewhat out of the ordinary. She took the drama classes and voice study that would have been acceptable as a hobby in a young lady of her standing, but regarded them seriously, and demanded a chance to go on the stage. Immediately after her summer romance with Leacock, which moved very quickly to his proposal and her acceptance, she set out from home for a year of study and stage work in New York.[23]

Although to go on the stage was a conventional dream for society girls at the end of the nineteenth century, very few of them actually made the attempt. More unconventional still than her stage career was her decision to marry Leacock who, whatever his charms and abilities around the social circuit, was just a high school teacher already at the limit of his salary potential and the apex of his community standing, with no family money or position to give promise of an improved future.

In 1899, his tenth year at Upper Canada College, Leacock had come up against the boundaries imposed in the teaching profession by lack of an advanced degree. Language study now held no interest for him. He was at last free from worry over his mother and younger brothers and sisters; he was engaged to be married and determined to start a family and a substantial career of his own.

Has Economics Gone to Seed?

I n the fall of 1899 Leacock left Toronto to study economics at the University of Chicago. Just as when he entered the University of Toronto in the autumn following his high school graduation, he was hard pressed to pay for even the first year of his intended studies; it cost more than the savings he had accumulated in his Upper Canada College career. Due to Agnes's improved finances, he requested and obtained a loan from his mother and brothers and sisters in the form of a $1,500 advance on Agnes's trust fund. An indenture dated 22 November 1899 was signed by all seven children, including himself, who were of age, as parties of the fourth part. Not only were they future legatees of Agnes's estate, but they would be responsible for repaying the money to the trust if Leacock proved unable to observe his repayment schedule, which provided for him to pay six per cent annual interest on the loan.[1] The risk taken evidences a firm determination to make a career in scholarship and university teaching, strong self-confidence, and, probably, an already-evolved plan for a way of affording the years necessary to obtain the doctorate.

Professor James Mayor of the University of Toronto had declined to encourage or help him in his studies of economics, and Leacock was, after all, the honours language student who preferred to risk his grade average on a subject he had never studied rather than face an algebra test. Why did he study economics if he was not equipped in mathematics? The question, sometimes asked by those who wish he had put all his genius into literature, is anachronistic, flowing from the mathematical essence of the economics mainly practised for the past seven decades or so. But in 1900 mathematics was not yet so central to the field. In part, the reason for Leacock's choice lies in the new academic discipline of economics as it existed at the turn of the twentieth century, when it had a distinctly bifurcated nature, scientific on the one hand, humanistic on the other. It was an aggressively modern study bent upon scrutinizing and even reorganizing economic life by means of the rigorous collection and analysis of data; but it was also a new emphasis within traditional humanism, strongly related to moral philosophy and history, and often considered a twin of political science, the descendant of the political philosophy of Plato and Aristotle.

As a separate field, distinct from history or philosophy, economics was only about a century old when Leacock began his informal studies at Upper Canada College. There were influential works on wealth, trade, labour, and organization dating back to the Greeks, but the modern study began properly with Adam Smith, who published his *The Wealth of Nations* in 1776. Economics, or "political economy" as it was usually called in the nineteenth century, was gradually being introduced to college classrooms at the very end of the 1800s. It was classed as one of the new social sciences; that is, within the traditional university curriculum it was considered an outgrowth of moral philosophy, and was linked to ethics or history in theory and in presentation. A university might decide to separate economics from the philosophy or history department, but the subject rarely became a department by itself, separate from other social sciences. At

McGill, for example, Leacock was hired to teach in the newly formed department of economics and political science; in fact, he gave the school's first political science course. Established universities looking to staff a department in the new field turned to history or philosophy departments for their experts. Mayor at the University of Toronto was a historian.[2]

In his book *Elements of Political Science* (1906), Leacock puts in a word about the difficulties of keeping the fields of political science and economics altogether separate.

> Inasmuch as the production and distribution of material wealth is very largely conditioned by the existing form of government and the institutional basis of economic life, the study of political economy is brought into an intimate relation with that of political science.

In a footnote, he comments on the academic consequences, as they then existed, flowing from the close connection of the two fields:

> The ambiguous relation in which the terms "political science" and "political economy" stand to one another is rendered still more confusing by the divergent usages of leading American universities. At Harvard "Economics" is a subdivision of the department of "History and Political Science." At Yale both "Economics" and "Politics" appear under the departmental title of "Social Sciences." At Chicago "Political Economy" and "Political Science" constitute separate departments.[3]

Looking back from Keynesian and post-Keynesian econometric science, some have disparaged Leacock the economist, while often praising the political scientist; this shows an instinctive awareness that his strength was in the disciplines conceived humanistically, for political science as a study has still not proved susceptible of any strictly statistic-analytical organization, and hence Leacock's approach has not been superseded. Yet it is also an error that applies subsequent standards to Leacock's work; it echoes the fact that in the 1930s Leacock engaged himself against Keynes's mathematical economics and for that reason does appear today somewhat as a rear-guard of a retreating phenomenon. It is good to recall, then, that during his training at the University of Chicago, and in the department he joined at McGill University, the division between the two fields was not as complete as it has since become. For Leacock, for the classic authors in the two fields, and for Leacock's professors, the social sciences were an outgrowth of history and ethics, not of statistics or, more generally, of the scientific method as it has come to be applied to the study of society, especially the economy, in the twentieth century. Leacock's growing ethical concern with the problems of modern society, together with his love for history and his success in his academic studies of it, were enough to attract him to economics seen as a distinctively contemporary descendant of philosophy and history that dealt with a new civilization. Economics and political science were fields growing up in direct response to the explosive social changes brought about by the Industrial Revolution.

If in the 1930s Leacock did not seem a forward-looking economist to some, he entered the field for forward-looking reasons and in a progressive fashion. So too he decided to take his degree in the United States rather than in Great Britain; he was impressed with the University of Chicago faculty in economics, which included J. Lawrence Laughlin, Henry Pratt Judson and Caspar Miller, luminaries of the field. But he chose Chicago largely for the sake of studying under a single very revolutionary thinker and teacher, Thorstein Veblen, who had been at the university since 1896. The American-born son of Norwegian immigrants, Veblen (1857-1929) published his first major book, *The Theory of the Leisure Class*, in 1899, the same year Leacock decided to attend the university. The book was a great intellectual event, widely and heatedly discussed; it was epochal and prophetic, catching the mood of the great nineteenth century's close — increasing dissatisfaction with the rapacious capitalism of the waning Gilded Age, an apocalyptic dread as misery for many seethed behind the carefree facade of the 1890s. The established order was beset now with rising tides of Marxism, socialism, anarchism, labour activism, somewhat feebly answered by a progressivism that sought political improvements to forestall the ripping apart of society's fabric in these stresses. Leacock may have read Veblen's book before he went to Chicago or he may have known of it through reviews; he may also have known of Veblen through the economist's publications in journals of the social sciences. *The Theory of the Leisure Class* became influential on Leacock's thought and is echoed strongly both in his economic writing (*The Unsolved Riddle of Social Justice*, for example) and in his humour (*Arcadian Adventures with the Idle Rich*).

For more than thirty years, Veblen's books exercised enormous influence; in the 1930s, for example, *The Theory of the Leisure Class* headed a list of "books that have changed our minds," placing Veblen above many scientists and philosophers whose names are today more familiar than his. Veblen was influential among economists but still more so among historians, journalists and intellectuals, who delighted in the acerbic social criticism he delivered in witty satirical prose intended to reach an audience beyond the specialists in his field. In selecting Veblen as his mentor, Leacock chose an outspoken man who can be seen as a model for Leacock's own use of literary power and humour to reach the general public with social criticism and iconoclastic political and economic views.[4]

Canadian students of economics usually went to Great Britain; Leacock and a handful of others are recognized by historians of education in Canada as being controversial importers from the United States of a new "scientific" (by the strongly humanistic standards of British academic economics) approach to economics.[5] Veblen's was not the science of the later twentieth century, but as an "institutional economist" he analyzed and commented on the actual circumstances of economic structures and behaviour. He departed from the theoretical principles of the nineteenth century to seek a ground in careful observation of fact for his judgments on finance and business. For all his attraction to this side of Veblen and of U.S. intellectual culture generally, Leacock was not tempted by the country as a theatre for his talents and a place to live; his academic year 1899-1900 in Chicago was his first and only extended residence in the United States. There was a good deal of traffic between Canada and the United States at the end of the nineteenth century, much of it draining population away from Canada. One million people went south in the 1880s, another half-million in the 1890s. Some of them were immigrants who decided to try their luck in more developed areas in the United States, after testing the Canadian prairies. Others were part of a "brain drain": authors such as Leacock's friend and editor at *Truth*, Peter McArthur, looking for audiences and markets, inventors and businessmen seeking capital and equipment. Alexander Graham Bell, for example, had moved from his father's home in the southern Ontario to the eastern United States, where in 1876 he patented his invention, the telephone, commenting that it had been conceived in Brantford and born in Boston. Several of Leacock's brothers and sisters lived in the United States at various times, but he, although he later wrote for U.S. audiences and considered North America in important respects one culture, had chosen definitively for Canada. Discernible already in his student approach to economics was an essential feature of his later written work, the playing off of American and British tendencies against one another, to supplement and correct each other's deficiencies, thereby developing a distinctively Canadian civilization and personality-type that would combine the best of each and transcend both.

During his first year at the University of Chicago, Leacock

completed six courses and received marks high enough to earn a fellowship in "political economy;" he had achieved another goal in that he was accepted to be one of a small group of students whose doctoral thesis work was directed by Veblen. When he went back to Chicago in the fall of 1900, he had Beatrix with him; in August they had married quietly at the Little Church Around the Corner in the New York's theatre district, where Beatrix had been working. Their first home together was a small apartment near the University of Chicago, but they had only been settled a few months when they moved to Montreal, where Leacock began work as a part-time lecturer in political science and history. Despite his fellowship, he evidently felt he could no longer afford to be without a job. He first applied to the University of Toronto, but Professor Mayor, now head of the economics department, refused to consider him. Backed by warm recommendations from Upper Canada College principal George Parkin, he was able to obtain an appointment at McGill.[6] McGill principal William Peterson wrote Parkin later that he had been impressed with Leacock from their first meeting. From 1901 through 1903, Leacock spent only one quarter of each year in Chicago, in residence at the university, and devoted the rest of his time to teaching at McGill.

At the time of his marriage, Leacock had just turned thirty-one. He was straight and slender, and gave the impression of being taller than his height of five feet ten inches. He had added a certain amount of maturity and dash to his face by growing a fashionable Edwardian mustache: combined with the square massiveness of his chin, it could help make him seem, at times, solid and respectable. Generally, however, he impressed people as looking, if anything, younger than his age. He often wore stylish and well-fitted clothes, and his untroubled if sometimes serious face was dominated by a striking head of dark, glossy and usually well-combed hair. However, the few informal photographs of him from this period leave no doubt that, away from the portrait camera, the rumpled and tousled Leacock of later years was developing.

Leacock's experience of working under Veblen, one of the great intellectuals of the time and still prominent in its intellectual history, can only be glimpsed through the humorist's later writings. In *My Discovery of the West*, published seven years after his former thesis director's death in 1929, Leacock wrote fondly and appreciatively of Veblen's theoretical powers but less positively about his writing style and classroom technique.

> Veblen had a beautiful and thoughtful mind, free from anger and dispute, and heedless of all money motive. As a lecturer, he had no manner, but sat mumbling into his lap, scarcely intelligible. But the words which thus fell into his lap were priceless....His writings, brilliant though they are, are too abstruse for popular reading, and not abstruse enough to be unintelligible and rank as gospel, like the Social Credit of Major Douglas.

Leacock devotes a paragraph to a curious anecdote about Veblen's highly unpopular class called "Primitive Economics of the Navajo Indians," through which most students apparently slept: "After a few minutes you could hear its [the class's] deep breathing." Leacock concealed himself behind the classroom's only pillar and so escaped the fate of one student refused credit by Veblen: "He told me after-wards the man had slept in his class." But was the class worth staying awake for? "Navajo is pronounced Navaho: I got that much out of it anyway." Leacock's judgment that Veblen was "too abstruse for popular reading" reflects his desire to be still more readable and influential, to express views more acceptable to society in both substance and rhetoric, and more likely to have a practical effect; it should be weighed against the wide acknowledgment of Veblen's work for its impact, profundity, importance, and literary panache.

The Theory of the Leisure Class illuminates the formation of

Leacock's thought on social issues. Veblen establishes several principles of historical and contemporary economic motives and organization, and then uses them to analyze various forms of human behaviour; often the result overturns accepted social values or reveals self-interest behind an appearance of altruism and objective truth. In *My Discovery of the West* Leacock outlined his concept of Veblen's key ideas, some of which he had heard in the classroom before they reached the public in printed form.

> The ideas of the lectures were gathered later into Veblen's books. The central point of his thought is that human industry is not carried on to satisfy human wants but in order to make money. The two motives do not work, thinks Veblen, to a single end as Adam Smith and John Stuart Mill had thought they do. They fall apart. Hence a lot of people get too much money. These have to find ways of spending it in "conspicuous consumption." This is the "leisure class," a sort of flower on a manure heap.
>
> Contrasted with the "money makers" are the "engineers," that is men who make *things* not money, — the "real boys," so to speak. They could satisfy all our reasonable wants if they guided industrial society. But they don't. The money getters, with their leisure class women and their "honorific expenditure," have entrenched themselves as "Vested Interests," — and there you are! What did Veblen propose to do about it? Nothing, so far as I remember.[7]

It may seem the simplification of Leacock's summary verges on the flippant, especially in his dismissal of Veblen's constructive suggestions. But Veblen was, in fact, little concerned with solutions, and Leacock's presentation does substantial justice to Veblen's quarrel with capitalism, a quarrel which Leacock made his own and was soon to introduce to the university classrooms of the English-speaking world via a best-selling textbook. Veblen attacked the work ethic, which justified the possession of wealth, by arguing that money was accumulated not by the honest effort to produce valuable objects (work) but rather in a barbaric attempt to prove superiority over other men through the possession of the most valuable goods. Money, once acquired, did not improve life for the community at large, as some economists argued, but effectively discouraged social improvements because the wealthy spent money only to drive home the point of their superiority. Veblen wrote:

> The institution of a leisure class hinders cultural development immediately (1) by the inertia proper to the class itself, (2) through its prescriptive example of conspicuous waste and of conservatism, and (3) indirectly through that system of unequal distribution of wealth and sustenance on which the institution itself rests.

Even activities one might suppose to be useful or at least harmless are undertaken because they demonstrate the leisured person's superiority in terms of absolute freedom from any necessity. Veblen argued this point in terms that bring before the mind's eye the young Leacock reading the controversial, cutting-edge book in provincial Toronto and receiving a disturbing confirmation of his own doubts about the education he had pursued at Upper Canada College and the University of Toronto:

> So, for instance, in our time there is the knowledge of the dead languages and the occult sciences; of correct spelling; of syntax and prosody; of the varied forms of domestic music and other household art; of

the latest proprieties of dress, furniture, and equipage; of games, sports and fancy-bred animals, such as dogs and race-horses. In all these branches of knowledge the initial motive from which their acquisition proceeded at the outset, and through which they first came into vogue, may have been something quite different from the wish to show that one's time had not been spent in industrial employment; but unless these accomplishments had approved themselves as serviceable evidence of an unproductive expenditure of time, they would not have survived and held their place as conventional accomplishments of the leisure class.

Finally, it is relevant to Leacock's career that Veblen's great book draws repeated attention to the questionable status of women in the leisure class. Men expect women to enjoy their position as recipients of leisure and wealth given them by their husbands, without admitting that this demand reduces women to "chattels" and "unfree servants." A wife busies herself with a round of social engagements and household duties that "prove on analysis to serve little or no ulterior end beyond showing that she does not occupy herself with anything that is gainful or that is of substantial use."[8]

In 1904 Veblen published *The Theory of Business Enterprise*, which considered the intricacies of money management rather than the social impact of "conspicuous consumption" by the wealthy. This more technical study, directly concerned with economic organization and less focused on social criticism, was based on the work Veblen was doing while he was teaching Leacock and directing his thesis. Shortly after the publication of the second book, he was asked to leave the University of Chicago; in his reminiscence in *My Discovery of the West* Leacock says only that "they 'let him out' of Chicago University," but the issue involved is well-known. Veblen was discharged because he travelled openly with a woman companion, his secretary, on an Atlantic crossing; at the time, he was estranged from his wife, who eventually divorced him. One might have supposed that the same university officials who admired Veblen for his outspoken attacks on his society's treatment of women would have expected unconventional personal behaviour from the economist. Apparently, they were prepared to endure his endless campaign against university regulations with regard to his classroom methods but could not accept the breach of marital propriety. From Chicago, Veblen went on to teach at Stanford and later in the midwest at a small college; after a second discharge for reasons similar to those that forced him to leave Chicago, he became a recluse and died alone in 1929.[9]

Leacock demonstrated his admiration for Veblen's insight by incorporating many of his teacher's complaints against society in his own work. He treated Veblen somewhat as he did Marx and socialist thinkers, drawing heavily on their criticism of *laissez faire* capitalism but rejecting their reconstructive suggestions and developing his own. Certain texts by Leacock display a rather direct use of Veblen's teachings; it is possible that Veblen's highly individual personal style, too, might have had an influence on Leacock's later self-presentation. How did the newlywed Leacocks react to the outrageous conduct of his teacher? On this point Leacock is silent, although it seems unlikely that he could have spent three years working closely under Veblen without observing and hearing about his personal life. When University of Chicago chancellor William Rainey Harper challenged Veblen regarding the possible impact of his conduct on the "moral health" of other professors' wives, Veblen is supposed to have replied, "I've tried them all. They are no good."[10] Leacock would have admired the witticism, if he heard it, but if there is a remote parallel between Veblen and Leacock on the intellectual question of women in society, there is none in the conduct of their personal lives. Leacock was comfortable in the traditional husband's role, and after Beatrix's death in 1925 was a devoted widower, contenting himself with relationships of complete propriety, or at least discretion. The question of women aside, he seems to have been tempted to imitate some of Veblen's careless sartorial style and his constant skirmishes against university regulations. Veblen refused to take attendance in class; students absent when he read the roll were not reported. Leacock's similar dislike of McGill's introduction of compulsory class attendance is well attested. Veblen disliked the university's requirement that teachers wear an academic gown and was notoriously negligent about his dress; Leacock's admirers outdo themselves in describing his tattered gown and generally untidy appearance. Veblen disliked keeping office hours and refused to take trouble over grading his students. Leacock on occasion is recorded as speaking quite cavalierly about assigning final marks. Still, there are differences that perhaps out-weigh all these similarities. By Leacock's account, and general agreement among other former students, Veblen had a poor classroom technique, whereas Leacock was remembered universally by his students as a commanding classroom presence; he adhered to the principles of teaching he recommended in his writing: strictness, forcefulness of delivery, clarity of organization, authority. More generally, Leacock developed into a thinker always concerned to encourage change only by setting the values he found in tradition against current abuses; thus he liked the puncturing of pious facades and hypocritical motives he found in Veblen as in Marx, but was deeply suspicious of the radical criticisms and remedies found in their work, grounded in the theoretical proposals of individual thinkers rather than the slowly broadened wisdom of an entire people working through its historic institutions.

Leacock's doctoral thesis was a historical study, "The Doctrine of Laissez Faire"; the subject shows Veblen's impact, whereas the approach may represent a combination of Leacock's interests along with the influence of his teacher's then-current research into the nature and history of forms of business organization. At his final oral examination, he was asked to discuss the tax system of the State of Illinois. Leacock refused, saying he knew nothing about it. He offered instead to speak on the theory of value.[11] A fundamental philosophical concept for nineteenth-century political economy, the theory of value deals with the idea of the valuable or the good; it was used to analyze the relationship between a price and the inherent worth of manufactured objects or services. Leacock spoke learnedly on this subject and was passed by the committee of examiners. In May 1903 he received his doctorate in political economy from the University of Chicago *magna cum laude*. He was now free to live year-round in Montreal, and he and Beatrix planned to return to Canada immediately. Throughout his life, though, he maintained a friendly acquaintance with the University of Chicago and with the city, where he was always much in demand as a speaker, both by civic groups and by Chicago-based lecture bureaus that served the midwest. As an alumnus of the university's graduate school, he recommended outstanding McGill undergraduates to the University of Chicago in not a few cases. A letter to his old department, which Leacock wrote on behalf of a female student in 1915, brought him this response from J. Lawrence Laughlin, who had been one of his favourite professors:

> It was a great satisfaction to get your personal note in your letter of recommendation for Miss Going. In fact, I had been on the point of writing you for a long time because your name and your books had become a household word with us. Mrs. Laughlin has had no end of pleasure and merriment out of your books; and her pleasure has been shared by my son....Of course, I claim that all this success has been due to the work you did in my economics seminar!

The students he met there remembered him just as vividly as did his teachers, and they too sometimes contacted him, directly or indirectly. One letter he received fifteen years after he had left the university provides a brief glimpse of his student days. Charles Starrett of the Chicago *Daily News* wrote to him:

> My friend and associate of the News, Mr. Leroy T. Binion, discovered me, recently, chuckling over the Nonsense Novels, and demanded to look at the volume. Thereupon he discovered that the author was one Stephen Leacock, with whom, he asserted, he had "gone to school" — that is, at the University of Chicago. Then he unfolded a number of anecdotes of the period, describing how the political economy class frequently became a debate between Leacock and the professor, in which the professor was as likely to be worsted as Mr. Leacock.[12]

Immediately after Leacock had received his doctorate, he was hired by McGill as a full-time lecturer in the department of economics and political science at a salary, with extra night-class duties, of two thousand dollars per year. During the summer of 1903, Stephen and Beatrix took a brief deferred honeymoon trip to England and France; it was the first time Leacock had been in his native country since his emigration in 1876. The opening of the fall term found them back in Montreal, established comfortably in a small flat near the university. They had spent much of every year in the city since 1901, but this time they were settling down permanently. Stories abound about Leacock at McGill, in the classroom and out. Relatively few of the first-person accounts of his antics date from these very early days, but even in his very first class, the one that began his life at McGill on the day before Queen Victoria's death, 21 January 1901, he had managed to make an impression. He had been hired to teach McGill's first-ever course in political science, and when it was concluded its students privately petitioned Peterson, the principal, to keep the young instructor on the staff because they had so greatly appreciated his ideas and technique as lecturer.[13] It was not an era in which student evaluations were relied on as a measure of teacher performance, and Peterson made no mention of the student support to Leacock at the time; he learned of it many years later from former students of the course.

Until 1903, Leacock taught history and political science. Once he had his doctorate in economics, he wanted to teach his specialty as well. A dispute arose between Leacock and the chairman of the department, Dr. A.W. Flux, when Leacock inserted courses in economics to be taught by himself into the McGill curriculum without receiving the chairman's approval in advance. Flux challenged Leacock's behaviour in letters to Peterson, and certainly Leacock seems to have been forcing his ideas through without attention to university procedure. More serious, though, were the accompanying charges Flux raised as to Leacock's competence to teach economics. Flux claimed to Peterson that he had made inquiries to Thorstein Veblen at the University of Chicago, that Veblen had replied in "curiously vague terms" and had shown a "hesitancy to praise." He did not, however, produce the letter for anyone else to read. Despite his assaults, Flux surrendered the point and allowed his junior faculty member to begin teaching economics. This incident is the first challenge to Leacock as an economist; it is interesting as well because Flux tried to use the words of Veblen, perhaps nonexistent words, against Leacock. If Veblen did write curtly to Flux, this is susceptible of quite a different interpretation than Flux gave it, especially in light of the fact that Leacock had just graduated under Veblen's direction with highest distinction. Veblen may well have been too preoccupied with his own growing troubles or simply uninterested in the squabbling of another university's faculty. If Flux, the department chairman, had been able to gain any support, surely he could have stopped one of his least senior subordinates from adding to the curriculum. Perhaps trouble arose simply because Flux saw that his newest faculty member would be difficult to handle, or because the chairman needed a political science teacher and was not interested in an economist. It is possible too that Leacock, with his Veblenesque tinge, was proving to be more controversial on economic issues than he was on history and political science.[14]

As soon as he found employment at McGill, Leacock began to publish sporadically, beginning with humour. "Children's Corner," a satire on a standard feature in newspapers and magazines, and a theme he reprised in sketches in 1925 and 1926, appeared in the December 1901 issue of *University Magazine*. From 1903 through 1905 he placed three humorous poems and three sketches in the *Montreal Herald*, *Old McGill 1905* and the *McGill Outlook* in Montreal, and *Saturday Night* in Toronto. One piece in the *McGill Outlook*, "Humor Unappreciated," in which he complains of the humorist's difficulty in finding acceptance, includes his influential version of the joke based on taking the common turn of phrase "died laughing" seriously. The sketch reproduces a letter of rejection he received from an editor unwilling to expose the public to the danger of a Leacock joke that had nearly killed the composing room staff with laughter when they tried to set it in type. Leacock incorporated versions of this idea into his later humorous lectures, whence it resonated through the twentieth century; the Monty Python troupe did an ingenious variation, about the British army seeking a way to use a lethally funny story against the Germans without killing its own men, almost seventy years after the appearance of "Humor Unappreciated."

The publishing of humour was almost entirely eclipsed in 1905, just after Leacock had established himself at McGill; for the next five years he devoted his writing time to serious, sometimes scholarly essays and articles, often based on addresses, that dealt with political and economic subjects, education, and occasionally history or literature ("The Rehabilitation of Charles II," "The Psychology of American Humour"). These were the fruit of his learning and teaching, and were calculated to enhance his reputation and influence as a commentator on the situation of Canada, its nature, and its best future course. His chief theme was the idea of a reorganized British Empire as a federation of equal nation states, a sort of super-nation with possibilities of unprecedented wealth and power. This subject, which he faithfully pursued throughout his career, was opened up to him in 1906 when Earl Grey, Governor General of Canada, began seeking a spokesman for the cause of imperial unity and received a warm recommendation of Leacock in response to his inquiries to Principal Peterson. Albert Henry George Grey, fourth Earl Grey, had been private secretary to Prince Albert and afterwards to Queen Victoria, and had served as administrator of Rhodesia 1894-97; an active, popular and public-spirited Governor General of Canada 1904-11, he was more than sympathetic with the pro-Empire sentiment that English-speaking Canada was known for, and worked to buttress it and to use it within the Empire for the strengthening of imperial unity.

As the result of Grey's investigations, Leacock was invited by the May Court Club (one of whose sponsoring members was Lady Alice Grey, the Governor General's wife) to give a series of six lectures in Ottawa on the subject of the British Empire. Delivered at Queen's Hall in Ottawa every second Friday from 12 January through 23 March 1906, these were "university extension lectures," arranged by the Club and given under the auspices of McGill; the lectures cost one dollar for the series or fifty cents for each individually, and were accompanied with a pamphlet providing an introduction to Leacock's ideas, the dates and titles of the lectures, summaries, a list of suggested supplementary readings, and even study questions for students. At the close of the course there was an examination for students who had attended. Leacock's topics were "The Making of the Empire: The Lessons of Its History," "The Constituents of the Empire: A Study of Self Governing Colonies," "The Economics of Empire," "Imperial Defense," "Imperial Federation" and "The Imperial Dependencies." The *Ottawa Citizen* and *Ottawa Evening Journal* reprinted the text of the first lecture; the last two were attended by the Governor General himself. Attendance was excellent, and upon conclusion of the series the *Citizen* (24 March) commented approvingly that Leacock had been both "inspiring" and "entertaining." He followed this up on 2 April with a related address, "The Imperial Crisis," to the Canadian Club, Toronto, which the Club reprinted in its 1905-1906 *Proceedings* and which was reported and in part reproduced in at least four Canadian newspapers and magazines. In these lectures and their published versions, Leacock was advocating a united parliament of the Empire with all its constituent nations participating, an equal imperial citizenship for individuals in all Empire nations, and a federal taxation to provide for imperial defence; he argued not simply that Canada's future was brightest within a federated Empire but that the country was of doubtful viability as the separate nation it would be in the event of the Empire's continued weakening or disintegration.[15]

Leacock's writing now already displayed the furious industry for which he became noted and which he maintained until death. Not only was he producing lectures, their published versions, and his occasional essays on education and literature, but he had begun to work on an important contribution to one of his academic fields. Since his days as a graduate student and a part-time lecturer at McGill he had felt that the still comparatively new university subject of political science badly needed a sound textbook on all aspects of the discipline. After working for three years, Leacock completed his manuscript in March 1905; the American publisher Houghton Mifflin accepted it, subject to small revisions, on 13 October, and in June 1906 he saw the release of his first book, *Elements of Political Science*, which turned out to be the biggest money-maker among all his published works, including the many volumes of humour he later wrote. After its initial release, the first American edition was reprinted eight times between 1906 and 1911; there was in addition an English issue of the book. Its long life included in 1913 a second American edition (revised), seven times reprinted, with an English issue, and in

1921 an English edition and a third American edition (revised and updated, with significant additions and deletions). It has been said that it was translated into nineteen languages, though this is without evidence; a Spanish translation is known. Certainly it enjoyed lasting popularity in the United States, Great Britain, and elsewhere in the Empire. A note Leacock wrote to a friend many years later states that "At one time it was used in 35 American universities and many British. It was, I understand, the first textbook used in China after the establishment of the Republic and in Egypt before the war...not quite dead in 1937. I still receive small cheques." Towards the end of his life, in *How to Write* (1943), he quizzically recalled its composition and history:

> So I took my pick and shovel to the college library and in three years I completed my Elements of Political Science. This book had an outstanding, indeed an ominous, success. It was no sooner adopted as the text book by the renovated government of China, than the anti-Manchu rebellion swept the former Empire. The Khedive of Egypt's attempt to use it as the text book of the Egyptian schools, was followed by the nationalist outbreak.

Reviews of the first edition were approving: "a useful textbook of the subject, brought well up-to-date," "clear-cut, well written, logically arranged, and convincing." Writing in *School Review*, Edward E. Hill worried, "It is almost too strong to be taken clear by the young student of political science, but will make an excellent diet when properly diluted with class-room discussion." The most serious objection raised was that Leacock offered "conventional" opinions, especially on issues related to the British Empire.[16]

For readers hoping to find either wit or impassioned social criticism, *Elements of Political Science* will be a disappointment. It is thoroughly a textbook, divided into three main parts — "The Nature of the State," "The Structure of the Government," and "The Province of Government" — and moving clearly and methodically through the essential topics: the nature of political science, the origin and nature and sovereignty of the state, individual liberty, forms and component parts of government, recent political movements and changes in political organization, and so on. Leacock's approach combines impartial presentation of topics with clearly stated value judgments. For instance, in the third part, which consists of chapters on "Individualism," "Socialism" and "The Modern State," he has this to say:

> Entirely opposed to the individualistic conception of government are the doctrines known as socialism, collectivism, communism, and which, subject to later distinction, may be spoken of together as the social-istic theory of the state. No socialistic state has actu-ally existed on any except a small and experimental scale. Socialism is therefore mainly an ideal rather than an actuality. But the doctrines it embodies have appealed so strongly to so many minds, have exer-cised such an important influence on actual legisla-tion and practical politics, and contain in spite of their fallacious nature so much that is of use and inspiration, as to merit a special treatment.

Leacock lists works by Marx among the chapter's recommended readings and balances his initial judgment as to the "fallacious" nature of socialist theory by presenting a very thorough summary of it. He disapproves of socialism for two reasons. First, he does not accept Marx's contention that a capitalistic economy must inevitably collapse due to its own wasteful politics. Second, he does not approve of the socialist remedy to capitalism's failings, that is, the substitution of public ownership through the agency of government for private enterprise. As with his relationship to Veblen's thought, Leacock's principal point of agreement with socialism is with its criticism of the present economic system. He welcomes the assistance provided by the socialist critique in stimulating political change.

> On more valid grounds the socialists draw attention
> to the wastefulness of the individualistic method of
> production and distribution. A vast amount of work
> is performed under it that has no social utility; a great
> deal of work is duplicated and even done several
> times over with no general advantage....From what
> has been said it will be easily seen that the critical or
> destructive side of socialistic theory contains a great
> deal that is true and extremely useful in indicating the
> proper direction of measures of social reform.[17]

Elements of Political Science devotes considerable attention to the development of the British Empire; this is attributable as much to the events at the turn of the century as to Leacock's supposed reverence for Great Britain. Complaints that his opinions are conventional and outdated almost certainly stem from his analysis of imperial politics in the early 1900s. He argues that the growth of a movement for complete independence of British dominions has given way to a resurgence of interest in imperial unity. The unity he proposes is not a return to colonial dependence for countries like Canada but the creation of a federation of nation states, an Empire that provides full and equal citizenship rights to every imperial citizen.

> The new wave of imperialism that has affected public
> opinion in all the great states of the world has fasci-
> nated the national ambitions of all the British subjects
> with the possibility of the future power of their

colossal empire. The smaller destiny of isolated independence is set aside in favour of participating in the plenitude of power possible in union. The combined efforts of Britain and the colonies called forth by the Transvaal War have done much to strengthen this feeling. But with the acceptance of this new point of view, the troubled question of interimperial relations again looms large upon the horizon....If independence is no longer to be the future ideal of the colonies, and since geographical reasons forbid a complete amalgamation, it looks as if the manifest destiny of the colonial system must now be sought in imperial federation....It does not seem possible that another generation can go by and find Canada and Australia still outside of the imperial councils; it hardly seems possible that the group of ministers who control the foreign policy of the empire can permanently remain the appointees of the electorate of the British Isles, to the exclusion of the British dominions beyond the seas.[18]

Soon after the June publication of *Elements of Political Science* Leacock was promoted to the rank of assistant professor, with a pay raise of five hundred dollars per year. Even more importantly, his lectures of January through April and the appearance of the book initiated his lifelong career as an advocate of imperial unity and his more general status as a respected if often controversial commentator on political and economic affairs.

Our British Empire

From April 1906 through March 1907, Leacock repeated his themes widely in addresses in Ontario and Quebec, and added to them such subjects as "Evolution and Socialism" and "American Humor;" the latter talk he delivered to a Canadian Manufacturers' Association meeting in Montreal, after the Association's secretary, Dacres Cameron, a former student of his, had reassured the doubtful businessmen that the professor could be witty as well as informative. With few exceptions, though, his speeches were serious. And they were attended to; for instance, during his May Court Club lectures Prime Minister Robert Borden had taken the trouble to disagree publicly with Leacock's interpretation of the U.S. Monroe Doctrine's application to Canada. He found himself engaged in debate on the highest levels of influence concerning matters of the national future, and he threw himself earnestly into such dialogue; on 18 January 1907, eleven months after Borden's riposte, he presented his further ideas on "The Monroe Doctrine and Its Application to Canada" to the Canadian Club of London, Ontario. A still more notable address was his "Greater Canada," delivered 25 February at the Windsor Hotel to the Insurance Institute of Montreal's annual meeting. Extensively quoted the following day by the *Montreal Star*, this "Remarkable Speech Delivered by Professor Leacock" chided Canada's timidity in taking its rightful role and argued that the country was ready to lead the reconstituted Empire. This address became an article printed in the *University Magazine* for March and was simultaneously issued as a twelve-page, ten-cent pamphlet, *Greater Canada, An Appeal: Let Us No Longer Be a Colony.*[1]

In the spring of 1907, his many lecture successes reached their high point when Earl Grey asked him to make a world lecture tour on behalf of imperial unity, to be sponsored by the recently formed Cecil Rhodes Trust. On 26 March, he responded in a letter outlining a route for the tour, the title of a lecture he would present ("Imperial Development and Organization") and a salary proposal of five hundred pounds per year. The major obstacle in the project's way was his work at McGill. Grey wrote Peterson asking for a two years' leave of absence for Leacock. "I think you will be doing a service to Canada and the Empire if you can see your way to allow him to do this work, for which he is by nature so admirably fitted."[2] He also enlisted the support of Leacock's former principal at Upper Canada College, George Parkin. Parkin had left Upper Canada College in 1902 to take a position with the Cecil Rhodes Trust; he was organizing the Rhodes Scholarship Program to bring students from British colonies past and present to study at Oxford University, a position which resulted in his being knighted in 1920, and which he retained until his death in 1922. Parkin, who had written strong letters of recommendation in support of Leacock's appointment to McGill, again praised his former subordinate and his suitability for the task; McGill's board of governors approved a one-year leave of absence and agreed to pay the expenses of the trip. The Rhodes Trust made a cash contribution, and Earl Grey offered to make up any difference between these sums and actual costs.

The lecture and the lecture tour was one of the great popular cultural forms of the day; it was descended from early and mid-Victorian origins, when new transportation technologies had suddenly made rapid long-distance travel possible, and new printing technologies together with mass education had made writers and thinkers widely known and their presences desired. The era of earlier European travellers, such as de Tocqueville, who merely sized up America for later publication, had passed into the era of European travellers such as Trollope and Dickens and Matthew Arnold who sized it up and meanwhile told it a few things for its edification and their profit. After this had gone on for several decades, Mark Twain had restored the balance richly with *Innocents Abroad* and several highly successful world trips on which he lectured and read from his novels and stories. In the summer of 1907, as Leacock was engaged in his tour, Twain made his last trip across the Atlantic, to receive, along with Rodin, Saint-Säens and Rudyard Kipling, an honorary doctorate from Oxford.[3] Unlike Twain in his famous turn-of-the century tours, Leacock had no international reputation to assure him audiences. He had been chosen by a private foundation and assisted by recommendations from government and university to be the official spokesman for a cause. Not an employee of government or an elected official, he was nonetheless expected to represent a position acceptable to governments in the Empire.

The clearest precedent for his trip was one made by George Parkin himself, five years before he became principal of Upper Canada College, on behalf of the Imperial Federation League. The League was founded in 1884 by residents of British colonies and of Great Britain who were convinced that the best course for the Empire was the type of unity Leacock was later to present in *Elements of Political Science*. A charter member of the league, Parkin in 1888 published his *Reorganization of the British Empire* and in 1889 accepted an invitation to tour Australia and New Zealand as the League's representative. Often finding himself without any audience to address, he gave interviews and met with private citizens and government officials to present the cause. He then returned to England and there published *Around the Empire* (1893), *Imperial Federation* (1893), and a study of Canada within the Empire, *The Great Dominion* (1895). He worked without pause as a thinker, lecturer and journalist on behalf of imperial unity, even after the Imperial Federation League collapsed due to internal difficulties in 1893, interrupting this activity and his residence in England only for his 1895-1902 service as Upper Canada College's principal. The Imperial Federation League had been organized to counter a threat that had, in some measure, disappeared by the mid-1890s because a renewed spirit of imperial unity had grown up due to British activities in India, the Sudan and southern Africa. Beginning in 1868, the year after Canada's confederation, Great Britain under Gladstone's first administration (1868-74) was being led firmly in the direction of freeing the former colonies on grounds that they merely distracted from reforming the home country. The League, which sought to counter this position of the great Liberal leader, was largely composed of opinion-makers from former colonies or continuing possessions who feared that these entities could not survive independently. But by century's end, rivalries between Great Britain and other European powers for control of world trade and shipping had renewed the Empire's importance to London and had made imperial reorganization and unity a stronger and more popular cause.

The key event in the years between Parkin's lecture tour and Leacock's was the Boer War (1899-1902). In the fighting to control the southern tip of Africa, Great Britain had relied on its former colonies — Canada, New Zealand and Australia — to supply troops and military equipment. In *Elements of Political Science*, Leacock held up the successful British war effort in South Africa as an example of imperial unity and a proof of its further possibilities: for once the colonies were not a drain on the home country's resources but rather a help in protecting her interests. Now in Europe, alliances among other

European countries had isolated Great Britain increasingly from its closest neighbours; without the far-reaching network of bases and supply points provided by the mature former colonies, there seemed little to bolster British security. The Boer War had received strong support in Great Britain; among the few dissenting voices raised against the campaign to protect the rights of English nationals living in the Boer states had been G.K. Chesterton, who emerged as a popular journalist through his writings on the war. He had humanitarian objections to the use of British military force against the Boers, but his chief objection was precisely the Liberal, Gladstonian stance that the Empire was a burden to the people of Great Britain; far from welcoming imperial unity in the fight, he objected to the acquisition of another imperial possession. In Canada, the cause had not met with universal approval, especially in Quebec, but Prime Minister Wilfrid Laurier had agreed to send several thousand troops. Leacock's view was just the opposite of Chesterton's; *Elements of Political Science* attests his approval both of imperial cooperation during the fighting and of the peace terms that brought a united group of British and Boer settlements into the Empire as the Union of South Africa. In a late work, *Our British Empire: Its Structure, Its Unity, Its Strength* (1940), he strongly regretted the military conflict and praised the Boers as "unsurpassed in the world's record of patriotic heroism"; this regret was not owing, however, to second thoughts concerning the war's upshot but to a belief that diplomacy would have better achieved the proper end, that is, admission of the area into the Empire.

> The tragedy of it is, as seen by many of us, that all that was ever gained by the war would have come naturally enough anyway, with patience and a lapse of time. People cannot, not even Dutch farmers, live forever on memories of Great Treks and kraals and assegais. Life must go on, and would have, and Dutch and British union under the Empire would

Beatrix Leacock, photographed about 1900.
Courtesy National Archives of Canada C-31937.

have come as easy and welcome destiny. It came another way.[4]

Leacock's imperialism in 1907 went beyond gratitude for British heritage and pride in Canada's contributions to the Empire's needs; it included an assertive sense of the proper Canadian leadership role in a renovated Empire that would be a sort of super-state and the dominant power of the emerging century. Already in *Elements of Political Science* he had reasoned the necessity of equal representation for all imperial citizens in an imperial legislative assembly. *Greater Canada, An Appeal*, the pamphlet and essay he published in March, was timed (as was the tour itself) to influence the Imperial Conference, which that spring was drawing government leaders from dominions and colonies around the world to London. He called for a "wider citizenship" for Canadians in the Empire as the one measure that would bring "the realization of a Greater Canada."

> Shall we still whine in our poverty, still draw imaginary pictures of our thin herds shivering in the cold blasts of the North, their shepherds huddled for shelter in the log cabins of Montreal and Toronto?...Or, shall we say to the people of England, "The time has come; we know and realize our country. We will be your colony no longer. Make us one with you in an Empire, Permanent and Indivisible."

Praising "the inevitable greatness of Canada," Leacock warned that there was an urgent need for a form of imperial membership beyond colonialism, something that was not satisfied by the ambivalent status of the Dominion, uncomfortably between a colony and an independent nation; without such imperial membership Canada would at best be trapped in "stagnation" and at worst be drawn into "the strife of races" within its boundaries and lost through the attraction of annexation with the United States.[5] The warning he gave was timely enough: disturbed by Britain's demands for military support and its concessions to the United States in the Alaska boundary dispute in 1903, Laurier was moving away from his former steadfast support of the imperial connection towards closer ties with the southern neighbour. In 1910, he concluded a trade treaty with U.S. President William Howard Taft, which was not enacted because of Laurier's defeat in the 1911 election, a defeat for which Leacock worked. For his part, Leacock tended to blame Great Britain only for failure to exploit its opportunities in Canada, not for spoiling the goodwill of Canadians through mismanagement of its role as maker of foreign policy for the Dominion. Rather, it was Canadians themselves on whom his criticisms fell in *Greater Canada, An Appeal:* they were failing to insist strongly enough that they would give up the comforts of living as "peasant pensioners" on the imperial bounty. He called on his countrymen to demand the wider, more strenuous role he envisioned they should have.

On 27 April 1907, Leacock and Beatrix embarked for England from Halifax on board the *Victorian.* He was now thirty-seven, and only eight years previously had been borrowing money to begin his doctoral studies. In sending him off, Earl Grey had cautioned him against being too negative about the United States (a country toward which Leacock grew warmer and warmer throughout his life): "It is quite possible to crow & flap one's wings without treading on one's neighbour's corns." Presumably Grey felt the rhetorically somewhat reckless professor did not need such a caveat regarding the mother country itself. But near his tour's beginning he created its most controversial incident by publishing in London's *Morning Post* for 17 May an article called "After the Conference: John Bull and His Grown Up Sons." In it he criticized the Imperial Conference for not taking positive steps towards unity among the dominions. The essay was written in American dialect, in the style of mock-backwoods naivete lampooning social and political topics, which had flourished from Seba Smith and Haliburton to Mark Twain and Artemus Ward; it concluded with the prophecy that antiquated ideas would be swept aside by the former colonies and Great Britain would find itself in a subordinate position or excluded altogether.

> The old man's got old and he don't know it; can't kick
> him off the place; but I reckon that the next time we
> come together to talk things over the boys have got
> to step right in and manage the whole farm.

Leacock was widely criticized by the British press; "John Bull" was reprinted and excerpted in Canada, too, where it was also discussed, deplored, and controverted. Peterson wrote to warn him against any further outburst: "Much of your offense consisted in rushing in where, by tacit compact, the genuine Canadian is afraid to tread." Winston Churchill referred to the article as "offensive twaddle."[6] Weathering the storm, Leacock lectured in London to the Royal Colonial Institute and also wrote a "Discussion" of a paper, "Some Phases of Canada's Development," delivered to the Institute by W.I. Griffith, Secretary of the High Commissioner's Office; the paper and Leacock's response were published in the Institute's *Proceedings* for 1906-7. In London he also addressed the Victoria League on "The Question of Canada"; at Oxford he spoke before a group of Rhodes scholars and dined at All Souls College. He reported in a letter to Peterson that he was being admitted to charmed circles: "I saw a great many people in London...went to lunch with Mr. [James Arthur] Balfour [former prime minister], stayed in the country with Rudyard Kipling and saw...Fabian Ware (Editor, Morning Post) and Amery of the Times."[7]

Reports of the tour continued in Canada from around the world as Leacock made his year-long progress from Europe to Australia and New Zealand, then to South Africa. After lecturing in England, Leacock and Beatrix took ten days in Paris and then travelled to

Marseilles, embarking on 30 May on board the *Macedonia* for Australia and New Zealand. He was in New Zealand from August through 12 September, lecturing at Wellington, Wanganui and Auckland; he then sailed for Australia and spent 16 September to 1 November in Sydney and 1 to 15 November in Melbourne, visiting and lecturing in Perth as well. He arrived in South Africa on 15 December and remained there until 1 February 1908. His lecture topics in these places included "The British Empire in the Twentieth Century," "Imperial Unity" and "Imperialism versus Democracy." He was sought out by government officials in all the Dominions and was greeted with special warmth at the University of Capetown. His proposed schedule had envisioned travelling from South Africa to Vancouver for lectures in the major Canadian cities from there to Montreal but this part of the trip was not undertaken; instead he returned to England, spent late February there, and embarked for Canada on 4 March, arriving on the tenth. Everywhere his audiences had been enthusiastic: always a quick learner, he had solved the problems of ill-calculated remarks and undiplomatic tone that had caused him to get off to a rough start. But he never again made such a lecture tour, although he remained faithful throughout his life to the ideal of imperial unity. Nor did he ever accept any similar role as quasi-official spokesman for a political entity or cause. He had learned he was ill-suited to such duty; he chafed under the restrictions it put on his expression of his own views in his own style, and he probably resented the odour of extreme respectable conformity which a politician of any sort, even a mere travelling expert, had to maintain if he was not to stunt his career. In later years, despite his long record of writings on political subjects, Leacock still carried in some official circles the reputation of being not quite safe enough to entrust with dutiful expression of the established positions. Although Earl Grey had obviously envisioned for his protégé a career as imperial apologist similar to that followed by Parkin, Leacock did not pursue this opportunity. The tour had helped teach him that the party line did not suit well with his flourishes.

Greater Canada, An Appeal, which was a platform address before and after it was a published essay, and press accounts of Leacock's performances during the tour, provide a view of the style in which he conveyed his political ideas at this time. Relying little on humour, he wrote and spoke in elaborate, flowing phrases rich in images and descriptions.

> And of all this take only our two new provinces, twin giants of the future, Alberta and Saskatchewan. Three decades ago this was the "great lone land," the frozen west, with its herds of bison and its Indian tepees, known to you only in the pictured desolation of its unending snow....

On 27 March 1907, the Vancouver *Daily Province* editorialized negatively on the pamphlet version of *Greater Canada, An Appeal*, pointing out that it had first been given before the Insurance Institute of Montreal; not only did the *Daily Province* find Leacock's ideas jejune ("Professor Leacock is a comparatively young man" and hence his remarks demand "post-prandial leniency" and "good-humored forbearance") but it felt that in his style "the orator runs amok" in a "diluted compound of Carlyle and the Prophet Downie, with a dash of epic poetry 'thrown in'." [8] Leacock displayed a strong command of the political manner of the day, flowery, emotional, inspirational and dramatic. He struggled to embody in this style a very personal approach to the political crises of the time. Above all, he was attempting to find a way to be both honorably Canadian and honorably British. Imperialism, he said in *Greater Canada, An Appeal*, was for many "a tainted word." So it is today, tending for many to remove a great part of his political theory to the curio cupboard, and leading some commentators to dismiss parts of even his humorous work as brutal rather than funny, bigoted rather than humane. On one point the verdict of history is clear: Leacock overestimated the future possibilities of the British Empire and the influence which, as an organized political entity, it could have for peace and civilization during the twentieth century. As the century progressed, he could see that the Empire was dissolving and becoming weaker. He was realistic about this, but never ceased to propose ways in which the process could be reversed or the remainder of the Empire could be renovated and strengthened. He saw the Empire effectively unite with the mother country in the titanic and crucial effort of the First World War, in an enactment of the lesson he had drawn from the similar but much smaller example of the Boer War; this reinforced his conviction that his faith was better put in the Empire, with its strongly protective defense of its own customs and traditions, than in international organizations like the League of Nations. At the time of his death, the spectacle of the Commonwealth countries' performance in the Second World War had reconfirmed him in his faith that the Empire, though its appearance might be changed, was a real force for good: an "inspiration, not a formula," as he once said.

If there is anything truly unfortunate about his imperialism it is that he that saw the Empire solely as an organization of Anglo-Saxon nations, and assumed that these nations would always want to be integrated as little as possible with the original populations of the lands they inhabited. The native residents of India or New Zealand were not to be thought of as true parts of the Empire, and certainly not as autonomous or semi-autonomous peoples with a right to representation and influence for their interests. More than unfortunate, it is disturbing that Leacock founded some of his praise of the British Empire on the idea of the superiority of the Anglo-Saxon peoples and the "white races" generally. In 1921 the revisions of the third edition of *Elements of Political Science*, which were intended to adjust its relevance and acceptability in changing times, included elimination of a section on "Criticism of Existing Systems; the Case of Women, of Negroes, etc." Yet in 1940 *Our British Empire* included such remarks as, "The rigor of the cold and the stimulus of effort bred the 'white races,' whose superiority no one must doubt." This he presumably regarded as a conclusion of the scientific geography for which he argued a central place in curricula until his last years. He drew a strong distinction between colonies like Canada, where British immigrants produced a population of mostly European origin, such colonies being capable of self-rule, and others in which non-white native populations remained under British authority. Although his view did not preclude the notion that such peoples might develop toward equality, such social evolutionism is presented as a reason for depriving natives of present-day rights rather than for speeding their empowerment.

> Still less could federation include the black subjects
> of the Queen now multiplying in Africa. These must
> remain as sleeping partners in the Empire, dreaming
> of their future heritage, and blessed at least with
> decent government and fair play.[9]

Leacock was of course not alone in positions of this sort. During the Second World War, the British Ministry of Education used *Our British Empire* as a morale-building tool, and none of the changes in the text the Ministry requested dealt with the passages on race. In a writer beloved for kindly laughter, this deliberate belittlement of some human beings as inherently inferior is deeply unwelcome. If in these attitudes he was a man of his time, a writer of his intelligence and originality can be expected to have transcended them at least in some significant measure. But the early Leacock was actually more mild in expressing these prejudices than the later. In his writings whether humorous or political, as long as he felt secure within the boundaries of his own Anglo-Saxon-derived North American community he was little inclined to be racially invidious. The assertion of the authority of British civilization over any other became more strident as the Empire granted the independence of former colonies in Africa and Asia.

Leacock returned from the tour on 10 March 1908. He had been away almost exactly a year, and in his absence, in July 1907, the Makers of Canada Series had published his second book, a study in the history of Canadian government and its evolution toward a separate and characteristic form; this was *Baldwin, Lafontaine, Hincks: Responsible Government*. The series was edited by Leacock's old friend Pelham Edgar together with the poet and man of letters Duncan Campbell Scott; they were later joined in the editorship by William Dawson Le Sueur, who had responsibility for Leacock's manuscript. Leacock, who had completed his book in the summer of 1906, then engaged in a prickly correspondence with Le Sueur, who was suggesting changes not only in style but in interpretation. Leacock ended by ceasing to respond altogether to Le Sueur's correspondence; he wrote to George N. Morang, head of Morang and Company Ltd., Toronto, the publisher, "I think Mr. Le Sueur's views on Responsible government quite wrong. I want to keep them out of my book." He visited the publisher personally on 20 March 1907, a month before leaving for England, and received the final proofs in May when in the midst of his first lectures and the firestorm over his John Bull essay.[10] Now as he returned to McGill he had a second book, as well as the tour, *Greater Canada, An Appeal*, and many magazine essays, to his credit; that spring the university named him William K. Dow Professor of Political Economy, a full professorship, and gave him a seat on the faculty of arts. His salary was raised to four thousand dollars per year. He was also appointed temporary chairman of the Department of Economics and Political Science; although the appointment was not confirmed until 1933, he served as chairman from 1908 until his retirement in 1936. As department head, he was in charge of determining which courses would be presented, and required each of his teachers to submit to him before each term began a page-long summary of new courses and those already offered: there would be no repetition of what he himself had done to A.W. Flux, as a junior faculty member forcing a course on the department chairman. In addition to his administrative and teaching duties, he continued to publish for scholarly magazines and conferences. In 1908, he addressed the American Political Science Association on "The Limitations of Federal Government" as well as making lectures to chapters of the Canadian Club, one at Orillia, Ontario on "The Asiatic Problem in the British Empire" and one at Montreal on "Union of South Africa." Articles based on his Makers of Canada study also appeared in the *American Political Science Review* and *Addresses Delivered Before the Canadian Club of Ottawa, 1903-9.*

He became involved in university publications through a student, W.E. Gladstone Murray, who went on to head the Canadian Broadcasting Corporation in the 1930s. Leacock loaned Murray ten dollars when they met one day in 1909 in the student union and Murray complained that he would be forced to leave school if he did not find work. Leacock later encouraged him to start *The McGill Daily* and frequently contributed to the newspaper. From his student days Murray was a regular contestant against the billiards-obsessed Leacock, experiencing "periodic humiliation" due to the professor's "superior skill."

> In 1911, after a game one evening, Dr. Leacock remarked that he was tired of these "unrelated and insignificant encounters." Whereupon he challenged me to 20,000-up, which he estimated we could finish in 20 years....The games took place in widely varying environments — clubs, private homes, grand hotels, but mostly in good old down-to-earth pubs. Actually the game ran for thirty years and was never finished, the final score being 18,975 for Dr. Leacock and 17,793 for me.[11]

McGill now supplied most of Leacock's society, and a favourite spot for conversation and billiards became the University Club, which opened on Dorchester Street in the spring of 1908; before leaving for his world tour, Leacock had attended a meeting to organize the new facility.

Among his closest, most important friends at the university and the club was Andrew (later Sir Andrew) Macphail, professor of the history of medicine. For a full view of Leacock's association with Macphail it is necessary to go back in time to near the beginning of his life in Montreal. The record shows no essays or articles published during his first two years as a sessional lecturer, 1900 and 1901, and only one lecture given, on "Anarchism" at Royal Victoria College. However, in 1902 Leacock became a member of the Montreal Pen and Pencil Club, in which Macphail was prominent, and this organization became one of two outlets for such continued attention to his genius for humour and literature as Leacock could manage in the decade prior to *Literary Lapses* (1910). At the Pen and Pencil Club, Leacock knew many Montreal artists, authors and literary amateurs of the time, most of them now forgotten. Among their number, however, were MacPhails's close friend, John McCrae, later famous as the author of "In Flanders Fields," and the painter Robert Harris, who was also a poet and memoirist. Until Macphail's death in 1938 he remained Leacock's chief literary mentor and confidante. Physician, historian of science and man of letters, he was a learned and elegant essayist in the best manner of the eighteenth and nineteenth centuries. He shared and helped confirm and strengthen Leacock's essentially classical sense of the meaning of literature as whatever is well written and intended by virtue of form, style and rhetoric as a contribution to general human culture, not simply as a specialist or scientific exposition. It is the definition by which literature includes not only poems, dramas, novels and stories, but the history of Gibbon and Macaulay, the political theory of Moore and Locke, the religious thinking of Hume and Newman, the critical work of Johnson and Hazlitt and Bagehot, the omni-curious essays of Bacon and Browne. Much of Leacock's work was eventually done in the tradition to which Macphail belonged, that of Johnson, Hume, Macauley and Arnold. In

Leacock, of course, the mixture was different and essentially lighter; to the list must be added his favourite humorists and Addison and Steele, Lamb, and near contemporaries who were masters of the light essay, such as Jerome K. Jerome and Robert Louis Stevenson.

Leacock's first recorded presentation to the Pen and Pencil Club was on 1 February 1902, when he delivered "Opening a Bank Account;" this doubtless is another title for "My Financial Career," which of course he had already tried out on Pelham Edgar and published in *Life*. Effective recycling of material became a constant feature of Leacock's career, as much in humour and literature as in economic and political writing. The Pen and Pencil Club heard a second contribution from him in 1902, one in 1903, two in 1904, and four in 1905. Even during the hectic period of late 1906 and early 1907, crammed with lectures to various bodies in Quebec and Ontario and preparations for his Empire tour and for his volume on the Baldwin-Lafontaine administrations, he presented three addresses to the Club. This material included poems ("We Are Seventeen," "Nothing"), humorous sketches ("The Passing of the Poet," "Merry Xmas"), and a literary-historical essay, "The Rehabilitation of Charles II." As his busy schedule of political lecturing developed in 1906-7, the Club increasingly heard versions of his platform addresses: "The Malthusian Theory," "The Future of the French Canadian," "The Monroe Doctrine and Canada" and "Greater Canada."

As if this was not enough, Leacock became the guest editor for the first two issues, January and February 1907, of the *University Magazine* (1907-20), which Macphail founded at the beginning of the year. The new magazine became the other support, along with the Pen and Pencil Club, of Leacock's continuing literary growth during the decade. In it he published, from 1907 through 1910, "The Psychology of American Humour," "Greater Canada, An Appeal," "Literature and Education in America," "Canada and the Monroe Doctrine," "The Apology of a Professor," and finally "The Devil and the Deep Sea" in the December 1910 issue, by which time his humour had become much in demand and was appearing widely in general interest magazines and in newspapers.

Leacock's friend and encourager was his senior by five years; born in 1864 in Prince Edward Island, Macphail came to Montreal to study medicine in 1884. A recent widower at the time Leacock met him, he was devoting himself increasingly to literature. The great literary passion of his life was Louis Hémon's novel of rural Québec, *Maria Chapdelaine*; in 1921 Macphail published its first English translation (it was superseded later in the same year by the still standard translation of William Hume Blake). It is likely that Leacock's presence was also a stimulus to the older man; in the first decade of the century Macphail produced *Essays in Puritanism* (1905), *The Vine of Sibmah* (1906), *Essays in Politics* (1909) and *Essays in Fallacy* (1910), all of them published in Boston or New York. His later publications included the volume on the medical services in the official history of the Canadian Forces in the First World War, in which he served as a medical officer. He edited a posthumous collection of poems by John McCrae; perhaps his best and most widely read book is *The Master's Wife*, a memoir of his family and of life in Prince Edward Island; it was published posthumously in 1939. Macphail and Leacock were inseparable friends at the University Club, at Macphail's lonely mansion, which he maintained in high Victorian decor, and later, when the Leacocks obtained a house, at Leacock's convivial dinner parties.

The two men shared a commitment to literature and equally a commitment to the British Empire. Macphail's influence helped confirm that of superiors such as George Parkin, Sir William Peterson and Earl Grey, whose intellectual work and rhetoric nudged Leacock toward an imperialism strongly tinged with "white man's burden" ideology; Macphail voiced the same excesses of white supremacy as grounds for excluding full citizenship to native people in the Empire that emerged in Leacock, especially late in life. Literary essays that Macphail's encouragement and the platform of the *University Magazine* helped stimulate are to varying degrees important for

Leacock's later work. In a 1916 volume he collected his study of Charles II, "The Devil and the Deep Sea," "Literature and Education in America," and "The Apology of a Professor: An Essay on Modern Learning." The latter is distinctly a forbear of one of the most famous pieces he ever produced, "Oxford As I See It" (1922). Many themes he later expressed in his humour emerge in these early essays, though there is little of his mature humorous approach in most of them; they can be soberly philosophical, and can modulate to impassioned pleading, for example when the subject is reform of the university system. After struggling for many years to attain the rank of university professor, Leacock was dissatisfied with the degree of authority it carried; his expectations, based on the Arnoldian example of the mid and late nineteenth-century British educational system in which he was nurtured, were disappointed. In "Literature and Education in America" he partly blamed the schools, whose passion for the methods of science had reduced the training of humanities students to an overspecialization that made them of little use to society.

> The pretentious claim made by so many of our universities that the thesis presented for the doctor's degree must present a distinct contribution to human knowledge will not stand examination....Our American process of research has led to an absurd admiration of the mere collection of facts, extremely useful things in their way but in point of literary eminence standing in the same class as the *Twelfth Census of the United States* or the *Statistical Abstract of the United Kingdom*.[12]

In the past, the university had "aimed at a wide and humane culture of the intellect." Now the doctorate was earned by writing "a useless little pamphlet called [a] thesis which is new in the sense that nobody ever wrote it before, and erudite in the sense that nobody will ever read it." While the universities corrupted the value of the professor by making him suited only to the very narrow bounds of his own specialty, society at large was confused in its search for authoritative information by the absence of respected authorities and the abundance of self-proclaimed "professors" of the banjo, of swimming and of patent medicines. In the debate over what a university should be, Leacock wholeheartedly joined the side arguing for an institution based on the liberal arts and humanities and higher sciences, rather than one providing professional or technical training of any kind. This debate of course continues, and today Leacock would be viewed as a partisan of the "elitist university" concept, as opposed to the university that is part of a system of mass public education intended eventually to provide, in theory, professional or quasi-professional career training to virtually the entire population. He was sensitive to the problem of elitism, however, and tried to propose ways in which even elitist universities could find students by applying standards of ability rather than of parentage or class. In lifelong controversial writings that began with early essays in the matrix of the Pen and Pencil Club and the *University Magazine*, he remains an effective champion of the idea of the university associated with Newman, based on intellectual merit and aimed at the development of generalist thinkers rather than professionals and experts. His early thought on this problem already had a breadth that took it beyond the question of university aims and structures because he saw how social changes were affecting education. Society's growing bias toward commercialism and materialism made publicity the most prized type of communication, with the result that most people had little capacity for or interest in exact knowledge of nature, society or human experience: "The only missionary we care for is an advertiser, and even the undertaker must send us a Christmas calendar if he desires to retain our custom."[13] Throughout his career, Leacock was drawn to two opposing poles of truth that must somehow, he felt, be maintained together. Education was being watered down to make it available to all; still, every member of a democracy must be well educated if the society is not to be at the mercy of an uninformed, uncritical electorate's opinions and decisions. How was this dilemma to be reconciled? He expected the university to supply an elite educated group that would in turn guide the rest of society. Within the man Leacock, the same duality existed. He aspired to be the kind of person that he thought the universities should produce; on the other hand, he was drawn to the popular press and the lecture stage as means of influencing a broader public. If some of his work seems at first glance to side with the common sense of the uneducated against the educated, a closer look always shows that his satire attacks the expert, the professional, the theorist and sometimes the pedant or reactionary exponent of an outmoded idea of learning. Common sense as he presents it is always subtly in tune with, and allied to, his concept of a well-trained, well-balanced philosophical mind. In general, he was successful in expressing his thoughts in a way that made them intelligible and forceful for a wide audience. His work rarely shows condescension; his experience gave him true solidarity both with the impoverished person whose struggles left no time for education and with the inhabitant of the academy. He knew in himself, in fact, that these two persons could be one and the same. He had real respect for any person who performed with honour in his own station and walk of life but did not believe that every person was suited to a university education and the intellectual and social tasks for which it prepared one. He satirizes the pretensions and failings of workmen, professionals, academics, divines, government and business leaders, sportsmen — but his most acid criticism is reserved for the influential guides of society who have been to university but have misunderstood, misused, or simply ignored what they learned there.

Some critics noticed early that Leacock at times seemed to side thoughtlessly with boorish philistines in making his points against the abuses of intellectuals and artists. He sometimes found himself accused of despising literature, education, even his own profession, of going overboard in identifying with the "common people," indulging their prejudices for the sake of effect when he made sweeping attacks on intellectual fashions. For example, his 1906 piece for the *University Magazine*, "The Passing of the Poet," jibed at the excesses of Romantic verse and the popular image of the Romantic genius:

> The undue access of emotion frequently assumed a pathological character. The sight of a daisy, of a withered leaf or an up-turned sod, seemed to disturb the poet's mental equipoise. Spring unnerved him. The lambs distressed him. The flowers made him cry. The daffodils made him laugh. Day dazzled him. Night frightened him.

Leacock's first home at Old Brewery Bay, which grew by progressive additions from the original "cookhouse" that Leacock and his brother Charlie built in 1908. This house was demolished when Leacock's new home was built in 1928.

Courtesy National Archives of Canada C-33107.

Leacock claimed to applaud the day that would substitute Huxley's *Physiology* for Gray's "Elegy in a Country Churchyard" or the police news of the *Dumfries Chronicle* for the verse of Robert Burns. Writing in a later issue of the *University Magazine*, Susan R. Cameron criticized him for dismissing poets "as futile creatures, tolerated in earlier, sillier generations than ours, and destined to become extinct as the race becomes full grown." Cameron was disappointed to think that Leacock, "an academic person of distinction," would be so mistaken about the value of poetry.[14] Yet it is important to notice that Leacock is not being facilely downright for effect, as humorously exaggerated as his phrasing may be. He is expressing a considered attitude that was not at all uncommon among intellectuals of the nineteenth century that had nurtured him, writers such as Thomas Love Peacock, Carlyle, and Macauley. Regrettable it might be, but poetry had decayed to a febrile attempt at freshness through faked simplicity and sensibility; the greatest poetry belonged to the childhood and adolescence of the race, when the youthful freshness and directness the art best embodied had been real and strong. But those times were past, succeeded by the current age, that of maturity and responsibility, of prose and fact. Leacock was not at all posing as a know-nothing to get a laugh; his satire was meant. In its later, more mature expressions it became deeply tinged with melancholy, a sense of *lacrimae rerum* at the inevitable fading away of good but preliminary things.

During his world tour, Leacock had written to his sister Daisy about helping him to purchase "a small place on Lake Couchiching" and in another letter had waxed lyrical over the home he would build there. Even earlier, on 30 May 1907, the day of his departure from France for Australia, he had sent a letter to his mother, and through her his brother Charlie, and enlisted them as his agents in making the purchase. This letter to Agnes shows that he had been considering a purchase of Lake Couchiching property for some time past. It also shows that a certain homesickness was increasing his desire for what he called "a place of my own" in Canada:

Tell Charlie to get a *place*: if the little point is not too wet I'd like it. If it is not obtainable then the Hughes point. On either of those, he may, subject to ratification by me, make an offer. And I'd like him to do something about it this summer so that I can take up the place next spring. The more I see of foreign parts, the less I think of them compared to Canada. And I want a place of my own.[15]

In 1908, with brother Charlie's help, he purchased thirty-three acres for sixteen hundred dollars. He christened the site "Old Brewery Bay" for a brewery reputed once to have been located nearby. A one-room shack was built during the first summer and became the nucleus for the first house Leacock built on the property. Writing to Daisy, Leacock spoke of a return to the Lake Simcoe area as "coming home."[16] Although he had fled the farm, he had spent his summers around the lake for many years, and his mother and brothers and sisters either lived in the area or visited frequently. His marriage had reinforced his ties to the Lake Simcoe region, where Beatrix, too, had family. The purchase of Old Brewery Bay marked a new age in Leacock's life: with it he confirmed a growing personal identification with Canada the nation and with his Canada, the intimate *terroir* of his emotional and intellectual growth. The world trip had convinced him that he was no party man, and that he would never sacrifice Canada for opportunities abroad. In 1909, securely established in the McGill University community, and rerooted in the soil of his boyhood at Old Brewery Bay, he found support in his family for a new endeavour, a return to the writing and publishing of humour.

Leacock (in wheelbarrow) and Beatrix (second from right) with unidentified friends, at Old Brewery Bay in 1908. Behind Leacock is the "cookhouse" from which his first Old Brewery Bay home evolved.

Courtesy National Archives of Canada C-31930.

Lapsing into Literature

I n the spring of 1909, Leacock signed a three-year lease on a semi-detached three-story house (the third floor had been servants' quarters) at 165 Côte-des-Neiges Road in Montreal. The agreement with owner William George Slack provided the option for an additional three-year lease; Leacock later purchased it.[1] Located on the east side of the busy Montreal street and eventually renumbered 3869, it remained his city home until shortly before his death in 1944. (In the 1950s, it was torn down to make room for construction of a new wing of Montreal General Hospital.) In Leacock's thirty-five years' residence, many memorable parties were held in the dining room; Leacock entertained McGill friends like Andrew Macphail, to whom the days of his celebrity added such visiting friends as Douglas Fairbanks and Mary Pickford, William Butler Yeats and P.G. Wodehouse. He delighted in reading fresh sketches as after-dinner entertainment, but parties always ended for him by ten o'clock. His work habit and inflexible will to achievement dictated to him the regular year-round practice, both in Orillia summers and Montreal winters, of rising early to write and study. The sketches read after dinner at Côte-des-Neiges Road often were written between five a.m. and the family breakfast, when Leacock was at work in his upstairs study. Attached to this study was a porch where he spent the nights on a small couch. He frequently extolled the virtues of sleeping outside. True, he nearly froze once when he became locked out on a particularly cold night, and he frequently had to wear his raccoon coat to a bed from which he had swept the snow. He was not alone among early-century litterateurs in the practice of sleeping out in the harsh Canadian winters: it was a health fad of the turn-of-the-century and after. As a Halifax teenager, Hugh MacLennan had practised it. Nellie McClung, bringing up a growing family in a Manitoba town, spent years sleeping in backyard tents for the reputed health benefits.

The Côte-des-Neiges house was the final element of a success story Leacock had been putting together for at least twenty-one years, since entering the Strathroy teacher training program determined to find a way to return to university. From his first doubtful step, studying languages while beginning to believe his future lay in economics, he had gone from achievement to achievement. Rising from temporary lecturer to chairman of the department of economics and political science in only seven years, he had secured respect as a political commentator. He had seen his mother through years of hardship following his father's decampment and now could visit her happily in her Lake Simcoe home where she was surrounded, especially in the summers, by a successful family of grown children and a growing flock of grandchildren. A healthy, active man in his fortieth year who had taxed himself heavily since high-school graduation with double duty as teacher and student, teacher and writer, teacher and lecturer, Leacock might have been expected to slow down and indulge his passion for teaching, polemics, scholarship and intellectual camaraderie, his fondness for masculine club life, sailing, fishing and gardening.

Instead, he began to discuss with his family and friends the possibility of collecting his humorous sketches into a book; his accomplishments to date were to be only a platform supporting not only redoubled activity in the career he had established but the addition of an almost entirely new one. Leacock had copies on file of the many pieces he had written before 1900 while he was working at Upper Canada College. These would form the bulk of his manuscript, but he could add to them the handful of more recent humorous pieces written for Macphail's *University Magazine*. It has been suggested that Leacock considered the book as a moneymaking venture to meet the increased expenses in Orillia. With not one but two households to maintain, he certainly must have felt the need of money. Not long before, he had asked for a salary increase at McGill, explaining that he was plagued by debts. Leacock's early pieces were not protected by copyright; he knew they were popular, because they continued to be reprinted, but for these reprintings he received no payment. By collecting them in a book he would hold copyright and thus earn money. There are several indications, however, that he was hoping for something more than a profitable collection of previously published work. Chief of these is his persistence, despite serious obstacles, in trying to publish in book form the collection he called *Literary Lapses*.

The project was a cooperative affair among family and friends. Beatrix and Marion Sandwell (née Street), who in 1908 had married Leacock's friend and former student Bernard K. Sandwell, compiled and prepared a selection of sketches from Leacock's files. Then Leacock discovered that Sandwell, at the time a drama critic for the *Montreal Herald*, opposed the project on the worry that publishing a book of recreational humour would damage the growing reputation of the economist and political commentator. Writing occasional humorous essays between serious projects was acceptable, Sandwell thought, but he warned that the new book would clash with rather than reinforce Leacock's authority.[2] Leacock was not daunted by Sandwell's zeal for his reputation, which indicated that his friend was certain the manuscript must be accepted. As it turned out, this was wrong. Leacock submitted *Literary Lapses* to the Boston and New York publisher of *Elements of Political Science*, Houghton Mifflin. In his submission letter of December 1909 his tongue was firmly in cheek in a way that bespoke complete confidence: "The dignified kind of humour which these sketches are supposed to represent is perhaps better without illustration....One might suggest that a photogravure of an Equestrian Statue of the author surrounded by the Houghton Mifflin firm might be inserted at the back of the book."[3] But the publisher, to its later chagrin, returned *Literary Lapses* without encouragement; in 1921, it tried unsuccessfully to purchase Leacock's U.S. publisher.

Leacock always credited his brother George that the project did not die with the first rejection. His closest friend among his many brothers, George was the first Leacock child born in Canada and eight years Stephen's junior. A man with little taste for education, George was highly regarded in the family as a wit and storyteller, and to him Leacock often credited his stories and ideas. In *Too Much College*, Leacock offers an analysis of the art of humour with help from a "story I can quote from memory, not actually of my own but of my brother George." Drawn from George's work experience with an Ontario electrical company, the story was given by Leacock in its bare outline as the basis for a discussion of different methods of humorous delivery. A workman is electrocuted while attempting to install a delicate new piece of apparatus. A team of inspectors from the company arrives to discover how the accident occurred. One bright fellow comes forward and offers to explain. He places his hands on the equipment, just as the dead man had done, tells the inspectors to turn on the power, and is electrocuted. Leacock said of the anecdote that he was always happy to end the story by revealing that the second man was only knocked unconscious, not really killed. "But when my brother George, who is a real storyteller, tells this story, he not only kills the second man but the chief of police — who undertook to explain it to the mayor of the town, and then the mayor and half of the town council. Nothing like Art for Art's sake."[4] Part of the charm of Leacock's humour derives from the success he has in recreating the rhythm, diction and tone of spoken language. In this art, apparently, George was especially gifted; family members agreed that if he had only been able to spell, he too would have been famous as a humorist; Leacock was always content to acknowledge him, and he remains a sort of half-legendary Mycroft Holmes of Canadian humour. In his professional life he was an electrical engineer, eventually becoming president of the Moloney Electrical Company of Toronto. In addition, he was an accomplished horse breeder. He had a summer home in the small town of Aurora, not far from Lake Simcoe.

On a visit to Montreal, George was told of his brother's rejected manuscript and asked to read it; his opinion that the work was good and deserved to be published made Leacock agree to keep trying. George had a hand, too, in deciding how the manuscript would get into print. He proposed that he and Leacock publish the book themselves and share the profits. The first contact with a Montreal printer, the Gazette Publishing Company, was made by George, who also provided a fifty-dollar deposit towards the costs. The plan was to make an inexpensive edition for sale on railway station newsstands. The brothers expected to earn seven cents per copy, with five cents going to George and two cents to Leacock. Before making final arrangements for the book's printing, however, Leacock returned the fifty dollars George had contributed and undertook arrangements for the book on his own.[5] There is no record of why he decided to do this, but it seems unlikely that he did so to deny profits to his brother, as has been suggested. At most, George's share of the profit of the first edition would have been slightly more than $140. Against that, he would have had to pay the larger portion of the upfront cost of producing the edition. George himself was untroubled that he did not share in the first edition's small financial success, remaining an enthusiastic supporter of his brother's career and an ungrudging source of ideas.

Under the plan Leacock now developed, the Gazette Publishing Company printed 3,000 copies of *Literary Lapses*, for which Leacock was charged fifteen and a third cents per copy payable three months after delivery. He arranged for the book's distribution by the Montreal News Company, which sold it for thirty-five cents ("a sum which raised it above the vulgarity of ten and twenty-five-cent 'railway' books," comments Robertson Davies, "but did not thrust it into the elegant company of the fifty-centers"). He would receive twenty-three cents per copy; he was to supply two hundred paper signs and a hundred cardboard placards to advertise *Literary Lapses*, and he also agreed to pay for any copies returned to him unsold. Thus, he was risking production costs of $461 plus the cost of the advertising materials for a possible net profit of $229. This seems a strong indication that Leacock was looking beyond this first edition towards future humour projects, which would make his initial risk worthwhile.[6]

Literary Lapses came out of the bindery on 9 April; it appeared on Montreal newsstands in the spring and summer. The book was 125 pages long and was bound in green boards with a green buckram spine. The title and author's name were stamped on the cover and printed on a label glued to the spine, which added the designation "A Book of Sketches." There was no biographical information about the author but a brief preface acknowledged several magazines, including *Truth*, where the bulk of his early work was presented under McArthur's editorship; *Life*, in which "My Financial Career" first appeared; *Saturday Night*; and several English periodicals, among them *Punch, Puck* and the *Lancet*. This first self-published edition of the famous book contained twenty-six sketches, at least four of which have come to be ranked as permanent classics in the history of humour: "My Financial Career," "Boarding-House Geometry," "The Awful Fate of Melpomenus Jones" and "A, B and C: The Human Element in Mathematics." Sales went "like hot pop corn,"[7] Leacock wrote; in October he reported the edition sold out. His contract with the Montreal News Company provided for the possibility of further editions, but the next appearance of *Literary Lapses* resulted from a transaction of an entirely different sort. Leacock found himself launched as a humorist in the international marketplace without having to risk another cent.

One of the buyers of the Montreal edition of *Literary Lapses* was the British publisher John Lane, whose firm was The Bodley Head in London. Lane was a frequent visitor to Canada and regularly stopped in Montreal in search of rare steel engravings for his collection. He was a successful prospector for Canadian literary talent as well. In 1895, he had published the first book by Ontario Mohawk poet Pauline Johnson, *The White Wampum*, after Johnson had visited his London offices to offer her work. More recently, Lane had been quick to see the promise of the Yukon balladeer Robert Service, and had acquired Service's first books for British publication. Both Lane and Leacock must have been hoping for another phenomenon such as that of Service, whose rise to world prominence had begun just two years before. Early in 1907, Service had been working as a bank teller in Whitehorse, Yukon Territory, and had sent the manuscript of his first book, *Songs of a Sourdough*, to Ryerson Press in Toronto, to be printed at his own expense for distribution to friends who had praised his recitations at parties in Whitehorse and Dawson City. Ryerson editor William Briggs, finding the manuscript extremely popular among the typesetters to whom it had gone as a commercial printing job, undertook to publish it himself and to pay Service a royalty. The book proved as popular among readers across the country as it had been in the composing room. By 1909, Service had produced two more volumes of his northern ballads and was receiving royalties from American editions and Lane's British ones.

Lane's most famous North American author was Mark Twain, whose death in April 1910 undoubtedly sharpened his eye for a likely successor. After returning to England, he cabled Leacock in early July with an offer to publish a British edition of *Literary Lapses*. Years later, Leacock recalled this first contact with Lane. "I cabled back, 'I accept with thanks.' Later on at a banquet Mr. Lane said he realised from the cable that I was the kind of man who would spend two shillings to say thank you."[8] Later in the same month Leacock received inquiries as to an edition from another British publisher, and in August was approached about an American edition by Harper & Brothers; his little vanity-published book had carried his name far and wide.

For Lane's edition, Leacock offered a great quantity of additional material, including even the humorous poems he had recited to the Pen and Pencil Club. The poems were rejected, but the new version of *Literary Lapses* was bulked up to thirty-nine sketches, with Leacock carefully governing the order. The great comic elan of the opening four sketches ("My Financial Career," "Lord Oxhead's Secret," "Boarding-House Geometry," "The Awful Fate of Melpomenus Jones") was not tampered with, but after that there were many insertions, such as the popular "A Christmas Letter" and "Men Who Have Shaved Me," the how-to sequence ("How to Make a Million Dollars," "How to Live to Be 200," "How to Avoid Getting Married," "How to Be a Doctor"), and his burlesques of Wordsworth, Tennyson and Longfellow gathered under the title "Half-Hours with the Poets." Leacock made a brief trip to England before the beginning of the 1910 academic year; though his book had not yet appeared, he found himself greeted already as the "Canadian Mark Twain," where just three years before he had been a serious and obscure authority on imperial organization and economics. Leacock returned final proofs of Lane's edition in October and it appeared in November 1910, although Lane dated the title page "1911," doubtless to keep it a new book longer in the eyes of periodicals and reviewers. The Bodley Head reprinted this edition of *Literary Lapses* four times in the next two years, and at least twenty-one times until 1941; this version is the *Literary Lapses* that remains in print nearly a century later in Canada. It was Leacock's introduction to readers around the world. The amazing sequence of events crowded into eight months, April through November 1910, brought Leacock into the select company of international celebrity authors, which included only a handful of Canadians, such as Service. Service left his teller's cage, but Leacock, interested in accommodating success as a humorist in his already busy schedule, could find recent precedent in several countrymen. In 1908, *Anne of Green Gables* was published in Boston and brought popularity to Lucy Maud Montgomery, a native and resident of Prince Edward Island, who never abandoned her domestic routine on the strength of her long-continued literary popularity; she cared for her grandmother and later became the energetic wife of an Ontario minister. The Reverend Charles Gordon, under the pen name "Ralph Connor," wrote a series of moral adventure novels set in the Canadian northwest, highly popular in the United States and Great Britain, as well as Canada, at the turn of the century. As with Leacock, Gordon's literary career began in the magazines, with a serial on his mission experiences in the west written for *The Westminster*, a Presbyterian church publication in Toronto. The serial became *Black Rock: A Tale of the Selkirks* (1898), the first of fourteen annual edifying books "Ralph Connor" published for the Christmas market; meanwhile, Charles Gordon stayed home, serving his Winnipeg parish and playing an active role in the city's social reform movements.

Reviewers everywhere liked *Literary Lapses*: "uproariously funny," "the form of these sketches is excellent," "the book is full of smiles." Some quibbled, though, that the pieces were not all of the same quality; some of the work was imitative and "written with a rapid pen."[9] Several pieces from *Literary Lapses* rank among Leacock's best, but many of the others have great merit and in addition are interesting as early attempts at themes that Leacock recapitulated in later humorous writings, with a more mature voice and sense of form. In the disparate sketches collected in his first book, which were written in the course of about seventeen years, Leacock was defining his territory: the plight of the little man troubled by technological changes and bureaucratic mass society, as in "Reflections on Riding" and "My Financial Career," or by social conventions to which he is an uneasy adherent, as in "The Awful Fate of Melpomenus Jones"; the pomposities of the rich ("Self-Made Men"), the learned ("The Poet Answered"), the enthusiastic ("Back to the Bush") and the upper classes ("Aristocratic Education"). Parody is included in "Lord Oxhead's Secret," though it is marred by a moment of racialism that ill assorts with the ideal of harmless laughter. Leacock was entirely aware of what he was doing in characterizing his Edwin Einstein and might have countered any criticism by pointing out that the character, and the story as a whole, hits on the English upper crust much more than on the Jews. This notwithstanding, the piece is a major advance over similar parodies going back to Leacock's school days, and fore-tells the *Nonsense Novels*, approaching their level of sublime satire-cum-nonsense. Of Gwendoline, the heroine, Leacock says, "She bore herself with that sweet simplicity which was her greatest charm. She was probably more simple than any girl of her age for miles around." In expressing her filial piety, the simple Gwendoline avers that she will never marry without her father's warrant, because "I am too much of an Oxhead for that." The old earl gazes at the portrait of his Elizabethan ancestor Sir Amyas Oxhead "whose pinnace was the first to dash to Plymouth with the news that the English fleet, as nearly as could be judged from a reasonable distance, seemed about to grapple with the Spanish Armada." This is the same Sir Amyas whose relationship with Pocahantas the embarrassed earl can only charac-terize as "not actually married": "'At least they loved one another,'" said Gwendoline simply. 'Precisely,' said the earl with relief..." Later, the earl fails in his attempt to calculate the pounds sterling equivalent of the fortune of Gwendoline's suitor in dollars: "It was bootless. His brain, trained by long years of high living and plain thinking, had become too subtle, too refined an instrument for arithmetic...."[10]

As "Lord Oxhead's Secret" looks forward to the *Nonsense Novels*, so "A Manual of Education" is a forerunner to Leacock's many humorous essays and sketches on education. One of the consummate successes in *Literary Lapses*, the sketch has a compact organization and simple delivery that manage to present all at once Leacock's humorous wonderment at the process of learning, his mingled sympathy and scorn for the amateurish bafflement with which so many people regard it, and an amused contempt for the popular creators of self-help methods of mental and personal improvement. "My book is intended to embody in concise form these remnants of early instruction," he explains, and promises in future a simple ten-sheet summary, suitable for carrying in the hip pocket, of the entire content of six years of college. (He later made good this promise in 1926 with the superb "The Outlines of Everything" in *Winnowed Wisdom*.) On astronomy, Leacock's "Manual" provides these insights:

> Astronomy teaches the correct use of the sun and the planets. These may be put on a frame of little sticks and turned around. This causes the tides. Those at the ends of the sticks are enormously far away. From time to time a diligent search of the sticks reveals new planets. The orbit of a planet is the distance the stick goes round in going round. Astronomy is intensely interesting. It should be done at night, in a high tower in Spitzbergen. This is to avoid the astronomy being interrupted. A really good astronomer can tell when a comet is coming too near him by the warning buzz of the revolving sticks.

The Aztecs are a "fabulous race, half man, half horse, half mound-builder....They have left some awfully stupendous monuments of themselves somewhere." Section III of the "Manual" is the "Remains of Botany," which in total are:

> Botany is the art of plants. Plants are divided into trees, flowers, and vegetables. The true botanist knows a tree as soon as he sees it. He learns to distin-

guish it from a vegetable by merely putting his ear to
it.[11]

The perils of real knowledge, as well as those of knowing a little and
not very accurately but very positively, are also examined in "The
Force of Statistics," "Saloonio: A Study in Shakespearean Criticism"
and "Half-Hours with the Poets." His worries about the deterioration
of education, or the unhelpful learning served up in the popular
media, or the evil example given society by its leaders — the rich, the
powerful, celebrities, highly publicized experts — are always paired
with a glance at the lives and plights of typical individual persons
grappling with modern conditions. His view of "The Life of John
Smith" reveals both sympathetic understanding and critical impatience, but it is his keen awareness of the typical quality of Smith that
generates the humour:

> In the boy's choice of a profession there was not seen
> that keen longing for a life-work that we find in the
> celebrities. He didn't want to be a lawyer, because
> you have to know law. He didn't want to be a doctor,
> because you have to know medicine. He didn't want
> to be a businessman, because you have to know
> business; and he didn't want to be a school-teacher,
> because he had seen too many of them. As far as he
> had any choice, it lay between being Robinson
> Crusoe and being the Prince of Wales.[12]

The simple things that perplex people draw Leacock's intense
interest: how to change trains, how to say goodbye to your host, how
to discourage a friend who insists on taking you camping. Not yet
present in most of the sketches is the mature voice of Leacock the
essayist, which wraps all it says in a warm humanity. The first person
frequently used in *Literary Lapses* is something different, a fictional

creation, or rather, many fictional creations, shifting sometimes subtly sometimes radically from piece to piece: the timorous aspirant in "My Financial Career" is not the same person as the acerbic critic of the rich who speaks in "How to Make a Million Dollars." These early pieces were never intended, of course, to establish a single comic voice, because Leacock wrote them over a long period for many different occasions and many different periodicals. This only makes *Literary Lapses* doubly interesting, for its own sake but also for the perspective it provides on Leacock's omnivalent potential as a humorist and thus on the features he later chose to emphasize, and others that he added.

In addition to teaching, serving as department chair, and seeing to the preparation of Lane's edition of *Literary Lapses*, Leacock that autumn used periodicals vigorously to follow up his success and growing celebrity in both political commentary and humour. After completing an extensive "Today in History" series for the *Ottawa Evening Journal* in which he wrote an article or a poem on a historical anniversary for each day in August, and placing some of his recent sketches ("Men Who Have Shaved Me," the how-to group) in the *Canadian Century* (Montreal), he immediately began a series of substantial articles for *Saturday Night* under the general title "Practical Political Economy." The first, "Theory of Value" (his doctoral dissertation topic), appeared on 12 November 1910, and thereafter instalments appeared weekly or biweekly, to the number of twenty-five, until the series was complete with "Socialism as a Political Force" in the issue for 29 April 1911. The development of topics sometimes mirrored *Elements of Political Science* but was far from a precis of the book, for Leacock incorporated analyses of current events and issues, and he oriented his remarks not to political science but to political economy as the series' title promised. No sooner were these articles well under way than he began another series, of an utterly different character, in the same magazine. "Novels in Nutshells I: Gertrude the Governess; or, Simple Seventeen" appeared in

Saturday Night for 10 December 1910, the same issue that carried
"Practical Political Economy V. — Bi-Metallism." A novel in a nutshell
appeared each week for ten weeks, the last being "The Man in
Asbestos: or, An Allegory of the Future" in the *Saturday Night* of 11
February 1911, where it shared the pages with the same author's
"Practical Political Economy XIV. — The Tariff System of the United
States."[13] If there had been any doubt, it was clear by now that
Leacock either was disregarding B.K. Sandwell's fears for the depres-
sive effects of his humour on his reputation as an economist or was
frontally attacking the potential problem, boldly thrusting the dual
nature of his interests and genius before Canadian readers.

The "Novels in Nutshells" were collected as *Nonsense Novels*
and brought out by The Bodley Head in the late spring of 1911. This
book, more than either Leacock's first New York publications in 1890
or *Literary Lapses,* marked the real beginning of his professional
career as a humorist. By so quickly producing sufficient new material
for another volume, Leacock demonstrated that he was ready to
produce on demand, and with greater skill and creativity than he had
yet shown. The concentrated achievement the new book represented
is striking; *Literary Lapses,* after all, had collected material from over
twenty years of writing. When the series began to appear in *Saturday
Night* on 10 December 1910 with "Gertrude the Governess," the
magazine's prefatory announcement said of Leacock, "Everybody
loves good clean humor. Everybody is attracted by it, for the real
humorist is a rare bird, and it is rarer still that one is captured on the
nest right here at home."[14] *Nonsense Novels* proved to be the most
successful of all of Leacock's humour collections; translated into
many languages, it has had more than three dozen editions and
reprintings. A notation in Leacock's papers from 1924 records that in
all editions it had sold 72,322 copies. It is *Nonsense Novels* in which
Leacock established a tradition that he maintained for most of the
next thirty years, publishing an annual selection of the pieces he had
produced during the previous twelve months for periodicals.

Nonsense Novels harked back to *Literary Lapses* in using narrative voices of shifting character; each of the ten stories has a different narrator, and as in *Literary Lapses* none of these voices is that of the Leacock character, as it emerged in later books, speaking and musing and making cracks. This is especially noticeable in the brilliant parodic uses of first person narrators, as in "'Q.' A Psychic Pstory of the Psupernatural," where the credulous victim is an even dimmer brother to the baffled bank depositor of "My Financial Career." In "Sorrows of a Super Soul; or the Memoirs of Marie Mushenough: Translated, by Machinery, Out of the Original Russian," Marie tells her story in terms that resemble Leacock's characterization of over-sensitivity in "The Passing of the Poet":

> Today in my walk I found a cabbage.
> It lay in a corner of the hedge. Cruel boys had chased
> it there with stones.
> It was dead when I lifted it up.
> Beside it was an egg.
> It too was dead. Ah, how I wept —[15]

This "novel" offers a rapid, knowledgeable and strongly opinionated run-through of Romantic nineteenth-century culture down to the early "existentialist" novelists, with even a glance at Nietzsche, or at any rate popular Nietzscheism. It submits yearning sensitivity and flirtation with the death-wish to a thorough satirical scouring, which reveals plain self-interest masquerading as poetic profundity, with one eye on the mirror, and partly fooling even itself with its act. It is a good example of the reason why Leacock was often credited with being a social and cultural critic in his humour.

Nonsense Novels possessed, in its veiled cultural criticism, a unity of theme, and in its parody a unity of form that Leacock's later collections usually did not provide, although there are notable exceptions, primarily *Sunshine Sketches of a Little Town* (1912), *Arcadian*

Adventures with the Idle Rich (1914), and *My Discovery of England* (1922). The "novels" are a distinctively Leacockian development of an established sub-genre of humour. Bret Harte had published his parodies of popular fiction, *Condensed Novels*, in 1867; the book had been reissued as recently as 1902. Leacock's hero, Mark Twain, had parodied the "medieval" novel in *A Connecticut Yankee at King Arthur's Court* (1889), where he had vented his own anger at Romantic idealism, which (through the novels of Sir Walter Scott) was to blame, he believed, for the hollowing out of modern character and the decay of civilization, especially that of the American South. Leacock's command of verbal humour is quieter than Mark Twain's but equal in its own way; in the shorter, more consistently lightsome flights of his "novels" he sought a more thorough integration of wit, commentary, scorn, and mellow wryness than *A Connecticut Yankee* had achieved. The success of *Nonsense Novels* was sealed and symbolized when U.S. president Theodore Roosevelt incorporated part of a passage from "Gertrude the Governess" into a speech with due credit to Leacock. The phrase Roosevelt borrowed is now part of culture:

> Lord Ronald said nothing; he flung himself from the
> room, flung himself upon his horse and rode madly
> off in all directions.[16]

Leacock presented parodies of ten distinct, familiar types of stories. "Maddened by Mystery: or The Defective Detective" is only the first of his many treatments of the follies of mystery fiction. "'Q.' A Psychic Pstory of the Psupernatural" introduces another oft-recapitulated theme, the distrust of spiritualism. (In later books, he attacked it directly.) "Guido the Gimlet of Ghent: A Romance of Chivalry" is a medieval novel that resembles Mark Twain's lampooning of Scott and Tennyson in nothing except its subject matter and the theme that only self-delusion and self-thwarting flows from a superinduced idealism or refinement. Leacock's narrator follows the long-distance romance of the hero and Isolde the Slender, for whom Guido regularly performed feats of daring, including killing a Saracen, "quite a large one"; the two have never seen one another, however, their love being based solely on reputation and on a locket each possesses of the beloved. When finally they meet, they see that "They were wrong about the miniatures. Each of them was a picture of somebody else."[17] Thus, "Guido was not Guido, and Isolde was not Isolde." "Gertrude the Governess: or Simple Seventeen" is a sentimental romance among the noble classes, which overturns the tradition of love conquering money, a reversal frequent in Leacock's puncturing of various errors, illusions and hypocrisies. "A Hero in Homespun: or The Life Struggle of Hezekiah Hayloft" follows a naive young man to the city and admiringly traces his route to social distinction through a life of crime. Other targets are the emotional memoir, the sea story, the Christmas tale, the science-fiction allegory and, one of his very best, "Hannah of the Highlands: or The Laird of Loch Aucherlocherty," a hilarious account of love's impact on an ancient Scottish feud.

In all the "novels," Leacock drew together plot and character devices that faithfully mirrored the type of fiction in question. At every point, the unlikeliness of situation and the excesses of expression in his originals are suggested by the variations he offers on the familiar elements, and the occasional excesses of nonsense or sarcasm which the risible clichés inspire in the narrator. Hannah, the beautiful Highland lass, is first seen "gathering lobsters in the burn that ran through the Glen." As she sings, "the birds seemed to pause to listen, and as they listened to the simple words of the Gaelic folk song, fell off the bough with a thud on the grass." Some fatal chance brings the new laird, Ian McWhinus, to the glen, where he offers a sixpence for one of the lobsters. It is love at first sight. But Hannah is a McShamus, and no member of her family has spoken to a McWhinus for nearly two centuries because of an ancient feud begun in a dispute about religion.

> Shamus McShamus, an embittered Calvinist, half
> crazed perhaps with liquor, had maintained that
> damnation could be achieved only by faith.
> Whimper McWhinus had held that damnation could
> be achieved also by good works.[18]

Heedless of the quarrel, Hannah determines to pledge her love to Ian. But she discovers that he is married to an American woman; in fact, he bought the lobster for her. With this revelation, the story moves rapidly to its inevitable climax.

In a brief preface to *Nonsense Novels*, Leacock alluded to some doubtful praises of his first book. Certain reviewers, he wrote, had "presumed, on inductive grounds, that he must be a young man from the most westerly part of the Western States, to whom many things might be pardoned as due to the exuberant animal spirits of youth." Leacock's ironic acknowledgment of criticism subtly parallels him to Mark Twain and his critics to those who could not comprehend Twain's comet-like apparition. These reviewers, Leacock went on, hoped that the author's intellect might improve as he grew older and better educated. As a matter of fact, such an "induction" from *Literary Lapses* was not far off the mark, although Leacock would not admit it: some of the pieces showed a brilliant writer who had not yet exerted himself or practised his craft very much. Leacock ignored this and turned to two other points, bringing home to his audience that he was an educator as well as a humorist, and making the first plain statement of his concept of humour:

> All that education could do in this case has been
> tried and has failed. As a Professor of Political
> Economy in a great university, the author admits that
> he ought to know better. But he will feel amply
> repaid for his humiliation if there are any to whom
> this little book may bring some passing amusement in

hours of idleness, or some brief respite when the
sadness of the heart or the sufferings of the body
forbid the perusal of worthier things.[19]

While most commentators could only praise the skill and genius of
Leacock's new book, it too, like its forerunner, received some
complaints, especially the cavil that parody did not permit "the
sounding of the heights of ideal humor." The *New York Times* and the
Nation agreed that Leacock suffered from a lack of restraint. Curbing
it might have improved the pieces marred by "facetiousness or horseplay," said the *Nation*; the *Times* opined that, "If the skits are sometimes quite funny they are more often little better than noisy horseplay
with words — a performance distinctly of the same class as that given
by the circus clown."[20] Some admirers of the book hoped for humour
of "subtler qualities" in future. Whether Leacock responded directly
to these comments or was himself questioning his work in similar
terms, "subtler qualities" are precisely what he worked to engage in
subsequent books and the creation of his mature voice. Yet the
charges aimed at his supposed lack of self-restraint are mistaken. The
extreme imaginative exuberance of some of his humour, displayed
throughout early works such as *Nonsense Novels* and never entirely
abandoned, is one of his great strengths, *pace* the *Nation* and the *New
York Times*. Then, too, *Nonsense Novels* displays a great advance over
the work collected in *Literary Lapses*: the pieces are longer, more
consistent in quality, more complex in structure and character. They
form a bridge to Leacock's next project, one of his most ambitious
and memorable books, in which he came close to writing a novel of
his own.

The Train to Mariposa

The years 1912 to 1914 form one of Leacock's primary creative moments. In this period he wrote and published *Sunshine Sketches of a Little Town* and *Arcadian Adventures with the Idle Rich*, books in which he explored the two environments he now inhabited simultaneously: small market town with conservative traditions, and mercantile capitalist metropolis of international and up-to-date pretensions. The history of *Sunshine Sketches*, written and published in 1912, goes back to 1911, when Leacock participated in the national election portrayed in the book's last two chapters, "The Great Election in Missinaba County" and "The Candidacy of Mr. Smith." And it goes back further, to the summer of 1908, when he acquired the property, with its spit of land into Lake Couchiching on Orillia's eastern outskirts, which he named Old Brewery Bay, and built there, with Charlie's help, his first cottage, called the "cook house." Leacock's income in 1909 was not sufficient for him to erect the house he wanted, and financial considerations kept the cook house little more than a summer cottage until after the First World War. Nevertheless, by 1908 Leacock had arrived in Orillia as a landowner and householder, a resident and a fixture of the town, even if he did occupy his property only seasonally. That he was considered something of a native son by 1906 is clear from the interested reporting by the *Orillia Packet* and the *Orillia Times* of his 1906-07 lectures and world tour; already in May 1906 he had given the Orillia chapter of the Canadian Club his lecture on "The Imperial Tariff Problem." He had now, in his time of maturity and achievement, struck his roots deep into the soil of his Canadian boyhood, which he was coming ever more clearly to see as a primary source of his character and creativity. During the summer of 1910, Leacock had also given his humour an Orillia root by beginning the composition of *Nonsense Novels* at Old Brewery Bay; it was the first of many works written there.

By 1911, his increased prominence was attracting opportunities in several spheres. Early in the year he accepted an invitation to become a member of the Fleming Electoral Reform Commission of Quebec. Not much later, he became more directly involved in politics, campaigning in the federal election of 1911. That spring and summer, the country's political passions, heightened by French-English tensions and debates about the economy and Canada's relations to the British Empire, came to a boiling point in the famous, and acrimonious, "reciprocity" campaign that resulted in Liberal Prime Minister Wilfrid Laurier's defeat on 21 September by Conservative Robert Borden. During the campaign, Leacock lent his support as a public speaker to Borden's Conservatives, which meant arguing against the Liberal party's free-trade economic position, even though he himself had taught the benefits of a limited free-trade policy to his McGill students. Leacock's seeming inconsistency arose first from his Conservative friendships and his own general conservatism, and second from the complicated issues of the election, which associated free trade with a movement toward the United States, while protectionism was associated with closer ties to the Empire.

A free trade agreement between Canada and the United States

had been negotiated in 1854 by Lord Elgin (James Bruce, eighth earl of Elgin, governor general 1847-54); it was abrogated in 1866. In 1910, political factors made U.S. President William Howard Taft amenable to a restoration of limited free trade with Canada. Laurier favoured freer trade both in principle and as a remedy to existing political and economic pressures, and in 1911 he negotiated a reciprocal lowering of tariffs between the two countries on many farm and resource products and some manufactured items. The move proved to be Laurier's greatest political blunder. It alienated the business community, which was used to the benefits of protective tariffs, and it aggravated deep-seated conflicts between French and English Canada, and to a lesser degree within each language group, about the country's relationship to the Empire. English Canadians were concerned about Laurier's action for practical and emotional reasons. Some feared the move would offend Britain, still Canada's major market for most goods; others saw Laurier's reciprocity agreement as flouting the mother country and taking a step away from the Empire, even a step towards union with the United States. Many French Canadians, on the other hand, welcomed a greater distance from Britain and closer ties to the United States.

To a great degree, the fears of English Canada were aroused and exaggerated by the anti-reciprocity Conservatives, with whom Leacock was allied, although he later parodied their inflated rhetoric in *Sunshine Sketches*: "it was a huge election and on it turned issues of the most tremendous importance, such as whether or not Mariposa should become part of the United States, and whether the flag that had waved over the school house at Tecumseh Township for ten centuries should be trampled under the hoof of an alien invader, and whether Britons should be slaves, and whether Canadians should be Britons, and whether the farming class would prove themselves Canadians...."[1] Laurier's defeat in English Canada proved that the organized farmers, who had pressured him for reciprocity, were no political match for the manufacturing interests that desired protective tariffs. The issue of continued strong ties between the Dominions and Great Britain seemed closely enough linked to the reciprocity issue that a vast majority of English Canadians voted for the Conservative party out of a combination of loyal sentiment and their understanding of the economic merits of the case. Leacock was now one of the most powerful expert proponents of a more important role for the Dominions in a renewed Empire. Apparently, his judgment that Canada saw the election as a plebiscite on the Empire was enough to make him disregard the incoherence of the argument that freer trade with the United States was in itself a move away from Britain.

If the election represented a conflict for Leacock, who had spoken and published as both a free trader and a champion of a federated Empire, he was true to his deepest nature in choosing the Tory, imperial camp over the Liberals. Laurier's Liberals championed an economic policy much closer to his own ideas, but he believed primarily in the inherited forms of political life, culture and civility, not in any analytical or technical concept. The Empire — the embodiment of Canada's link to British civilization — was among the most important of these inherited forms. Nor was his view a simple fear of change, or a clinging to the status quo, or an example of class solidarity, for his writings early and late show his understanding that the British system of society and government was to a great degree unfair and ponderous; it often benefited the undeserving, excluded the able and impeded the establishment of the justice that was its own *raison d'être*. On the other hand, he thought modern economic, industrial and political systems entrapped people in ways that were still worse: the systems were devoid of humane and civilizing values or goals, and were open only to change that occurred for mechanical, inhuman reasons. Once Leacock decided to enter the political arena, he was attracted to the Tory camp not only by his upbringing as a son of old England but by half a lifetime of personal effort to develop ideas and a literary sensibility that would give depth to the beliefs first imparted to him in childhood. It is clear that he chose his political side in order

to be where he felt he belonged and not because he opposed reciprocal tariff reductions on principle. He was able to persuade himself
that free trade within the Empire, as a means of strengthening its ties
and paying for its defense, was a different matter from free trade
directed outward, and in 1910-11 gave several anti-reciprocity
addresses as far afield as Quebec City and Saint John, New
Brunswick. The object of his warnings in at least one of these lectures
was, however, the German empire and not free trade in general or
reciprocity with the United States.

Leacock's satirical view of the election may have emerged in the
hindsight of 1912, as he worked on *Sunshine Sketches*. If it existed
during the campaign, it did not prevent him from vigorously
supporting all the Conservative positions in speeches given in
Montreal and Simcoe County. His public advocacy of anti-reciprocity
occasioned a well-known jibe by Professor J.C. Hemmeon, his friend
and colleague in the Department of Economics and Political Science.
Hemmeon stated in class that economists are all free-trade advocates,
and a student objected that Leacock was a protectionist. "I repeat,"
Hemmeon replied, "all economists are free-traders."[2] This sarcasm
has been construed as a slight to Leacock's ability as an economist,
but it seems more likely to have been aimed at his involvement in
politics, which caused him to oppose what Hemmeon knew he
taught: as an economist he was a free trader, as a politician a protectionist. In Montreal, Leacock participated in the election at the local
level and the national level. He had been persuaded to assist the
Conservatives' national publicity effort by the rising politician Richard
Bedford (later Viscount) Bennett. With the help of an acquaintance
who had once worked in England for the *Westminster Gazette*,
Leacock wrote full-page newspaper advertisements, published
nationally, which played up the claim that Laurier's reciprocity agreement meant "selling out" to the United States. Leacock worked in a
Montreal riding on behalf of a lawyer, John Hackette, QC, the only
Conservative member of parliament elected that year from Quebec.

(In that province, Laurier's smashing defeat was at the hands of the Nationalistes.) In his home riding of East Simcoe, he supported another winner, Conservative candidate L.B. Bennett, who defeated Liberal Manley Chew of Midland.

In the East Simcoe riding, his role was an important one. On Friday, 1 September 1911, he delivered a major political address at the Orillia Opera House (built in 1896 and still standing downtown at Mississaga and West streets). Known locally ever since as "the reciprocity address," the speech made an impression on many local residents. In the audience was Leslie M. Frost, later a premier of Ontario, who recalled that Leacock "made a very devastating attack on the whole reciprocity idea" and that the people of Orillia felt his speech "had considerable to do with the election of an anti-reciprocity Conservative."[3] He was serious about the 1911 election, and his addresses were packed with factual material, convincing arguments and even, it appears, emotional rhetoric. Although he had moved away from the oratorical style of the day, and would seldom if ever use it again, he had founded his platform career on that style in his British Empire tour of 1907. The Orillia *Packet*, the town's Conservative newspaper, reported Leacock's speech at the Opera House thus: "Professor Leacock discussed the question on the highest plane and the audience hung on his glowing periods for nearly an hour." On the other hand, the Liberal organ, the Orillia *Times*, paraphrased his remarks in a way that may have influenced his own parody of political speech-making in *Sunshine Sketches*: "the foundations of the British Empire will be shaken [by a Liberal victory] ...Canadians will become hewers of wood and drawers of water for the Yankees...will be their bond slaves and their hired men."[4]

Leacock was questioning himself as well as politics and the follies of the voter when, in the last two chapters of *Sunshine Sketches*, he derided political positions and rhetoric. He satirized the use of economic arguments and statistics by portraying speakers who have no idea what they are talking about and listeners who claim, out of vanity or party prejudice, to follow and be convinced by purely nonsensical lines of thought. In the end, the fictional election is won through the cunning of the hotel keeper, Josh Smith, who has no political ideas and runs as a Conservative only because there is already a Liberal candidate. Smith wins because he uses the telegraph and newspapers to convince the townsmen that there is a Conservative landslide and that, to be on the winning and influential side, they must vote for him. In September 1911 there was in reality a national Conservative landslide; one senses in this satire Leacock's likely assessment of what really swayed the election in Orillia, and how much the various opinions on reciprocity, his own and others's, really counted. This did not prevent him, however, from publishing in the *National Review*, London, "The Great Victory in Canada," a serious praise of the Canadian electorate's great service to the Empire, although he later echoed its title in the derisive "The Great Election in Missinaba County," the tenth chapter of *Sunshine Sketches*.

The end of the campaign and the election coincided rather neatly with the opening of the 1911-12 academic year at McGill. That fall there arrived to Leacock a request from the *Montreal Star* that he should provide it with a series of sketches. According to B.K. Sandwell, the idea originated with Sandwell's friend Edward Beck, the *Star*'s managing editor, who wanted to persuade the humorist to create a specifically Canadian work. The official request to Leacock came after the project was approved by Sir Hugh Graham, the *Star*'s owner and publisher, who had co-founded the newspaper in 1869 with George T. Lanigan, himself a humorist, known for the once famous poem "The Ahkoond of Swat: A Threnody." Sandwell introduced Leacock to Beck, and the three men decided that the work would take the form of a serial rather than a series of unconnected pieces and that it would have a Canadian setting. In Sandwell's belief, this agreement represented, at the time, "the only really large-scale commission ever received for a fictional job to be done for a purely Canadian audience."[5]

In creating *Sunshine Sketches of a Little Town*, Leacock filled this bare format with the life and charm of the town of Mariposa. It is possible that Leacock already presented the basic concept in the early meetings with Beck and Sandwell. There exist two pages of his notes, dated 7 January 1912, which are headed "Plan and Ideas for a series of sketches about a little country town and the people in it: Each sketch about 4000 words: General title — SUNSHINE SKETCHES OF A LITTLE TOWN."[6] The first page gives the general concept of *Sunshine Sketches* as a whole, and the second outlines the story that became "The Speculations of Jefferson Thorpe." Leacock records the titles for "sketches up to date" (those already conceived): "The Hostelry of Mr. Smith," "The Speculations of Calverly Short" and "The Tidal Wave of Local Option." The last of these was never written, although its subject, prohibition, was to serve Leacock in future essays. He says to himself, "For Calverly try *Madison* Short" and, on the second page, not satisfied with either name, he devises the title "The Speculations of Jefferson." Here he was using, for this tale of a small town barber's adventures on the stock market, the name of his own barber in Orillia, Jefferson Short. But only the first name satisfied him; sometime between 7 January and the appearance of the sketch in the *Star* on 2 March, he arrived at the surname of "Thorpe."

Sunshine Sketches was written at Leacock's Côte-des-Neiges house. Having made his first notes for the project on 7 January, he worked quickly and the first completed sketch appeared on 17 February. This piece, "Mariposa and its People," and the second, "The Glorious Victory of Mr. Smith" (24 February), were later combined to make the opening chapter of the book version, "The Hostelry of Mr. Smith." Instalments appeared at intervals of one to two weeks, until the series was completed with the twelfth instalment on 22 June. B.K. Sandwell wrote that "the stories were shaped out at the dinner table" of Leacock's home, where the humorist would narrate the ideas he had developed during his early-morning work sessions, thus testing and improving them before committing a final version to paper. His chair was customarily placed well back from the head of the table so he could leap up and move about the room enacting his words when the spirit moved him.

Leacock's notes of 7 January support the oft-repeated claim that characters in the series were based closely upon his Orillia friends and acquaintances. The notes name several of his models: "Jim Smith, Lach Johnson, McCosh, Canon Greene, Jeff Short" and others. He not only knew these people, he counted several of them among his close friends and sporting companions, he frequented their businesses and used their services. The fact that he maintained the associations just as warmly after the book was published as before, together with what testimony can be still gathered from Leacock's Orillia friends and their descendants, indicates that the familiar story of the town's high dudgeon over the book is mainly legendary. For the book form of the series, Leacock began sending the sketches to John Lane in London, mailing the first group in late February and others in early and mid-March. By 20 March he had sent Lane the first five chapters comprising 35,000 words, but two weeks later he told Lane he was dissatisfied with the completed portion of the manuscript and would keep the succeeding chapters in his possession for a thorough revision. In a 24 February letter, he had estimated to Lane a book of 50,000 words. Ultimately the revised manuscript was more than 62,000 words. Having completed the serial instalments and his academic term work, on 12 May 1912 Leacock left for a vacation in France; from Paris he sent Lane the final manuscript, and may have read proofs before embarking for Canada from Le Havre on 15 June. *Sunshine Sketches of a Little Town* was issued in London by The Bodley Head on 9 August, and in New York by the John Lane Company on 20 September, with a Canadian issue appearing simultaneously with the American.

The series had just finished appearing in the *Montreal Star* and the book version was in production when in late June Leacock returned to Orillia to spend his summer at Old Brewery Bay, surrounded by the people and scenes of which he had written. He expected no storm of protest from the locals and he experienced none. If he made any changes on the advice of Orillia friends, these were minor. Towards the end of his life, he wrote that in 1912 he had received a letter from his friend Mel Tudhope, an Orillia lawyer and judge, threatening, tongue in cheek, to sue for libel on behalf of some of the people portrayed in the newspaper series. This, Leacock said, "led the publisher to think it wiser to alter the names so in the book edition they are changed."[7] A different account came from Charles H. Hale, who, with his brother Russell, published the *Orillia Packet and Times,* having merged the two papers; Leacock combined the brothers to form the Mariposa journalist Hussell, and their newspaper became the *Mariposa Newspacket.* On information derived from Hale, J.V. McAree of the Toronto *Globe and Mail* wrote in 1958:

> Mr. Leacock consulted Mr. Hale who advised him to be a little less precise in his description of the various people at whom he poked gentle fun. This he did. In a preface, he also said that the fictional characters were really fictional and that the setting might be any small Canadian community. This did not satisfy all of them and there were mutterings about libel suits. These died down, however.[8]

Charles Hale was an intimate friend of Leacock's; it is possible Hale advised the author in these terms. Leacock never mentioned having heard any serious indication that libel actions were considered; he stated that the letter from Tudhope had been "in fun." The addition of a preface to the book, possibly as a result of grumblings from Orillia citizens and Hale's advice, was a much more substantial change than any of the alterations in characters' names from the newspaper versions to those in the book. As to alterations in characters' descriptions, there are none. Among the changes of name Leacock made, only two were important. Judge Pepperleigh in the book had been police magistrate McGaw in the *Star* serial; he was based on John McCosh, who was mayor of Orillia in 1886, 1903 and 1904, and was later appointed the town's police magistrate. George Mullins of the Mariposa Exchange Bank in the book had been George Popley in the *Star*; his original was George Rapley, manager of the Traders Bank, which stood at 82 Mississaga Street East and which employed John Stephens, the model of Peter Pupkin, suitor of Judge Pepperleigh's daughter, Zena. Perhaps there is some significance to the fact that Leacock changed the names only of such pillars of the community as a bank manager and a prominent local politician. Other changes between the original serial and the book version are negligible. Transitional summaries, needed to remind newspaper readers where the story left off, were eliminated or shortened, and a few other slight changes were made. For example, the name of the township was changed from Medonte, a township just west of Orillia, to Tecumseh, also a real township but one which lies far to the south.

Josh Smith, the wily and gargantuan hotelier, one of the chief unifying presences of *Sunshine Sketches*, had his original in Jim Smith, proprietor of the Daly House.[9] The real Smith, who weighed more than three hundred pounds and had a wife who weighed less than one hundred, loaned even his physical characteristics to the fictional Smith; the Daly House, on which Smith's Hotel was based, stood at the corner of Matchedash and Mississaga Streets until it was destroyed by fire in 1949. Jefferson Short, Leacock's barber and the original of the speculating barber Thorpe, had his shop at 152 Mississaga Street East; in 1977 his barber's pole, mentioned in *Sunshine Sketches*, was found in the basement of a building on this site. It was being used to support a crossbeam. Like Thorpe, Short had a daughter named Myra who was known locally as an aspiring actress. Golgotha Gingham, the Mariposa undertaker, was based on Horace Bingham, an Orillia undertaker; the Liberal MP John Henry Bagshaw on Judge R.D. Gunn; Netley's Butcher Shop on Hatley's;

McCarthy's office block on Mulcahy's; Missinabi Street on Mississaga Street, and so on. John McCosh, the original of Judge Pepperleigh, had a son, Percy, who, like Neil Pepperleigh, went to the Boer War in South Africa. The model of Zena Pepperleigh, the judge's daughter and Peter Pupkin's light-of-love, was Ovida McCosh. The McCosh home, now the Mundell Funeral Home, still stands at 79 West Street North.

In creating the book version of *Sunshine Sketches*, Leacock added to it as a preface a lively autobiographical essay he had contributed to the British periodical *Canada: An Illustrated Weekly for All Interested in the Dominion*; this appeared on 23 December 1911 under the title "Stephen Leacock: Professor and Humorist" and early in 1912 was reprinted in the *Montreal Star*, the *Orillia Packet* and *Saturday Night*. But to create the book's preface he added to his essay three concluding paragraphs that qualify the apparent resemblances between Mariposa and Orillia:

> Mariposa is not a real town. On the contrary, it is about seventy or eighty of them. You may find them all the way from Lake Superior to the sea, with the same square streets and the same maple trees and the same churches and hotels, and everywhere the sunshine of the land of hope.

Nor are the residents of Mariposa to be seen simply as portraits drawn from Orillia life:

> The Reverend Mr Drone is not one person, but about eight or ten....Mullins and Bagshaw and Judge Pepperleigh and the rest are, it is true, personal friends of mine. But I have known them in such a variety of forms, with such alterations of tall and short, dark and fair, that, individually, I should have

much ado to know them. Mr. Pupkin is found whenever a Canadian bank opens a branch in a country
town and needs a teller.[10]

As with characters, so too with incidents: Leacock adapted,
combined and transformed actual happenings in Orillia. The burning
of Dean Drone's Church of England Church in "The Beacon on the
Hill" was based on the burning of Saint James Anglican, whose
incumbent, the Reverend Richard Green (rector 1888-1911), was the
model of the "Rural Dean." Leacock's fire broke out late one night in
April, and the citizens of Mariposa desperately fought to keep it from
spreading through the wooden town. The fire that destroyed Saint
James broke out just after nine o'clock in the morning on Sunday, 19
March 1905, and like the fictional fire it left the church "nothing but a
ragged group of walls with a sodden heap of bricks and blackened
wood...." Even the financial situation surrounding the fire provided
elements for Leacock's fiction, in which the dean, hard-pressed to
meet the mortgage payments for the needlessly elaborate church, is
rescued as by providence from his financial quandary when the
overinsured building burns. Although the insurance on Saint James
did not cover the rebuilding costs, it did exceed the value of the mortgage, as the *Orillia Times* had noted:

> St. James church was erected in 1890, at a cost of
> over $18,000. The organ was a $3,000 instrument,
> and it is doubtful if both could be replaced to-day for
> less than $25,000. There is a mortgage of $7,100 on
> the building. The building and organ were insured
> for $12,300....[11]

Leacock added and embellished, but his fiction had one of its roots
thrust into fact.

Perhaps the best known of his chapters, "The Marine Excursion of the Knights of Pythias," is also the best example of the way in which he modelled his material not only from factual happenings but also from Orillia's institutions and ideas. In narrating the ill-fated excursion of the *Mariposa Belle*,[12] Leacock suggests that its disastrous "sinking" is in fact a customary event. Indeed, such incidents were not uncommon among the steamers that plied lakes Simcoe and Couchiching during Leacock's Orillia days as a student summer vacationer and, later, as a new householder. Professor Arthur Lower has traced the origin of "The Marine Excursion" to the sinking of the lake steamer *Enterprise* at its dock in Barrie in August 1902. On the other hand, Professor Ralph Curry points out that the steamer *Islay* sank while skirting the Couchiching shore in a manner similar to that of the *Mariposa Belle*. While the *Enterprise* is probably the physical model of Leacock's steamer, the third of the three boats that served Lake Couchiching around the turn of the century, the *Longford*, has perhaps the strongest claim of all to being his inspiration. It did not sink; one warm afternoon in October 1898, it ran aground on a sandbar, just as the *Mariposa Belle* later did, during a businessmen's outing. At the wheel was Captain Laughlin ("Lockie") Johnson, the original of Leacock's Captain Christie Johnson. The details of this incident — and the mixture of affable deadpan description and wisecracks with which an unnamed *Orillia Times* reporter recorded it — are so incipiently Leacockian that the *Longford*'s misadventure, too, must have gone into the saga of the *Mariposa Belle*. On 27 October 1898 the *Times* reported:

> The annual outing of the business men of the town, on the steamer Longford, has come to be as much a feature as Thanksgiving Day, and neither Messrs. Thomson or their guests would feel that the boating season had been properly closed if the event did not take place. Thursday last was a beautiful day, nearly as warm and bright as July, and when Mr. Geo.

Thomson appeared on Main Street, and announced that the Longford would leave at 11 o'clock, everybody who could, put aside business and started for the dock.

Crossing Lake Couchiching, the boat called at Longford, where Mr. Win. Thomson was taken on board, and after a short time spent at Geneva Park, steamed down to the Portage, where the Longford Co.'s herd of cattle was inspected and lunch partaken of. The day being so delightful, Mr. Thomson suggested a run down to Beaverton, and everyone being willing, the Longford was headed for the Narrows. When east of Ship Island, and within a short distance off Horse Shoe, a sudden jar was felt, and the party found themselves stranded on Sanson's shoal. Captain Johnson had miscalculated the course, or had failed to allow for the low water, as ten feet further east would have cleared the shoal nicely. The life boat was lowered and the anchor taken out a short distance, with a cable attached to the winch. All hands manned the capstan, but were unable to draw the boat off. Mr. Dean happened along with his steam yacht Dolly, and took Mr. Geo. Thomson and a crew to Longford, where they rigged up the Curlew, and proceeded to take the crowd home to Orillia. With all hands on board, the Curlew was just getting nicely underway when she, too, bumped on the shoal and came to a standstill. The life boat from the Longford was put in commission, and the schooner, lightened of her human freight, floated free. The party got aboard again and sailed into Orillia without further mishap. The only loss was the loss of the P.M.'s head-gear which went overboard and sank. Police Magistrate Lafferty may be strong on points of law but he is decidedly weak on a capstan. Capt. Johnston [sic] was heard renaming the shoal. As he did so in Gaelic, the reporter was unable to catch the title, but it sounded like "Howingehennadididothat." Capt. Johnston has been sailing these lakes for over thirty years, and this is the first shoal he has discovered.

How the Longford got out of the course is a mystery but it is supposed that the electricity generated by the heated discussions of the voters' list court deranged the compass and drew the needle in that direction.

With the first shock there was a general rush for life preservers. Commodore Haywood never goes to sea without one of his own. As he reached for his hip pocket, he had several offers to assist him "Blow" it, but as the preserver would not go around, he was forced to decline. Moral…"Consider the lilies."[13]

"Why, it is just the little things like this," comments the narrator of "The Marine Excursion" as the *Mariposa Belle* settles onto a reed bank, "that give zest to a day on the water." In *Sunshine Sketches*, Leacock's imagination was able to combine many forms of humour — wit, satire, verbal play, caricature and exaggeration, understatement, nonsense in plot and in dialogue — to a degree that very few writers have achieved. And yet, the book's tone springs from something more fundamental than its humour: Leacock's comic view of the world, which suffuses his portrait of Mariposa with a kindly but melancholy light in which everything is clear yet subtly muted, softened and distanced. A loving depiction of the present is mysteriously blended with nostalgia, and a tenuous sense of foreboding that perceives fragility and an invisible decay. When Leacock was writing, the small-town Canada he described was in full vigour; he adhered to a real model, yet there is a sense of a lost paradise, of times remembered, in his depiction of Mariposa. In *Sunshine Sketches*, his perfected style — simple yet ever varied, supple, intimate, preserving the accent of speech within his own distinctive version of the essay's sophistication — embodies a vision of an apparently changeless world that in fact is slowly changing and passing. Mariposa is a benign, privileged mode of existence, but as such it is only an island always threatened, from within and without, by the corrosive realities of the great world and of human nature.

Leacock's narrator sees Mariposa from the perspective of an established resident, a community member: Leacock's own perspective as he looked out at Orillia and environs from the home he had established on Lake Couchiching. The book reveals affectionate and critical insights into small-town existence that Leacock had been gathering since childhood, but it does not convey a child's or adolescent's vision remembered in adulthood. It keeps revealing facets of the complex attitude of a grown man, a citizen, who is distanced from his fellows by his insight into society and human motives but who nevertheless chooses to belong, even to the point of closing one eye to folly and ranging himself with those he satirizes: with their better selves and their hopes, but also with their foolishness and failures. Mariposa is not Orillia but a dissection of Orillia that is also an imaginative idealization, carrying a great charge of thanks and praise. Leacock wrote, "The inspiration of the book — a land of hope and sunshine where little towns spread their square streets and their trim maple trees beside placid lakes almost within echo of the primeval forest — is large enough."[14] Mariposa contains the creative latitude for a glancing, multivalent, ironic sensibility that can love and mock in the same breath. Such a sensibility is often viewed with suspicion in any real town; it is Mariposa where Leacock is actually at home and a citizen.

True to the nature of comedy, *Sunshine Sketches* shows us a world in which crises are not of ultimate seriousness, a world that beyond injustice and disaster renews itself through the always-repeated rituals of life and the loves and marriages of the younger generation. Yet the marriage of Peter Pupkin and Zena Pepperleigh does not have a central, symbolic role; it is not the climax of the main plot. Leacock was disappointed he had not developed *Sunshine Sketches* as a unified novel; he thought this failure stemmed from his inability to make the Pupkin-Pepperleigh romance a thread that ran through the entire book. In fact, the book seems to indicate that he could not create such a unity because he did not believe in it. The minor importance of the romance is in tune with his constant sense, both here and throughout his writings, that motives of self-interest, covetousness and status-seeking underlie romantic sentiments. Like many of his heroines, Zena professes a love-inspired asceticism, but when she learns of Pupkin's family wealth, "she bore up as bravely as so fine a girl as Zena would, and when he spoke of diamonds she said she would wear them for his sake." Leacock looks at these workings of the human mind mildly but clearly; his attitude is not condemnatory, but he realizes that such ready abandonment of avowed principles is what ultimately erodes the human happiness, here represented by Mariposa, that people miraculously manage to find for themselves from time to time. Zena's attitude, magnified, is exactly that of the plutocrat who, in the final essay in the book, "L'Envoi: The Train to Mariposa," sits in the Mausoleum Club in the great city and dreams of going back to his home town, although the journey never will occur. His self-will and acquisitiveness have exiled him and will keep him in exile. Leacock's narrator sits next to this plutocrat in the Mausoleum Club and stage-manages the empty dream of returning. The reader cannot help feeling the ghost presence of Leacock, Montreal professor and political expert, resident and partisan of small-town Canada. Indeed, the narrator had presented himself in these terms, as a sort of parallel to the Mausoleum Club plutocrat, in the "Preface" that balances "L'Envoi" and frames the book. "L'Envoi" is only one of many occasions in *Sunshine Sketches* on which the narrator, who generally distances himself from the foibles under examination, identifies with what he satirizes. In life, Leacock had one foot in Mariposa and one on Plutoria Avenue. He lived a myth of small-town Arcadia and made it more than a myth; at the same time he hungered for, and to a large measure achieved, the success in the climate of the larger "outside" world that is everything to the millionaires, academics and divines of the great city, which he would soon explore in *Arcadian Adventures with the Idle Rich*. Leacock could not be content with the retired, unknown life of a cracker-barrel philosopher. When we read of Peter Pupkin's father, the Maritime millionaire with forestry and real-estate interests and a hand in government and law, we may recall that it was Leacock, of all those on the Orillia scene, who was related by marriage to a similar figure, Sir Henry Pellatt, owner of a magnificent summer estate in Orillia.

It is fitting and effective that *Sunshine Sketches* reaches its climax not in a marriage but in politics. In the election, the falseness of the outside world intrudes most seriously upon Mariposa; the election reveals how prone the people of Mariposa are to be governed by their own foibles. Once the vote is over and this tempest has been stilled into amusing inconsequentiality, the magic power of Mariposa to resist worldly venality and pretension is dramatically confirmed. At the same time, this power is revealed to consist of nothing but the town's ever-vulnerable smallness and harmlessness. The people of Mariposa resemble, in all respects, the people and forces of the outside world. But in them everything that is dangerous has been reduced in scale and placed in a setting where it does not seem to matter. Leacock's melancholy undertone rises from the subtly expressed fact that these dangers do matter, despite appearances. Influences tending towards a more ruthless world do pass into Mariposa. Perhaps they change it for the worse; at any rate, they drive some people out of it to seek a supposedly greater arena, and it is lost to such people, perhaps forever. Even if Mariposa remains always present, always possible, it may move somehow beyond reach, beyond our ability to live in it anymore. This is why the narrator, at the end, is not in Mariposa but seated beside the plutocrat in the Mausoleum Club, dreaming of "the little Town in the Sunshine" but magnetized by the promise of the city. And so the sense that Mariposa's crises and stumbles are not of ultimate seriousness, are always healed in the ongoingness of a small-town Arcadia, must be qualified. In the midst of humour and praise, Leacock's melancholy inscribes a real threat and a real loss.

Through the summer of 1912 Leacock continued to participate happily in the life of Orillia, despite the jocular warnings of Mel Tudhope, Horace Bingham's complaint that Golgotha Gingham has been too obsessed with his business and barber Jeff Short's protest, "I never thought he was going to put in a book what I told him." Tudhope and the Hale brothers, especially Charles, with whom Leacock played cricket, were among his closest friends, as was

This picture, taken about 1913 at Old Brewery Bay, shows Beatrix (seated left) with her mother.
Courtesy National Archives of Canada C-31938.

Doctor Edward Ardagh, his billiard companion, who was the model for Doctor Gallagher in *Sunshine Sketches*. He pursued his devotion to fishing, often employing as a guide Orillia's famous world-champion oarsman, Jake Gaudaur. As years passed and both his worldwide reputation and his local rootedness became more established, he began receiving requests from city officials to appear at local events. For example, he spoke at the opening of the bridge over the narrows connecting lakes Simcoe and Couchiching and at the dedication of Orillia's monument to Champlain, who in 1615 had spent nearly a year at the Huron capital, Cahiague, just west of the city's site, and had fished at the narrows. In the preface to *Here Are My Lectures and Stories* (1937), he recalled being introduced at an Orillia function as "one of the foremost humorists of East Simcoe." Also in 1912 the annual writing routine of his Orillia summers was definitively established. Working at earliest morning, beginning close to dawn, he began producing the sketches that would constitute the first of the many annual humour collections that became the axle of his career. These books, although they often had one or more unifying themes that linked some of the sketches, resembled *Literary Lapses* more closely than Leacock's other humour works to date, *Nonsense Novels* with its central thread of literary parody and *Sunshine Sketches* with its unified portrayal of a social milieu. The book on which he was now at work, eventually entitled *Behind the Beyond* after its most elaborate piece, was not quite the pure miscellany that *Literary Lapses* had been, collecting as it did the disparate work of two decades. It took book form primarily as a means of bringing together and republishing the essays and sketches Leacock was moved to write over the course of a year. Immediately after returning to Canada from his May-June visit to France, he had begun making hay of his new fame; from 13 July until 13 September, *Saturday Night* carried six sketches on Paris. These began under the general heading "A Humorist in Paris," but after the second instalment the series title was switched to "Gazing on Gay Paree." Combined, edited and revised, the sketches soon became the third part of *Behind the Beyond*, five essays grouped in the book under the subtitle "Parisian Pastimes."

When Leacock returned to McGill in the fall of 1912, he was engaged in expanding his department, an effort authorized by McGill's principal Sir William Peterson, as part of an overall upgrading of the faculty of arts. Leacock's methods as chairman featured careful selection of professors, complete loyalty to his staff and scrutiny of the department's offerings. During the academic year he took time to consult with the American representatives of his British publisher in New York, where he made a hit as a speaker at the Lotus Club when he filled in extemporaneously for a guest of honour who never arrived. His schedule as a guest lecturer was relatively light during the 1912-13 academic year but included an appearance in February as guest of honour of the Victorian Club of Boston; at the Westminster Hotel he addressed the Club on "Imperial Unity." In 1913, when the University Club moved into a new building (the one it still occupies at 183 Mansfield Street), Leacock provided an analysis of moving costs that proved it would be cheaper to drink the bar's stock and buy again than to move the bottles, but the membership did not accept his logic.[15] An event of 1912-13 that proved to be important was the arrival of Professor René du Roure, who would soon become one of Leacock's best friends and a fast University Club companion. The physical antithesis of Leacock, du Roure was a slight, short and impeccably turned-out Frenchman who had immigrated in 1909 to teach at the Université Laval in Quebec City. After three years there, he joined McGill's department of romance languages.

Whereas in 1910-12 Leacock had published seven scholarly essays, in addition to his books, lectures and popular series of articles on economics and politics, in 1912-13 he produced only one, "The Canadian Senate and the Naval Bill"; and even this, since it appeared in July 1913 in the *National Review*, London, may have been written or at any rate completed after the spring term had ended and he was back to Orillia. The reason for his markedly slowed pace in articles on political-economic themes was the effort he was putting into books, all of them popular in character. In 1911 he had agreed with Thomas Morang, the publisher of the Makers of Canada Series in which he had published his *Baldwin, Lafontaine, Hincks: Responsible Government*, to provide books for a new series, The Chronicles of Canada for Boys and Girls. Already in 1911 he had completed the manuscript of one of his contributions, *The Mariner of St Malo: A Chronicle of the Voyages of Jacques Cartier*. The series, however, was transferred from Morang's company to another, and then another, before finally achieving publication with Brook & Company of Glasgow. One of the things which preoccupied Leacock during the fall 1912 term was the writing of volume one of the series, *The Dawn of Canadian History: A Chronicle of Aboriginal Canada and the Coming of the White Man*; his notes show that he began the manuscript on 1 October and completed it on 4 December. It appeared in 1914, followed in the same year by Leacock's two other contributions, the Cartier book and *Adventurers of the Far North: A Chronicle of the Frozen Seas*.[16] In 1912-13, he was also busily producing humour with a view towards completing *Behind the Beyond* for the autumn 1913 publishing season and the Christmas trade. During the academic year he began publishing his series of "Familiar Incidents" in the *Saturday Mirror*, Montreal; he continued to produce this series during the summer of 1913 at Orillia, and the *American Magazine*, which reprinted the earlier instalments, became the first publisher of the final instalment, "The Dentist and the Gas," in July. This series is comparatively weak, with the exception of "My Unknown Friend," which appeared in Montreal in March and again in the *American Magazine* in November. The relaxation and routine of Orillia bore humorous fruit that summer. The contents of *Behind the Beyond* were basically set when the title essay, "Behind the Beyond: In Three Acts and Two Drinks," had appeared in the *American Magazine* and "The Retroactive Existence of Mr. Juggins" in the *Popular Magazine*, both in August, and "Homer and Humbug" in the *Century Magazine* in

October. The manuscript had already gone to John Lane and on 31 October was published by The Bodley Head in London and the John Lane Company in New York; it was Leacock's fourth consecutive best-seller. The nearly 4,000 copies it sold by the end of the year earned Leacock $541.35, which raised his annual income to more than $10,000 for the first time.[17]

Four of the five short "Familiar Incidents" excepted, *Behind the Beyond* maintains a high level of humour and style, and displays Leacock in many different moods and manners. The title piece, renamed for the book as "Behind the Beyond: A Modern Problem Play," is only one of the essays and stories in the book that is linked to the ideas Leacock had developed in *Sunshine Sketches* and was further exploring as he thought about the composition of *Arcadian Adventures with the Idle Rich*, which he had already proposed to the John Lane Company in a letter of 5 November 1912.[18] "Behind the Beyond" shows how people are easily swayed by the ridiculous attitudes disseminated through popular culture, especially that strain of it that acquires the cachet of seriousness, becoming something that everyone with pretensions to culture is supposed to know and discuss. This is a noteworthy thread in *Sunshine Sketches*, and had already dominated the parodies of *Nonsense Novels* and many of the essays in *Literary Lapses*; a constant of Leacock's work, the theme is especially strong in his earlier books. In *Sunshine Sketches*, for instance, the romance of Zena Pepperleigh and Peter Pupkin definitely has elements of satire that have their roots in *Don Quixote*'s excoriation of the effects of fantasy literature, and in Mark Twain's similar stance in *A Connecticut Yankee*. The romantic maiden, Zena, shapes her notions according to novels of chivalry she reads when her fierce father is not present to keep her attention fixed on the reading matter he has assigned, *The Pioneers of Tecumseh Township*. When her shy suitor can do no more than whiz by her porch on his bicycle every evening, she sees "a sort of dim parallel between the passing of the bicycle and the ride of Tancred the Inconsolable along the banks of the Danube." In "Behind the Beyond," Leacock incorporates both the drama and its audience into his story, masterfully suggesting what the play is like by conveying the audience's reaction to it. The theatre-goers hang spellbound, despite the patent foolishness of plot and characters, and the shoddy stage business that emphasizes the transparent artificiality of it all. The door is obviously cardboard, the valet enters before the bell sounds for him, Sir John "reads" letters without looking at them and announces that it is eight o'clock when the stage clock tells another time altogether. Nevertheless, the audience is deeply impressed, even as it clings to the pretense of intellectual superiority by disparaging the play. Leacock displays the watchers' gullibility by treating them as a huge chorus that goes through synchronized stages of feeling; there seems to be no individual with a divergent opinion. When one of the play's characters, Jack Harding, who is "meant to typify weakness," promises to carry off Lady Cicely to a romantic port of her dreams (she mentions Para Noia), the audience is with him: "Any man in the audience would do as much. They'd take her to Honolulu." The men are so absorbed in the play that they become Jack Harding, except that their idea of a romantic destination is amusingly mundane next to the fictional playwright's ignorant flight of geographical nonsense. The agreed-upon judgment that it is a "perfectly rotten play, but very strong" shows the theatre-goers adopting attitudes they profess to analyze and judge, just as the citizens of Mariposa deprecate but ape the notions that come to them from the city and from books, magazines and newspapers.

The five acerbic travel essays, "Parisian Pastimes," look forward to *Arcadian Adventures*, in their stinging depiction of the follies of wealth and fashion, and the ignorance and vulgarity of social climbers who wish to associate with the *haute monde* and yet claim to rise to a position superior to it in understanding. Other aspects of Leacock's art can be seen in even comparatively weak sketches. "Under the Barber's Knife," for instance, uses "cinematic" literary effects to create a barber-shop like the one that became a staple scene of comic films and animated cartoons. The barber dominates the cowed customer, muffles him in hot towels, talks to him mercilessly while wielding a careless razor. The choleric, dictatorial editor of "Making a Magazine," a much more accomplished sketch, is Leacock's early contribution to another character that became a favourite comic type in later literature and film (where, however, he often turned out in the end to have a kindly heart). These and many other early Leacock characters and situations are similar to elements of film and literature from the 1920s through the 1940s. As his era's greatest and most prominent literary humorist, Leacock drew from but also influenced the tone, setting and imagery of American movies in their "golden age." He was acquainted with Charlie Chaplin, who suggested he write for films, an idea he entertained but never enacted; and his work was a model for other literary humorists who did become involved in the film industry: Robert Benchley, for example, and S.J. Perelman, who wrote for the Marx brothers. It is worth noting that *Sunshine Sketches* too is an example of Leacock's contribution to the development of popular motifs. In 1912, North America was a conti-nent of small towns that remained in many respects as they had been since the late nineteenth century, but American and Canadian writers were engaged in a literary and philosophical war over the value of this heritage. Was the small town a needed source of values and a spiritual oasis, or was it a narrow milieu breeding conformism and self-satisfaction; did it produce human ennoblement or dehumanizing provincialism and drudgery? Leacock presented the optimistic view in *Sunshine Sketches*; the very force of his satire on the small town, by the fact that it did not destroy but mysteriously enhanced its object, gave force to his assessment. By the end of the same decade, Sinclair Lewis, a satirist but no humorist, had drawn the negative picture of cultural isolation and pettiness in *Main Street* (1920). Leacock's vision, persuasive because it was both vivid and balanced, fed into the towns much like Mariposa that appear in the films of Frank Capra, in the

Andy Hardy series and numerous others; although this familiar filmic town may derive more directly from Booth Tarkington and other American literary models, it is Leacock who provided its most enduring expression.

Behind the Beyond possesses a general unity and shape, despite its primary character as a collection. The opening piece, "Behind the Beyond," satirizes contemporary literature in the form of the drama, and is mirrored by the final essay, "Homer and Humbug," in which Leacock skewers the reverence with which some regard the Greek and Latin classics to the depreciation of modern writers. "Familiar Incidents," with its five depictions of a somewhat hang-dog if wry everyman bewildered by typical North American situations, is followed by the five "Parisian Pastimes" sketches satirizing the fashionable European world and those who gaze in at it with hungry faces pressed to the window. In the final movement of the book, "Homer and Humbug" is preceded by the haunting if hilarious "The Retroactive Existence of Mr. Juggins" and the slashing "Making a Magazine: The Dream of a Contributor." Juggins's quest for the roots of things leads him to childishness; soon he will "back up clear through the Curtain of Existence" to "die, or be born, I don't know which to call it." His disastrous approach to life had included a never-completed study of French that gradually regressed to a demand to learn the lost "ancient Iranian, the root-language underneath." If Juggins, under the laughter, is a metaphysical allegory of a too-great fascination with the original and the underlying, so "Making a Magazine" levels the balance, rating the clichés, fashions and competitiveness which haunt contemporary literary life and everything that preens itself on being up-to-date and forward-looking. Coming at the end of this calculatedly if loosely organized sequence of sketches, "Homer and Humbug" emerges as an argument against pretension and received ideas, and for honesty and first-hand knowledge, in the formation of taste.

In late 1913 and early 1914, Leacock was seeing the fruits of the success achieved by his first books. These had already established him in the minds of the most perceptive onlookers as the leading English-language humorist and as the man who was redirecting and reinvigorating literary humour in the twentieth century. Since the publication of *Behind the Beyond*, Leacock's acuteness as an observer of the drama and his potential as a playwright had been commented upon; in November, James L. Ford approached him for permission to turn "Behind the Beyond" into a play for production by the New York Stage Society; on 2 February 1914, Ford wrote him to report on a production of the play that was held in a private New York home for a high-society audience. Ford and Leacock divided the proceeds. On 5 December 1913, he received a request from British humorist E.V. Lucas to contribute to a humour anthology, and in January came a letter from Frederick Eckstein of Doubleday Page & Company, New York, attempting to lure him away from the John Lane Company as his American publisher. Eckstein offered Leacock a leather-bound edition of his works, similar to editions Doubleday had made for Kipling, Conrad and O. Henry. The editor wrote that "now nearly everyone here has the Leacock 'bug.' We have been through various stages of the Kipling 'bug,' the O. Henry and the Conrad ditto, but of all we seem to have the first in the most virulent form."[19] Leacock remained with Lane. In early 1914 Leacock's mail was also bringing him many requests to provide material to the most prestigious, widely circulated periodicals in England and the United States, and was providing another reflection of his popularity in the form of fan letters. One from a New Orleans architect perceptively touched on the many roles and points of view Leacock had adopted in his works. The writer asked, "But are you an optimist or a pessimist? Your writings show the melancholy cynicism of Bernard Shaw, the good-natured banter of Gil Blas, the hoping-for-better satire of Aristophanes. Are you a Proteus?" Other fan letters he began receiving at this time came from the likes of Faith Baldwin (1913), F. Scott Fitzgerald (1916) and Kenneth Roberts (1917). On 22 May, Claire Hellwig wrote from Munich to ask for the rights to translate *Nonsense Novels* into German; she had already secured the consent of a far-off Leacock admirer, the novelist Gustave Meyrink, to provide an introduction and find a German publisher for the translation;[20] Leacock was eventually translated into German, but this particular initiative was soon lost in the bitterness of the approaching war.

In the 1913-14 academic year, Leacock was extremely busy with his writing, although the period was outwardly uneventful. He was offered the job of chairing a committee in Ottawa to study cost of living, a subject on which he had produced several recent addresses and articles, but rejected the post in early December.[21] In his stead he recommended Professor James Mavor, the man who had turned him down for a University of Toronto professorship. In 1913 Leacock and J.C. Hemmeon founded and directed McGill's Political Economy Club, and throughout the fall contributed a series on current events and issues to the *Montreal Daily Mail*, including such titles as "The Cry of the Consumer" (on cost of living), "Temperance and Legislation; a Plea for Fair-Mindedness" and the two-part "Social Reform in the Coming Century," which decried unjust distribution of wealth, pro-claimed the philosophy of individualism a failure, prophesied the advance and the benefits of technology, discussed the changing role of women, and rehearsed his view of socialism as an invalid idea of government but an important expression of the need for social change.

In March 1914, the pieces that Leacock would gather in his next annual humour collection, which he ultimately titled *Moonbeams from the Larger Lunacy* (1915), began appearing when "Aristocratic Attitudes or Little Anecdotes of Great People" was published by the *Century Magazine*; Frank Crowninshield, its then-prominent editor, had cooperated in James L. Ford's adaptation of "Behind the Beyond." In short order, Leacock brought out other sketches destined for the collection in the *Popular Magazine*, the *American Magazine*, and *Vanity Fair* in New York, and *Methuen's Annual* in London. Simultaneously he was writing the second of his two parallel books of linked stories, *Arcadian Adventures with the Idle Rich*, about the denizens of the Mausoleum Club on Plutoria Avenue in the great city, who had been glimpsed by the narrator of *Sunshine Sketches* in "L'Envoi: The Train to Mariposa." The eight chapters of *Arcadian Adventures* were begun in the spring 1914 academic term, Leacock completing the first on 19 February and three others before the term ended; the final three sketches were written and the completed manuscript prepared at Old Brewery Bay by August. The first five chapters appeared in the *American Magazine* from July through November. In book form, *Arcadian Adventures with the Idle Rich* was issued in October, and by November Leacock was reading the "most glowing reviews...from all over the United States, longer & better than I have ever had before."[22] He had feared his satire was too pointed, and literary taste too dull, for the book to be a success, and indeed it was never one of his most popular and profitable titles, but among critics and committed Leacockians it immediately gained and has always retained the status of one of his finest accomplishments.

Leacock's fundamentally nontechnical view of all that is comprehended in economics, political science and sociology can be clearly read in *Arcadian Adventures*, his most Veblenesque book. Like Veblen, he uses economic and social insights to construct a form of satire that unmasks the true motives behind class behaviour. This unmasking is applied to the pretensions and self-conceptions not of a single class but a broad spectrum of classes, and also to the theories and rationalizations of economists and social observers who claim to explain social systems accurately. Leacock had even less faith than Veblen in technical and theoretical approaches to socio-economic situations; far from admiring or adopting, he derided approaches that stem purely from a disinterested, scientific examination of a problem and that might require the imposition of a new political or economic system on a society. Rather, as *Arcadian Adventures* and *Sunshine Sketches* clearly indicate, Leacock felt that the basis of society had to be the individual person acting intelligently from good motives.

Conservatism and an emphasis on the individual person underlie *Arcadian Adventures* and make it an indictment of the greed and foolishness that burden a potentially benign world. If individuals would act well, the existing social and governmental forms would function properly and improve; meanwhile, these forms represented an order and an inheritance too valuable to tamper with. Between Leacock and the scientific economist there is the difference between the person who believes social change must spring from personal change of heart and one who believes it comes with change of means. The two views seldom exclude one another absolutely; the technical view usually admits the necessity of enlisting the individual's enthusiasm, and the humanistic view will state that any change of public spirit must be made practical through effective methods. But the difference in their starting points marks them, and there was something antipathetic to modern economic science in Leacock's belief in the economic importance of the individual's attitudes, and in his conservatism, which would rule out (in a most unscientific manner) the possibility of changing certain social institutions.

Does Leacock regard any of the systems and institutions he depicts in *Arcadian Adventures* — capitalism and mercantilism, the modern university, organized religion, democratic government in a metropolis — as good or bad in themselves? The systems seem evil because the people who operate them seem to be inevitably either foolish or greedy or hypocritical. Leacock focuses his satire and implicit condemnation on persons and the relationships they form, not on the systems those persons adapt to govern their social and economic activities. In Leacock's book, college presidents are somehow not corrupted by the system of modern higher education; quite the opposite, they are mere promoters with no essential interest in education, hence contributing to injure it and lessen the respect in which it is held. Financiers are ignoramuses who attribute to their own acumen the results of birth, luck and blind economic momentum; clergymen are concerned only with prestige. And all of them change their opinions as the wind blows. Venality and hypocrisy, profiteering, unprincipled opportunism: these constitute the real problem, as Leacock sees it, and much of the hilarity of *Arcadian Adventures* comes from the way in which he repeatedly drives the point home.

In the first chapter, "A Little Dinner with Mr. Lucullus Fyshe," each time the financier Fyshe begins to proclaim his revolutionary socialist tendencies, something occurs to make him contradict himself and spout commands or insults at the lower classes. The very predictability of these occurrences becomes funny, underlining Fyshe's complete inability to be honest with himself, to compare what he does and what he says. Leacock implies that if Fyshe would act on what he claims to understand, there would be no labour unrest and no revolutionary socialism because there would be none of the social conditions that cause them. Throughout the book, the reader sees that the "Idle Rich" have become so wholly pragmatic, so cynically intent on their own advantage, and so willing to change with the opportunities of the day and the moment, that they are no longer even capable of realizing they are dishonest: long corruption has not left enough of the human in them for that. It has become impossible for them to change, or even — except perhaps in rare moments of nostalgia or frightening vacancy — to recognize what they have become. For Leacock, then, the humanistic belief that the individual's attitudes determine society does not amount to faith that the individual can be converted and society thereby improved: *Acadian Adventures* bitterly implies that the drives for power and wealth will continue to cause many to convert themselves into ruthless, hollowly polite, utterly self-deceived simulacra of human beings, who will be a permanent source of social debility and injustice.

In the story of the inadvertent multimillionaire from Cahoga Country, told in "The Wizard of Finance" and "The Arrested Philanthropy of Mr. Tomlinson," Tomlinson is saved from the corrupt city (where his sudden wealth places him) only by a complete lack of comprehension. And this lack of comprehension comes from the fact that the healthier rural attitudes of his native region on the banks of Lake Erie are embedded in him, just as corrupt and trivial attitudes are embedded in the Plutoria Avenue financiers and lawyers who prey on him when he comes to the metropolis. Leacock portrays a world in which there is little opening for change; paradoxically, however, this very changelessness makes the vicious and stupid actions of the rich seem humorously inconsequential. Life appears to go on much the same, no matter what they do, for if shallowness and injustice are ever renewed, so is innocence. Months after Tomlinson's fortune has vanished, the debits and credits of his empire neatly resolving themselves into a nought, President Boomer of the university and Lucullus Fyshe are still involved in their heedless money-grubbing and their efforts to seem impressive; Tomlinson is back on his Lake Erie hillside, where he now sees "nothing but the land sloping to the lake and the creek murmuring again to the willows." However, in the world of *Arcadian Adventures*, just as in that of *Sunshine Sketches*, a slow change is in fact occurring, although it is nearly invisible, impalpable. There is evidence of this change in the decay of the university under Boomer's control, and in a subtle fact that is almost buried near the end of the tale: "the development capital had disappeared." Those who seeded real gold in Tomlinson's creek, where only fool's gold was to be found in the rocks, managed to get what they wanted out of the ten-days'-wonder of the nonexistent gold strike. Leacock's emphasis is on the way in which the "Idle Rich" act, but there are indications here and there of the effects they have, too; as in *Sunshine Sketches*, the result is a sense of melancholy and even foreboding that veins the predominant humour.

At the outset of *Arcadian Adventures*, Leacock justifies the title of his book by comparing the "Idle Rich" to shepherds and shepherdesses. They live in an Arcadia of their own imaginations, as did the courtiers during those ages that produced pastoral literature with its decorative landscapes and rural characters. Such literature was sometimes artificial and foolish. At its best, however, it was used to create an ideal country world as a means to examine the sophisticated court and city. *Sunshine Sketches* created a true and fascinating Arcadia in this classic sense, although Leacock's version was highly personal and original. Ineffably pleasant and yet far from perfect, Mariposa shows up the fallaciousness of the worldly attitudes that intrude, and also the vices of the Mariposa people and their vulnerability to all that could harm them. *Arcadian Adventures* concentrates more on the satirical dimensions of the pastoral, emphasizing the corruption which becomes apparent whenever the "Idle Rich" congratulate themselves on their goodness and simplicity or whenever a real shepherd from the environs of Mariposa, such as Tomlinson, wanders among them. Both books are idylls: they present an almost timeless world that appears to absorb human folly without too much ill effect. Together, they portray very winningly a North American version of La Belle Époque, the golden calm before the storm of the First World War. But they also show Leacock penetratingly, prophetically aware of the aggressive cupidity and the culpably ignorant contentment that haunt good times and help to call down such storms as the one that was about to descend.

Some Just Complaints About the War

G reat Britain declared war on Germany on 4 August 1914 and Canada, as a Dominion of the Empire, with her foreign affairs controlled from Westminster, was automatically at war; the first Canadian contingent, 33,000 troops, arrived in Plymouth, England on 16 October. In August, Leacock was nearing his forty-fifth birthday; he was at the end of his annual summer sojourn at Old Brewery Bay; the book version of *Arcadian Adventures* was in preparation, and the fateful month saw the appearance of its second chapter, "The Wizard of Finance," in the *American Magazine*.

Although the outbreak of violence caught many by surprise, Leacock had warned for years in lectures, articles and his university classes that German militarism posed a threat to world peace. He considered that he knew the German nation and German culture well. His language training had included German; he was one of three McGill faculty members the university relied on to review doctoral theses written in that language. During his student days in Chicago, he had frequented German neighbourhoods to practise the language and felt that he had met even there a nationalistic spirit. Already at the turn of the century he was keenly and angrily aware of Germany's aggressively competitive stance toward the British Empire, and he remained so throughout his life; during the Second World War, he wrote that the seeds of both global wars had been sown by Germany when it urged the Boers into conflict with Great Britain in 1899. Throughout the 1899-1914 period, he had feared that German militarism and imperial expansionism would lead to hostilities, but his criticism of Germany went further. In his "The Devil and the Deep Sea: A Discussion of Modern Morality," a 1910 essay that first appeared in book form during the war, Leacock attributed to German philosophy a large measure of the breakdown he saw in civilization generally. The lessons taught by religion had been repudiated by humanity, which had "called itself a Superman, and headed straight for the cliff over which is the deep sea." This charge is a serious version of the same analysis of the failures of Romantic individualism that he often sounded lightly, for instance in "Sorrows of a Super Soul" and "The Passing of the Poet"; a widespread corruption of modernity, it was located he believed particularly in German culture. For him, rampant individualism was a sister phenomenon to the xenophobic Romantic nationalism of *der Volk*. His attitude is closely parallel to that of Bertrand Russell, who wrote of the nineteenth century, "a profound revolt, both philosophical and political, against traditional systems in thought, in politics, and in economics, gave rise to attacks upon many beliefs and institutions that had hitherto been regarded as unassailable." In its "romantic" form, said Russell, this "revolt passes from Byron, Schopenhauer and Nietzsche to Mussolini and Hitler..."[1]

At the war's beginning, Leacock's patriotism was buoyant and his attitude toward the Axis powers triumphal; they would soon be defeated, the fighting would be brief. It was a general conviction, he claimed, that the war would last only a short time because the world's industries could not produce sufficient weaponry quickly enough to sustain it, whatever the desire of the combatants to continue.[2] One reason the prediction did not come true was Canada, which began the war years supplying agricultural products but quickly created a new industrial base of factories producing war materials. Canada also provided more than six hundred thousand men, including four army divisions. The vast majority were volunteers; conscription, which proved one of the most divisive wartime issues, especially in French Canada where the war was unpopular, was not instituted until 1917. Men from McGill made up six infantry companies and provided a siege battery and a five-hundred-bed army hospital; a member of its staff was Leacock's friend at the Pen and Pencil Club, Doctor John McCrae, author of "In Flanders Fields."

Leacock's circle of friends was altered considerably by the departure of student and faculty soldiers. Gladstone Murray, who started the *McGill Daily* with Leacock's help, became a flying ace. Professor René du Roure, who had worked in the French diplomatic service before coming to Canada, returned home to enlist soon after the war began, and was seriously wounded in the first action he saw. He spent three years in German hospitals as a prisoner of war. Even Leacock's friend Andrew Macphail, three years his senior, joined the armed services and served in the medical corps. But Leacock had no such skills as those of a physician and found his war work at home as propagandist and fund raiser.

In the fall 1914 term, Leacock spoke on the financial aspect of the war to the McGill Political Economy Club and published an essay on the "American Attitude" to the world situation in Macphail's *University Magazine*. Meanwhile, pieces that would be collected in his 1915 humour miscellany continued to appear in the most popular magazines of the day, such as *Vanity Fair* and the *Century Magazine*; he published his essay, "American Humour," a subject he had approached in earlier lectures, in an issue of the *Nineteenth Century and After*. Soon the war had entered its second year and the pattern of trench warfare along the western front, which would last until 1918, was already well-established. The war Leacock once had thought must end in months became a static, nightmarish quagmire of casualties and destruction. In January, the Canadian government approached Leacock to help raise money for the Belgian Relief Fund that had been established in aid of casualties and refugees of the overrun country. He eagerly agreed, and gave his services without pay; the money raised went primarily to refugees housed at Nantes during the war. At the same moment when he embraced this cause, which occupied him periodically until the war ended, the Leacocks learned that Beatrix, then in her mid-thirties, was pregnant. In January 1915, they were in their fourteenth year of marriage; they had begun to think that their hope for a child would never be realized. Preparations for the birth did not alter the family routine until very shortly before the event. Witnesses have said that home life on Côte-des-Nieges Road was dominated by Leacock's personality, tastes, and schedule. Frequent, expansive dinner entertainments around the centrepiece of the avuncular master, warm and witty but not liking to be interrupted, were held in late Victorian style perhaps modelled on what he had experienced in Macphail's home. Guests dressed for dinner, which was served by a properly uniformed French maid; afterwards, there was the ritual separation of the sexes, the ladies retiring to the parlour together and the men lingering at table for wine, tobacco, and bluer, more raucous conversation. Private home life revolved around his heavy demands for writerly seclusion in his cluttered study, and his absences to travel for lectures; now at the beginning of Beatrix's pregnancy, these absences became especially frequent with the demands of his war work.

Touring for the Belgian Relief Fund was one of Leacock's first experiences with humorous lecturing, which before the war he had done on only a handful of casual occasions. Most of his addresses had been given as an economist, an imperial apologist, or a campaigner for the Conservative party, although the sprinkling of humour he sometimes had given them had helped make him much sought-after. For the fund-raising appearances of winter and spring 1915, he developed the format and manner he would use throughout his future successful career as a humorous platform speaker. Presenting himself in the guise of a popular lecturer on fiction or drama, he wove together parodic accounts of the literature under discussion with wry comments on its shortcomings. An intriguing glimpse of his lecture-circuit adventures at this time comes in a passage from the essay "We Have With Us To-Night," which appeared in *My Discovery of England* (1922). There, he described some of his early public speaking woes, including one experience explicitly identified as belonging to the war tours.

> I recall in this same connection the chairman of a meeting at a certain town in Vermont. He represents the type of chairman who turns up so late in the evening that the committee have no time to explain to him properly what the meeting is about or who the speaker is. I noticed on this occasion that he introduced me very guardedly by name (from a little card) and said nothing about the Belgians, and nothing about my being (supposed to be) a humorist. This last was a great error. The audience, for want of guidance, remained very silent and decorous, and well behaved during my talk. Then, somehow, at the end, while someone was moving a vote of thanks, the chairman discovered his error. So he tried to make it good. Just as the audience were getting up to put on their wraps, he rose, knocked on his desk and said: "Just a minute, please, ladies and gentlemen, just a minute. I have just found out — I should have known it sooner, but I was late in coming to this meeting — that the speaker who has just addressed you has done so in behalf of the Belgian Relief Fund. I understand that he is a well-known Canadian humorist (ha! ha!) and I am sure that we have all

been immensely amused (ha! ha!). He is giving his delightful talk (ha! ha!) — though I didn't know this until just this minute — for the Belgian Relief Fund, and he is giving his services for nothing. I am sure when we realize this, we shall all feel that it has been well worth while to come. I am only sorry that we didn't have a better turn-out tonight. But I can assure the speaker that if he will come again, we shall guarantee him a capacity audience."[3]

Lurking behind this anecdote is, perhaps, Leacock's reason for one of his most striking and oft-commented-upon stage mannerisms: as he would move toward a humorous peak in his delivery, he would begin to smile and laugh himself, until he was convulsed and could hardly seem to get out the crowning point of his joke. Though sometimes criticized, this bit of business proved infectious with his audiences and served the purpose of informing them unequivocally that he was a humorist. Among his other influences upon modern popular culture, he is an inventor of the canned laughter device.

His initial lecture for the Belgian Relief Fund was called "Frenzied Fiction," a title he later used for a humour collection and for other, similar lectures. His notes show that his 1915 lecture consisted basically of an adaptation from his works: he wove together "Behind the Beyond" with two pieces that were to appear in book form as the opening and closing sketches of *Moonbeams from the Larger Lunacy* (1915), "Spoof: A Thousand-Guinea Novel. New! Fascinating! Perplexing!" and "In the Good Times After the War," which mocked both journalism and politics in its purported account of a farcical British House of Commons session held in the euphoria of war's end, which Leacock was then dating to 1916. The flavour of the 1915 "Frenzied Fiction" lecture is best suggested by a popular sketch that he created on the same model and published in *Further Foolishness* (1916). "The Snoopopaths; or, Fifty Stories in One" combined Leacock's commentary with scenes and dialogue from the type of story he designated as "snoopopathic:"

> This is a word derived from the Greek — "snoopo" — or if there never was a Greek verb snoopo, at least there ought to have been one — and it means just what it seems to mean. Nine out of ten short stories written in America are snoopopathic.[4]

His commentary makes the sketch "not so much a story as a sort of essay. The average reader will therefore turn from it with a shudder. The condition of the average reader's mind is such that he can take in nothing but fiction. And it must be thin fiction at that..." The main characters in his snoopopathic tale of love are "A MAN" and "A WOMAN," which may remind readers today of a snoopopathic film that was popular many decades later. He explains, "I put these words in capitals to indicate that they have got to stick out of the story with the crudity of a drawing done by a child with a burnt stick." The drama rises suspensefully to a surprise ending while in every sentence Leacock mocks its fatuous excesses:

> As soon as The Man comes into The Woman's room — before he knows who she is, for she has her back to him — he gets into a condition dear to all snoopo-pathic readers.
>
> His veins simply "surged." His brain beat against his temples in mad pulsation. His breath "came and went in quick, short pants." (This last might perhaps be done by one of the hotel bellboys, but otherwise it is hard to imagine.)
>
> And The Woman... "She turned and rose 'fronting him full.'" This doesn't mean that he was full when she fronted him.

Leacock and Beatrix with Stevie at their Côte-des-Neiges Road house, about 1916.

Courtesy National Archives of Canada C-31967.

Newspaper reports show that he devoted ample time in his lectures to the serious business at hand, discussing the war effort, praising gallant Belgium and conveying the suffering of her soldiers and people. Hearers reported the lectures as wildly funny at first, then modulating to sombre and ultimately uplifting tones of patriotic fervour, with optimistic predictions of the war's speedy and successful conclusion.

On 7 January 1915, before the Philadelphia Browning Society, he made the first test of this new lecture format by mixing the humour of "Behind the Beyond" with a plea for the defense of English-speaking civilization in the form of an address to Theodore Roosevelt; the Browning societies, which had been established far and wide in the nineteenth century to elucidate and spread the gnomic wisdom of the great poet, were themselves an example of the world in which Leacock had been nurtured and which would be swept away by the war. The Belgian Relief Fund lectures got well under way in February and March, during which he spoke at Saint John, Halifax, Quebec City, Montreal, Toronto and Hamilton. He was now setting himself an extraordinarily taxing schedule of activities, adding these lectures to humorous and scholarly writing, teaching, and administrative duties as department chairman. On 15 March, the *McGill Daily* published (and *Maclean's* soon reprinted) another of his skewerings of German culture and character, "Side Lights on the Supermen: An Interview with General Bernhardi." As the war progressed, a combination of Canadian successes and German atrocities prompted him to adopt a still more forceful stance. In April, the Canadian First Division distinguished itself at the Battle of Ypres, and then, on 7 May, German torpedoes sank the passenger liner *Lusitania*. After an end-of-term hiatus, Leacock returned to the lecture stage with a tour of Ontario cities; from 24 May to 11 June, he spoke in Welland, Galt (now Cambridge), London, St. Catharines, Guelph, Brantford, Fort William, and Sault Ste. Marie.[5] In the aftermath of the *Lusitania*'s loss and the proof of Canadian military prowess, he was publicly recommending that Kaiser Frederick Wilhelm II be hanged once the war was won, and that the Dominions, including Canada, should take the lead in insisting upon this.

In the summer of 1915, at Old Brewery Bay, he continued to write and publish humorous essays and sketches. The summer routine went as usual until Beatrix felt that the time was nearing for her to give birth. Having almost started the trip too late, Leacock and she hurried back from Orillia to Montreal, where Stephen Lushington Leacock was born on 19 August. Leacock wrote immediately to Agnes to invite her to the city; his happy letter is veined with the stress, pain and danger of what proved to be a difficult delivery for Beatrix.

> My Dear Mother — Young Stephen was born at a quarter to three this afternoon. He is a fine young boy, in fact a regular corker, and weighs eight and a quarter pounds. Beatrix had made an error about the date of his birth, but thank heaven, we left Orillia in time or the journey might have been too much for her. He had a close run for his life as he had decided to throw himself into the world wrong end first. We had the three best men in Montreal and four nurses. Peters told me that without those seven people working at it, there would have been no chance. Beatrix was taken ill at 6 this morning and I drove her over to the maternity hospital. She had a bad time but it is over now & she is resting & doing fine. The baby looks just like Barbara and little Stephen [his niece and nephew] and me and all the rest. Beatrix was awfully well right up to the end except that she had a bad fall two days ago. But Peters says the baby is not a premature baby being if anything over developed. Beatrix will have to stay where she is for some

time, I don't know how long, two weeks I should think. How soon can you come down? We must take up the arrangements for the christening right away. I want my friend Mr. Symonds the rector of the cathedral to do it.

I sent a wire to George [his brother] today. Will you please tell Charlie [his brother] and the rest. Teddy [his brother] is probably still with you....I gave the telegraph company a dollar to take the message from Sutton to the Grange. So don't let them charge you for it....I could only stay with Beatrix for a little while this afternoon as they wanted her to sleep but I am going over after dinner and we'll see the baby together. I never yet saw a baby that looked so complete, so all there, so little like a red monkey as Stephen does: indeed he seems to me a most remarkable child. Please write and tell Carrie [his sister, Mrs. Jan Ulrichson, mother of Barbara and "little" Stephen] that her present hit it just right because it arrived at the very hour that he was born. I'd write to her myself but I have no address. Beatrix won't be able to write for some days. Be sure to let me know right away just how soon you can come, and come as soon as you can.

Your loving son

(Old) Stephen Leacock

P.S. Tomorrow I am going to make my will and appoint trustees, guardians and a staff of godfathers, godmothers, proxies, and assistants. We have decided that from the boy's birth there shall be no extravagance on him. We got from Eatons a plain basket for him to sleep in, — there — I guess this is as much as it is fair to inflict in one dose.[6]

Another family member was heard from when on 26 August Dr. Rosamond Leacock — Dot — wrote from Calgary agreeing to be the new baby's godmother. Soon Beatrix had returned home, well and happy, with Stevie, as he came to be called, and all seemed in a flourishing state, the addition heightening still further the sense of an enchanted and fortunate realm that surrounded the busy, successful life the Leacocks had created.

An entry from Agnes's diary carries the story forward a few weeks, to 5 September, when she wrote at her home in Sutton:

> It is a long time since I have written anything but letters, and a great event has taken place. My first Leacock grandchild was born on the 19th of August, Stephen's boy. He and Beatrix have been married a long time and this longed for child has taken up all my thoughts of late. I hope very soon to see him; at present he and his mother are in the maternity hospital, and it's not much use for me to go to Montreal till they get him home to Côte des Neiges, as one can see so little of people in hospital, but Stephen writes often of the boy and he's a chip off the old block I'm sure — like Stephen and my father. He is to be called Stephen Lushington.[7]

Stephen honoured his mother's family by giving his son a family name, Lushington, just as she had done in giving her now famous son the name Butler.

With the exception of the arrival of the "most remarkable child," the 1915-16 academic year closely followed the pattern of the

Leacock holding his son at Old Brewery Bay, about 1917.
Courtesy National Archives of Canada C-31914.

previous one. September saw the publication by John Lane in London of a minor work, *The Marionette's Calendar*, an engagement calendar gift book that had been proposed by Lane to Leacock and A.H. [Anne Harriet] Fish, who had produced the stylish drawings for *Behind the Beyond*. Fish made twelve drawings suggesting a love story between the Harlequin puppet characters Pierot and Pierrette, and then Leacock provided verses. Another enterprise that came to fruition at this time was a dramatization by English playwright Basil Macdonald Hastings of "Q: A Psychic Pstory of the Psupernatural" from *Nonsense Novels*. Hastings's "*Q*": *A Farce in One Act*, starring Charles Hawtrey, premiered in London on 29 November 1915 in a program of plays at the London Coliseum; it received very warm notices and was frequently performed in Britain over the next twenty years. That fall Douglas Bush, later to become a famous scholar and critic, published an article praising Leacock in the *Toronto Star*; Bush, at the time a University of Toronto undergraduate, characterized Leacock as a humorist superior to Mark Twain. This elicited from Leacock a letter of thanks and a gift copy of *The Adventures of Huckleberry Finn* in refutation of the idea.[8]

In July, Leacock sent the completed manuscript of *Moonbeams from the Larger Lunacy* to Jefferson Jones, his editor at the John Lane Company, New York; the American edition appeared in October, followed by the English edition in December. The collection was warmly received by critics, one of whom called him "the court jester of the day," and readers, who bought it out through at least six impressions through 1920. In a preface, Leacock referred ironically to his own now-established practice of making humour miscellanies: "The wise child, after the lemonade jug is empty, takes the lemons from the bottom of it and squeezes them into a still brew. So does the sagacious author, after having sold his material to magazines and been paid for it, clap it into book-covers and give it another squeeze." Many of the pieces were parodies of follies, other than this one of his own, that he observed in literature and more generally in the realm of celebrity:

"Who Is Also Who. A Companion Volume to Who's Who," "Aristocratic Anecdotes: or, Little Stories of Great People" and "Spoof: A Thousand-Guinea Novel. New! Fascinating! Perplexing!" The latter, which he used in his war lectures, burlesqued the clichés of romantic fiction, but also mocked, in a way that has not lost any of its relevance, the marketing ploys of publishers: "Readers are requested to note that this novel has taken our special prize of a cheque for a thousand guineas. This alone guarantees for all intelligent readers a palpitating interest in every line of it." In "The Reading Public: A Book-Store Study," a clerk cunningly sells several copies of the same book "as a sea story, a land story, a story of the jungle, and a story of the mountains," as indicated by the preference, along with the inability to read and judge for himself, of each prospective customer who enters. Leacock, who had written light verse since his student days and was an admirer of the poetry of W.S. Gilbert and Lewis Carroll, composed some good "bad poetry" to exemplify the work of the poet he invented in "Ram Spudd: The New-World Singer. Is He Divinely Inspired? Or Is He Not? At Any Rate We Discovered Him." The mystical, bathetic Spudd, who is in part a glance at such literary phenomena as Rabindranath Tagore and Canada's own Wilson Pugsley Macdonald and Bliss Carman, is not above stealing the old jokes of the famous humorist, Stephen Leacock. For instance, in his "Spring Thaw in the Ahuntsic Woods, Near Paspebiac, Passamoquoddy County," Spudd writes:

> Where I am standing I find myself practically sur
> rounded by trees,
> It is simply astonishing the number of different
> varieties one sees.
> I've grown so wise I can tell each different tree
> by seeing it glisten,
> But if that test fails I simply put my ear to the tree
> and listen,

And, well, I suppose it is only a silly fancy of mine
  perhaps,
But do you know I'm getting to tell different trees
  by the sound of their saps.[9]

Pieces directly related to the war included, besides "Sidelights on the Supermen" and "In the Good Time after the War," a number of the brief vignettes from "Afternoon Adventures at the Club" in which Leacock depicts instances of vanity and ignorance among men discussing the war in much the same way that he customarily mocks the pedantry and pretension of businessmen or outdoorsmen. (This genial grouping of scenes from club life includes the much anthologized "The Hallucination of Mr. Butt"). "In the Good Time After the War" pictures a chaotic session of the British parliament, the members delirious with the euphoria and bonhomie of victory, in which strong brotherly feeling created by cooperation in the war effort defuses permanently the issue of Irish Home Rule. Leacock's hope that the war might make some real difference in the question was at best a poor prophecy, at worst a careless dismissal of the issues lying behind the Irish campaign for independence. "Sidelights on the Supermen" made comedy, as he often did, out of the two sides of his career, economics and humour. German General Friedrich A.J. von Bernhardi visits Leacock late one night at his office. When asked how he managed to get by the janitor who acted as doorman, Bernhardi replies, "I killed him....His resistance was very slight. Apparently in this country your janitors are unarmed." The general has come to praise Leacock's humour as it is displayed, for example, in *Elements of Political Science* and to bemoan the failure of the English-speaking public to understand the solid German humour found in the general's own works, such as the light irony of: "A surprise attack, in order to be justified, must be made only on the armed forces of the state and not on its peaceful inhabitants. Otherwise the attack becomes a treacherous crime."[10] Catching the spirit of the game, Leacock reduces

Bernhardi to a deflated bag of wind by citing to him from the same German text: "In the event of war the loosely-joined British Empire will break into pieces, and the colonies will consult their own interests." What begins as a witty exchange ends with the patriotic but routine notion of the braggart revealed in his true insignificance; in this case, the impressive uniform of Bernhardi is punctured by the stiletto peak of his helmet and shrinks "into a tattered heap." Leacock's early pieces on the war were filled with pride and optimism, as were his Belgian Relief Fund lectures, with which they overlapped. While he never lost the pride, the lessons of the war did temper his jauntiness. By the time the fighting ended he was bitter.

In January 1916, surveying the appalling and mounting cost of the conflict, he contributed a vision of the future to *Maclean's*, "After the War — Ruin or Prosperity?: A Fifteen Year Prophecy." Simultaneously his recent humorous work was appearing: *Vanity Fair* published "The Snoopopaths or Fifty Stories in One" in February. Writing that month to Pelham Edgar to turn down a request to speak in Toronto, he said that he was about to spend a week making Belgian Relief Fund appearances in eastern Ontario, then speak at two cities in the southwestern part of the province, then fulfill an engagement of his own to speak at a New York literary banquet and, finally, give more Relief Fund lectures, an extensive U.S. tour. That spring he took the stage in New York, Buffalo, Pittsburgh, Cleveland (twice), Baltimore (twice), Wellesley (Massachusetts), Ithaca (New York), Indianapolis and Chicago. At the same time, his social life among Montreal business leaders, writers and artists remained a full one. He provides a glimpse of his activities, and his wry way of looking at the world around him, in his comments to Edgar:

> Funny damned thing here the other night: — a banquet was arranged for Brymner the artist in congratulations on his C.M.G. [Companion of the Order of St. Michael and St. George; William

Brymner, a painter, had received the honour in 1910]. Mr Baker of the C.P.R. kindly placed the C.P.R. station dining room at the disposal of the committee...It was the first time the Railway dining room had ever been so used & hence all the staff from the chef down were on their mettle. They wanted to show that when it came to banquets the C.P.R. could break all records. But of course being a station dining room, their one idea of efficiency was high speed. Time was everything. Oysters and soup flew through the air. Dish succeeded dish like lightning & the poor little banquet, never a very costly one or elaborate even as planned, was over in thirty-five minutes. Over its corpse, three or four speeches were made. But as it turned out that all of the speakers were men of few words, each relying on other people to do the talk, the whole banquet which began at 8:30 was over at a quarter to ten. The gay revellers were out on the street at ten o'clock, and the dining room cleaned up...and closed tight within five minutes of their leaving. The whole thing is felt by the Railway to be a triumph of management. They think, with a little more practice, that they'll be able to run a banquet through in about twenty-five minutes.[11]

Despite his keenness for all he encountered, Leacock could now sometimes feel a tiredness that was compounded of his heavy demands upon his energy, a sense that he was aging, and the realization that the war was ending forever the world he had known in his childhood and his prime. Around this time he began to express directly, in his own person, the melancholy *tempus fugit* attitude that is embodied implicitly in *Sunshine Sketches:* ultimately no human effort or accomplishment is of significance in the vast abyss of time, nor can it avail to stop or retard the passing away of what a man has loved. He shares with other English essayists concerned for moral issues, notably with Samuel Johnson, a sense that the task of life is to fill up, honorably and with as much goodness as possible, the weary expanse that stretches toward death. Like Charles II, of whom he had written before the war in an essay he would soon publish in book form, he had become one of the rare persons able to understand that "nothing really matters very much." In his February 1916, letter to Edgar, after narrating the C.P.R.' s speed banquet, he turns aside to muse,

> I am also getting old. Are you. I had expected to stay young for ever and always felt as if I had not begun yet and was still planning what I would do when I grew up. Now I find, almost suddenly, that it is nearly over. I feel like the indignant miller at the ballot box, who said, — " Is *that* all, boss, is *that* all you do?" — And so with life: one asks, "Is *that* all, boss?"

In December 1915, just before his heavy winter and spring schedule of war lecturing began, Leacock had sent to the John Lane Company, New York, a manuscript of selected serious essays. In April it appeared under the title *Essays and Literary Studies*; it was a book of which he was extremely proud. That he anticipated scant interest in it, however, is perhaps indicated by those introductory words to "The Snoopopaths": "This particular study...is not so much as story as a sort of essay. The average reader will therefore turn from it with a shudder." The earliest of the pieces included was "A Rehabilitation of Charles II," from the *University Magazine* of May 1906, but several of them had been produced during the war years, including "The Woman Question," which first appeared in *Maclean's* in 1915. Several others, including "The Apology of a Professor," "The Devil and the Deep Sea" and "Literature and Education in America," were 1907-10

University Magazine contributions. After seven well-received books of humour, Leacock was guaranteed attention for this departure. In general, reviews were positive, although one critic questioned whether the seriousness of the subjects addressed was matched by the author's avowed reliance on "the half-truth"; one of the essays concluded, "The half-truth is to me a kind of mellow moonlight in which I love to dwell. One sees better in it."[12]

In *Essays and Literary Studies*, Leacock expanded his efforts as a popular author. Although he never again published a volume devoted entirely to his essays on education, literature and social issues, henceforth his humour collections often featured at least one essay with a distinctly serious subject and tone; a well known example is "Oxford as I See It" from *My Discovery of England* (1922). In many of these essays, the division between the serious writer and the humorist almost disappears; there is simply Leacock, the human observer who commands satire, logic, persuasion, evocative power over language, and the knowledge that his subject requires. The development of a mature style as an essayist brought to many of his later works a softer, more thoughtful approach to humorous pieces as well; the surface glitter of exaggerations and absurdities became sometimes secondary to the sympathetic penetration of very human and simple scenes — a man fishing or gardening or simply growing old. The master of first-person narration, who gave himself anarchic freedom of verbal play and commentary, began to use style to create an engaging self rather than to display imaginative virtuosity. However, in his earliest essays, Leacock was not yet writing about "himself," the fictional Leacock he gradually created to speak his musings and embody the melding of satire and sympathy that he touted as the highest and rarest human achievement. The pieces in *Essays and Literary Studies* are in general the most serious short prose compositions he ever published in book form; their blending of humour with the primary intentions of analysis, argument and persuasion varies greatly in tone and in effectiveness. They provide a key to the dominant attitudes of his early maturity; beyond that, a few of them are classics of the essay form. In the memorable "A Rehabilitation of Charles II," the first-written piece which stands last in the book, Leacock sets out to refurbish the reputation of one of England's less respected monarchs. He explains:

> Thus it is that we live in an age of historical surprises. We know now that Rome was not founded by Romulus, that the apple shot by William Tell was not lying on his son's head at the immediate time of the shooting, and that America was not in the true sense of the term discovered by Christopher Columbus, who had spent eighteen years of tearful persuasion in trying to prove that there was no such continent.

Leacock's busy search through the career of Charles II for commendable achievements is conducted with an admirable display of historical scholarship, but the best he can find are negative attributes: Charles did not really care about his religion and he was not overly interested in politics. In sum, "He had grasped as few men have done the great truth that nothing really matters very much." *Essays and Literary Studies* also included appreciations of Dickens, O. Henry and "American Humour," the first of the many theoretical examinations of humour he would publish; in it he states his general principle that the best humour must be kindly:

> The short comings of our existence, the sad contrast of our aims and our achievements, the little fretted aspiration of the day that fades into the nothingness of tomorrow, kindle in the mellowed mind a sense of gentle amusement from which all selfish exultation has been chastened by the realization of our common lot of sorrow.[13]

In that sentence, penned in 1907, may be read the literary aspiration that he embodied later in the ineffable attitude of *Sunshine Sketches* and *Arcadian Adventures*, and his late essays' balanced tone of mockery and compassion.

His fall 1916 humour collection, *Further Foolishness* contains a theoretical discussion of humour, just as had *Essays and Literary Studies*, published earlier in the same year; this marked the beginning of Leacock's tendency to dart back and forth over the line that separates the humorist and the critic as his growing celebrity and the gradual development of the Leacock comic persona made his own writings and appearances increasingly the subject of his work. "Humor as I See It," the concluding entry of *Further Foolishness*, elaborates the theory of a kindly and lenitive species of comedy, and illustrates the idea with examples. It is the source of many phrases that came to be associated with Leacock, including the definition that "it is a prime condition of humor that it must be without harm or malice, nor should it convey incidentally any real picture of sorrow or suffering or death."[14] One spur, he claimed, to these reflections on humour was a review in which a critic had said, "What is there, after all, in Professor Leacock's humour but a rather ingenious mixture of hyperbole and myosis?" He replied, "The man was right. How he stumbled upon this trade secret I do not know. But I am willing to admit, since the truth is out, that it has long been my custom in preparing an article to go down to the cellar and mix up half a gallon of myosis with a pint of hyperbole. If I want to give the article a decidedly literary character, I find it well to put in about half a pint of paresis." What was his real opinion? It would never occur to people such as this critic that the making of humour "is hard, meritorious and dignified. Because the result is gay and light, they think the process must be."

The war drew Canada away from its closest neighbour, the United States, and this too became a concern of Leacock's and an object of his powers to prod and persuade, as evidenced by several of the pieces collected in *Further Foolishness*. All but the first of the five stories grouped under the heading "Peace, War, and Politics" include excoriating mockery of U.S. cultural values and of its foreign policy toward Turkey, Mexico and Germany. The first story in the group, "Germany from Within Out," is mirrored by the last, "The White House from Without In," which lashes the Wilson administration's neutrality policies by means of fictional extracts from the president's diary. Leacock scornfully attributes to Wilson a naive eagerness to believe German protestations of innocence in relation to the submarine attacks on shipping, the issue that eventually drew the United States into the war. "Cables from Germany. Chancellor now positive as to *Torpid*. Sworn evidence that she was sunk by some one throwing a rock." In another of these stories, "Over the Grape Juice; or, The Peacemakers," the central character is the president of Haiti, "melancholy with the broken pathos of the African race." When he dares to tell a banqueting group of prominent Americans that the "sad spectacle" of war "shames our polite civilization," and to compare his own violence-riven country, then occupied by Marines, to the "poor white folks...murdered on the *Lusitania*," he is answered by "a chorus of dissent and disapproval:"

> "My dear sir, my dear sir," protested Mr. [William Jennings] Bryan, "pray moderate your language a little if you please. Murdered? Oh, dear, dear me, how can we hope to advance the cause of peace if you insist on using such terms?"
>
> "Ain't it that? Wasn't it murder?" asked the President, perplexed.
>
> "We are all agreed here," said The Lady Pacifist, "that it is far better to call it an incident...."
>
> "True, quite true," murmured The Eminent Divine, "and then one must remember that there are

always two sides to everything. There are two sides to murder. We must not let ourselves forget that there is always the murderer's point of view to consider."[15]

Just as Leacock's attack on Germany's militarism was underpinned by an ironically given thumbnail analysis of perversions in German culture, so he traced what he saw as American spinelessness to a self-deceiving and self-satisfied materialism. All at the American peace-makers' banquet congratulate themselves that they have no other object than doing good, whether they are "producing oil, or making steel, or building motor-cars." The American "Philanthropist" preaches that "the true way to end war is to try to spread abroad in all directions goodwill and brotherly love," and the "way to inspire brotherly love all round is to keep on getting richer and richer till you have so much money that every one loves you." This febrile, hypo-critical do-goodism is symbolized in Bryan's stand for temperance. No one at the bloodless gathering will drink, but neither will anyone protest, the beverage he has supplied for the dinner, made from grapes "picked in the dark" and "carried, still in the dark, to the testing room" where "every particle of alcohol is removed." When the globe-trotting narrator of all five "Peace, War, and Politics" stories enters Mexico, where the American army is pursuing Pancho Villa, his attempts to travel through the impoverished, backward countryside finally bring him to the scene of a battle. Comedy is suddenly ripped apart by two paragraphs of thrillingly circumstantial description of a cavalry column being ambushed. But soon the dead soldiers have picked themselves up from the ground, and a film director is shouting complaints about flaws in the scene's performance: it was all staged for the movies. Governments had been accused long before this of creating foreign adventures as diversions, but Leacock's story is an extremely early use of the notion of a war purposely produced to be broadcast by modern mass entertainment media for the purpose of enthralling and bamboozling a gullible public. Ever since *Further*

Foolishness appeared, the image has been repeated in various guises by American satirists of government, including ones working in film.

In one of his earliest wartime lectures, that given at Philadelphia in January 1915, Leacock had tried to cajole the United States out of neutrality; in that lecture, he had appealed to the name of Theodore Roosevelt, an admirer of Leacock's humour since 1911 and a vocal proponent of U.S. military participation in the war from its outset. But the United States remained neutral until 1917. On what basis could he condemn the distance that Wilson maintained between his country and the European combatants? In the 1911 election, depicted by Leacock in *Sunshine Sketches*, Canada had made a strong choice to continue close ties with Great Britain and the Empire and to draw back from proposed closer relations with her southern neighbour. He himself had worked hard for this result. Published almost at the moment of the war's beginning, *Arcadian Adventures with the Idle Rich* in large part expressed his conviction that the materialism and boosterism of U.S. culture were deleterious influences for Canada. He worked strenuously for stronger Canadian power within the Empire, and this was in part because he distrusted close association with the United States, which, he felt, might absorb his country and put an end to its unique national character and values. Although the course of the war brought changes to Canada's relationship with Great Britain, Leacock never expressed regret that imperial ties had drawn the country into the costly fighting.

The main plank of his persuasive platform was that the United States must join a battle for the preservation of civilization; further, the cultural and militaristic corruption of Germany meant that civilization was now more than ever entrusted to the Anglo-Saxon nations, of which the United States was, in his view, one. In his war work, Leacock asked for American dollars to help refugees, but he primarily laboured to have the United States enter the war. The effort continued in his speeches, and in sketches, stories and essays he published in 1916 and 1917 and collected in his 1917 humour miscellany, *Frenzied Fiction*. Here again U.S. foreign policy with regard to Europe and Central America is often castigated. But between the composition of many of the pieces and the publication of the book in December 1917, the U.S. entry into the war intervened. Early in 1917, Germany felt confident that a submarine blockade could starve Great Britain into surrender within six months, and that the American reaction this might provoke could not become effective within that period. Unrestricted submarine warfare was resumed and soon eight American ships had been lost; President Wilson asked Congress for a declaration of war on 2 April; it was passed on 6 April. By 17 April, Leacock had completed his congratulatory essay, "Father Knickerbocker: A Fantasy," in which he implicitly associates himself with the early American humorist and author Washington Irving to generate a sentiment of fraternal sympathy between the United States and her embattled English-speaking sister nations. The piece was published in *Hearst's Magazine* in June; it concludes, "And I knew that a great nation had cast aside the bonds of sloth and luxury, and was girding itself to join in the fight for the free democracy of all mankind." If Leacock did not see his polemics bring the United States into the war, at least he had the satisfaction of knowing that his arguments and prophecies had been correct and that the action he had recommended had proved necessary. So too judged Theodore Roosevelt, who wrote Leacock in 1919 to invite him to dinner in New York, sending along an article he had written praising Canada's role in the war.[16]

Frenzied Fiction was far from being entirely taken up with the war; in fact, it was less so than *Further Foolishness* had been, and was welcomed by critics as one of the best of his titles. The sketches, stories and essays are long and well developed over an impressive range of subjects and moods, from the sentimental "Merry Christmas" to the hilarity of "My Revelations as a Spy;" there were sometimes uproarious, sometimes genial treatments of health fads, modern university curricula, spiritualism, fishing, and temperance. Leacock did not publish a book in 1918, the last year of the war, because of the demands of his lecture work for the Belgian Relief Fund. When the armistice of November 1918 had stilled the guns, and the 1918-19 academic year had concluded, he turned happily to favourite interests. He was famous for leaving Montreal the first moment that the end of classes and examinations would permit in order to be able to spend the longest possible time at Old Brewery Bay. With Beatrix, he now began planning an addition to the house there. They also planned a boathouse, whose second story served as his office for many years. René du Roure had returned to Montreal and his friendship with Leacock; they had shared teaching duties for a new program on French government and culture that McGill established. Besides being a popular dinner companion at Côte-des-Neiges Road, du Roure was now the Leacocks' most frequent summer guest as well. When the fall 1919 term began, Leacock encouraged the establishment of the *McGill News* and was the paper's first editorial board chairman. He also began teaching courses in the university's new sociology department. His writings and his war work began to bring him honorary doctorates. The first was conferred in 1919 by Queen's University, Kingston, and three others followed in 1920: Dartmouth College, Brown University and the University of Toronto.

Another pleasant addition to his life that came with the end of the war was the friendship of American humorist Robert Benchley, with whom Leacock began to correspond in 1919, after he had lectured at Benchley's *alma mater*, Harvard University. Throughout his life a loyal admirer and professed imitator of Leacock's, Benchley was told by a friend that the professor had praised Benchley's work in magazines, and had opined that Benchley ought to publish a book. An early letter shows Leacock providing the younger writer with practical advice and encouragement in developing his work; he sends along an advertising flyer from an etiquette instructor who promised customers absolutely reliable tips on meeting royalty:

It doesn't quite become me as a loyal subject to get too funny about kingship. But I wonder if your nimble wit couldn't do something about this new coming of the King to America....Some hotels will have notices (*Kings not admitted*), others will cater to the king trade. — I see a title like *Kings Wanted* or *What Shall We do with our Kings*....Possible openings ought to supply you with plenty of ideas. Go to it.

Leacock provided the preface for Benchley's first book, *Of All Things*, in 1922, and Benchley in return sent a copy inscribed, "To Stephen Leacock, who certainly *ought* to like most of the stuff in this book as he wrote it himself first."[17]

Leacock's final book of war humour was filled with a bitter triumph over his enemies. *The Hohenzollerns in America*, whose title page added the subtitle *With the Bolsheviks in Berlin and Other Impossibilities*, contains a number of amusing "impossibilities" about education, the movies and polite conversation, similar in manner and subject to many pieces in *Further Foolishness* and *Frenzied Fiction*, but for the most part comparatively tepid. Most of the book is devoted to reflections on the war. In 1917, a poem in *Punch* praised Leacock: "And yet though so freakish and dashing, / You are not the slave of your fun; / For there's nobody better at lashing / The crimes and the cant of the Hun." During the war, Leacock had moved from rather detached exposures of German pomposity and ironic criticisms of German intellectual culture to increasingly specific attacks on German war policy: diplomatic lying to the United States, destruction of neutral shipping, use of poison gas. As the attacks grew more specific, they also centred on more specific personal targets. The title piece of *The Hohenzollerns in America* refers to the Kaiser; the Hohenzollerns were the royal family that had ruled Prussia since 1701 and the German Empire since 1871, and which the German defeat had deposed. Leacock's fantasy pictures the Hohenzollerns as having been turned into typical refugees, forced to immigrate to the United States to seek a new life. For narrator, he creates the voice of a family member, a minor princess accompanying the deposed Kaiser, his son and other relatives. The Kaiser's son, "Cousin Willie," is revealed to be a drunkard; the princess notes, "what a sneaking face Cousin Willie has." Another relative, who steals furtively from the family's meagre purse, is described in some new clothes: "he has got hold of a queer long overcoat with the sleeves turned up, and a little round hat, and looks exactly like a Jew." The princess tells of his "command of Yiddish" and his plans to become a tailor in New York. The Kaiser himself is portrayed as a senile fool unable to understand his changed circumstances any better than he had understood the plight of Germany during the war: "It was pleasant to hear Uncle William talk in this way, just as quietly and rationally as at Berlin, and with the same grasp of political things."[18] For at least some readers it was not pleasant to see the master of sunshine with so little grasp of his own principle, which he had recently enunciated: "it is a prime condition of humor that it must be without harm or malice."

Some of the pieces in the book had already been written by war's end, including not only humour but the now customary sprinkling of serious essays; for instance, in October 1918, just before the Armistice, *Vanity Fair* had carried "Some Just Complaints About the War; Criticisms of the Way in Which It Is Being Conducted." It was clear by then, however, that Foch's relentless pressure was close to exhausting and collapsing the German army; by 1 November, Leacock had completed the first chapter of the six chapter title section of his new book, and in December, *Vanity Fair* published it as "The Hohenzollerns in America; Leaves from a Royal Diary, Dealing with Their Voyage Across the Atlantic." The other parts of "The Hohenzollerns in America" were swiftly written and the book appeared in the United States in April, in Great Britain in July.[19] It was not the least popular of Leacock's collections, but its literary reception was better in Great Britain than in the United States, where several reviewers criticized it harshly. According to the *Saturday Review*, "We reach the conclusion that Mr. Leacock has fatally impaired his reputation by this work. Our particular quarrel with Mr. Leacock arises from his treatment of the ex-Kaiser." By the author's standards, the humour of *The Hohenzollerns in America* is not of a high quality. If literary humour should draw people closer through their sympathetic understanding of life's difficulties, then much of the book is not humour at all; certainly, German readers could not draw any sympathy from Leacock's performance, nor could Jews, to whom the Germans had been mockingly compared in an aside. Leacock was offering his readers the temptation to share with him a cruel glorification of the sufferings of enemies now defeated. Formerly, Leacock's chosen subjects had lain too close to his own traditions and loves to permit such a thoroughgoing destructiveness. In the wake of the war, however, the world had changed; he drew the strong conclusion that his own country, no matter what its internal problems and follies, was a shield against other peoples and countries that threatened his way of life. Leacock's personal suffering and fear showed in the bitterness with which he allowed himself to lash out in victory against the losers of the war.

Unsolved Riddles

L eacock was far from unconscious of or indifferent to the venal-
ities, injustices, and lost opportunities, or the structural
economic and political problems, that characterized the
English-speaking democracies and that had contributed to the
disaster of 1914-18. On the contrary, his reinvigorated sense of Anglo-
Saxon cultural patriotism, even chauvinism, made him increasingly
anxious to see these difficulties resolved out of his tradition's own
resources, for the sake of its honour and future success and domi-
nance. One of his first writing projects after the war was a seven-part
newspaper series for the *New York Times* entitled "The Unsolved
Riddle of Social Justice," which was featured prominently in successive Sunday editions from 31 August through 12 October 1919, when
the *Times* headlined the final instalment, "Social Control for Equal
Opportunity: A Forecast of a Future Somewhere between the
Iniquitous Conditions Brought about by Individualism and the
Vagaries of Socialism. The Road to Freedom: — Vision of the Future."
The articles, along with a related lecture that he had published in
pamphlet form, were crafted into the book version of *The Unsolved*

Riddle of Social Justice, which the John Lane Company of New York issued in January 1920.[1] Critics praised Leacock's clarity of presentation but most complained that the riddle remained unsolved at the end of his study. This cavil was wide of the mark; if neither Leacock nor anyone else has found a simple key by which a single person or party can bring about social justice in the face of all the powers and tendencies opposing it, he did lay out an insightful analysis of its causes and its form in the post-war era, and provide an advanced, even prophetic sense of steps necessary toward the goal of what is now called the "mixed economy."

The book is one of the few works in which he makes even oblique references to the social unrest brought to his own country by the war. As an enthusiastic supporter of the Empire, he had reserved his wartime criticism for the enemy and for those outside of Canada who dragged their feet in joining the British cause. He had not satirized Canadians except those who thought they were supporting the war effort — for instance, by fund drives or political arguments — but were in fact unwittingly failing, in his view, to help as they should. Nor at the war's end did he give his views on the social tensions that arose in Canada or on the dramatic transformation taking place in Canada's relationship to the Empire. In *The Unsolved Riddle,* many of these silences are broken to a degree. He refers to two of the most difficult problems Canada had faced in the immediate past, conscription and labour unrest. But he does not comment directly on specific Canadian events; he focuses on the general and worldwide economic problems of which these events were the local manifestations.

In 1917, Canada had divided dangerously along ethnic lines on the issue of conscription. Conservative Prime Minister Robert Borden reversed an earlier pledge that a draft would not be used to fill projected troop quotas for overseas service. Opposition in Parliament to a draft led to an election, which brought forth violent demonstrations against conscription, especially in the province of Quebec. A bomb destroyed a wing of the home of publisher Lord Atholstan (Sir

Hugh Graham, Leacock's publisher for the initial periodical version of *Sunshine Sketches*, who had been made a baron in 1917, because his newspapers supported a draft). Leacock did not enter this political fray, which like the 1911 election was won by the Conservative party. But conscription is an important topic in *The Unsolved Riddle*, where Leacock lays down the principle that any government instituting it should expand social protection for all citizens. The issue of post-war labour unrest came to a head in Canada with the Winnipeg General Strike of 1919, the only general strike in Canadian history. More than 20,000 civic employees walked out in sympathy with a strike that had begun in the local metals and building trades; in actions associated with the strike, several demonstrators were killed by police gunfire. Borden's successor, Conservative Prime Minister Arthur Meighen, took harsh measures to punish the strike leaders and showed small sympathy for labour protestors and their demands for reform. Again, Leacock did not enter the public debate, but in *The Unsolved Riddle* he declared specific measures, such as a minimum wage,[2] necessary in order to redress injustice to workers.

The Unsolved Riddle approaches the question of social justice from two perspectives: the unique historical situation created by the First World War, and the century-long evolution of economic theory from the free traders of the early nineteenth century to the prominent socialist thinkers of the twentieth. It deplored the terrible waste of the war, the loss of life and the misuses of an incalculable amount of the world's wealth in the production of war machinery. But the war had taught industrial society an important lesson: necessity could produce a level of productivity previously thought impossible. In peacetime, free choice returned society to a much more haphazard and therefore inefficient mechanism of supply and demand. Leacock argued that freedom was preferable to enforced efficiency, but he also warned that a return to the old economic theories and to the inherent injustice of an unregulated capitalism would contribute to economic inefficiency, unnecessarily low productivity and prosperity, and a growing gap between rich and poor that was a threat to the survival of society. Just as he had in *Elements of Political Science*, Leacock acknowledged that socialist thinkers had understood correctly the evil of existing economic structures in the industrialized west. He objected, however, to the socialist solution of collective ownership and redistribution of wealth, primarily on the pragmatic grounds that such a state would produce a more terrible tyranny than was possible under the checks and balances of a democratic system. Without controls on its managers, the socialist state could only guarantee perfect equality among perfect people; as a goal of social evolution it was utopian and unworkable, as a form of government in actual effect it was a prison house of tyranny by elected bosses.

The proper system for restoring an equitable sharing among all citizens of a society's wealth and power would use government protection of workers to balance the economic strength of those who controlled the industries. Leacock argued that government should supply work for the able-bodied, and financial support, especially medical care and education, for children, the handicapped and the aged. He gave two reasons to justify this new direction for industrialized nations: first, society had to repay its debts to its citizen soldiers; second, the round of violent labour unrest and workers' revolts would continue unless the social evils that they protested could be removed by government intervention. Leacock warned that socialism won its adherents from those disenchanted by the inequities of the economic order in western democracies: for the periodical instalment on the subject, the headline desk for the *New York Times* had summarized his thought in the formulas, "Socialism: A Machine Which Won't Work: Born in the Bitter Discontent After the Napoleonic Wars, Utopian Dream Has Misled Thousands of Visionaries."

A traditionalist, Leacock nonetheless spoke strongly, even intransigently, on behalf of advanced causes. His underlying motive was conservative: he feared that the society he loved would be destroyed by or because of the economic injustices it contained. For the sake of his society as well as from his real desire for the good, he desperately wanted a just prosperity to spring from the political culture that had nourished him. He saw the dark possibility that the drive for radical change inspired by inequalities would sweep away the entire structure, replacing it with systems hostile to it, innovated and rootless systems that proclaimed their ability to deliver a better future. True to the English conservative tradition, he embraced grad- ualism, but he was urgent that in the present circumstances change should not be *too* gradual. He spoke boldly for measures not associ- ated with the conservative philosophy of his time when, for instance, he urged that the higher taxation required by the war be continued in peace as a means of financing the immediate expansion of govern- ment social programs. Perhaps his own childhood experiences and the birth of his son had much to do with the central social measure he preached: "No society is properly organized until every child that is born into it shall have an opportunity in life."[3]

His preoccupation with these serious sociological, economic and philosophical matters did not abate the flow of his humour but if anything enriched it. In 1920 he wrote a fresh series of literary paro- dies, which he published in *Harper's Magazine*; the July issue carried the first of the "New Nonsense Novels: Winsome Winnie, or Trial and Temptation"; the general title was chosen by the magazine, and Leacock did not like it.[4] He completed the book manuscript of *Winsome Winnie* in late August and, as had become his procedure, mailed it to Jefferson Jones of the John Lane Company, New York; there his books were corrected and set in type, the proofs then being sent to England as the basis of the version to be published by The Bodley Head. When *Winsome Winnie* arrived at the John Lane Company offices, Leacock was informed that the book was not accepted, the first rejection he had suffered since Houghton Mifflin had returned *Literary Lapses* twelve years earlier.[5] There may have been many considerations behind the company's decision. The nega- tive response in the United States to *The Hohenzollerns in America* may have caused fear that a new Leacock book would not be well received. The publisher's editors, somewhat panicked by critical grumblings about the mixed contents and variable quality of *Further Foolishness* and *Frenzied Fiction*, may have decided that the new parodies were not as good as earlier ones. However, the principal issue was money and it is quite possible that the rejection was merely a means of pressuring Leacock for a concession. In October 1919, he had signed a contract with Lane for three future books, in which he had negotiated for himself an unusually high twenty per cent royalty on all copies of American editions. *Winsome Winnie* was the first of the three books he delivered; the company now argued that this royalty made American editions unprofitable and it would be publishing Leacock at a loss. He counterproposed in friendly terms, offering to accept a royalty of fifteen per cent on all copies after five thousand; the new arrangement was accepted and publication of the book went ahead, the American edition appearing in November.

Winsome Winnie proved to be one of his most popular collections and a hit with critics from its first appearance; novelist Robertson Davies thought it one of Leacock's very best books, superior even to the original *Nonsense Novels*. There were eventually eight reprintings; the first edition of five thousand copies sold out in 1920 and three thousand more copies were sold by the end of 1921. Critics almost unanimously reported that the eight parodies were uniformly excellent. According to the *New York Times*, "Despite his delicious drolleries, Mr. Leacock's book of verbal cartoons contains an amazing amount of truthful criticism — doubly effective because its form and oblique method of delivery rob it of all malice." The few murmurs against the book were aimed at a lack of the "fresh spontaneity" of his early books. An isolated caveat came in a quirky *London Times Literary Supplement* review claiming Leacock's jokes were often good for only one laugh because they were based on "verbal surprise" or "the technical improvement in an established joke."[6] The parodies in *Winsome Winnie* go to the heart of the literary forms that he mocks and deal with the assumptions shared by writers and audiences; the humour is often dry and depends less on jokes than on a thorough parody of the overall characteristics of literary genres and the attitudes underlying them. The parodies include a romance among rich families, in which the heroine, Winnie, is bankrupted by her speculating guardian; a domestic drama, in which a wife is saved from deserting her husband by the opportune arrival of a family fortune; a political melodrama, in which the fate of an empire hangs on the social gifts of a minister's wife; a murder mystery; a ghost story; a historical tale of the American Civil War; and a tale of shipwrecked lovers. One of the most charming of the lot, "The Kidnapped Plumber," is a story of the new age, in which Leacock portrays the "true" rich as highly paid tradesmen and makes them the object of the same threats, and the heroes of the same adventures, that are traditionally associated in popular fiction with aristocrats and business tycoons. These delightful, daring men of the kitchen sink save the police the trouble of rescuing one of their own from the grip of crime. The story begins: "But we were talking as only a group of practicing plumbers — including some of the biggest men in the profession — would talk." The stories have an ease and polish that evidence Leacock's mastery not only of comedic concepts and timing but also of narrative flow and the art of constructing beautiful, varied phrases and sentences. "Buggam Grange: A Good Old Ghost Story" begins in consummate yet loopily skewed Gothic style: the narrator describes how night was coming on "as the vehicle in which I was contained entered upon the long and gloomy avenue that leads to Buggam Grange."[7]

The success of *Winsome Winnie* was a bright spot in a period when Leacock found himself hard-pressed to maintain the two sides of his intellectual activity, humour and work in economics. Demands on him for writing in both fields, along with invitations to deliver lectures, mounted steeply in the post-war years. Existing correspondence from this period shows that he had many periodical commitments; he was sometimes late in delivering his copy and was having great difficulty finding time to do the work necessary to accept some promising opportunities that were offered to him. During the winter of 1919 and the spring of 1920, soon after the periodical version of *The Unsolved Riddle of Social Justice* appeared in the *New York Times*, the owner of the *New York Sun*, Frank Munsey, approached the owner of *Maclean's*, Colonel J.B. Maclean, about the suitability of Leacock as a writer for his newspaper, especially on economic and social subjects. During the First World War, Leacock had published several essays in *Maclean's*, including "The Woman Question," "Let Us Learn to Speak Russian" (a pre-revolution forecast that Russia would emerge as an important world power after the war) and "Is Permanent Peace Possible?" Maclean's first report to Munsey was mixed: "As an economist...he is rather flat, heavy, but I believe he would adjust himself under the tuition of men like Wardman and Mitchell to the brilliant style of the Sun." After several months of gathering information on Leacock and attempting unsuccessfully to draw the author into the discussion, Maclean wrote to Munsey: "He is not dependable in work or correspondence. We have to write and telegraph several times to get a copy of promised articles." Munsey also heard from *Maclean's* regional editor in Montreal that "as an economic writer, there is a good deal of difference of opinion. Some like him; others do not. There seems a fairly general opinion that he tends to be rather dry, and if he wanders off what might be called 'strict' economics, he is inclined to be rather radical in his views." Munsey was not discouraged altogether by these reports. He had heard Leacock speak at New York City dinners, one at which novelist John Galsworthy had been honoured and another at which Munsey himself had received the Legion of Honour from the French ambassador to the United States. Munsey abandoned his intelligence-gathering efforts via *Maclean's* and invited Leacock directly to visit him in New York at the first opportunity. Leacock agreed to do so but wrote, "I am afraid that as far as doing any writing goes, I have at present more than I can manage." Clearly Leacock was aware that he had made too many commitments. Thus he turned down the chance to become part of the *Sun's* brilliant stable of serious, penetrating wits, which included Don Marquis among others. In 1921, *Collier's Magazine*, one of Leacock's best outlets in the United States during the 1920s, asked him to write a series of long articles on current economic conditions. Although Leacock responded with a proposal for three features, he never submitted finished articles; two years later, the magazine's editor was still trying to get confirmation through Leacock's agent that he would eventually write such a series. He never did, although he continued to publish in *Collier's*.[8]

The success of *Winsome Winnie* did not end the distracting process of negotiating with publishers. During the early 1920s, John Lane was attempting to sell his American firm, the John Lane Company, and in his letters to Leacock he argued that the size of the humorist's American royalties were hurting his efforts to attract a buyer. Lane's views on this matter during the first two years of the 1920s are well summarized in a letter to Leacock dated 4 November 1921.

> I said that the fact that you were paid a 20% royalty in America caused the publishers I have been in negotiation with to remark that although I give such importance to your name I must be losing on every copy of your books sold, which is quite true, or was true until you arranged with Mr. Jones to accept a 15% royalty on all copies sold after 5,000 of *Winsome Winnie*.

Lane said that Leacock's audience, although strong, was somewhat elite and selective because his books were "not made up of sentimental trash which the great public here swallows by the million. In fact, you thrust your rapier at them all the time, and you guy all the things they stand for." The American firms that considered buying John Lane's business noticed that Leacock's recent books generally were not the best-sellers his earlier titles had been and continued to be. Lane repeated some of the complaints that his editors said they had been hearing a year earlier, at the time of the initial rejection of *Winsome Winnie*: "you are doing too much, and there is a very general feeling, even in Canada, that you are now writing snippets for high prices, and these are too short for book form, which is a sure way of losing your hold on book buyers." Finally, Lane warned that copyright protection was not perfect in the United States, especially for Leacock's important first three books, *Literary Lapses*, *Nonsense Novels* and *Sunshine Sketches*, which had not been printed in the United States but manufactured in Britain and imported.[9] The success of *Winsome Winnie* had quieted some of these complaints both about expensiveness and supposed declining quality, but Leacock began taking his own steps to improve the management of his periodical work and books in the United States and England. In 1921 he engaged agents in both countries; he was soon dissatisfied with his British representative and changed to another. His American agent, Paul Reynolds, remained with him for many years, although their relationship was sometimes strained, especially at the beginning, by Leacock's occasional efforts to sell on his own to magazines he was well acquainted with. Reynolds wrote repeatedly to complain that this was interfering with his efforts; he would call periodicals only to find that they were in direct contact with the author.[10]

In the spring of 1921, arrangements were being made for Leacock to make a three-month lecture tour of Great Britain during the last quarter of the year. Despite Lane's complaints about quick writing of brief sketches, Leacock was pressed by Lane's companies from both New York and London to produce a book which could be sold during the tour. He promised at first that the book was possible but by the summer was forced to recant. As an alternative means of benefiting from the tour, Lane arranged to reprint six of Leacock's

Beatrix with Stevie at Old Brewery Bay, about 1917.
Courtesy National Archives of Canada C-31906.

Leacock and Beatrix presiding over tea at Old Brewery Bay, about 1920. Also shown in this picture are Freddie Pellatt and Mrs. May Shaw ("Fitz"), holding Stevie.
Courtesy National Archives of Canada C-31948.

early books. He also prepared in England a deluxe edition of *Nonsense Novels*, illustrated by John Kettelwell; the economics of this project required Leacock to agree to a reduced royalty on the book.[11]

Another troublesome circumstance of 1921 was his inability to finance the construction of a new house in Old Brewery Bay, despite the fact that he was in the midst of the most lucrative year of his career to date. During the ten years from the land's purchase until the end of the First World War, the original "cook house" had grown steadily if irregularly by *ad hoc* additions. In 1919, Leacock and Beatrix had arranged for the construction of the boathouse, the upper story of which became Leacock's sanctuary and prime summer writing space, and for renovations to the existing cottage. But their real goal was a new house. In July 1921, Leacock wrote to his friend Alfred Chapman, an architect, who had already begun to plan the building, that he was forced to delay due to the loss he would have to take, in the economic depression of the early 1920s, if he were to sell stocks, the only means he had of raising the funds for construction.

> I am sorry to say that I am finding far more difficulty
> with the financing of my house than I had expected.
> I knew of course the whole cost as 20,000 at least. In
> going over my stocks I find that owing to the depres-
> sion I must sell at least 25,000 of my holdings...to
> realize this. I fear this goes back beyond housedom.[12]

He told Chapman that his brother George advised him that to sell the stocks would be disadvantageous because they would eventually return to full value, and that money spent at the time would buy less than the same amount spent later, under improved economic conditions. Chapman agreed, saying that the house would not be in use until the following summer in any case. When 1922 arrived, however, Leacock felt he had to decide to postpone the building again.

If 1921 was his most successful year in financial terms, with his income rising to more than $20,000, this was in large part because he spent much of the year taking advantage of many offers to do lucrative lecturing; it was these commitments that forced him to refuse new writing projects and to leave the humour book originally promised for late 1921 unfinished. Lured by high fees, Leacock planned his tour of Great Britain for the fall of 1921 while, in the spring, he travelled extensively in the United States. As soon as the 1920-21 academic year concluded, he made a very rapid tour of the northeastern and upper midwestern states, giving lectures which each paid him three hundred or three hundred fifty dollars. Beginning with an appearance in New York at the city's Graduate Society of McGill University, he spoke in Boston and Andover, Massachusetts; Lancaster, New Hampshire; Cleveland and Toledo, Ohio; Chicago and Evanston, Illinois; Milwaukee, Wisconsin; St. Louis, Missouri; Burlington, Iowa; and Louisville, Kentucky. The tour agent was the Coit Lyceum Bureau of Boston and Cleveland, which arranged, among other appearances, a speech in Toledo for the Jewish Men's Club and one in Cleveland for the Adventuring Club.

Also adding to his 1921 income was the appearance of a revised edition of his most successful book, *Elements of Political Science*; the updating, which focused especially on incorporating the events of the First World War, gave new life to the durable college text. Though Leacock was forced to turn down offers to make periodical contributions, the reverse side of this coin was that during the years 1919 to 1921 he provided many articles on crucial economic and political topics to the era's most prominent publications, including not only the *New York Times* but *Collier's* ("Is Disarmament Possible" and "Painless Tax"), and in Canada, *Maclean's*, for which, despite Colonel Maclean's apparent impatience with him, he was writing regularly. Simultaneously he was publishing humour voluminously in *Vanity Fair*, *Harper's* and a variety of other publications in the United States, the United Kingdom, and Canada.[13] In addition, he used many of his academic holidays (e.g. at Thanksgiving and Christmas) to travel and

Stevie, about 1919.
Courtesy National Archives of Canada C-31912.

speak at functions in the United States and Canada. For example, he was able to dash to New York to be one of the featured speakers at the centenary commemoration of James Russell Lowell (22 February 1819-12 August 1891) celebrated by the American Academy of Arts and Letters. Among the other distinguished literary guests were Alfred Noyes, Edgar Lee Masters, and Barrett Wendell. Many years later, in a reminiscence published by the New York *Herald Tribune* in December 1933, Leacock recalled this event:

> I remember...at the Lowell Centenary at Columbia University, ten or eleven years ago, meeting good old — no, I won't name him, the famous old Harvard professor of English who played such a large part at the gathering — all right, then — Barrett Wendell. He shook me warmly by the hand and said heartily, "I'm so glad to have the opportunity of meeting you, my children read your books." I returned, "Thank you! My mother reads yours."[14]

Other instances of this feverish lecture activity can be seen at the beginning of the next academic year, in the fall. In late November 1919 he dashed down to Boston and gave a warmly received lecture, "Literature of Today and Tomorrow," announced by the *Harvard Crimson* on 28 November as an upcoming appearance by "A Great Humorist" and reported by it the following day under the headline, "The Worst Is Yet to Come, Says Leacock/Heroes and Heroines of Novel of Tomorrow May Become Even Sillier Than at Present. Humorist Warmly Received." Then, in December after the holiday break had begun at McGill, he spoke at Auburndale, New York, twice in Pittsburgh, and in New York City at the New England Society annual dinner, before returning to Old Brewery Bay for Christmas. From the beginning of 1920 until the end of May 1921, when he paused to spend the summer writing and preparing for the British tour, he made at least fifty-seven speaking appearances, mainly in the American east and upper midwest, crisscrossing these regions from New York to Milwaukee, from Boston to Louisville.

During the summer of 1921, Leacock was visited in Orillia by Professor William Caldwell, whose series, "Impressions of Ontario," ran in the *Canadian Magazine* for several issues in 1922. Caldwell provided an informative glimpse of Leacock in the midst of his first whirlwind year as a popular lecturer, right down to the one-year-old McLaughlin touring car he had bought and insured for himself a few months earlier.

> There was Leacock bursting into the hotel and shouting in his loud voice towards the desk: "Is Professor Caldwell here; I want him at once. His room is off, do you hear, cost or no cost, say what you like or say what he likes, he is coming out to me till over Monday and I will attend to everything." I mention all this as characteristic of the man either in his ordinary daily life or in his play, for Leacock has all the insouciance and all the impulsiveness, all the abandon of the creative artist, or the child of nature — a veritable Playboy of the Western World. Characteristic, too, was his summer get up, half covered as he was by a hastily thrown on winter overcoat over his semi-boating or semi-lounging outfit, an ill-fitting and bedraggled crushed and rain-softened canvas hat and an equally sloppy clay-covered and mud-covered pair of white duck trousers that had once been new and fashionable. The whole bohemian effect was in the most delightful contrast to the fairly opulent car outside the door (no country doctor's or country minister's Ford for Leacock) earned by his own pen, and the superior, easy, commanding manner with

which he bossed the whole hotel staff and hailed half
a dozen people at the same time that he was shouting
for me.[15]

Caldwell had hoped to learn how Leacock composed; his only real conclusion was that "Leacock has simply to get worked up now and then to the boiling point, and then dash home to that upper room and work off his steam." The dashing-home part of the formula was drawn from Caldwell's experience of being driven at top speed along the country roads near Orillia to see Leacock's favourite fishing and boating areas and the homes of his friends. According to Caldwell, Leacock refused to interrupt his summer holidays with lecturing or university work but wrote daily and received a constant flow of mail and visitors from the outside world, many of them "the New York and London editors who are exploiting him." Leacock's correspondence includes a note from J. Jefferson Jones, the John Lane Company editor who had become a fast friend, to say regretfully that in 1921 he would not be able to spend his customary holiday in Old Brewery Bay.

Caldwell also captured Leacock the gardener who worked "just as long as he feels like it and no longer." Much of the work was in the hands of Leacock's long-time assistant in caring for the grounds, Bill Jones, a retired army private, whom Leacock had hired in 1918 and immediately "promoted" to Sergeant. The charming picture of a man and his gardener provided in later years by Leacock, who portrays the homeowner as taking credit in his conversation for the hours of shovelling, planting and harvesting done by his assistant, seems to have been drawn from life. An ardent gardener, Leacock was forever starting schemes for raising vegetables to sell at market in Orillia and always finding that other activities pulled him away from finishing the work, which was left to Jones and others, although the humorist still referred to it as his own. He took pride in the menus for the Orillia house being made up largely of the produce of the property. Caldwell concluded by wishing that Leacock "would make the effort somehow to put together the human nature that he knows so well with the political economy and the political science that he teaches at McGill." This was especially important in the post-war arena, he felt, since the world required a new social vision.

Caldwell shows Leacock in his country place. It is rarer to catch a glimpse of him at home in Montreal, but his son's pediatrician, Doctor Alton Goldbloom, left a memoir that provides some insight into his long-time friend's home life. The doctor described Leacock as the courtly, sophisticated presiding genius of many of the most memorable gatherings of professional and literary men he had ever attended. Even during the casual summer months, Leacock saw dinner as a formal occasion, for which men were expected to wear black tie. If his own tie was inclined to come undone, his suit was impeccable. The maids at the Côte-des-Neiges house wore smart uniforms and spoke French. A former student tells a story of Leacock arriving late for a meeting at the Political Economy Club wearing his black tie in its customary imperfect condition. Everyone else was dressed in the formal wear that he required of them for club functions, but when Leacock removed his raincoat, he was wearing a loud check suit rather than a dinner jacket. Interrupted while dressing, he had never finished changing his clothes and had finally rushed to the meeting as he was.[16]

Another significant initiative of Leacock's in the fall of 1921 began in a private dinner with writer friends B.K. Sandwell, Pelham Edgar, and John Murray Gibbon (future publicity director of the Canadian Pacific Railway); the four authors met to discuss what they felt were troubling implications of a recent initiative to change Canadian copyright law. Throughout the early twentieth century, various efforts had been made to formulate international copyright laws that would end the piracy, common on both sides of the Atlantic, of works by popular authors in Great Britain and North America. Such laws could mean higher royalty costs for publishers, and since copyright laws were determined primarily by legislatures, not by international agreements, national publishing industries often applied pressure against them. A Canadian publisher had presented to Parliament a recommendation to change the country's law to benefit the native publishing industry by limiting copyright protection in Canada to authors whose books were printed in a Canadian edition. Under this proposal, if a book by a Canadian author were published and produced in New York or London but not in Canada by a Canadian firm under a co-publishing arrangement, a Canadian publisher would be permitted to reprint it without paying the author or original publisher. This effort to foster the publishing industry by creating a sort of legal piracy hit directly at the livelihood of Canadian authors, and the four friends determined to organize a meeting of the country's writers to protest the proposed legislation. On 7 December this meeting was held at Montreal and the Canadian Authors' Association, the country's first national writers' organization, was founded. More than one hundred writers (including novelists Frank Packard and "Ralph Connor" and poet Bliss Carman) made Gibbon the CAA's first president and Sandwell its first secretary. At the time Leacock was out of the country on his tour of Great Britain, but he was included as a founding member.

We Have With Us To-night

On 14 September 1921, Leacock, with Beatrix and Stevie accompanying him, sailed from New York on the *Metagama*, bound for Liverpool. His tour resulted from an invitation he had received in the spring from the prominent firm of booking agents, Christy & Moore Agents Ltd., which approached him as a result of both his literary fame and his success as a North American lecturer during and after the war. The invitation had prompted him to request leave from McGill's new principal, his old friend and former student, General Sir Arthur Currie; Currie approached the board of trustees for the leave, which was granted during the summer. Not since his 1907 world lecture tour on behalf of the Cecil Rhodes Trust had Leacock been absent from the university during the academic year. Christy & Moore provided him with first-class passage as part of their service for the three-month engagement.

At that moment, the transatlantic commerce in celebrities was brisk. Screen stars, royal personages, influential political commentators, and society ladies turned novelists were making tall black headlines travelling to the great cities of Europe and North America to give audiences a personal glimpse of themselves and a chance to listen to their remarks. H.G. Wells was in Washington for a world disarmament conference. Margot Asquith was giving out exclusive photographs and interviews to Montreal and Toronto newspapers as part of her promotional tour for her first book, an international bestseller. When Leacock arrived in London, he did so simultaneously with Charlie Chaplin and just days ahead of the movie dream couple, Douglas Fairbanks and Mary Pickford. In the fall of 1921, Leacock was fifty-one and would turn fifty-two on 30 December, just after his tour ended — old, it might seem by modern standards, to enter on the career of a worldwide celebrity. But he was heir to a tradition that for nearly a century had brought revered writers, such as Charles Dickens and Mark Twain, to the lecture circuit relatively late in their lives.

Leacock travelled inconspicuously and seemed simply a busy professor taking advantage of an unusual change in his routine to combine business travel with a family holiday, much as he had done in 1907. Then he had indeed been, as he appeared, simply an obscure intellectual. But now the reaction to his arrival in the British capital proved that, in Great Britain at least, his fame was easily a match for that of Chaplin, Fairbanks, or Pickford. On his first morning in the city, he found himself surrounded by reporters eager for interviews. British readers evidently hoped to hear about Leacock as much as they looked forward to hearing from him. He too was, much to his surprise, a celebrity. Back at home in Canada, the newspapers reported that "it looks as though Stephen Leacock may become as much an idol with the middle class in England as Charlie Chaplin is with the populace. Chaplin gives the impression of hiding from his admirers but since Leacock's arrival on Sunday interviews with him abound." Leacock was charming the British by declaring that "he would rather have written *Alice in Wonderland* than the *Encyclopaedia Britannica*" (a line from the famous autobiographical preface to *Sunshine Sketches of a Little Town*). The *London Morning Post* article that described his arrival, reprinted in New York, identified Leacock as a worthy successor to Mark Twain in the role of ambassador of humour from America to England. In fact, he was even more welcome than Twain because of the special quality of his Canadian humour. "His fantastical ideas are often in the nature of American hyperbole but they are developed in English fashion as a rule, in a quiet and close-knit narrative which has none of the exuberance of the typical American humorist." The *Morning Post* reminded its readers that before publishing a humour collection, Leacock had achieved wide popularity in England through reprintings of his early magazine pieces, such as "Boarding-House Geometry." The interviewer speculated that, far from hindering the humorist, a background in political economy provided the right touch of unlikeliness to mark him as a memorable character. "No doubt, Mr. Leacock owes something to the fact that he himself is an incarnation of the incongruous, being Professor of Economics at McGill University, whose humour is taken more seriously than his political economy — more seriously, we repeat."[1]

The most enthusiastic of many prominent interviews appeared in the *London Times* on 27 September 1921. It gives a strong impression of Leacock, and Leacock himself put it to a good use in creating a running tongue-in-cheek skirmish with the London press that lasted through much of his tour. The *Times* interviewer, writing under the headline "A Master of Satire," reported:

> Mr. Leacock is a burly man in a light tweed suit; the sort of man it is hard to imagine wearing anything but a light tweed suit. He has a broad, strong face, with a wide forehead, half-covered by masses of low-growing hair and a thick moustache over a well-set mouth. Take him feature by feature and he might remind you of Thomas Carlyle.

With his eyes "twinkling," Leacock talked "in the most impartial

manner of the beauties of economics and laughter," He proved something of a journalistic problem at first because, against all the laws of
celebrity, he did not want to talk about himself:

> It was not so easy to persuade Mr. Leacock to let the
> public into the mysteries of his craft or to talk about
> himself at all. First, there was a substantial barrier to
> be crawled over and under and around. That barrier
> was O. Henry. Every reader of Mr. Leacock must be
> aware that he adores the stories of O. Henry on this
> side of idolatry. He has been blamed by stern critics
> for extravagance of worship. "I don't care," he says.
> "I stand by every word I've written of that magician."
> There happened to be in the company a man who
> had known O. Henry personally and this man was
> obliged to stand and deliver. All that O. Henry had
> ever done and said in his presence, what O. Henry
> had earned and where he had spent his money, why
> O. Henry was shy and whence he had drawn his
> inspiration, this — and much also to similar purpose
> had to be debated and threshed out, accompanied
> by recollections of this plot and that, with zealous
> eulogy, before Mr. Leacock would condescend to
> realize that he himself was also a writer and an inter-
> esting person.[2]

Was this reticence due to zeal for O. Henry, or to a failure to realize
his own importance, or to native modesty? It is most likely that
Leacock, besieged by questioners probing the secrets of his personal
life and his professional successes, indulged in a bit of leg-pulling by
displaying an "extravagant" interest in the private doings of another
writer.

Once he got started, though, he was willing to unburden himself. He said that "political economy had saved him from being considered merely a 'funny man'" and reminisced about his early disappointments in trying to publish a collection of humour. He said his manuscript was returned with the explanation that "humour was dangerous." According to the *Times*, it was his brother George who discovered a publisher for him. "Reading the rejected 'trifles,' he observed fraternally, 'Oh hell, these are good,' and sent them into safe and profitable harbourage." The story is slightly skewed, because of course the Houghton Mifflin rejection slip really had said that "humour was too uncertain," suggesting that the danger posed by the humour, in the company's admittedly shortsighted eyes, was financial failure. Ten years later, Leacock had published his ten books of humour with another firm and was contentedly giving out the secrets of his method to the London press: early rising, sleeping outdoors, getting the idea down fast, and so on. He also reminisced to the *Times* about his teaching days in an Ontario high school:

> Fathers and mothers too — you know how tiresome they can make themselves by interfering with the school master? I remember a man who used to check his son's lessons. Once, opening the boy's exercise book, I came on a note, "How is it that after being with you three months Robert knows no Latin?" Under this note I wrote another: "Probably his ignorance is hereditary." Another boy was helped by his relatives; I went over his Latin prose with him and pointing to one sentence said, "I don't agree with your grandmother's view of the dative," and to another, "Your grandmother fails in her declensions." The treatment was effectual.

There was much more of the same, all positive, all witty, and all excellent advance publicity for his lecture appearances; like a born showman, Leacock left them begging for more.

The tour did not begin in London. Instead, his first engagement, on 4 October, was held in the Yorkshire city of Thirsk. Fifty appearances to give humorous lectures were scheduled from early October to late December; he would go to England, Scotland and Cardiff, Wales. Britain was a small country by North American standards, as Leacock himself was quick to point out, but to crisscross it as he did for fully three months from Bournemouth to Aberdeen, with several stints of daily appearances, was a stern task. For the most part, his wife and young son remained in London at 58 Romney Street, Westminster, while he travelled alone to meet the various audiences arranged for him. Leacock or his agents had preferred to take the show out of town before attempting the capital; however, he was not idle between the opening in Thirsk and his first scheduled London appearance on 17 October. On the contrary, the Sunday before he was due to speak in London, Leacock published in a London paper his own account of being interviewed.

> I pass over the fact that being interviewed for five hours is a fatiguing process. I lay no claim to exemption for that. But to that no doubt was due the singular discrepancies as to my physical appearance which I detected in the London papers.
>
> The young man who interviewed me immediately after breakfast described me as "a brisk, energetic man, still on the right side of forty, with energy in every movement." The lady who wrote me up at 11:30 reported that my hair was turning grey, and that there was a "peculiar langour" in my manner. And at the end the boy who took me over at a quarter to two said, "The old gentleman sank wearily

upon a chair in the hotel lounge. His hair is almost white." The trouble is that I had not understood that London reporters are supposed to look at a man's personal appearance. In America we never bother with that. We simply describe him as a "dynamo." For some reason or other it always pleases everybody to be called a "dynamo," and the readers at least with us like to read about people who are "dynamos," and hardly care for anything else.

In the case of very old men we sometimes call them "battle horses" or "extinct volcanoes," but beyond these three classes we hardly venture on description. So I was misled. I had expected that the reporter would say: "As soon as Mr. Leacock came across the floor we felt we were in the presence of a 'dynamo' (or an 'extinct battle horse' as the case may be)." Otherwise I would have kept up those energetic movements all the morning. But they fatigue me, and I did not think them necessary. But I let that pass.[3]

Leacock said without "any spirit of elation or boastfulness" that he had been interviewed eighteen times in all and that, from the question of his appearance right through to the question about the relative merits of American and French drama, he had felt off balance.

With this article, he moved from celebrity guest to a participant deeply embroiled in the heady give-and-take of London letters. His jests at his supposed unfamiliarity with the methods of the British press gently mock the whole process of "selling oneself." He holds no brief for the methods of American newspaper people, whom he portrays as jingoistic promoters of their individual cities, looking only for some controversial or complimentary remark to hang on each distinguished visitor's well-known name. At the same time, he calls into question the reliability of the reporting process, even when undertaken in the presumably high-mindedly British style. He questions just what a reporter can hope to see: will it really be everything, will it be true? He himself changed during a day of interviewing, and it was precisely the interviewing that did it. He also implied a distinction between what he was prepared to give his interviewers and what the interviewers were attempting to get from him. He preferred to spin yarns of his own choosing and reveal himself in that way rather than to provide direct answers to questions about his personal life or to be treated as an enigma suitable for dissection. His article enabled him to enter his own opinions about how impressions should and should not be gathered and won him fresh headlines only the weekend before his London opening.

It also drew some prickly words from the humour magazine *Punch*. *Punch*'s 12 October number carried a brief paragraph about Leacock's claims on the quantity of his interviews. It seems he said he had been interviewed eighteen times, sixteen times by men and four by women. *Punch* replied, "We are not saying it in any spirit of superiority, but we make it twenty." Considering the form of Leacock's remark, and its source, we may suspect that he intended a slight on his female interviewers. At any rate, he did not change its wording or offer any explanation when he later republished his newspaper piece in the book he wrote about his trip, *My Discovery of England* (1922). More important, though, was another article in the same issue of *Punch* by Ernest Jenkins entitled, "Mr. Stephen Leacock, An Interview Gone Wrong." Jenkins, offering a mock apology for his failure to provide a thorough physical description of Leacock, explained:

> I called one morning soon after Mr. Leacock's arrival in this country. I made full notes as to his eyes, their position, quality, flash-point, and colour. I took particulars of his hair, its shade, density, specific gravity and cube root. With callipers and tape-measure I arrived at the area in square millimetres of his jaw. I also

made a rough sketch of the suit he was wearing and took a sample for chemical analysis. But on opening my evening paper I discovered that most of this, if not all, had been done by another interviewer.[4]

Jenkins was mocking the *Times* as well as Leacock's protestations. But he went on to recount some of the questions he had put to Leacock on subjects of literature and economics, the British press and political celebrities and suggested an inadequacy in the answers he received. He concluded with a stab at the humorist's discussion of his special subject:

> And finally, when I asked him for a few hints as to how to write humorous sketches, he responded with great readiness and fluency, yet without giving me any real encouragement to believe that now I knew exactly how to do it. At this point I concluded my enterprise, made a courteous bow — and took my leave a little disillusioned.

Leacock, it seems, had not impressed everyone equally with his ability to be funny and to describe how to be funny. But he had certainly established himself as a name to contend with and argue over and all without once speaking publicly in London. It was an auspicious beginning.

Fifty appearances within eighty-one days was arduous, but Leacock was so much a match for the pace that he added several other engagements to this pre-arranged speaking schedule and managed a busy social life as well. Although fifty-one, the Leacock of this era was the hearty, energetic figure of the *Times* interview, the one doubtless given at an early-morning hour. Some of his most famous pictures and portraits date from his final years, when he lived primarily in Orillia and presented the aspect captured, for instance, in

Yousef Karsh's photographs of 1939: a gray-haired, stoop-shouldered, wrinkled but smiling country sage. But in 1921, Leacock's thick unruly mop of hair was brown touched with gray; his face, though lined, was full of colour, and the contour of his jaw was firm and square. His most striking feature was his eyes, gray-blue and (as the *Times* said) always twinkling, the kind of eyes that promise candour and inspire confidence. His lips turned easily into a smile. He did not always wear tweeds, but his well-tailored clothes somehow came to every occasion rumpled and a little the worse for wear. His ties would not stay tied but always seemed to be inching loose so as to give him freer rein to look about and speak easily. He was of middle height and carried his compact body erectly, although with a slight stoop at the shoulder. His voice, trained by years of teaching and storytelling at home, in his club and on the lecture stage, was deep and full, with an educated accent. His laughter, "a laugh a humorist would be proud of," according to the *Times*, sounded frequently when he spoke, as a welcome and a cue to his audience. Although it suited his own sense of a proper comic manner, his laughing on stage sometimes aroused resentment. He recalled one disgruntled listener who objected: "Well, I will say, you certainly do seem to enjoy your own fun," to which he had replied, "If I didn't, Madam, who would?"

Thousands would and did. Leacock said later that so many people came to hear him during the British tour that he calculated his earnings worked out to about thirteen cents a person, but he admitted that the crowds had been consistently excellent. In his famous essay, "We Have With Us To-night," from *My Discovery of England*, he makes light of his treatment on this trip, especially of the horrors he endured at the hands of confused, self-important or dues-seeking chairmen. But on 17 October, the night of his first engagement in London, he had at the Aeolian Hall a chairman who must have pleased him with the warmth and insight of his introduction. Sir Owen Seaman, editor of *Punch*, taking as his theme the special qualities of Leacock's Canadian humour, praised its appeal for the British.

"Now Mr. Leacock's humour is British by heredity, but he has caught something of the spirit of American humour by force of association. His humour contains all that is best in the humour of both hemispheres." Seaman said ruefully of the Americans, "When we fail to appreciate their humour, they say we are too dull and effete to understand it, and when they do not appreciate ours they say we haven't got any." Leacock was safe on both counts. Events proved that he appreciated the humour of the British and the British appreciated his, to the point that he could honestly conclude that "all the good old jokes about the lack of humour in the British people are a pure myth."[5]

For his tour Leacock used a rotation of four speeches, "Frenzied Fiction," "Drama As I See It," "Laugh with Leacock" and "Literature at its Lightest." The latter two were compilations of passages from previously published work. The first two, which proved the most popular, were essays on the foibles and foolishnesses of contemporary popular fiction and drama. Readers can find three "Frenzied Fiction" lectures in a book published late in Leacock's career, *Here Are My Lectures and Stories* (1937); he had used the title "Frenzied Fiction" for a number of talks during the First World War and hence when he compiled some of his lectures he had three different ones under the same title. Formally, they are similar to many lectures Leacock wrote in the pattern that is found in "The Snoopopath; or, Fifty Stories in One," in which he had said, "This particular study in the follies of literature is not so much a story as an essay." What may be called his platform essays were illustrated not with samples from the writings and authors being mocked but with his own parodies of fashions in literature and drama. The flavour of these addresses can be found in his enduringly popular "The Great Detective," closely based on one of the "Frenzied Fiction" lectures, which begins, "I propose tonight, ladies and gentlemen, to deal with murder. There are only two subjects that appeal nowadays to the general public, murder and sex; and, for people of culture, sex-murder."[6] In these essays, Leacock developed a flexible, seemingly easy form and style that allowed him to retain the touches of pure fancy and parody familiar from the *Nonsense Novels* and *Behind the Beyond* and at the same time to produce a new creation, the fictional Stephen Leacock, who seemed — but only seemed — to be the man Stephen Leacock himself, in his own person and with no mask or reserve between himself and his audience. The fiction of these essays is that they contain no fiction, that what we hear is simply a man speaking to his equals about drolleries and disasters of the world in which we find ourselves. The London *Spectator* gave the name of the "magnifying-glass method" to the characteristic Leacockian technique of holding some aspect of life up to a view so clear that it became clearly foolish. This approach suited Leacock's stage manner, which was that of the witty raconteur, a demeanour stationed midway between the lecturer and the out-and-out show business performer. Some commentators have said that Leacock modelled this manner, with its ease and informality, on his classroom technique, although Leacock's former students unanimously maintained that he rarely seasoned his teaching with jokes.

It is likely that he modelled his performance and persona on what he knew of Mark Twain's platform style, adapting this to his own very different personality and vision. The *Morning Post* was insightful in referring to Leacock's style as "a quiet and close-knit narrative which has none of the exuberance of the typical American humorist." The typical comic performer of the day delivered rapid-fire, disconnected jokes, accompanied with broad physical humour, and projected an extravagant persona that was a version of one of various time-hallowed, clownlike types, enacted with little regard for consistency should a gag require something completely out-of-character. Humorists who took the stage, like Brett Harte or George Ade, were more organized, often basing their performance on their published texts, but depended also on the projection of exaggerated types, such as the frontiersman or the man of the backwoods who reveals an unexpected, naive wisdom that proves to be more shrewd than innocent; this comic approach, which persists from Haliburton's Yankee peddler through Will Rogers to the present day, tempted even Leacock in his old age. But Leacock's own approach was entirely different and fresh, a rare example of a comic invention. Clemens had read from his works and had expressed the serious concerns of a great writer, but he had also maintained the fictional mask of Mark Twain, the rude westerner and river man; he set the example of what could be done by consistent presentation of a deeply imagined persona, but represented the apotheosis and exhaustion of the American humour of the nineteenth century rather than a way ahead. Into this gap Leacock stepped, literarily in the 1910s and as a public personality from about 1920, to produce the character of the erudite philosopher who is yet one of us, scorning equally the follies of intellectuals, specialists, leaders, and ordinary people, laying bare the ways they are ruled by simple and low impulses self-deceivingly garnished as faith in some supposed wisdom, whether it is called science or common sense. A contemporary audience sees the influence and tradition of Leacock whenever it sees a comic performer who presents a fairly unified script of jokes and portrays himself or herself as no clown but a dignified person, perhaps quicker and wittier than the norm but just as beleaguered by modern life, riding it out with the help of an ultimately forgiving sarcasm. There have been and continue to be many such humorists.

Leacock lectured three more times in London and on each occasion was presented by a distinguished journalist: on 19 October by J.A. Spender, editor of the *Westminster Gazette*; on 20 October by Sir Campbell Stuart, editor of the *Times*; and on 21 October by J. St. Loe Strachey, editor of the *Spectator*.[7] All of the speeches were triumphs. During the next seventeen days, Leacock took two breaks, one for three days and the other for four, while speaking in the middle and southern sections of England, from Shrewsbury on the Welsh border to Folkestone near Dover. He made his single visit to Wales, an appearance in Cardiff, on 7 November. This began the most crowded period of the hectic tour. For the rest of November he was scarcely free for more than one day at a time while making a lengthy foray into Scotland with appearances at Glasgow, Edinburgh and Aberdeen. A return to the London area early in December was followed by a brief swing through Scotland and northern England and then south again for the conclusion of the tour. His recollections of the tour lectures — described in two of the essays from *My Discovery of England* (1922), "We Have With Us To-night" and "Do the English Have a Sense of Humour?" — present two different sides of his experience. The first, though it acknowledges his warm reception during the tour, emphasizes the doubtful pleasures of being a public speaker, who is subject to various unfortunate circumstances, unforeseen complications, and incompetent introductions. Once he was introduced as a criminal.

> Witness this (word for word) introduction that was used against me by a clerical chairman in a quiet spot in the south of England:
>
> "Not so long ago, ladies and gentlemen," said the vicar, "we used to send out to Canada various classes of our community to help build up that country. We sent out our laborers, we sent out our scholars and professors. Indeed, we even sent out our criminals. And now," with a wave of his hand towards me, "they are coming back."[8]

On the other hand, Leacock said frequently that he found his audiences, like his interviewers, eager and appreciative. If they had any fault, it was only that they hoped to hear something from him and not simply to look at a famous person. In "Do the English Have a Sense of Humour?" he called this perhaps the most significant difference between his audiences in North America and in Britain.

Being a celebrity meant that Leacock was sought out by kindred celebrities, and he found the time and energy to take advantage of invitations from John Galsworthy, Hugh Walpole, Arnold Bennett, Dean Inge and Sir Gilbert Parker. He discussed the nature of humour with G.K. Chesterton, after a game of billiards. Chesterton joined the onlookers at the Oxford and Cambridge Club, where Leacock was engaged in the game with his old friend from Montreal, W.E. Gladstone Murray. Afterwards, Leacock and Chesterton talked privately; according to Murray, Leacock felt that this conversation "helped to crystallize my conception of humour as, perhaps, the highest product of civilization." Actor Cyril Maude took Leacock to Westminster to meet playwright J.M. Barrie, then sixty-one, whose *Peter Pan* was enjoying a revival in London. Their encounter was a command performance conducted in the eccentric style Barrie demanded: he reclined on a sofa in a darkened apartment and his guests were ushered in to amuse him. This unlikely pair, the languorous Barrie and Leacock the dynamo, found common ground in O. Henry. Years later, Leacock wrote an account of the visit as a memorial to Barrie, whom he remembered as one of the few people in England at the time who had read O. Henry and "was crazy over his stories." Leacock was able to supply Barrie with firsthand information about O. Henry's life thanks to accounts of the author's acquaintances, perhaps including the one he discovered at his press conference. Barrie was reluctant, in the end, to let Leacock go.[9]

The circumstance of O. Henry's name cropping up on the tour is not as much by chance as it might seem at this distance. His death in 1910 had spurred a new admiration for his works in America and England, an interest they had not enjoyed during the writer's life. In 1916 Leacock had written a strong defense of O. Henry in which he attacked those critics who found fault with O. Henry for publishing some inferior material, presumably for money. Sympathizing with the financial pressures that might cause an artist to publish inferior work, Leacock criticized critics who would dismiss the good works of a contemporary author because of a few bad pieces but would praise a classic author on the basis of his greatest efforts. He eulogized O. Henry as an author very little swayed by the modern machinery of syndicates and press services. Leacock's praise of O. Henry, amounting perhaps to a kind of identification, came at a time when Leacock himself began to be criticized for writing too fast for the sake of earnings. In discussing O. Henry and the private tragedy of want and neglect that lay behind the production of his stories, Leacock showed a keen understanding of the difference between good writing and commercial success, the purity of aesthetic judgment and the writer's life; either tardy or early financial rewards always put great pressure on the writer. Leacock found himself having to deal with the opposite of O. Henry's experience: fame and financial rewards came to him if not early in his life, then at least relatively early in his writing career; he never suffered anything like the poverty and neglect that beset O. Henry, but he had powerful ambitions to derive influence and wealth from his writings beyond those that his profession as scholar and professor provided.[10]

Leacock the intellectual and educator took short busman's holidays on the tour by visiting several universities. He had a special text, "The Economic Man," intended for such serious occasions. One of his most satisfying stops was at Oxford, where he had spoken during his 1907 Rhodes Trust visit to England. It was a rare family outing: his wife and son went along to stay at the famed Mitre Inn. After addressing the Oxford Union, Leacock was also entertained at a breakfast by former McGill students. These events formed the basis for one of Leacock's most famous essays, "Oxford As I See It," a very serious praise, illumined with wit, of education at the British university. As Leacock's career continued, the theme of quality education would engage him more and more; much of his basic concern that education be tailored to developing the gifts of individual students, rather than being made into a wholesale commodity, emerges clearly in the Oxford essay. He took an opportunity to stir up controversy during a visit to the London School of Economics, where on 12 December he was the guest speaker at the inaugural meeting of London's Canadian Club; he was introduced by Sir Gilbert Parker, a transplanted Canadian living in London, whose novels of Canadian adventure were best-sellers. Leacock used the occasion to make some much-appreciated jokes about a recent Liberal election victory back home. Turning to British politics, he said that complaints about income tax, common at the time of his visit, failed to take into account the heavier burden of hidden and indirect taxes borne by citizens of other countries. Leacock maintained that Britons were, in fact, well off with respect to taxation. This brought a storm of letters against him in the press, which Leacock invited the London School of Economics students to answer on his behalf if they agreed with his remarks. The students complied with the request readily, and in gratitude he treated them to lunch during a return visit to London.[11]

Nor did Leacock find respite in Britain from publishing business. At the time of the tour, John Lane was in New York attempting to complete the sale of his American company. Leacock met several times with The Bodley Head's directors and editors while he was in London. Letters to him in England from the New York and London offices indicate that he had seriously begun to consider changing publishers. Writing from New York, Lane cited statistics of Leacock's poor recent sales and suggested that the quality of most of his latest work would not long maintain his reputation. But he promised continued service if Leacock would resist the temptation of large advances offered by other firms. At the same time, Lane's people in London were evidently stung by Leacock's many complaints about his recent dealings with the firm. After one meeting with Leacock, director B.W. Willett wrote to him:

> I gathered from your general conversation and atti-
> tude at our interview that our rivals in the trade, such
> as literary agents and others, had been pretty busy
> poisoning your mind against us as a firm. Might I

suggest that if you want to make enquiries about us
— which, of course, you are perfectly justified in
doing — you should go not to people who are preju-
diced against us, either as rivals or for other reasons,
but to unprejudiced people in the trade, such as
booksellers. I do not believe that there is any
publishing firm in England who could have worked
up your books in the way that we have done in the
last ten years.

Lane and his editors urged Leacock to remember that his published
books would remain with Lane if he changed publishers. A new firm
would not be interested in promoting these old books, but Lane
would continue to build sales for all his books as each new one
appeared. In the end, Leacock remained with Lane's Bodley Head in
England and Dodd, Mead and Company, which bought the John
Lane Company, though he consistently refused Dodd, Mead's
requests[12] for multi-book contracts and courted and entertained (but
never took up) serious offers for his humour books from such firms as
Harper Brothers and Doubleday Doran.

One of the most remarkable performances during the tour was
Leacock's speech on 8 December at the London Society. An account
in the *Times* places the speech in the third person but still reproduces
clearly the flavour of Leacock's remarks. Just as he turned the tables
on his interviewers with his article on being interviewed, so here
Leacock turned the tables on English impression-gatherers in
America by giving his impressions of England and some impressions
on forming impressions.

He came here a raw Canadian; he was now a cooked
Londoner. He had nothing but admiration for his
hosts' fellow islanders who crossed the Atlantic to
pick up impressions like huckleberries on the other

243

side. As far as he knew, Mr. H.G. Wells had outdistanced all rivals in that art, by having formed 2,758 impressions in a fort-night, or at the rate of four and one-half per second! (Laughter) Personally he could only pick up impressions somewhat laboriously, although he had sold them before he landed in this country. (Laughter) He had been told that among the first places which he must see in London were the Tower, in which there was the most marvellous collection of instruments of torture in the world, and the British Museum, with its most extraordinary collection of Egyptian writings; but he had become a sophisticated Londoner in that he had not seen those places, although he had seen the splendid spectacle entitled Cairo. (Laughter) Among the monuments of London, one which he could not too much admire represented Sir Wilfrid Lawson drinking tea. When he and some Americans were told that it represented the first prohibitionist all that they wanted was that there should be placed beside it in equal majesty a statue of the last prohibitionist.[13]

Complaining of his troubles in gaining impressions about the workings of British government, Leacock made this report on the House of Commons:

He would describe the situation of the luncheon-room, the tea-room and the bar but of the actual chambers, not a good deal. He would explain that the legislative chamber was very little used, because at the present time legislation was not conducted there but elsewhere as, for example, in the home of Mr. Lloyd George, or in Ireland, or in any other

convenient spot and then at the earliest convenient
moment the members were summoned together to
hear the latest thing in legislation and were expected
to cheer or groan or, if they chose, to do both.
(Laughter)

The tour came to an end in Bournemouth, Hampshire, on 23
December. The *Bournemouth Times* noted that Leacock made his
final appearance in his home county of Hampshire, which he had left
at the age of six. Some of Leacock's friends and colleagues made
much of the humorist's British birth in trying to characterize his
special brand of transatlantic humour. In writing *My Discovery of
England*, Leacock said little about his feelings on returning for only
the third time in more than forty years to his home country, and for
the first time in all those years to his home county. Years later, in
drafting his autobiography, he did tell a story about his Hampshire
visit of 1921: a car trip with E.V. Lucas, a writer for *Punch*, whose
humorous work Leacock very much admired. The trip was urged on
Leacock by Lucas because there were special souvenirs of cricket,
Lucas's favourite sport, near Hambledon Village at Bury Lodge,
which as it happened was the ancestral home of the Butlers,
Leacock's mother's family. Leacock relates that Lucas was much
more impressed by the ancient cricket scores kept in Bury Lodge than
by any sentimental associations the place held for his companion.
Leacock himself had approached the village pub, he reported,
expecting a warm scene in honour of "the return of the native" but
got scarcely a nod of interest. Even in a work intended as autobiography, he presented his single account of a visit to his place of origin
in terms that more conceal than reveal his feelings.[14]

He spent Christmas and New Year's in London, and then took
his family to Paris, where he helped prepare French translations of his
work. The Leacocks sailed for home from Le Havre on 14 January
1922. Leacock wrote to Christy & Moore that he had enjoyed the

tour. That year, lecture fees from the tour boosted his annual income to more than twenty thousand dollars for the first time. Despite his success, however, he did not follow up his new-found fame or ever again interrupt his McGill routine to mount a lecture tour on the same scale. After his Bournemouth engagement, Leacock told a *Times* correspondent that he did not expect to return.

> As far as I know, it is not very likely that I shall ever have the opportunity to be free from my college work to come back again, but I leave with very great regret. I have met with such extraordinary kindness, and such generous appreciation from the audiences who have heard me all over England and Scotland that the experience is one which I shall long cherish. I am afraid that when I go back to Canada, and say how I have been treated, it will let loose upon these shores, a flood of Canadian humorists and economists. I hope, for my sake, that they will be treated as I have been treated. From my experience here, I am convinced that all the good old jokes about the lack of humour in the British people are a pure myth. I have made during the last three months a very handsome livelihood out of the British sense of humour and I am properly grateful for it.[15]

Full of impressions he planned to sell in the form of *My Discovery of England*, Leacock said his grateful goodbyes.

Women and Whiskey

W hen Leacock returned to Canada, the time and work pressures that had plagued him in 1921 continued. *My Discovery of England* was the first book he wrote for Dodd, Mead and Company in New York, and the editors there moved quickly from praising him as a great "adornment" in their list of authors to urging him to finish his book before public interest in his trip had died away. He wrote back that responsibilities at the university were pressing him hard, but that he wished even more than they to have the book appear by 1 April.[1] In some measure, *My Discovery of England* corresponded to Professor Caldwell's hope that Leacock would combine his humorous sympathy and his scholarly expertise to bring a new social vision to the world. It was at first somewhat disappointing to Dodd, Mead because it contained so many non-fiction essays on serious subjects and humorous pieces tied closely to social concerns, but the book proved popular with critics and the public on its publication in the fall of 1922. It went through several printings both in the United States and England. (It was not as popular in Canada, where a second impression was never made from the first edition.) Reviews were generally enthusiastic; it was "bright with the humor which bubbles irrepressibly from the writings of this Canadian 'Mark Twain,'" wrote the *Boston Transcript*. In England it was called "not only amusing but shrewd" in its analysis of English politics and press. Robert Benchley filed an encomium in the *New York Tribune*, and a glowing assessment came from New York's *Outlook* magazine: "Mr. Leacock's humor has never been more enjoyable than in this book. He contrives to touch up the foibles and follies of English and Americans alike, and without giving offense in either direction. Capital reading!" There were occasional quibbles that the book's "blithe conception" was not uniformly realized. In *The Nation*, Lawton Mackall wrote, "Philosopher, pedagogue, political economist that he is, the responsibility of being unflaggingly roilicksome becomes at times almost an anxious duty."[2] Leacock the grammarian and nonpareil stylist probably would not have respected the opinion that could produce such a sentence, but Mackall's reservation does graph one of the book's special characteristics, its explicit blending of the serious and the humorous.

Born and nurtured in the literature and attitudes of the middle and late nineteenth century, Leacock in his career exhibited an arc familiar among the great Victorians, from the exuberance of early creativity through an increasing submission of art to social relevance, resulting in late works that always seemed questionable to the first admirers of the early ones. Tennyson is a famous example of this pattern; Charles Dickens, who was himself seen as a humorist in the somewhat different definition of those days, and Mark Twain are other examples; Thackeray is a catastrophic one. The late-century movements of art-for-art's-sake and decadence were in a measure responses to the freighting of art with public significance, as was the Victorian upsurge of nonsense, which produced Leacock's beloved *Alice's Adventures in Wonderland* and *Bab Ballads*, and in which his own humour first germinated. Oscar Wilde wrote the manifesto of this impulse in his essay "The Decay of Lying," defending pure literature and attacking the literature of the world's sorrows and necessities, descended in his view from Wordsworth, who had been the saint of Matthew Arnold's Victorian high seriousness and the subject of brilliant Lewis Carroll lampoons. Wilde brought paradox, contradiction and irony to their high point, and was often funny, but he was no humorist, and it would be hard to name a spirit more at variance with Leacock's, despite points of coincidence. It is the example of Dickens and Clemens that Leacock in his own manner followed. Since 1916, with the publication of *Essays and Literary Studies* and the inclusion of an essay touching on serious concerns in *Further Foolishness*, he had been experimenting with explicitly bringing his views into his literary production. *My Discovery of England* is a watershed in this regard, defining the nature of his most characteristic humour for the remainder of his career. Henceforward he would not produce a unified work but collections containing pure humour and parody, increasingly rare, alongside humorous essays that employed wit and hilarity in the expression of his themes and concerns. He would never write another *Nonsense Novels* or *Sunshine Sketches of a Little Town*, but from his later books can be culled a body of inimitable essays that make him a successor of Addison, Lamb, and Stevenson. Such work, beginning with *My Discovery of England*, also placed him in the ranks of contemporaneous writers who as public figures were social reformers, such as George Bernard Shaw, G.K. Chesterton, H.G. Wells, and of similar writers before, including his beloved Dickens and Mark Twain — literary artists who defined the age as much through the opinions for which their creative work gave them a platform as through the work itself. In his new book, the brilliant wit was subordinated to a sage's quite serious teaching on the nature and proper methods of education. There can be no doubt that Leacock purposefully augmented this aspect of his work during the last twenty-five years of his life, consciously linking himself to the tradition of author as wise man and social adviser. Thus the 1921 tour, from which so much of the concept and impetus for this change of direction was derived, can be called a major turning point in Leacock's career, both in establishing his fame and public persona and in determining the nature of his future writing.

Over the years, *My Discovery of England* has lost favour among his humour collections, although two of its pieces, "Oxford As I See It" and "We Have With Us To-night," are among his best and most frequently anthologized. Leaving to one side the question of the book's merits, it must be admitted that it was produced with a speed rivalling H.G. Wells's pace as an impression-former. The manuscript was at the publisher in March, but even that fact scarcely indicates the rapidity with which Leacock had worked. Two of the pieces were prepared and presented during the trip itself. A third was published in *Outlook* in February 1922; this was Leacock's answer to the question, "Do the English Have a Sense of Humour?" Several other sections were published in *Harper's* early in 1922. Although the crowds in Britain had already enjoyed lecture versions of his work and although prestigious magazines were eager for the pieces, Leacock found that the completed manuscript did not enthuse his publisher. A Dodd, Mead and Company editor reported on it, "I must confess to a feeling of disappointment that it is not actually fiction."[3] Is *My Discovery of England*, especially given what we know of its manner of preparation, a sign of one critic's claim that Leacock's ambition to be "an imaginative writer" had faded after 1915? The book was specifically undertaken as a highly individual response to a particular event; it required Leacock to develop something that would believably seem his own voice, the voice of Leacock the man, in a form "more like an essay than a story." In writing "Parisian Pastimes" for *Behind the Beyond* (1916), he had already used a similar approach to discuss the objects of travel and how to travel. The London trip had also encouraged him to make the attempt of speaking as a recognized author responding to his established audience. The danger that this course held for him was not that he would cease to be funny, or even that he would no longer write fiction; the excellence of his comic control of parodies, character sketches and vignettes did not require that he move solely in the direction of sustained narrative. Rather, his danger was a temptation to believe that his individualized manner of treatment, with wit embodying a humane and informed but commited approach to the subject in hand, would guarantee a successfully humorous and persuasive attack on any subject he chose. Already in *My Discovery of England*, there are jokes which, however sound, seem ill-assorted with the depth and breadth of the subject he seeks to handle through witticism.

Among the many public questions besides education that *My Discovery of England* addressed were women's rights and prohibition, two issues that occupied a great deal of Leacock's attention throughout the 1920s. Both movements gained their first significant success in Canada during the First World War, and he always associated them with the social upheaval the war had created, and the end of the pre-war world in which he had come to maturity. He wrote relatively little on the question of women's suffrage, although before the vote was given to women in Canada he published the essay, "The Woman Question," in *Maclean's* in 1915 and reprinted it in *Essays and Literary Studies*. Although it begins lightly, in the manner of one of the club scenes in *Further Foolishness*, it is in fact a very serious argument on the question of the social roles proper to women. Leacock opens with a conversation he overhears; two women are agreeing that if they had the vote, there would have been no war. While doubting this claim, Leacock does not challenge seriously the right to vote. But he challenges the fundamental principle on which the extension of suffrage would rest: that men and women are equal. By 1920, women could vote in federal elections and in provincial elections except in Quebec; the first woman member of parliament, Agnes Macphail, was elected in 1921. But in 1915, "Women need not more freedom but less" Leacock had opined, in opposition to the current of the times. "Social policy should proceed from the fundamental truth that women are and must be dependent." His principal argument was that society needed to have women in the roles of wives and mothers, but he did not refrain from suggesting that women were not suited to the professional requirements of many important positions: "The only trouble is that they can't do it." Just as he would later do in *The Unsolved Riddle of Social Justice,* he urged that society would treat its women fairly only when it guaranteed sufficient financial support for them without requiring them to work. This would allow them to devote themselves to child-rearing. Mechanical inventions had freed women from much housework, he admitted, but no invention could release them from their nature and duty as mothers: "No man ever said his prayers at the knees of a vacuum cleaner." Society was criminally liable for expecting young women to support themselves before marriage in a world without jobs suitable for them, and it was "the most absurd mockery of freedom ever devised" that a widow would be left to provide for herself and her young children after her husband's death.[4] Later in his career, when women persisted in seeking social emancipation in education, in property ownership and even in matters of etiquette — smoking in public, for example, or frequenting bars — Leacock would occasionally turn from his belief that women were seeking work unwillingly to snap that social ills were being created by these emancipated females. In *Humor: Its Theory and Technique* (1935) he charged that when women turn away from their role as a sort of preserve for the purest moral principles, the result is the phenomenon of a literature filled with blasphemy and profanity.

Even more than the general question of women's place in society, the immediate question of women's place in his classroom plagued Leacock. During the First World War, the numbers of women students at McGill increased sharply; when the war was over, the balance shifted slightly but women remained a large proportion of the student population. Invariably polite to his women students, Leacock continued until the end of his life to criticize what he saw as the follies of university education for women. In 1921 he wrote an article for *Collier's* called "We Are Teaching Women All Wrong," in which he said that women had been failing elementary physics at McGill for twenty-five years and it was time to take the subject away from them. Women could not reason or think, he wrote, but they could argue. Their supposed lack of capacity for the university life was not, however, his only or even his chief complaint. If women did have to attend school, they should study something that would be valuable to them in their future homes, such as nursing. He contended that preparation for a profession was wasted on them because eventually they married and then their training was of no use to society. Especially during the 1930s, he complained that valuable space in the country's universities should not be wasted on women who would never enter professions while many deserving male students could find no place on campus. Co-eds came in for much of the scorn he aimed at all of the denizens, male and female alike, of the type of university developing in the early century as schools moved away from the classical curriculum of the 1800s but not towards the strict and heady regime of hard modern studies that Leacock championed. As well, campus atmosphere and activities were changing. In many humour sketches, he portrayed his consternation at fictional students' accounts of modern university life, many of them placed in the mouths of eager co-eds, who seemed to him to prove that no valid work was being accomplished. He once addressed a McGill sorority on the subject of women college students, comparing the qualities of North American girls (who chewed tobacco) with those of British girls (who were addicted to gin) and finding little merit in either.[5] In "Oxford as I See It," he confessed that the sight of female students at the august university had been upsetting to him, and worried that the male students must find it difficult to work.

Leacock was fond of baring the absurdities of human thought and behaviour; it is sometimes difficult to determine whether he is using his humour to expose an institution or group as wholly valueless or only seeking to remedy flaws by exposing them to ridicule. The combination of his serious essays, "The Woman Question" and "Oxford as I See It," with his many humorous portrayals of the empty-headed girl student seems strong evidence that he sincerely wished to limit or end altogether higher education for women. But perhaps he was adamant precisely because he saw that a complete end was impossible, and exaggerated his disapproval in an effort to secure whatever change he could in the direction that he favoured. He had said that he preferred "half-light" as exposing truth more clearly; in *The Garden of Folly* (1924), he reiterated this: "A half truth, like half a brick, is always more forcible as an argument than a whole one: it travels farther." He is clearly attempting to explain and justify his use of hyperbole and litotes — exaggeration and understatement — for the humorous sharpening of serious points. His confidence that he could wield his half bricks without confusing his audience was evident, but some readers wished for something different. "When he argues about the woman question, he makes one wish that he would lay aside his facetiousness oftener," said one critic, expressing the puzzlement readers sometimes felt when faced with serious arguments mixed with light and highly coloured jibes that might or might not be intended as conveying a truth.

The question becomes even more complex when Leacock's personal life is placed beside his public statements. His wife, Beatrix, a well-educated woman who had contemplated a career, devoted herself after marriage mostly to domestic concerns. However, she did help him with his work: for instance, she and Marion Sandwell had selected the stories that went into the first edition of *Literary Lapses*, the foundation of his career as a humorist. Leacock's mother too was, by the standards of her age, a very well educated woman; because of her determination Leacock had received his own education, and he had received at least the rudiments of it, including some of his most formative reading, from the woman herself. Yet Leacock spoke of her as a hopeless teacher of her children, explaining that "she was only mother." Leacock's youngest sister, Dot (Rosamond), remained single for many years while she practised medicine, first in Calgary and then as a distinguished pathologist at Toronto's Hospital for Sick Children; by all accounts Leacock was very close to Dot, whom he chose as his son's godmother. He paid university tuition for his long-time secretary and niece, Barbara Nimmo (daughter of his sister Carrie), while she lived with him in Montreal, and then adopted Barbara into his household when his secretary, Grace Reynolds, left for further training. Although his own circle of professional and literary intimates admitted no women, he supported, at least on one occasion, a woman faculty member. Maude Grant, warden of the Royal College of Victoria, was fighting a proposal from Sir Edward Beatty to divert the college's endowment to other uses. Leacock upheld Grant's cause, although his tone was patronizing; he approached Grant and told her, "I won't let them do anything bad to you, dear." Leacock's correspondence shows that he enthusiastically recommended at least one of his female students for admission to graduate studies in economics at the University of Chicago.[6] Thus, he could make exceptions to his rule against education for women. But it seems that no amount of personal experience or concern for his own nearest and dearest ever swayed him from the conviction that society's development was being turned in a poor direction by allowing women to study on the university level for professions of their own choosing.

Women in his classroom annoyed him but prohibition made him furious; it rendered one of his favourite pastimes difficult because illegal. Prohibition was enacted in Canada as a conservation measure in the last years of the First World War, but when the war ended all the provinces kept the law on the books. Even before the war, many towns had voted to be "dry" in much the way Mariposa had done in *Sunshine Sketches*. Orillia had been a hard-drinking place in the boom time of the lumber camps, the little town possessing nineteen taverns, but by the late nineteenth century it had become a stronghold of temperance opinion; from the First World War until the 1960s, the lakeside beauty spot and gateway to the farther north was one of the driest jurisdictions in Ontario. In *Sunshine Sketches* Leacock depicted the temperance campaign there as a political trick to win votes; once the fictional election was over, his characters ignored the prohibition against alcohol, and eventually the law was dropped. The story shows his essential approach in his long fight against prohibition: since hypocrisy and political maneuvering lay behind any attempt to stop the sale of alcoholic beverages, he and all sensible citizens could refuse to accept the apparent judgment of society that drinking should be given up. In *Further Foolishness* he staged a "temperance peace conference" and in *Frenzied Fiction* presented a frightening vision of a dry Toronto: workers move with dreadful efficiency from homes to factories and back again, but beneath the surface the determination to drink succeeds despite the ban, as characters secretly import liquor from Quebec and sell it in special brokerage firms. In *The Hohenzollerns in America*, Leacock describes life in a postwar Germany beset by continuous revolutions. A principal German official, now ousted, is preparing with delight to return to his former job as a waiter in Toronto when Leacock reveals that in that city there is no more beer garden and no more beer. The official decides to stay in Germany and risk execution. There are worse things, he explains, than death.

Leacock's campaign continued unrelentingly in his humour collections through the time of his British tour and for the next twelve years. By 1927 all Canadian provinces except Prince Edward Island were selling alcoholic beverages in licensed stores, restaurants and taverns, but Leacock pressed the offensive until the prohibition amendment to the United States Constitution, passed in 1920, was repealed in 1933. In July 1919 he gave an account of the prohibition situation in North America, "The Warning of Prohibition in America," for England's *National Review*; this struck the British as a notable article, and a version of it was picked up in August by the London *Sunday Pictorial* as "The New Tyranny That Threatens Us: How Prohibition Became the Law in America — a Warning to Britain." On 2 April 1921 he gave a ringing Toronto lecture, "The Case Against

Prohibition," to the Citizens Liberty League, meeting in the Foresters' Hall on College Street to launch a campaign against the Ontario Temperance Act; this address, in which Leacock "Pour[ed] Imprecations on Prohibitionists and the O.T.A." and called the act an "Unjust Immoral Thing," was voluminously reported and quoted in five Toronto newspapers, other newspapers across the country, and the *Canadian Annual Review* for 1921, as well as being quoted and controverted in the *Christian Guardian*.[7] He promised to "write articles against prohibition at any time for any paper for nothing." The question also influenced his career as a lecturer, and not simply in the sense that he chose it as a frequent subject. In 1922, Charles Schwab, the president of Bethlehem Steel, invited him to speak at a dinner for Pennsylvania's two senators. Leacock discussed the invitation with Colonel Maclean but decided to turn it down. Maclean relayed his thinking to Schwab:

> It is utterly impossible for him to make an enter-
> taining, mirth-provoking after-dinner talk to a prohi-
> bition gathering. I know that he has refused to speak
> at any such gathering anywhere in Canada where
> they have prohibition. Personally, he is a violent anti-
> prohibitionist.[8]

His practice of carrying a flask of whiskey with him when he travelled led to at least two confrontations with United States customs officials. Once, he left his flask behind in his train compartment while visiting the club car. A customs officer found it and approached him to say that it would be confiscated, which Leacock declared he would not permit; he led the officer outside the train, where after emptying the flask he was allowed to keep it. On another occasion, when travelling to a lecture engagement in Buffalo, he was told by a border official that he could not enter the country with a flask of liquor. He thereupon telegraphed the lecture's sponsors, "No hooch. No spooch." It is not known what arrangements were made to resolve the crisis but Leacock kept his appointment.[9]

The fullest statement of his serious opposition to the prohibition movement had been delivered in his 1919 article "The Tyranny of Prohibition." The vehemence of its attack on religious groups associated with the movement drew an angry response from British clergymen in letters to the press; Leacock persisted, in *My Discovery of England*, in praising Great Britain's rejection of prohibition. In "The Tyranny of Prohibition" he attributed the movement to hypocrites, fanatics, political opportunists and big business. In later years, he added the charge, similar to today's complaints against "political correctness," that many people had feared to speak out against prohibition because the forces supporting it were attacking "the personal fortunes and political position of anyone who should dare to oppose them." Although he allowed that a handful of sincere individuals might believe that "they are doing the work of Christ on earth," he likened these to Torquemada and Philip II of Spain for the damage they did in the name of good intentions. But he attributed the chief power of the prohibition drive to "organized hypocrisy" practised by politicians who saw a cause that would win them votes, and to the unlimited dollars of business interests concerned to secure a docile work force. This he took so far as to claim that there was no basis in fact for the charge that drunkenness was damaging family lives and incomes. Instead he drew a picture of "a sober industrious working man" whose evening pipe and glass of ale turned his drudgery into a pleasant life for a brief moment; it was discrimination against the poor, Leacock said, to interdict this single pleasure.[10] He exhibited no awareness that the two sides of this argument are contradictory. If the picture of this meek labourer with his pathos-laden evening soporific is accurate, then there can be little sense in the contrasting picture of Machiavellian prohibition-mongering capitalists and politicians, with its implication that these figures see their interests threatened by a pot-valiant working class.

Then, too, Leacock pointed out, morality was used as an argument for prohibition but he did not need the law to tell him right and wrong. Statutes against murder or robbery were used to reinforce the social conscience of the community; those against drinking, on the contrary, left him torn between the law and his own convictions. He could not agree with the restrictions and would not obey them. He went out of his way to convey publicly that he was not abiding by prohibition laws. Once in 1919, when his Orillia farm truck was cited for lacking proper safety lights, he paid the fine but took the opportunity to note on the requisite form, which inquired, "Temperate or intemperate?" that "I drink every day." By Leacock's own testimony and that of many friends and colleagues, he drank regularly. Visiting friends were invariably greeted with the offer of a drink. To spare them any worry, he kept his bar well-stocked; as he remarked, the flow of liquor was never completely stopped. Pharmacists did a brisk business with prescriptions for alcoholic beverages throughout the most stringent period of regulation. Everyone — the rich, criminals, and ordinary citizens — found ways to get a supply. In a popular song of the period, a railway employee telephones a homeowner to tell him, "There's a box of books here for you, Bill, / And it's leakin' all over the station." Leacock, whose favourite tope was Scotch, continued throughout the prohibition period to make drinking a regular part of his social gatherings, club meetings and dinner parties. Stories abound, especially from McGill associates, of eccentric Leacock performances after drinking: the night he passed out Jehovah's Witnesses leaflets in the street; the night he unscrolled a roll of toilet paper, on which he claimed was written the lengthy extemporized free verse poem he chanted loudly; the night he supposedly called out from the bushes to ask a student for an arm home because he was having difficulty walking. It may be that these are apocrypha, manifold exaggerations from a few amusing but milder incidents, much like the hyperbolic tales of his incompetence as a sailor, which he himself helped to foster. For all the years of his drinking, there is not one recorded instance of an ugly scene, public nuisance, time lost from work or other signal difficulty associated with excessive drinking. Leacock himself commented, in "The Tyranny of Prohibition," that he knew judges, lawyers, professors, doctors, clergymen and many other professional people who drank, but this did not translate into drunken judges on the bench or professors coming incapacitated to class. He concluded that drinking did not lead inevitably to excess and was therefore a matter of private discretion.

The Toronto *World*'s 4 April 1921 headline on Leacock's address to the Citizens Liberty League, "Professor Leacock Opposed to Prohibition as a Matter of Principle,"[11] registers his claim that to him the issue was not personal. But was all his intense propaganda on the issues of prohibition and women's rights truly evoked by principle? These issues drew from him arguments whose extravagance and doubtful cogency weakened rather than strengthened his cause in a way that bespeaks psychological anguish. In *The Unsolved Riddle of Social Justice*, a very different-seeming Leacock had argued that society was obliged to provide able-bodied men and women with meaningful work or guaranteed financial support for the medical care and education of their children. In discussing issues like the debt Canada owed to its war veterans and the elimination of poverty, he could vehemently protest the plight of the working man who was forever cut off from the dignity and pleasures of life enjoyed by the rich. These broad economic and social views contrast vividly with his opinions on prohibition and women's rights. Writing on women's rights, he did not offer to champion women's search for meaningful, productive work; on the contrary, he urged women to be satisfied with domestic roles. Writing about prohibition, he presented a picture of the eternally downtrodden worker to whom society owes not comprehensive justice but the right to drink after work as the only solace for his serf-like status. In these two areas, Leacock seems to feel merely stung by appeals to his social conscience, in which he was in many respects distinguished and advanced. His unreasonable tenacity in argument shielded him from any thought that his views might be incorrect or at least might benefit from the addition of positive proposals to address the social imbalances that drove the issues. Why?

In a deeper way than he perhaps recognized, the issues of women's liberation and prohibition were indeed matters of principle to him, and further were linked to one another. His father represented a failure to accomplish the masculine role and enter the masculine world as these had existed in his day. Leacock had conquered what had unmanned his father; from the standpoint of his childhood passage into and through adolescence, his chief accomplishment had been the protection of himself and his family from his father, his supplanting of his father, and then his rescue of the family from ruin, the slide into the lower classes, which still threatened as an aftermath of his father's incompetence. In this, Leacock had been abetted by his mother, a strong woman who nevertheless accepted the traditional role of wife and mother, effacing herself in her contributions to her children and her partner, who as it turned out was finally not Peter but, by default and by the power of his will, her son Stephen. Leacock on his side had experienced a mother and a passel of sisters — surrogate daughters — threatened by paternal drunken weakness and perhaps violence; he had experienced the implicit condemnation of such a male that emanates from the helpless victimization and the consequent sense of a higher moral being of women in a threatened position such as the household of his childhood. It became essential to his identity that he should dominate his father's demon, indeed that he should toy with it repeatedly and come away unscathed, and that he should be honoured for this performance. And it was similarly important that acknowledgment should come from women who remained in their sphere, leaving unopened the disturbing possibility that the male accomplishment he had perilously achieved, at the cost of ousting his progenitor and first self-image, was a moral dilemma easily surpassed by, or nonexistent in, the other sex. In his joke about women's chauvinism as to their own sex in the area of politics, he could gingerly harken to the female quip that women in charge of government would mean no war, but then — as if briefly remembering and quickly dismissing a nightmare — he had to fly to aspersions on women's professional competence, and to praises of special feminine qualities which supposedly precluded operation in the sphere where he had fought, suffered, and survived.

Temperance and suffrage not only brought women into the public realm, but through their linkage these issues also brought the theme of the "moral superiority of woman" into politics. It is easy to forget that beginning in the second quarter of the nineteenth century and for more than a hundred years, temperance was an advanced social cause in large measure led by women, and that in early twentieth-century North America women secured the franchise largely through alliance with politicians who wanted their votes in support of prohibition. Leacock was not wrong in seeing this phenomenon as a movement to control and forcibly refine the male, implicitly thus characterized as crude and dangerous, by means of women-supported government initiatives. A further implication is the judgment that the method of offering males the general influence of civilization and morality for them to accept freely has been tried and has not worked. Leacock's accomplishment was implicitly demeaned, disregarded, and he was confronted by a company of what he could only consider jill-come-latelies, issuing advice and commands as if he had not already achieved their goals and at a cost they could not imagine; further, they were threatening to take away from him the dragon alcohol that he had tamed. The source of his unnoticed self-contradiction when portraying working men in "The Tyranny of Prohibition" can be here glimpsed. On the one hand Leacock had to assert the anarchic or self-willed freedom of the male, hence the picture of the government-capitalist alliance forcibly sobering its labourers; and on the other hand he had to assert that this freedom is already, and best, contained by the will of man himself, hence the picture of the industrious family man bringing home his pay from factory or mine and finding a tragical anodyne to self-imposed servitude in his one glass of beer in the parlor. The problem is of course that these two images, coherent from his own psychological standpoint, are completely incoherent on the social and political plane into which he projected them. So too with most of his efforts to express himself on women's rights and temperance; the closeness of these issues to great psychic stresses put them beyond his capacity to transmute life into art.

Leacock was heir to a Victorian tradition that had paid great honour to the special qualities of women and had prided itself on its wise and paternalistic care, keeping them in situations which supposedly were helpful to themselves and society, and protecting them from their limitations. The identity Leacock had forged for himself in the crucible of his adolescence had taken this pattern, and in turn Leacock had received from late nineteenth-century society significant reward in the social-political arena where adolescent accomplishments must be worked out to their adult expressions. As those Victorian social forms began to be criticized, judged inadequate, and dismantled, a pain rose in him which he never cured and never became entirely used to, for this social transformation was the macrocosmic rejection of what microcosmically he was.

In 1923, Leacock published *Over the Footlights*, which took its title from the book's centrepiece, a group of ten nonsense plays. His interest in popular drama and in satirizing it had been stimulated by the response of theatre people and audiences alike to "Behind the Beyond" and its English dramatization. His parody plays first appeared in *Harper's*, and were based on one of his lectures in Great Britain, "Drama as I See It"; just as the "Frenzied Fiction" lectures had done with the novel and story, this one skewered the stage, with illustrations of its follies in the form of Leacock's own satirical dramatic scenes. Negotiations for publication of *Over the Footlights* were complicated by his problems with his agents and with Dodd, Mead. Having been approached directly by several other publishers and periodical syndicates for his future work, he kept his options open by refusing to give Dodd, Mead the three-book contract it requested but did publish *Over the Footlights* with the firm. For all its mockery, the book indicates Leacock's growing interest in writing for the stage, which in the form of rights ownership questions became the source of friction between him and John Lane. Since the 1915 production of "Behind the Beyond," Leacock had been concerned to obtain the dramatic and movie rights to his work in contracts. This had been a point of contention between him and Lane's representatives during his meetings in London. Bodley Head editor B.W. Willett had represented to Leacock, as a point indicating both his expensiveness as an author and the benefits for him of remaining with the firm, that Lane had left these rights available to him and had even gone to the trouble, at a financial cost and with no return, of stopping illegal productions of "Behind the Beyond" in Australia and New Zealand.[12] The Bodley Head never did, however, play any effective role in bringing Leacock's work to the stage.

The ten *Over the Footlights* playlets are scripts with brief introductory remarks. There are many types: "Napoleon at Home" (historical drama), "Cast Up by the Sea" (love on a tiny Pacific island among victims of shipwreck), "Dead Men's Gold" (a western treasure hunt). A modern romance, "The Soul Call," is characterized as a "piffle play" in which well-to-do men and women "analyze themselves" as their souls outgrow their bodies. It is the sort of play, he wrote, that you hear about before you see it; its complex romantic quadrangle is the topic of heated argument at every social gathering. Should Lionel and Helga leave their spouses in pursuit of Bergsonian illusionism? He went on to make general asseverations on contemporary stage craft which, allowing for their lighter tone, were more or less identical to those W. B. Yeats expressed in a poem fifteen years later:

But actors lacking music
Do most excite my spleen,
They say it is more human
To shuffle, grunt and groan,
Not knowing what unearthly stuff
Rounds a mighty scene...

Leacock remarked that the craft of acting had so deteriorated that directors no longer looked for skill but were concerned only with appearance. "When they want a man to act as a butler, they don't advertise for actors — they advertise for butlers." The concept of theatre as a created illusion to entertain and instruct is replaced by "realistic" revelations of personal life, with the result that theatre patrons are no longer audiences but peeping Toms.

The twelve non-dramatic pieces that fill out *Over the Footlights* include some charming and memorable sketches, for example, "My Affair with My Landlord," "My Lost Dollar" and "Personal Experiments with the Black Bass." In "Roughing It in the Bush," Leacock begins by criticizing the outdoor pretensions of his friends and ends by narrating an expedition of his own with several companions, notably his brother George. Against the express preference of all the intrepid adventurers, George's luxurious automobile conveys them into the wilderness; George had wanted to pack in on burros, while Leacock had thought that perhaps a wild moose might be useful. Meals were taken at a local inn, and in general the men adapted splendidly to the rugged demands of the outdoors. Several sketches turn on the Leacock character's own quizzical befuddlement at some of the most popular advances of the time, such as the radio: "One more item has been added to the growing list of things I don't understand." The younger Leacock tilted in mainly impersonal, objective fashion at institutions that indifferently abused unwilling victims: boarding houses, banks and so on. His humour now presented a version of himself as a narrator who feels a sorrow laced with scorn that life is moving away from him. In "The Approach of the Comet," he laments that there is more information in the hands of normal people than they can possibly use; moreover, they don't understand it and aren't equipped to act on it. When a scientist informs him that a comet is on a collision course with earth, Leacock is thoroughly alarmed. Unable to interest the scientist in the humane question of mankind's survival after the event, he is reassured by another acquaintance, who explains that the collision will only be with the comet's tail. But alarm rises again when he hears a school-child ask his mother about the report, and she replies that the comet will destroy the world over the weekend and there is nothing to be done about it.

Over the Footlights was well received; a second book he published in 1923, College Days, gained and merited little critical attention. It was an assemblage of occasional verses written primarily for campus events at the University of Toronto and at McGill, genial occasions at which Leacock had presented remarks: graduations, retirements and others. The earliest piece is from 1902 and was written for a short-lived McGill publication; many date from the war years. Leacock said the book had "an uncommercial and ideal character" but with few exceptions the verses are too limited in reference and too slight to warrant reprinting. Perhaps Leacock believed in the quality of the work, or perhaps he simply thought it was appropriate to his life as a college professor and member of the university community that his writing for university occasions should be published. Leacock would return to the subject in a much more satisfying volume, Too Much College (1940), which is weighted with many serious topics — the teaching of psychology, the proper instruction of a foreign language, etc.

Lectures, the publication of two books, the accumulating royalties of his existing publications, and university salary all contributed to his income's reaching forty thousand dollars in 1923, its high water mark. Fan mail reinforced the message of his popularity, as did the appearance of the first book-length study of him as a writer, by Peter McArthur, who combined biography with a brief anthology of Leacock's works. He apparently enjoyed his fan mail, and although more letters to him than responses from him are preserved, testimony survives of the kindliness with which he regarded his readers. In 1920 he responded to a request for a piece of manuscript from a Mr. Saunders:

> For many years I have kept manuscripts with the feeling that sooner or later a request such as yours must come. I have at present about two barrelsful. The supply far exceeds the demand. It is with great pleasure I send you a "chunk" of my writing.

What he sent was five handwritten pages of the draft of an essay included in *College Days*, "English as She Is Taught at College," about the variation between English as taught in university classes and English as used by distinguished authors. Fan letters were filled with compliments, which were often phrased in terms intended to be facetious, in honour of the author's style. A young girl from Cape Breton Island sent Leacock a watch case she had made, embroidered with a blue flower and green, yellow and pink edging, which is still preserved in his files in Old Brewery Bay; she thanked him for "a pretty Novel which I Sure Enjoyed Reading." Another fan who addressed him by letter was explorer Vilhjalmur Stefansson, who called himself "an extravagant admirer of your humorous writings." Stefansson thanked Leacock for saying "pleasant things about my work."[13]

Peter McArthur's book *Stephen Leacock* (1923) reprinted a choice selection of Leacock's work and offered a biographical sketch and a critical appraisal. The biography is not detailed; McArthur admitted that he had limited his investigations largely to what Leacock had written about his early life. McArthur recalled that

University of Toronto students had appreciated Leacock's wit long before it was widely published; but he did not mention that he had been the editor at the New York magazine *Truth* responsible for its publishing many of Leacock's pieces that had formed the core of *Literary Lapses* in 1910. McArthur claimed little personal acquaintance with Leacock, saying that he had only been introduced to him once while Leacock was playing billiards. The distance between the two Ontario humorists may be explained by McArthur's having adopted, in 1908, just when Leacock was moving toward prominence, a retired life at his rural childhood home near Appin, from which he published his own humour, largely in Toronto newspapers, becoming known as "the Sage of Ekfrid."

In McArthur's view, Leacock was a humorist rather than a satirist; he lacked the fierce and unrelenting nature of the best social critics, and he also seemed less interested in solving problems than in analyzing them. But McArthur denied that the master was a "trifler" because of his humour, which was a rare and precious form of literary genius. Touching only lightly on themes of the work, and then in terms of the man who presumably lay behind it, McArthur said, "Possibly he finds forgetfulness himself in his outbursts of fun-making." He did not explain precisely what he thought motivated Leacock's putative search for forgetfulness; possibly he was referring to the undertone of sadness evident in some of the writings, such as the introduction to *Sunshine Sketches*, with its account of Leacock's childhood years, and the clear sense of loss and nostalgia in the book's tone. Or he may also have been thinking of Leacock's confrontation with the features of society he found deeply objectionable — the sense of weariness, of having been put aside by a world going wrong, that can be found in Leacock, as opposed to the satirist's icy self-confident anger and passion for correction. McArthur wondered if Leacock's popularity was hurting his writing, spurring him to produce too fast for "the publishers, syndicate managers and directors of lecture bureaus."[14] He disapproved of *Winsome Winnie*, a second volume of nonsense novels, seeing it as evidence that Leacock was pressured to produce more of his most popular kinds of work rather than develop and explore his potential; in this disapproval, he goes against the common critical praise of the book as one of Leacock's most fully successful. Thus McArthur became another voice who raised — probably just because by now it was becoming familiar — the question whether Leacock's popularity was a deleterious influence on his writing.

In the critical cavils that were directed at his work during the 1920s, those associated with popularity — that it seduced him, or that he wrote too quickly in order to exploit it — were often linked with the idea that he was out of touch with the mass audience, whether because he was an intellectual, or a cynical philosopher who actually scorned the common man behind his affable mask, or a cranky and backward conservative, or because he was a Canadian, not sufficiently in tune anymore with the situations either of Great Britain or the United States. When in his 1916 essay for the *New Republic*, "O. Henry and his Critics," Leacock had defended that author and, by implication, himself against critics who judged by the hastiest and worst work rather than appreciating the best, he had been answered in suggestive terms by the distinguished American critic William Trowbridge Larned. O. Henry had indeed been seduced to write too perfunctorily in his last years, Leacock's essay had granted, by promises of the first real financial success he had known, but this did not remove the value of most of his work, which was best proved by his popularity with the general public. Larned, responding in a later issue of the magazine, questioned judgment by popularity: "The plain people have come to be a pest." He wrote that popularity had been known to ruin an author, and continued, "As an old and fervent admirer of Stephen Leacock's humour long before the plain people and the plain people's editors found him out, I can only hope that he will never become really popular with us." Finally, Larned had questioned Leacock's ability to understand the flow of critical opinion in the United States, which tended to raise up idols and then destroy them quickly; he suggested that Leacock's Canadian background might make it impossible for him to understand the United States.[15] In other words, he was warping his genius to gratify a fickle audience which he could never comprehend or secure, at least not permanently.

Larned may be seen as a sympathetic, sensitive and honest commentator who tried gently to nudge Leacock toward the realization that in fact his attitudes and subject matter were high brow and his true popularity among a rather select, erudite, and ironically inclined readership, one which could negotiate the literary, historical, and philosophical foundations of many of his jests and of his humour in general. Leacock was not in fact what is commonly called a "popular" author, not even in terms of the magnitude of his sales, despite his canny Mark Twain-like use of the device of identification with a mythical common man. However, Leacock was unwilling to let go of the idea of his mass appeal, or at least to let go of his desire to exploit it in order to bolster his finances and his favourite causes. His 1924 collection, *The Garden of Folly*, was widely reviewed and those negative comments that it received showed the way in which certain complaints were now becoming usual, such as the idea that he was repeating and thinning his formulae: "Now and again one would like to weep at the spectacle of his dragging humour around by the scruff of the neck."[16] Just as Larned had predicted eight years earlier, British reviewers too now wished for something more suited to their audiences. As for his inclusion of opinions and profundities, the brief remarks on humour that opened the book were often dismissed as the sort of sententious nullities that characterized many humorists' theories of their art.

The Garden of Folly contains some fresh and charming pieces: a series of romances delivered in the style of advertisements, for example, and an investigation into the historical importance of beards. But the principal articles are indeed too long and too thin. The book presents a section of "Letters to the New Rulers of the

World," including ones "To a Prohibitionist" and "To a Spiritualist" in which Leacock hits predictably at favourite targets. The first of the letters, to the League of Nations, attempts to use humour to express his political and social ideas. On behalf of a small town, Leacock congratulates the League — ironically, it hardly needs to be said — on its many important diplomatic successes, and then requests some practical help on problems faced by the town. In this way he mocked the hope and possibility that the League could deal with the international situation in a way that would have any real beneficial effect within Canada and for Canadians — or within any particular country, for that matter. His own belief, of course, was that in world affairs Canada should act through the British Empire, and this, rather than verbal demolition of an obviously impotent body, was the underlying point. Here too the ideas he sought to promote by stretching his humour seemed out of step. He could not expect his sarcasm at the League's expense to prompt strong pro-Empire action from the Canadian government of the day under Liberal Prime Minister Mackenzie King, or from the populace which had put it in office. The Liberals, elected in 1920, would remain in power, with one major interruption, until the end of the Second World War. King showed little interest in following up the initiatives of Conservative Prime Minister Robert Borden and his successor, Arthur Meighen, to strengthen Canada's independent role within the changing imperial community as it had begun to develop during the First World War. But King was not concerned, either, with demonstrating a nonimperial international role in the League of Nations or anywhere else. His government concentrated instead on Canada's internal economic problems and led the country into partnership with the United States, whose growing investments in Canada during the 1920s helped bring a gradual improvement from the post-war depression. Leacock was now a rather forlorn voice on behalf of strong imperial ties.

At the midpoint of the 1920s, Leacock found himself beset with worries that his career would be difficult to sustain, and overburdened by the combined demands of humour writing, questions of politics and economics, his academic work, and his campaign against prohibition. Despite a growing drumbeat of criticism against slight and repetitive humour, too laden with political commitments and backward ideas, he showed no willingness to purify his humorous writing, or limit his expression of political views to appropriate vehicles while seeking for some of them a more nuanced, rhetorically powerful form. It seemed he had reached a crisis of adaptation; his behaviours no longer suited some aspects of his changing environment yet he was unable to wish to change them. The second half of the decade did not solve these problems but rather trumped them with others far direr.

Family Sorrows

During the 1924-25 school year, Leacock resumed intense activity as a humorous lecturer. Since returning from England, he had made sporadic sallies into nearby areas of the United States; he went often to New England, New York, Pennsylvania and Ohio, states particularly rich in colleges and universities, which provided many of his engagements, and occasionally he had ventured as far afield as Iowa and North Carolina. By 1924 his customary fee had increased to five hundred dollars; with the help of his agent Paul Reynolds he organized two extensive though condensed tours in the United States and other brief trips. The first of the tours, a foray into the American south, probably originated in part with associations he had formed at the University of Richmond, Virginia, where on 2-6 April 1923 he had presented four lectures on successive days detailing "The Evolution of Democracy," from the origins of the concept, through the French and American revolutions and the nineteenth-century era of "laissez-faire," to the democracies of the 1920s.[1] His fall 1924 southern expedition occurred in September and took him first to Virginia, with three lectures at the university in Richmond and two engagements at Roanoke, and then to Rock Hill and Charlotte, North Carolina, Atlanta, Georgia, and Johnson City, Tennessee. His notes in planning the trip show that to inaugurate it he chose the topic "Charles Dickens" but that for the most part he used humorous lectures on "The Wreck of My Education," "The Lighter Side of Literature" (i.e., one of the "Frenzied Fiction" talks) and "What I Don't Know About the Drama."

In Richmond, Leacock was interviewed by John Archer Carter, a reporter for the Richmond *News-Leader*, who many years later published an account that illustrates the humorist's reserve towards the press, and his continued attempts, as in England, to control its presentation of him, including a disarming ability to forget, seemingly, his own rules. Having asked for an interview, Carter went to the Hotel Jefferson, where he was greeted by a man who did not correspond to his idea of a humorist, a "big man, with a large, longish face and a mass of greying hair parted on the side," who looked like a "mortician or chief mourner." Leacock handed the reporter five sheets of hotel stationery covered with handwriting. It was the interview, he explained, written while he had been waiting. It ran:

> Professor Stephen Leacock, of Montreal, head of the Department of Economics at McGill University, who is lecturing this week at the University of Richmond, had a brief chat this morning with a representative of this journal.
>
> Dr. Leacock spoke in his characteristically humorous vein of his increasing difficulty in being interviewed by the press. "I have grown to have so many friends," he said, "in so many places and of such different ways of thinking that I can't say anything at all without losing some of them. For example, I hold very strong views on the Volstead Act, but I daren't say what they are. I'd like to tell you how beautifully the Quebec system of government

control works, but I mustn't. I have strong views on Evolution and Fundamentalism. In fact I truly believe that all adherents of one side are soft in the head, but I won't say which. I either think that Mussolini is the hope of the world or the death knell of democracy. People who fly across the Atlantic are either damn fools or heroes. In fact, all my opinions are too violent for friendly intercourse.

"But I am here on a mission which fortunately is not controversial at all. I am giving three lectures out at the university on the relation of the great humorists of the world to social progress. The lectures are to deal with Charles Dickens and Mark Twain, and O. Henry, with a hint here and there on the side that I am doing a little good myself. That's why I don't want to give an interview. Good-bye."[2]

When Carter asked to step into the hotel to read the "interview," Leacock agreed and they were soon talking convivially. Leacock readily allowed Carter to use a few items of their conversation as the basis of a story to satisfy his editor. One of the anecdotes that interested Carter concerned Leacock's efforts to collect O. Henry manuscripts. An advertisement announcing that he was collecting unpublished material for a possible future edition and would pay for any he used, had brought him an unexpected flood of stories, many of them, to his disgust, obvious frauds. He confessed to Carter that he had angrily told one lady the story she had submitted had been written by O. Henry "after his brain had been removed." Carter received his interview, but Leacock had entirely controlled their meeting, which had thus remained a discussion of his professional rather than his personal life, and he had made sure that even a newspaper story about an appearance on the popular lecture stage referred to his philosophical interests and scholarly credentials.

During the 1920s, in *Winnowed Wisdom* (1926) and *Short Circuits* (1928), he continued to broaden his criticism of interviewing techniques. It wasn't only being interviewed that bothered him; he didn't like reading interviews very much, either. The essays "International Amenities" and "New Lights from New Minds" (*Winnowed Wisdom*) question the value of reporters' eager attempts to manufacture news out of the impressions provided by visiting celebrities. In the first, Leacock concocts an international incident out of the way in which press reports prompt escalating insults from American visitors about Great Britain and British visitors about America; with tongue-in-cheek self-reflexivity, he draws the idiotic mischaracterizations of each country by the other from his own account, in his lecture to the McGill women, of the differences between American and British students. In "New Lights from New Minds," he suggests that the whole boring interview process would be brightened up if celebrities commented on fields other than their own: industrialists could assess universities, sports stars could judge architecture and so on. This proposal for a supposedly new type of celebrity journalism represents, of course, Leacock's opinion of the form as it exists and the value of the "expert" responses it elicits. One of the sketches in the group called "Save Me from My Friends" in *Short Circuits* presents an exasperating encounter between Leacock the visiting lecturer and a reporter assigned to cover his speech but who had failed to be there. He catches up with Leacock at the station as the train is about to leave and breathlessly asks him for a quick summary. With a few leading questions, the reporter is able to provide extensive coverage of Leacock's address under the headline, "Thinks Aldermen Pack of Bums." All of these stories and essays are pointed exaggerations that express Leacock's criticism of the modern press as he saw it from his social critic's standpoint and as he experienced it in his role as a public figure. His analysis of the press roughly parallels his view of the drama — not surprisingly so, because both critiques spring from the same principles. As the drama is in essence a serious examination of life now being demeaned to voyeuristic representations, so too the press is a foundational element of a free democratic society being polluted with pointless sensationalism. To his frustration, Leacock continued to experience eager press curiosity about his personal life, which he refused to indulge, and continued to battle the press's tendency to portray him as a mere funny man, making even his intellectual accomplishments simply part of the by now tiresome joke that he was a humorist who was also an economist. He found that entering into the public spotlight meant being tagged with characterizations that one could not control or shake off; the definitions of one's work, one's worth, even one's personality, were in the hands of others. Characteristically, however, he would not accept being defined; this problem would preoccupy him throughout the 1920s and especially during the 1930s. He tried to contradict the facile portrait of himself that he often saw painted, and the easy dismissal of his views, with a new insistence upon the value of his economic and political thought and an ever increasing emphasis on his philosophy of the civilizing nature of humour — the idea, in other words, that even his humour itself was underlyingly serious and philosophical.

His final lecture in the south was in the last week of September and by 9 October he was off again on his second extensive tour, a six-day swing through New York and Massachusetts that took him to Potsdam, Syracuse, Cortland, Cooperstown, Utica, Troy, the Washington Irving School in New York City, Smith College in Northampton, and Buffalo, to conclude with separate addresses to two organizations in Rochester on 15 November. One of his standard talks at this time was a "Frenzied Fiction" lecture called "Heroines in Literature," and a member of the audience at Smith College later recalled Leacock's description of one western heroine whose cowboy protector chivalrously left her in the tent and went out to sleep on the cactus.[3] Mockery of the fatuous portrayal of women in popular novelistic and dramatic heroines had always, of course, been a staple of his humour, but it became explicit as a theme of literary and social satire with sketches from *Over the Footlights*, including "Abolishing the Heroine"; the material used in his lectures was similar to that which appeared in published essays of the 1920s such as "Hunt for a Heroine" in *Short Circuits*. His lecture notes and titles from this period indicate that he was using material developed for his British tour and earlier but at the same time was discovering fresh perspectives on his traditional themes; his files show that, as crowded as these trips were, he was working during them to perfect new outlines and passages. Thoughts on his old subject of the ridiculous heroine became grist for future essays on the subject; lectures on Mark Twain and Charles Dickens served as germs of the biographical-critical studies of those authors that he would later write, expressing not only admiration and insight but, obliquely, his own self-image and self-defense.

Leacock was out lecturing again within a month, travelling in mid-December to New England for humorous lectures at Danbury, Connecticut, and Springfield and Westfield, Massachusetts; during December he also gave three serious lectures in Montreal, on "The Place of Letters in National Life," "The Canadian Economy," and the value of the classics in a sound general education.[4] Once his frenetic autumn had concluded with his final Montreal lecture, on 17 December, he took Beatrix and Stevie to Nassau, Bahamas; he hoped the trip would help Beatrix, who had been ill for more than a month. Even on this holiday, however, he continued to make news, give his opinions, and lecture. The Leacocks embarked from New York on 19 December, and the following day the *New York Times*, under the headline "Professor Leacock Sails: Canadian Writer Resents Rule Regarding Income Tax Proof for Voyagers," quoted Leacock's arguments against the regulation that had required him to prove he had earned no income in the U.S. before departure. Then on 30 December, in Nassau, he found the opportunity to present one of his "Frenzied Fiction" talks.[5]

At this time, nothing dire was suspected of Beatrix's condition; the trip's chief purpose, in fact, was to give Stevie a change of climate, and when Leacock returned to Montreal for the beginning of classes after the Christmas-New Year's hiatus, he left mother and son at Nassau to spend the winter months. When in the spring of 1925 Beatrix arrived in Montreal, she was feeling poorly enough to give up her customary round of university and social functions, but her condition was still not considered so serious as to require medical attention. The family spent the summer of 1925 in Orillia as usual, hoping that this change of air and activities would improve her health. During the fall, however, she went to her doctor in Montreal accompanied by one of her closest friends, Mrs. H.T. (Fitz) Shaw. In consultation with a visiting specialist, Blair Bell of Liverpool, the doctor diagnosed her condition as breast cancer. Bell came into the case because he was known to Leacock through a friend, a former McGill professor of pathology, Doctor George Adami, who had been appointed vice-chancellor of Liverpool University in 1919; in response to Leacock's questions about cancer therapies, Adami had written that Bell's new lead treatment was achieving good results. Beatrix's disease was taken by the doctors to have sprung from a severe blow from a golf ball that had hit her during the summer of 1924 in Orillia. When an operation failed to improve her condition, it was pronounced untreatable. During the fall 1925 academic term, Leacock was frequently absent from classes, visiting Beatrix daily in Ross Memorial Hospital. Refusing to admit that her case was hopeless, he decided to take her to England, to Doctor Bell, although Bell did not think her cancer could be reversed. Elizabeth Kimball, Leacock's niece, records that Beatrix did not want to go to England but preferred to accept the findings of her Montreal doctors. Nevertheless, Leacock arranged the trip, with help from his friend Sir Edward Beatty, chancellor of McGill and president of the Canadian Pacific Railway, who arranged to have a Canadian Pacific ship, scheduled to leave just two days after Leacock made his request, outfitted with a private infirmary and a staff of two nurses. Leacock and Beatrix, accompanied by Stevie and Beatrix's mother, Mrs. Kate Hamilton, sailed to Liverpool, where

Beatrix was admitted to Doctor Bell's private hospital. But she was never strong enough to begin treatments. She died on 15 December 1925, only a few months after the first diagnosis of her condition. Among the many messages of sympathy that arrived in Liverpool was a telegram from McGill principal Sir Arthur Currie, "Courage, Stephen, we are all with you."[6]

After a memorial service at Saint Luke's Church, Liverpool, conducted by Doctor Adami's father-in-law, the body was cremated and taken back to Canada where, on 31 December, the ashes were buried in Toronto's Saint James Cemetery. The burial thus took place the day after Leacock's fifty-sixth birthday; Beatrix had been forty-five at the time of her death. Leacock intended to move his wife's remains to the Leacock burial plot at Saint George's Church near Sutton, but the change was never made. He returned to his classroom early in 1926, but it took almost two years before he reestablished the routine of work and amusements he had followed since Beatrix had helped him to publish *Literary Lapses* in 1910. There was no book in 1925, and *Winnowed Wisdom*, which appeared in 1926, drew largely on material written for magazines before his wife's illness had been recognized. When he did produce a new collection, *Short Circuits*, in 1928, its themes were a determined opposition to contemporary society and a strong nostalgia for the past. Late in life, he wrote that husbands who adored their wives proved it by ignoring them, showing temper, and discovering too late how much they wished to express their love.[7] It has been suggested that this conceals Leacock's own regret. What neglect on Leacock's part, if any, can be inferred from the scant evidence now available of the couple's private and nuptial life? Kimball is the only witness to refer to Leacock as being drawn to other women during his marriage, and she writes merely that Beatrix "forgave him readily for his occasional philanderings."[8] No definition or example is given of what type of unfaithfulness, if any, had been involved. The most that other witnesses to the marriage say is that Beatrix seemed content to remain in a sphere of activities separate from her husband's, as a sportswoman, clubwoman, and chatelaine, and that she may have felt somewhat left behind as Leacock's success brought more and more distinguished visitors to her Montreal table and to the guest rooms at Old Brewery Bay. On the other hand, there is no evidence to contradict the notion of Leacock as a careless, perhaps neglectful husband, whose self-absorption required a corresponding selflessness of his wife. He dedicated himself first to his career, or careers, and this required relentless energy channeled into a strictly observed schedule that must have accounted for twenty-four hours of the day during the academic year. Of course, a small portion of this time and a large portion of the summers were set aside specifically for socializing and relaxation; even in such zones, however, Leacock was sometimes focused on his image and his act, and was never forgetful of the famous routines that could leave Beatrix alone after 10 p.m. to shepherd a party he had organized so that he himself could retire in order to rise and be writing by five in the morning.

Family photographs are one indication that Beatrix relished her life and that her relationship with her husband was easy and equal. Pictures abound of Beatrix as a smiling part of social gatherings, outings on the lake and quiet meals with her family. Photos show her with Leacock, holding the new infant, sitting on benches on the crowded porch of the "cook house," and driving with the baby Stevie in a pony cart. Professor William Caldwell wrote of her smooth management of the busy Old Brewery Bay household, with its constant flow of celebrities, local friends and family. Nor was she absent from the scenes of Leacock's professional life, whether helping to create the original version of *Literary Lapses* or accompanying Leacock during the Rhodes tour in 1907 and during the British lecture tour in 1921. Leacock's secretary, Grace Reynolds, tells of packing Beatrix's evening gowns for the hopeless 1925 voyage to Liverpool; Leacock said his wife would need them when he took her to the Riviera to recuperate after her treatment.[9] But there are very few existing or available documents, such as the letter announcing

Stevie's birth and Agnes Leacock's diary entry of the event, that testify to Leacock's warmth of feeling for Beatrix and for the family he was building with her. Adding these indications together, the likely inference is that Leacock and Beatrix mutually agreed, though perhaps without the explicit communication often recommended today, on a form of relationship governed by nineteenth-century ideas of the distinctive qualities and roles of the sexes, and held each other in respect and affection within such a framework. The style of marriage Leacock preached is not to contemporary tastes, but his reverence for the woman's role as wife and mother, a centre of moral values through her influence in the family, is also a praise of the role Beatrix filled in his life. Both Leacock and Beatrix were children of marriages that had failed. Both had experienced weak fathers who had shrunk from or been defeated by the demands of the masculine role. Both clung to the family ties, friends, and social circles that had been theirs as adolescents and young adults, when they had begun to forge their own identities; they had found one another within that social world, and they worked throughout their lives to maintain it. Beatrix had risked much to marry Leacock when he was an aspiring student economist, but her marriage ultimately turned out to demand of her only one major sacrifice: she could not pursue an independent career. Everything else that had composed her life before the wedding — amateur theatricals, charitable work, sports and social gatherings among large circles of well-to-do friends and family — remained her province throughout her married life. Although his frequent meetings with celebrities are well documented, Leacock spent most of his time by choice with his close neighbours, his relatives and the families of professional associates. Beatrix, with her prominent Toronto family background, was as comfortable in such society as her husband, or more so, and this social talent and experience was a part of what she contributed to their union.

One sorrow they had shared, and which would now remain to afflict Leacock alone for the remainder of his life, was the physical abnormality of their son. Within his first few years, they had become concerned about his uncertain health and especially about his slow rate of growth. Kimball reported him as a delicate child who already wore glasses from the age of two or three. Increasingly concerned about Stevie's physical problems, Leacock consulted friends at the McGill Medical School and selected a thirty-six-year-old specialist, Doctor Alton Goldbloom. No precise diagnosis is given in Goldbloom's published account of the case, although it is clear that Stevie's condition involved very slow growth. Letters to Goldbloom from Leacock refer to the father's fears on this score and his hopes for Goldbloom's treatment: "I think he's growing. But I hate to measure him." Goldbloom, however, did measure him; in 1927, Stevie, at twelve, was three feet nine inches tall and weighed forty-four pounds seven ounces. In a later letter, Leacock wrote, "You will be very much pleased to learn that Stevie at last shows a definite and apparently rapid growth," and the doctor records his own opinion that his treatment had been successful. Perhaps both these views are in part correct but they seem in some respects to be wishful thinking; Stevie never reached five feet tall. Goldbloom's claim of success actually suggests, in fact, that he had feared the child might die, and Leacock once introduced the pediatrician to Agnes as "the most fortunate doctor in the world — his patients live."[10] Care for his son never ceased to be an absorbing worry for Leacock. Convinced of the need to provide him with financial support, despite Stevie's excellent school performance, Leacock used much of his earnings to establish a large trust fund. This preoccupation probably accounts for at least some of the projects he undertook for high fees towards the end of his life.

In The *Garden of Folly*, Leacock had included a laudatory character sketch of an Ontario physician he had known in childhood, Doctor Charles Thompson Noble, whom he admired greatly for his expertise and compassionate care. But in many of his books, Leacock satirized modern medicine. Sometimes his target was the public's garbled and gullible pretensions to knowledge, as when his narrator mocked at the pseudoscientific pronouncements of acquaintances who proposed to treat themselves with "nitrogen" and "potash" for reasons they felt were informed but that in fact were nonsense. Sometimes he satirized the medical scientist or professional practitioner who lacked Noble's insightful support of the whole person and instead offered his patients complex, incomprehensible formulas of doubtful merit. On the basis of his writings alone, Leacock might have been judged a skeptic on the value of modern medicine, but his care for his wife and son shows a different side of his mind. Eager for a scientific miracle, he demanded of medical science more than he allowed others to believe it might provide; the skeptic and the spirit of hope existed in him, painfully, side by side, and he was eager to believe where he could not. Doctor Goldbloom saw in Leacock a mixture of "sheer brilliance intermingled with naiveté and medical credulity."[11] Just as Leacock searched beyond Montreal for help for Beatrix, he persisted in consulting other physicians about his son even after engaging Goldbloom, casting about for treatments that seemed feasible or at least possible. In Liverpool he visited a noted pediatrician, and he made a special trip to New York to meet a specialist in endocrinology. His wife's death led him to donate a thousand dollars to the McGill Medical School; the money was to be used to establish the lead cancer treatment. He later offered to match, dollar for dollar, any funds raised for cancer research by McGill. For many years, he made speeches to raise money for cancer research and frequently introduced the cause into other speaking engagements. At a luncheon of the New York Cancer Committee, he once proposed the death penalty for anyone proved to be tricking people with fraudulent treatments for the disease: an oblique, enraged recognition of his own vulnerability.

For two summers after Beatrix's death, Leacock did not reside at Old Brewery Bay. In 1926, he accepted an invitation from René du Roure to stay in Montreal, where du Roure operated a French summer school. Leacock did not prepare a book for publication in

1927. That year, concern for Stevie's health led Goldbloom to suggest a trip, and Leacock made plans to travel to the French resort, Biarritz, for the summer months, in company with family friends, the Shaws. H.T. Shaw was a Montreal businessman; his wife, Fitz, was the friend of Beatrix who had accompanied her to the doctor in 1925. They brought along their daughter, Peggy, and her governess, who was to care for Stevie also. The final member of the party was Grace Reynolds, the young secretary whom Leacock had hired in 1924 and whom he would invite in 1926 to move into the house to help also in Stevie's care and in household management. The group arrived in London early in May. Unlike his other visits to London, this trip was strictly for pleasure. Apart from contributing an article, "On Literature," to the *London Times* and making a brief visit to his publisher, Leacock spent his time with Stevie, the Shaws and Grace Reynolds; they visited tourist attractions and devoted evenings to the theatre. The trip to Biarritz also included a stop in Paris and a visit to northern Spain. The vacation signalled the importance of his friendship with the Shaws, especially Fitz Shaw, who remained close to him until his death. In his will, he left her five hundred books from his library and the copyright of his autobiography. The precise nature of their connection is not known. Fitz Shaw separated from her husband and was frequently in Leacock's company both in Montreal and in Orillia, where she had a house very near his and connected with it by a path; during his final illness in 1944, Fitz took a room in Toronto near his hospital to be able to visit him daily. No secret was made of their friendship. Fitz dined with Leacock in Montreal, including at the University Club, and she was present at many parties and dinners at Old Brewery Bay. She sometimes accompanied him on visits to his mother at Sutton. There was a rumour in Orillia that Leacock was having an affair, although an anecdote about the gossip shows that perhaps many people thought Fitz Shaw was not the other party involved. Leacock received a telegram that said, "I will be with you tonight. René." Talk soon filled the town that the name of Leacock's lover had been revealed as René. The telegram was of course from René du Roure.[12] No evidence or testimony exists to confirm or disprove the existence of a physical relationship between Leacock and Fitz. On his return from Biarritz, he arranged with his sister Carrie that her daughter, Barbara Ulrichsen, should come to stay with him in Montreal; Barbara would replace Grace Reynolds, who was leaving to attend university. Leacock offered to provide Barbara with college tuition at McGill and general financial support if she would work as his secretary and manage the household. Ultimately she became his indispensable assistant, doing research, preparing manuscripts and conducting business. As mistress of his household, she packed his flask when he was lecturing, provided female dinner companions for the bachelor professors of the department of economics and political science when they visited, and sorted his correspondence. After his death, she helped prepare the book *Last Leaves*, which contains her illuminating memoir of his final years. Leacock chose to retain in his home a family atmosphere, and he chose someone from his family to help achieve it.

During the fall of 1927, he was also arranging another piece of family business, the construction of the new house in Orillia, which he had planned with Beatrix in the early 1920s. His architect, Kenneth Noxon, accomplished the work during the summer of 1928 and by 1 September, Leacock was writing to thank him warmly for the nine-teen-room house, which he said would be a joy to him until the end of his life;[13] it was accurately described at the time of its construction as possessing the "long lines and steep roof of French Canadian domestic architecture." It was built on a rise about one hundred yards from the shore of Lake Couchiching. thus standing farther away from the water's edge than did the original house and providing a better view of the lake. A porch ran nearly the full length of the front, and at the back an enclosed sun porch looked out on a garden. The house included living room, dining room, guest bedrooms and a basement billiard room; Leacock's bedroom and study were in a separate wing, at the east end of the ground floor near the library. Fireplaces in the principal rooms and the bedrooms were the primary source of heat. (Although the family came to Orillia for the Christmas holidays, Leacock found the new house uncomfortable the only winter he attempted to spend there.) Before construction began, Leacock had attempted to buy adjoining property to construct a trout stream, but when this fell through, he leased a stream in Oro Township, south of Orillia, and stocked it with trout at a cost of fifteen thousand dollars. A tennis court was built on the grounds, and the garden contains a sundial with two inscriptions: "Grow old along with me! The best is yet to be" (Browning) and "Brevas Horas — Longos Annos," Leacock's own ambiguous coinage, mixing hope and sorrow. It is not extravagant to suppose that the two inscriptions together express the absence of Beatrix and the defeat of Leacock's hope to build this house for her and live in it with her.

After Beatrix's death, home life revolved around Stevie; Leacock devoted many hours to his deeply loved son. A sense of the latitude he was given comes from an anecdote told by a student who had come in the evening to Leacock's Montreal house to consult with the professor. The student was distracted from his work by Stevie, who was firing a pea-shooter at him from the doorway of his father's study. Leacock calmly asked his son to leave, which Stevie did, only to return a few minutes later. The scene was repeated several times, until at last Leacock suggested that the boy go downstairs into the hallway, where another student was waiting, and fire at him until it was his turn to come up to read. Stevie obeyed immediately. Life in Orillia, too, was organized in large measure for the boy's amusement. Elizabeth Kimball writes of being called to Old Brewery Bay, along with other cousins spending the summer in the area, to play with Stevie. One memorable occasion was a birthday party for him. Leacock determined to hold the party on an unoccupied farm owned by his brother Charlie, where, according to Kimball, the hot August weather combined with the desolate landscape to make an unpleasant

The Old Brewery Bay Players in Red Riding Hood Up-to-Date, 14 August, 1929. Left to right, front row: Stevie as Lord Wolf, Peggy Shaw as Riding Hood. Left to right, back row: Virginia Smithers as Clarissa, Margot Castillon as Lady Hood, René du Roure, director, Jeddie Steward as The Dowager Lady Hood, David Ulrichsen as Gaffer Gammon, Barbara Stephens as Jane.

Courtesy National Archives of Canada C-33109.

day for her, but father and son appeared satisfied with the gathering. Stevie was a prominent player in the Leacock-engineered amateur theatricals popular at Old Brewery Bay. A playbill from New Year's Eve, 1929, announced the production, "Beauty and the Boss, or, The Sorrows of a Stenographer." The character of Mr. Jack Jackal, "He eats Stenographers," was played by Master Stevie Leacock. Other cast members included Peggie Shaw and children from many prominent Orillia families, including some whose members had been models for characters in *Sunshine Sketches*; for instance, two Tudhope daughters, whose industrialist father was the chief Liberal party supporter in Orillia, were among the "bevy of stenographinettes" seeking employment in the production, which was managed by Captain René du Roure. The playbill noted that guests were to come by sleigh because cars would not be able to negotiate the road from town. A sleigh service had been arranged through Anderson's Livery in Orillia.[14]

Many of the surviving stories of Leacock at McGill also date from the 1920s. A woman student in his 1925 class regretted that Beatrix's illness had kept him away so often, but admired the way he required students to follow up questions raised in class with independent library work, on which he invariably remembered to ask for a report. Some students valued Leacock's capacity in economics or political science less than the "humanity" he conveyed in his lessons. Leacock argued forcefully for his own conservative views ("And he, before Winston Churchill, saved the British Empire every Monday, Wednesday, and Friday at three o'clock in Room 20," according to colleague John Culliton) but he was sometimes cavalier in his treatment of campus regulations. Impatient with the rule that he must take attendance, he devised many techniques to avoid marking anyone absent. He sometimes delayed attendance taking until every student was present, no matter how late in the hour this occurred; on another occasion, he called a student's name repeatedly without answer and finally asked if the boy had any friends, inviting anyone to respond for him. Leacock's academic gown was legendary. He seems to have worn the same one throughout his entire career, although it gradually degenerated into a tattered green affair with trailing bits of cloth that reached to the floor. In the early 1920s, a class presented him with a new gown, which he wore once, but then abandoned for his old favourite. On one occasion, when Leacock heard that a housemaid had expressed her admiration for him by telling Beatrix she wished she could kiss his gown, he promptly tore off one of the garment's ragged ends so that she could kiss it at home whenever she wished.[15]

Leacock was generous with money for campus activities, including the Political Economy Club he had founded. He often paid to have students' theses and papers published. For the annual class book of 1925, he wrote an article suggesting that McGill needed a literary magazine, and during the fall of 1925 was interviewed by the university newspaper, the *McGill Daily*, on the topic. He averred that there was an urgent need "for some kind of journal which will afford to the students a proper vehicle of literary expressions and a proper training ground for learning to write." Although himself a founder of the *Daily*, he found it "nearly useless...as a vehicle of culture," while several other universities, smaller and less prestigious than McGill, had outstanding literary magazines. "It is quite plain to me that in this matter of a college journal we either lead the world or else come at the tail end of the procession. I think I know which we are doing." Leacock mentioned a campus controversy over a literary supplement to the *Daily* and said that although he did not wish to enter a debate properly reserved for the students, he did wish to recommend a new magazine. That fall, several students founded the *McGill Fortnightly Review*, which in its two years of publication was one of the country's most influential literary magazines, the first publication in which Canada substantially felt the influence of the new literature that had emerged earlier in the decade under such names as Ezra Pound, T.S. Eliot, and James Joyce. The inaugural issue, in November, included a front-page article by Leacock, in which he said he had sent the

Leacock at Old Brewery Bay with Stevie and Peggy Shaw, about 1928.

Courtesy National Archives of Canada C-31981.

editors a dollar, a "more substantial testimony" of his support for their cause. Several important writers began their careers on the *McGill Fortnightly Review*; its founders were poets A.J.M. Smith and F.R. Scott; for managing editor they chose an eighteen-year-old sophomore, Leon Edel, later the biographer of Henry James. Smith had been the editor of a controversial literary supplement to the *Daily* in 1921, and although he made it a nationally acclaimed publication, the student council of McGill withdrew funding for it after one year; Scott, in addition to his distinguished career as a poet, became one of the country's most prominent constitutional lawyers and scholars, a pioneer socialist, a founder of the Cooperative Commonwealth Federation, and a pioneering translator of French Canadian poetry. Edel remembers Leacock as an inspiration to these and other campus writers: he not only suggested and supported the *McGill Fortnightly Review*, he offered living proof that literary success was as close as one of their own teachers.[16]

Leacock published three books in the five years between 1925 and 1929: *Winnowed Wisdom* (1926), *Short Circuits* (1928) and *The Iron Man and the Tin Woman* (1929). Of the three, only *Winnowed Wisdom*, which was composed primarily of pieces written before his wife's illness, was a critical success.

> After several volumes in which the humour was spread thin, Mr. Leacock is himself again,

one review reported, although the *New York World* opined that

> those who have not read Stephen Leacock in the past...will derive more pleasure from *Winnowed Wisdom* than those who will be setting it up against Mr. Leacock's old books.

It includes several of his best-known sketches, among them "How My

Wife and I Built a House for $4.90," "How We Kept Mother's Day," "The Give and Take of Travel," and "The Laundry Problem." A great many of the pieces are commentaries on journalism, including "An Advance Cable Service," "The Children's Column," "Are We Fascinated with Crime?" and "The Next War." The book returns to several forms and topics Leacock had used before, including "outlines" of scholarly subjects, ostensible transcriptions of the outrageous debating style in the British House of Commons, the conduct of public meetings with the attendant sorrows of visiting speakers, and the questionable economic policies of charitable organizations. To these themes, in most instances, he brought a refreshing new twist, as in his discussion of evolution, which purports to answer criticism of Darwin's work by offering an exemplary passage from the *Origin of Species*: "On the Antilles the common crow, or decapod, has two feet while in the Galapagos Islands it has a third. This third foot, however, does not appear to be used for locomotion, but merely for conversation." In "The Crossword Puzzle Craze," he uses his familiar technique of transferring a standard vocabulary from one activity to another:

"Good morning, Short-for-Peter."
"Hullo, Diminutive-of-William. How do you experience-a-sensation in four letters this morning?"
"Worse than a word in four letters rhyming with *bell* and *tell*."[17]

The creative pause surrounding *Winnowed Wisdom* doubtless reflects a difficult and prolonged adaptation to Beatrix's death. One other literary project that did go forward during the 1926-27 period came to Leacock serendipitously, although it came to represent for more than a decade a satisfying aspect of his career. In October 1926, a Jesus College, Cambridge, history don named V.C. Clinton-Baddeley wrote Leacock that several years earlier he had adapted "Behind the Beyond: A Modern Problem Play" for stage presentation at a private occasion of the Cambridge University Amateur Dramatic Society. Now he sought permission to publish the play and arrange public performances and in letters exchanged through December he obtained it. His adaptation was performed first at a Cambridge Christmas revue, and then moved to London, where it had an excellent run (at least eighty-four performances, through 27 March 1927) at the St. Martin's Theatre, on a bill as a curtain-raiser for "Berkeley Square" by J.C. Squire and John L. Balderston. In 1932, Clinton-Baddeley published in England his *Behind the Beyond: A Play in Three Acts* and two other Leacock adaptations, *Winsome Winnie: A Romantic Drama in Three Acts* and *The Billiard-Room Mystery*, based on "Who Do You Think Did It? (Done After the Very Latest Fashion in This Sort of Thing)," which appeared in August 1920 in London's *Bystander* magazine but was never collected in a book; a fourth adaptation, *The Split in the Cabinet*, also based on one of the "new nonsense novels" collected in the *Winsome Winnie* volume, followed in 1938.[18]

Short Circuits, the first book that collected pieces produced by Leacock since Beatrix's death, appeared in June 1928 and paid Leacock that month an advance against royalties of $1,000. The book was welcomed by hungry Leacock aficionados: by August it had sold about 5,000 copies and earned Leacock an additional $1,000. But it did not get a warm critical response: "The rich vein of Mr. Stephen Leacock's humor seems to have become exhausted," said one reviewer, and another commented, "Even Stephen Leacock nods now and then." Many pieces in the collection had been written at the request of Dodd, Mead, which had wanted Leacock to stretch his original manuscript for the book to fifty thousand words. On 7 February 1928, Frank C. Dodd had written to Leacock, "*Short Circuits* is a bully title, and I am glad you can squeeze it out to 50,000 words. The more the merrier." The old saying did not apply in this case. Leacock's final text was squeezed out even further, giving a lengthy, ten-section volume (nine groups of essays and the epilogue) of 384 pages; a smaller proportion of the pieces had previously appeared in magazines than was the case with earlier collections. B.W. Willett of The Bodley Head, in contact with Leacock over preparation of the English edition, noted in a March letter that *Short Circuits* "is a very much longer book than any of your others. We had, therefore, to decide to publish it at 7/6d."[19] To pad, Leacock took some of the series he had written for magazines, such as one under the general heading "Save Me from My Friends," which provided the book's fourth section, and added additional essays on the same subjects: Lane's complaint that Leacock had begun writing "snippets" perhaps had not applied to his work at the beginning of the 1920s but came partly true with *Short Circuits*. Leacock identified the book's theme as "the contrast between yesterday and to-day, between to-day and to-morrow" and throughout it he betrayed a clear preference for the past, a fact that is underlined by the imitation of Gray's "Elegy in a Country Churchyard" with which the volume ends: "The Epilogue of This Book: An Elegy Near a City Freight Yard." Modern man is portrayed as living and dying in an ugly landscape of factories, stock-yards, tenements and train tracks. The grim humorist warns of the loss of domestic animals, backyard playgrounds for children, the simple pleasures of county fairs, and the security of growing up in a family home. Although many of the book's pieces are so slight as to be mere sketches, still there are examples of Leacock at his best even in this predominantly exhausted, sad-voiced, almost defeated collection. Memorable essays include "Old Junk and New Money," "A Lesson on the Links: The Application of Mathematics to Golf," "Softening the Stories for the Children" and "The Great Detective."

Undeterred by critical cavils, The Bodley Head remained anxious to receive new Leacock titles quickly and regularly, and Frank C. Dodd continued to ask for longer manuscripts. *Short Circuit* was scarcely out of the gate when Willett, in December 1928, was prod-ding Leacock for assurances that his new book would be ready soon enough for Lane to advertize in the spring; in February, Dodd wrote,

"I am delighted to hear there is a prospect of having a volume of sketches this year. We ought to have at least 60,000 words to make a book of respectable bulk — 70,000 would be better." Leacock had 30,000 words ready for Dodd in March, but he accepted the publisher's direction and in August wrote:

> I am glad to say that I have now plenty of sketches from which to choose the book (same terms as before I understand)....For this title I propose to use a title of one of the sketches. The Iron Man & The Tin Woman And Other Such Futurities. It sounds to me a good selling title and would illustrate well. The only objection is that it is only a title [of] one sketch but...the subtitle shows that the sketches hang together.

"The same terms as before" referred to Leacock's twenty per cent royalty, which had to be made specific since his multi-book contract had expired with *Short Circuits*; Dodd asked him to lower the rate to fifteen per cent, since it was "pretty difficult indeed to show a profit and pay that rate, especially on a $2.00 book," but said he would defer to Leacock's decision, concluding, "We are proud to have your books on our list and I certainly would go a long way before losing you." Leacock offered only to descend to fifteen per cent on the next book if Dodd, Mead should lose money on this one, and in September received a new one-book contract on his old terms: twenty per cent royalty and $1,000 cash advance. The book, almost as long as *Short Circuits*, appeared in November and by 1 February 1930 had sold over 5,000 copies, earning Leacock more than an additional $1,000. The British edition appeared from The Bodley Head almost simultaneously; the two books differ slightly, the American version lacking five pieces present in the British version but containing one other.[20]

If the essays and sketches in *The Iron Man and the Tin Woman* hang together, it is around a satirical science fiction or science speculation theme: mockery of the brave new future predicted by journalism and applied science, and of the "advanced" aspects of the present as well, which are held up for ridicule against a nostalgic, golden vision of the past, of the commonsensical, of the norm: the "majesty of a peaceful public anxious only to be let alone," as Leacock put it in one of the book's mellowest entries, "Eddie the Bar-tender." Taken with *Short Circuits*, *The Iron Man and the Tin Woman* forms a kind of diptych, both of them preferring the past to the present, the former mixing nostalgia with satire of the present day, the latter attempting to concentrate its fire upon technical progress and the atmosphere of boosterism around the idea of a better future. Both the British and the American wrappers featured an illustration of male and female mechanical robots, and three of the book's seven sections bore the titles "Pictures of the Bright Times to Come," "To-Day and To-Morrow" and "Futurity in Fiction." As the latter section title indicates, Leacock adapted his traditional concerns — in this instance, parody of popular literature — to his present theme; the book is similar to *Short Circuits* in that a very few fine pieces leaven a group of rather flat ones that transparently repeat Leacock formulae. Among the fine essays included, "Further Specialization" develops the sound idea that overspecialization is interfering with the proper performance of jobs; the story describes the enormous concatenation of experts it will one day take to give a man a shave. In "Mr. Chairman, I Beg to Move," Leacock returns to the hopeless confusion of women's-club meetings, and "The Hero of Home Week" follows a long-absent visitor whose insistence that he remembers the vanished old days in his home town is weakened somewhat by the discovery that the old days still exist there unchanged in the shape of former friends, community characters and landmarks.

In all three books of the late 1920s, Leacock's opinions on women's rights and prohibition are well represented. Satisfied as he was by the introduction of licensed liquor outlets in Canada, he continued to hammer away at prohibition in the United States. In "Literature and the Eighteenth Amendment" (*Short Circuits*), he offered American writers the use of Montreal as a setting for their stories so that traditional scenes of merriment and intrigue featuring alcoholic beverages could be staged legally. In "Eddie the Bartender" he laments the removal of a character type and the entire element of life it represented:

> Perhaps, under Prohibition, they took to drink. In the cities, even their habitat has gone. The corner saloon is now a soda fountain, where golden-headed blondes ladle out red and white sundaes and mushy chocolates, and smash eggs into orange phosphates.
>
> But out in the solitude of the country you may still see, here and there, boarded up in oblivion and obliquity, the frame building that was once the 'tavern.' No doubt at night, if it's late enough and dark enough, ghostly voices still whisper in the empty bar-room, haunted by the spectres of the Eddies — 'What's yours, gentlemen?'[21]

Where is he now? Eddie and all the other Eddies, the thousands of them?...

Women are portrayed primarily as his narrator claims to have met them at the meetings of women's clubs, for which he shows very little sympathy or respect, despite their having provided Leacock with a high proportion of his speaking engagements. In his "Appeal to the Average Man," which introduces *Winnowed Wisdom*, the Leacock character's scientific sifting of current reports yields little to recommend either the average man or woman. The average woman might be consoled that his analysis finds her, on the whole, superior to the average man, but there were a few reservations: women cannot do arithmetic beyond improper fractions, they each eat about four tons of candy in a lifetime, and they read nothing but love stories. His own goal, he said, was "to start the movement for getting above the average."[22] In his continuing emphasis on a sharp differentiation between men and women and their roles in society, Leacock never refers to but perhaps reflects a Canadian controversy unfolding in the late 1920s, the "persons" case. After Canadian women received the vote in all provinces but Quebec (which did not grant them the franchise until 1940), and women representatives were elected to the House of Commons, the legality of an appointment of a woman to the judiciary was challenged. It was argued that, under the British North America Act (the law that established the Dominion of Canada), only "persons" could hold such offices and women were not persons under the law. Author Emily Murphy, whose appointment to the bench in Alberta had been challenged, took the case to court, and in 1928 the Supreme Court of Canada ruled that, in fact, women were not "persons" under the law. In 1929, however, that decision was reversed by the British Privy Council, which held final authority over the Act.

The two books proved at the least that Leacock the humorist was back in the saddle. In the fall of 1929, he sent a new program of lectures to several bureaus in the United States, offering programs from talks on literature and economics to readings from his own humorous writings. Response was so strong that he was booked for all the holidays of the 1929-30 academic year. Between 1925 and 1929, his interest in expanding his career beyond magazines and books continued. His social life also found a new equilibrium. Among the many visitors to his Montreal home at this time were Douglas Fairbanks and Mary Pickford, now friends, who came for one memorable dinner at which they urged him to write a screenplay in which they could star. Encouraged by such feelers as this, and his new association with Clinton-Baddeley, Leacock was again beginning to think about how to parley his longstanding satire on drama and film into participation in the worlds of the stage, filmmaking, and even radio. His agent, Paul Reynolds, was negotiating with the Hollywood movie company, Famous Players-Lasky Corporation, on the sale of screen rights to his books. In 1927, Leacock also began contributing articles on the Canadian provinces to the *Encyclopaedia Britannica*, a somewhat ironic task in view of his oft-quoted line that he would rather have written *Alice in Wonderland* than that entire reference work. In September 1929, Leacock was the chairman of the Upper Canada College centenary banquet, held at Toronto's Royal York Hotel. It was a memorable evening, one of the school's most famous graduates and faculty members entertaining a large gathering of distinguished alumni, including provincial and national government officials. Only one month later, the world economy that had seemed so prosperous and stable suddenly fell apart. In Canada, the collapse began on 24 October at the Winnipeg Grain Exchange with a dramatic fall in wheat prices. Five days later the New York stock market crashed: the ensuing depression was to be one of Leacock's chief concerns in his career as an economist.

Back to Prosperity

The New York stock market crash corresponded in Leacock's calendar to the beginning of the 1929-30 academic year. By this time he had recovered fully from the period of relative silence that surrounded Beatrix's death; during the next five years he returned with all his former energy to a demanding schedule of teaching and writing. There were new humour collections, but most of his writing was serious work, directed at the Great Depression of the 1930s, which he considered the most challenging crisis he ever faced as an economist, even including the First World War and its aftermath, and the later outbreak of the Second World War. It was "a failure of society, and economists in particular," he thought, that the crisis had not been anticipated and avoided. Just as he had done during the war, he responded quickly to the national situation, producing two books and several brief works proposing directions for economic recovery.

He began his campaign against the Depression on an old theme, Canada's participation in the British Empire. The imperial harmony he had praised during the First World War and had held up as a model for economic organization in *The Unsolved Riddle of Social Justice* had not continued when the fighting stopped. During the war, Conservative Prime Minister Robert Borden had demanded and won an independent voice for Canada in the war councils of Great Britain, and after the armistice had secured an independent seat for the country at the League of Nations. Perhaps under continuing Conservative leadership such moves towards an independent voice within British imperial decision-making would have eventually fulfilled Leacock's hope, expressed ever since his 1907 Rhodes tour, for an imperial government that truly represented all the dominions of the Empire. However, Liberal Mackenzie King governed throughout most of the 1920s, coming to office in 29 December 1921 and remaining in power until August 1930, except for Arthur Meighen's three-month government of the summer of 1926. Under King, imperial relations — and, in general, any international involvement outside the Americas — were not pursued. King refused a request from Britain for troop support in a military action in Turkey in 1922 and consistently avoided involving Canada in any general imperial defense programs during the 1920s; he was to continue this policy in the 1935-48 period, after he had returned to power yet again in October 1935, following the five-year Conservative interregnum of Prime Minister Richard Bedford Bennett. At the same time, King drew back from developing an independent international role for Canada through the League of Nations, preferring to pursue closer ties with the United States in the expectation that Canada's location in North America would protect the country from threats of war in Europe and Asia. Against King, Leacock steadily championed the importance of imperial cooperation as a safeguard for Canada and a base for economic growth, pointedly commenting, for example, in a 1924 Montreal speech, "The silliest thing this country could do would be to cut itself loose from the help and co-operation of the British people."[1]

In the fall of 1929 Leacock reduced his lecturing beyond the McGill classroom to almost nothing, quit writing humour for magazines and syndication, and started writing a general work on "political economy" of which nothing now is known, although doubtless it was meant to respond to the economic crisis. By November, however, his interest had shifted to a manuscript entitled "The Economic Integration of the British Empire," which he claimed to have begun considerably earlier. He engaged his younger colleague, Professor John Culliton, to do statistical research for him and kept a stenographer busy for several months as he steadily completed the draft of what was eventually a 256-page book. The draft was sent in March 1930 to the Macmillan Company of England, which then refused publication — the first time a Leacock title had been rejected since 1909, when Houghton Mifflin had turned down *Literary Lapses* — on the opinion given by its outside reader, John Maynard Keynes, that the book was "extraordinarily commonplace." An alternative publisher, Constable & Company, Limited, was quickly found and the book was issued in July; Leacock's concern over the delay occasioned by the Macmillan rejection caused him to press for such speed that the book itself bore, on binding, dust jacket, and title pages, the new title he had chosen, *Economic Prosperity in the British Empire*, but the running heads had to be left reading "Economic Integration of the British Empire," a circumstance explained to the reader in a note on page v.[2]

The book propounded Leacock's remedy for the Depression as it affected the countries within the Empire. He called for the lowering of tariffs towards the goal of free trade among the dominions, and a system of imperial finance and investment to develop the still untapped resources these countries held. This book's impact, the general nature of its proposals, and additions to the proposals which Leacock made later are all summarized accurately (if proudly) in a blurb he wrote for a 1932 book on the same subject, *Back to Prosperity*:

> Professor Leacock of McGill University published,
> just before the conference of 1930, a book on

Economic Prosperity in the British Empire. His book was widely read by statesmen and economists both in England and the dominions. It is no exaggeration to say that it greatly influenced public opinion. Dr. Leacock's new volume, The Coming Imperial Conference and the Return to Prosperity [later retitled], deals with the work that can be achieved at the new conference of 1932. He advocates an imperial super-tariff, together with a system of "three cornered preference." The existing preference he admits has been largely... "humbug"..., since Canada will not admit any imperial imports calculated to injure her manufacturers. Professor Leacock approves of this but finds the remedy in turning over to imperial, as opposed to foreign, imports the vast Canadian market for tobacco, cotton, oil, coffee, tropical fruits, rubber and things not producible in Canada. Canada receives in return the British market for wheat, and Great Britain the colonial tropical market. The three parts of the trade are carried on in "quotas" or "blocks" of imports at arranged prices.

Professor Leacock also urges joint action with a view to establishing inter-imperial currency, joint action to create a (limited) imperial debt, and joint action to stimulate the silver market and raise prices by increasing the monetary use of silver.[3]

Leacock also suggested a new program of immigration within the Empire: settling immigrants in undeveloped regions would promote imperial prosperity. He wished to bolster the population of British descendants in the Empire outside the United Kingdom; the second chapter of Part I: Until Now, is entitled "The Possible Expansion of the

White Race within the British Empire." Saying that the dominions did not wish to involve their own economic survival with the other races who occupied the British Empire, including the native populations of India, South Africa and New Zealand, he spoke of a conference "between nation and nation, between white men and white men." *Economic Prosperity in the British Empire* found eager support among pro-imperial groups; the board of trade in Orillia bought a thousand copies, which were mailed to British members of parliament and newspaper editors. Reviews quickly appeared in the London *Times*, the *Express*, the *Morning Post*, the *Spectator*, and other newspapers and periodicals. The book was reviewed in the main favourably or was summarized by the press respectfully and without counterargument. Indeed, a representative sample of reviews from throughout Leacock's career shows that this was the constant response to his works on imperialism and to his economic works generally. The *Times Literary Supplement* sounded a note of criticism that would continue to be used against his writings by his opponents and that echoes down to today in critical judgments of his political and economic work: he lacked the care for scientific statistical information and the mastery of recent economic theories necessary to address the new economic conditions and crises. According to the *Times*, "Few economists will be impressed with the shortcuts the author takes 'through the jungle of statistics,' or with his pieces of 'financial magic' in which something is made out of nothing."[4] But for the most part, newspapers and writers who entered quibbles generally did so with regard to individual points within a discussion that was well-disposed to Leacock's views. It is part of the myth that has grown up around him, fostered by writers interested in his humour and not overly concerned for history, and by ideological opponents seizing on his humorous writings as a convenient means of dismissing him, that he was gently accepted as a duffer in political and economic matters.

In fact, Leacock's own statement that *Economic Prosperity* was "widely read by statesmen and economists" and "greatly influenced public opinion" was as precise as it was self-confident. His ideas were questioned by experts who held divergent opinions and favoured different methods, which they liked to present as more advanced, but this was the sort of "dismissal" that Leacock himself courted and encouraged, for he wished to participate in the forum of ideas and prove that his own were beneficial and superior. As to the charge of inaccuracy, he was well aware of it and continued to hold the considered opinion that the condensations and shortcuts he took with economic statistics never affected the truth of his argument and served the useful purpose of making it more readable and therefore more influential. For instance, in 1940, when his book *Our British Empire* was read in manuscript by the British Ministry of Information, which was going to buy copies to give away, Leacock contemptuously dismissed the long list of adjusted statistics, altered dates and new shades of phrasing suggested by the ministry's history expert; he rejected several "corrections" that he knew to be wrong and allowed the ministry and his publisher to satisfy themselves on the others, since none of them had any bearing on his message and none reflected an inaccuracy of importance to the general reader.

Economists can scarcely be expected to cede influence to one of their number, unless to a few magisterial figures such as Keynes. But the influence of Leacock the practical economist on politicians and working experts involved in government was real and is well documented. One example of the impact of *Economic Prosperity in the British Empire* involves a fellow Canadian of the greatest importance in Great Britain: Max Aitken, Lord Beaverbrook, Ontario born and New Brunswick reared, who became a British newspaper magnate and later an influential politician, Winston Churchill's most trusted advisor during the Second World War. Aitken must have read the book as soon as it came from the press, and on 31 August 1930, he wrote to Leacock:

During a yachting journey in the Channel I have been reading, for the second time, "Economic Prosperity in the British Empire."

If I may be allowed to say so, I am more impressed than ever with your statement of the case for economic re-organisation...

In the Second Part of the book, the definition of mass production and standardisation will serve to instruct many an ignorant person.

I do not agree with your policy in relation to The Argentine. I would like to buy all our Wheat imports from Canada and Australia, selling to these Dominions the imported requirements of their farming population.

The need for agricultural development in Britain is very pressing.

Very few of our economic writers know anything about it. In fact, I am very glad to get the opportunity of redressing my own viewpoint to some extent....[5]

Aitken invited Leacock to propose methods of getting the book into the hands of as many influential men as possible. His letter shows that Leacock's ideas were often developed not solely out of his debates with professional economists, but through the dialogue that his public prominence allowed him to carry on with powerful figures in government and elsewhere: Leacock modified his ideas on wheat imports along the lines indicated by Aitken in his remark on Argentina; the change was reflected in *Back to Prosperity* when it appeared in 1932.

Leacock's reputation as a humorist received a boost in 1930, despite the relative lack of success of his recent books, with the nearly simultaneous appearance of the two earliest major anthologies of his work, published on the occasion of his twentieth year as an author of humour; he was now sixty. The idea appears to have originated with

Frank C. Dodd, who proposed it to The Bodley Head during a trip to England. In the event, The Bodley Head and Dodd, Mead and Company, rather than cooperating, each came out with its own selection, respectively *The Leacock Book* and *Laugh with Leacock*. The British book appeared in August 1930 and the American in October; Dodd appealed to Leacock to keep *The Leacock Book* out of Canada but he refused and the two books were both sold in Leacock's home country, by different distributors.[6] *The Leacock Book* is perhaps the best and most generous selection ever made from the humour of Leacock, although he has been the subject of many judicious anthologies. Under five headings it collects eighty-three essays and stories spanning the nineteen works he had published with The Bodley Head between 1910 and 1929, from *Literary Lapses* to *The Iron Man and the Tin Woman*; the selection gives the two series of nonsense novels and *Sunshine Sketches of a Little Town* and *Arcadian Adventures with the Idle Rich* virtually complete, presenting the latter two books, in a section called "Narrative," as a collection of separate pieces with the original chapter headings as titles. *The Leacock Book* was chosen and introduced by the British comic novelist Ben Travers, a Bodley Head stable mate of Leacock's. Dodd's *Laugh with Leacock* was chosen and edited by company staffer Raymond T. Bond, included thirty-four pieces, and sported a preface composed of a note "to Professor Leacock" by Bond and tributes from fourteen of Leacock's colleagues among American humorists: Irvin S. Cobb, Charles ("Chic") Sale, George Ade, Robert Benchley, Harry Leon Wilson, Homer Croy, Lawton Mackall, Christopher Morley, Ellis Parker Butler, Donald Ogden Stewart, Will Cuppy, Nunnally Johnson, George S. Chappell and Gelett Burgess. Of the group, only two, Benchley and Sale, were close friends of Leacock. Sale was a former vaudevillian from Nebraska whose best-selling book on the construction of outhouses, *The Specialist*, sold one million copies in 1929; he was an occasional guest of Leacock's in Montreal and in Old Brewery Bay. Benchley repeated his earlier compliment that he was greatly indebted to the master's work: "I have written everything that he ever wrote — anywhere from one to five years after him." Another of the group, George S. Chappell, praised him as more than a humorist and mentioned "one little contact" with him at a lecture engagement, in which he had spoken with the same charm Chappell found in his work. The fifteen humorists extolled Leacock for his many roles, from critic to college professor, and especially singled out his capacity to admire other humorists, to promote his art and — picking up a theme that he himself increasingly insisted upon — to analyze human folly with kindliness.

Only a handful of the fifteen once-famous writers have had anything approaching Leacock's durability. Judging from his own humour anthologies, a number of them were favourites of his, especially Benchley and George Ade, whose historical importance in American humour is great although the taste for his work has gone by. Many of the fifteen were Leacock's close contemporaries, including Irvin S. Cobb, "The Sage of Paducah," best known for his stories of his Kentucky hometown where he began his career as a reporter; Ade, who made his mark with the series of *Fables in Slang*, based on his column for the Chicago *Morning News*, beginning in 1897; Harry Leon Wilson, author of the once-celebrated comic novel *Ruggles of Red Gap* and a successful screenwriter; Ellis Parker Butler, remembered primarily for his 1906 story "Pigs Is Pigs;" and Gelett Burgess, who tired of the fame of his one well-remembered piece, the poem "The Purple Cow" from 1897. The younger writers acknowledged their indebtedness to Leacock's example; Cuppy called him "the real grand-daddy of the best ones of the day still."[7] These humorists were of a few types: rural newspapermen who had become known through their characterizations of their regions; college and cosmopolitan wits like Benchley and Morley; and writers for the movies, including Nunnally Johnson, who penned, among other famous screenplays, *The Grapes of Wrath*, *How to Marry a Millionaire* and *The Keys of the Kingdom*. In a comparison with these admirers, Leacock's distinction stands out starkly. He worked neither in regional journalism nor in that of the large publishing centres; he refused to exploit local colour in portraying his locale as a quaint backwater, and he refused equally to take his talent to the capitals of opinion and fashion, there to make a niche through original handling of whatever was already accepted as prestigious in the literary and intellectual worlds. His originality was to stay at home and transcend the limits of regionalism by purposely bringing Montreal and Orillia into the great world through the force of his literary culture, creative imagination and international presence as a social scientist. In himself he demonstrated to the outside world what his milieu had produced, and to that milieu what it was capable of. Against all odds, he worked to make an Aegean of Lake Simcoe, a Greece of Canada, an Athens of Montreal. He was cosmopolitan, but on his own terms and in his own way, which for the most part neither Canadians nor others have yet caught up with.

The anthologies were quickly followed by *Wet Wit and Dry Humour: Distilled from the Pages of Stephen Leacock*. The collection originated in Frank Dodd's desire to exploit his author despite the humorist's stubborn diversion of his energies to economics and politics. On 19 October, Dodd wrote that Raymond T. Bond was suggesting "that if you have no new book for 1931, we might bring out a collection of your essays dealing with prohibition. He tells me that there are enough of them to make a small book, and it ought to be very amusing. Would you have any objection to this?" Leacock agreed and proposed to add some new material; he also suggested the title. The new pieces included especially the opening essay, "The Dry Pickwick: England's Greatest Writer Adapted to America's Greatest Legislation," which Leacock liked so much that he now wished to name the book after it, a suggestion that Dodd defeated.[8] The bulk of the book was made up of Bond's culling of not only anti-prohibition but generally pro-bibulous pieces from various Leacock collections, beginning with *Literary Lapses* and extending to *The Iron Man and the Tin Woman*: the full 1910-29 range the earlier anthology had covered. *Wet Wit* includes "A Butler of the Old School As Transformed and Enlarged Under the Eighteenth Amendment," which describes a dealer in vintage water whose sources range from the Johnstown flood to ancient village pumps. With this story in mind, an anecdote told by a member of Leacock's academic staff shows how his published humour was interwoven with his daily life and conversation. Every year Leacock invited his professors to a dinner party to mark the opening of the new fall term. One year, when all the men attending were unmarried, he asked Barbara Ulrichsen to arrange for some dinner companions for them from among her friends at McGill. At cocktail time, one of the co-eds asked for a drink of water. "Water? Water?" Leacock answered. "Ah, yes, I remember water about forty years ago. Barbara, get out that very good water we've been saving for forty years."[9]

In July 1930, while the two anthologies were taking shape, the influence of *Economic Prosperity in the British Empire* was being felt, and Dodd, Mead and Company was germinating the idea of *Wet Wit and Dry Humour*, Prime Minister Mackenzie King and the Liberal Party dropped the writ for a federal election. King had refused to take any action to counter the economic effects of the New York stock market crash and its aftermath on the grounds that the separation of powers prescribed for Canada by the British North America Act left social service programs in the hands of the provinces, not the federal government. When he called the election, he expected to receive a mandate to continue this policy. Instead, the Conservative party, under Richard Bedford Bennett, a friend of Leacock's since the 1911 campaign against Sir Wilfrid Laurier, was elected; the Conservatives took office on 7 August 1930. Leacock had been invited to run for Parliament as a Conservative in this election but had declined. There is little indication that the new government's first steps to ease the effects of the Depression were influenced by Leacock, but as the years passed Bennett made increasingly clear his reliance on some of the professor's ideas and introduced programs very close to ones

Leacock had proposed. The initial Conservative measures, taken before 1930 was out, included establishment of a fund for social relief, the money to be distributed and administered by the provinces. As well, a high tariff was set to protect Canadian business from foreign — especially non-imperial — competition. The specific and unmistakable alignment with Leacock's views first became apparent at the 1932 Imperial Conference, when Canada participated in the joint lowering of tariffs among Commonwealth countries while standing by its high tariffs for other foreign nations. The close contact between Leacock, his friend Bennett and Bennett's government is witnessed by existing correspondence, press accounts, and statements of contemporaries. Leacock resisted repeated attempts by the Conservatives to increase his influence by increasing his direct involvement in the government; he turned down several invitations to serve in various capacities, apparently because he preferred to maintain the freedom of his views and his impact as an impartial, academic commentator.

In 1931 the status of the Empire had changed dramatically with passage of the Statute of Westminster, by virtue of which all the former dominions were acknowledged as full nation-state partners with Great Britain under the traditional British monarchy; the new partnership thus formed was called "the British Commonwealth of Nations." To Leacock, the Commonwealth was a step in the wrong direction: it provided for more independence of action by the dominions, but Leacock continued to campaign for cooperation among its members along the same lines he had proposed for the Empire; in *Our British Empire* (1940) he would even argue that the Empire, as he conceived it, still survived despite the changes involved in creation of the Commonwealth. Throughout 1930 and 1931 Leacock had been writing, as he informed his editor at the Macmillan Company of Canada in November 1931, "a lot of stuff (syndicated) on current economics affecting the empire (gold standard, prosperity, silver, etc.)"; he now proposed to make some of these writings the basis of a quickly produced book on imperial economic reorganization. The working title was "The Coming Imperial Conference and the Return to Prosperity" and the goal was to influence the opinion of the public and politicians in Canada and England in the run up to an imperial economic conference that would meet in July 1932 at Ottawa. Produce it quickly he did; the manuscript was published in Canada in January and in the United States in early February. In England, however, Constable & Company, which received the manuscript early enough to bring the volume out simultaneously with the American edition, dithered until 21 March. Leacock was convinced that he had lost significant income by this delay, which he considered a virtual breach of contract. But he felt a much more profound "disappointment and indignation that the publication of the book should have been delayed till after the great tariff debate [in the British Parliament] on the introduction of protection" in England.[10] The book, whose title finally became *Back to Prosperity: The Great Opportunity of the Empire Conference*, constituted a proposal, with arguments in support, for measures that should be taken at the July conference. He suggested, as he had in 1930, that the dominions would find their best chance of overcoming the continuing effects of the Depression through co-operation in trade and finance. In the United States, where there was, naturally, a hungry eagerness for any news of constructive action to relieve the Depression, the North American Newspaper Alliance asked Leacock to report on the conference for its members, but he declined, another instance of his attempt to reserve his time and energy for objective, scholarly analysis and advocacy in respect to the world economic crisis.[11] The Imperial Conference enacted, to some extent, the lowering of tariffs among the Commonwealth countries that Leacock had proposed, and Canada played an important role in bringing in the measures, which were implemented at home as part of the Conservative battery of designs to ameliorate the Depression. On 2 July 1932, just before the conference opened, Prime Minister Bennett had sent Leacock a "memorandum on monetary reconstruction," warning him to regard it as completely confidential because it was tentative and "has not yet been passed upon by the government." Bennett wrote: "it raises questions of importance, some of which are highly controversial. I shall be very glad if you can find an opportunity within the next ten days to express your opinion...." Treating the Canadian government on the same principles he had used with the American newspaper syndicate, Leacock refused and returned the consultancy fee the government had sent him. In September, Bennett wrote again to offer the compliments of the Cabinet and to ask privately "to discuss with you the monetary situation."[12]

Canada was not the only one with a troubled monetary situation; in the early 1930s Leacock's expenses were going up and his income was going down. To compare the pre-crash and post-crash Leacock fiscal situation, it should be noted that in 1928 his income from dividends and bonds was $5,837.92, and from literary work $14,015.99; his gross income was $26,171.13. In 1929 his gross income was similar, $24,461.24, but in 1930 he earned only $17,183.36. His income continued to decline; the Depression affected the performance of his investments, while his earnings from humour writing suffered from lack of time and attention. In 1931 his gross income was $14,719.30; he derived $2,898.20 from stock dividends and bonds and $3,466.06 from royalties, magazines fees and lectures. In early 1932 he commented in a letter to his British editor, "Like all people here I fought this hard winter low dividends and acutely unstable etc. Hence these tears."[13] The specific reasons for his declining income were several. One was the disappearance of his syndication fees from humour. During the 1920s syndication had brought him between five hundred and eight hundred dollars per month; it had formed the largest single source of income from his creative writing. In the aftermath of Beatrix's death he had gradually let fall the highly successful syndication of his pieces in newspapers throughout North America, which had been accomplished for him by his agent Paul Reynolds, although he had rebuilt it to some extent at the end of the decade. Except for some relatively meagre returns for syndication of economic and political articles, this income was now entirely eliminated by his abandonment of magazine humour to save time for economic work. Although the anthologies sold well, each bringing him substantial advances and royalties, his humour books of the 1930s were not as popular as his earlier ones had been, and they faced the additional challenge of the severely depressed book market. The same challenge faced the economic works; he hoped that these serious efforts would also sell well and would compensate him for the change in concentration of his writing work, but this hope was only partially realized. In reporting to him in February 1932 about *Back to Prosperity*, Hugh Eayrs of the Macmillan Company of Canada wrote, "The book is getting interesting attention. So far its sales have been light, but then frankly there isn't one book of any sort or kind that is selling. In all my years in the game I have never known the book business quite so bad."[14]

Then, too, in 1930 and 1931 Leacock overburdened himself with nonremunerative college work, which also deprived him of the time to seek periodical publication of portions of his books in progress. He had added to his teaching duties the direction of the McGill Monographs Economic Studies Series: National Problems of Canada, and threw himself into this, acquiring and editing manuscripts, arranging publication through Macmillan of Canada, soliciting advertising from many large corporations, and making arrangements with printers. In fact, the monographs were produced by Hale Brothers of the Orillia *Packet and Times*. Despite his best efforts to reduce costs, the series had to be discontinued for insufficient funding; because of a commitment he had made to the project, Leacock was left with responsibility for $270; McGill paid this for him and then deducted forty-five dollars a month from his salary. Another project touched by Canada's economic troubles was a book he prepared for Graphic Press of Ottawa. At the invitation of its director, the historian Lawrence J. Burpee, Leacock edited and wrote an introduction for the largely fantastical memoirs of a seventeenth-century French soldier and explorer in Canada, Louis Armand de Loin d'Acre, Baron de Lahontan. *Lahontan's Voyages* was actually on the presses, and a few copies had been printed, when financial failure forced Graphic Press to close in 1932. Leacock was never paid for his work on the book; in the depressed book trade of those years, he made two attempts to find another publisher for this work that would have small sales potential at the best of times, but was unable to do so.[15] An inscription by Leacock in a presentation copy of the book states that "Lahontan was in my opinion not a liar but a great explorer the first in upper Minnesota. His opposition to the church occasioned his exile and defaced his reputation." He made the material of his 5,000-word introduction the substance of "Lahontan in Minnesota," a paper delivered to the Minnesota Historical Society in October 1933 and published in the journal of that body two months afterwards. Leacock was one of several Canadian authors hurt by the collapse of Graphic Press, an event of some importance in the early literary history of Canada. Others included Prairie novelist Frederick Philip Grove, and the brilliant young poet and novelist Raymond Knister, who died by drowning in August 1932.

Two humour collections appeared in 1932, *The Dry Pickwick* and *Afternoons in Utopia*. *The Dry Pickwick*, published only in England and for the Commonwealth by The Bodley Head, was an aftereffect of the American *Dry Wit and Wet Humour* but in no way a duplication. Leacock had thought that Bond's idea of anthologizing his *cris de guerre* against the Volstead Act would have little appeal in England but he found B.W. Willett interested. He entered into negotiations to produce a book based on the American one but with additional material; it would lead off with and take its title from "The Dry Pickwick," a satirical fantasy nicely poised to flatter the English as much as it had cajoled the Americans. Preoccupied with his economic work and other activities, Leacock received his contract in March 1931 but failed to return it properly signed until April 1932;

forty thousand new words of copy, however, arrived at The Bodley Head in November 1931, and the book was published the following February. The new material for the American book plus the new material written specifically for the British one allowed *The Dry Pickwick* to overlap *Wet Wit* only partially and to be in the English context a completely new work, containing no pieces gleaned from collections previously published in Britain. It includes the title essay, in which one of Leacock's favourite Dickens characters has a nightmare of what life would be like under the restrictions of the Volstead Act. Other essays are "The Perfect Optimist," a rueful monologue on the joys of visiting the dentist, and "Ho for Happiness," in which Leacock proposes a happier sort of plot resolution than modern fiction commonly provides. Initial sales of the book in England and the colonies amounted to about 3,000, earning Leacock a gross royalty of £85; there is no record that it sold much after that.[16]

Afternoons in Utopia was somewhat unusual among his later books of humour: he produced it in a single concerted effort. In December 1931 he sent letters to Dodd, Mead and The Bodley Head:

> I plan for the spring a new book to be called Afternoons in Utopia, to be made up of a series of stories and sketches all turning on our economic future.
>
> Not *one* of the stories is written yet so there will hardly be time to get more than one or two of them in and out of magazines. But I won't wait. Life is too short. Now, — when can I have them done: I am crowded with college work and have one other book (80,000 words) to write at the same time. If I say *spring* and it's *summer* does it matter much?[17]

The book was to be a discussion of the dangers of socialism in a form, humour, that would reach the people. Leacock always liked the book and looked upon it as a serious achievement; in his last economic book, *While There Is Time: The Case Against Social Catastrophe* (1945), he cited it as one of his works on the subject of proper economic restructuring and the danger of socialism. Nevertheless, it was one of Leacock's least successful books, and never earned back his $1,000 advance on royalties. Like *The Iron Man and the Tin Woman*, it was cast generally in the form of speculative futurist fiction and essay, and could be seen as a thorough excoriation of modern tendencies, not simply the economic-political theories of socialism and communism. Groups of essays satirically considered trends in medicine and higher education and the concluding chapter, "The Fifty-Fifty Sexes," returned to Leacock's attack on the reappraisal of the relative roles of the sexes and the reimagining of the human personality generally.

Another disappointment in this period came with Leacock's work for radio. In 1931 he was approached by two different firms. Richard Marvin of the J. Walter Thompson Company Limited, an international advertising agency, visited Leacock in his campus office; the company invited him to propose a program for a client, and later asked him to quote a price for use of material from *Sunshine Sketches of a Little Town* on radio. Both projects fizzled out. In February, producer W.N. DeFoe of R.D. Broadcasting Company came to Montreal to suggest to him a series of ten-minute radio talks. Though he responded positively, the programs never went beyond the planning stages. When in 1934 Leacock did get a program on the air, it provided some welcome cash but proved a surprising letdown for all concerned. The former editor of a Toronto humour magazine, Joseph McDougall, who was working for an advertising agency, knew Leacock well and had printed several of his pieces; he approached Leacock on behalf of his agency, which was planning a radio show to be sponsored by Pompeiian Hand Cream. Leacock, the agency, and the sponsor settled on twenty-six broadcasts in thirteen weeks; he would be paid $1,300 for writing and delivering the series. The good humour surrounding the negotiations is suggested by an unusual clause in the contract. Leacock planned a dinner party before each broadcast and was permitted to bring his guests to the studio, or, if he preferred, he could broadcast from his home. "I don't like talking to a box on a stick," he said.[18] The initial broadcast was made from station CFCF in Montreal on 27 March 1934; the next three were also done in Montreal and the last twenty-two in Orillia. According to McDougall, Leacock might have been able to make a success of the broadcasts on television, but radio audiences, who could not see his face and expression, seemed offended by his customary style of leading the laughter. The series was not continued after the contracted episodes. After this experience, he never again consented to return to the microphone, despite various offers.

His furiously active 1932, which had produced the financially unrewarding Back to Prosperity, The Dry Pickwick, Lahontan's Voyages and Afternoons in Utopia, brought forth yet another book, a short biography and critical study (168 pages) of Mark Twain. This was a foray into a field of nonfiction new to Leacock, one that would prove to be a basis for the reconstruction of his income from popular writing. His Mark Twain answered a need that had been felt especially, perhaps, since 1924, with the appearance of the immense, confusing, but deeply impressive selections from Clemens's uncompleted Autobiography edited in two volumes by Albert Bigelow Paine. As Mark Van Doren had written in a review for The Nation, "the book as it now appears is a jumble of things some of which are consequential and some of which are not...But the Autobiography, shapeless and disappointing as it is, must still be called a great book."[19] Leacock provided a survey and interpretation of the man and his humour divided into eight chapters, beginning with "Childhood and Youth — Mark Twain as Tom Sawyer 1835-1857" and concluding with "The Evening of a Long Day 1900-1910." The book was part of a series of brief biographies published in England by Peter Davies Ltd. and in America by D. Appleton and Company; the English edition appeared in November 1932 and the American the following

February. Sales records do not survive but the book garnered excellent reviews from such periodicals as the London *Times* and *Evening Standard*, was reprinted in a cheaper British edition in 1935, was reprinted again by Thomas Nelson & Sons Ltd. in 1938, was included (minus the chronology of Clemens's life, bibliography and index) in a 1956 American university literature textbook, and was issued in a photographic reprint of the first British edition in 1974.[20] The book is in a sense a typical product: series of short works about leading writers and thinkers have proliferated for nearly as long as there has been a mass press, intertwined as that institution is with the self-education impulse characteristic of the modern era. But Leacock's *Mark Twain* belongs more particularly to the tradition of short comprehensive biographical and critical studies of an author that had developed in the eighteenth and nineteenth centuries, in such works as Samuel Johnson's *The Lives of the Poets*, the essays on individual writers produced by Thomas Carlyle and Matthew Arnold, and the many monograph-length studies that Victorian scholars often produced as introductions to editions of classic authors. The expansion of such writing to the length of short books published independently had been pioneered in the twentieth century by the brilliant studies written by G.K. Chesterton on Browning (1903), Dickens (1906), and George Bernard Shaw (1910). Chesterton's books are not works of biographical research; he was content to summarize the author's life from existing, readily available sources, which he did not question. And he was more interested in his own generalizations about his subject than in close literary analysis. His studies, then, provided a model for the analysis and criticism of culture through the example of great writers that ran parallel to the method Leacock favoured in his economic and political works. In his Twain biography, Leacock displayed an easy mastery of what may be thought of as the Chestertonian critical biography that depended less on close reading than on the insights and brilliance of an outstanding writer and critic. Such a biography was not so much an attempt at objective interpretation as the confrontation between a mature thinker and a parent figure, to argue and agree over the shape of history and the future.

Leacock praised Mark Twain as the originator of American humour and American literature in that he created a style and a literary attitude that could not have been produced elsewhere; he commented that in this sense there was yet no Canadian literature, but he was certainly thinking of his ambition for his own work. He was also concerned with his great predecessor as a model of both the good and the bad in creating a public persona: "side by side with Mr. Clemens, who is dead, there grew an imaginary person, Mark Twain, who became a legend and is living still." He paid honour to Twain's fierce love of justice, including his hatred of imperialism, even presenting for admiration his anger against the British Empire's war on the Boers, where Twain's view had been the opposite of Leacock's. But Leacock did strongly fault Twain for suppressing his anti-British views out of fear that they would damage the image of Mark Twain as a lovable sage. Again, Leacock can be seen defining himself both with and against Twain, implicitly defending his determination to speak his mind, even in humour, against those who complained that polemic only distorted his art and image. He described what he found essential in Mark Twain, and by implication in himself:

> His humour lay in his point of view, his angle of vision, and the truth with which he conveyed it. This often enabled people to see things as they are, and not as they had supposed them to be — a process which creates the peculiar sense of personal triumph which we call humour. The savage shout of exultation modified down to our gurgling laugh greets the overthrow of the thing as it was. Mark Twain achieved this effect not by trying to be funny, but by trying to tell the truth.[21]

At the same time, he was concerned with Twain's uniqueness. Twain had been brought up "solely in his own country...in the days when American was America." He had lived "before the motion picture industry had flickered the whole world with similarity." Leacock mused that his great originality might also have owed something to his relative lack of education, in a way that recalls the old image of Shakespeare as an untutored genius, "warbling his native woodnotes wild" with a spontaneity that surpasses art. Like Shakespeare and Dickens, said Leacock, Mark Twain had received little schooling: "He thus acquired that peculiar sharpness of mind which comes from not going to school, and that power of independent thought obtained by not entering college." A good example of one of his half-bricks that travel far, this remark suggests he knew himself to be too refined and intellectual, and living in too thoroughly settled a world, ever to have an impact like that of Twain the wild westerner on an age to which he was a fresh, astonishing phenomenon. A few pages later, Leacock reattaches the other half of the brick:

> There seem, indeed, to be two distinct means by which a man of native genius may succeed in life. The one is by receiving a sound and complete education; the other by not getting any at all.

It's not as simple as staying out of school; whether in or out, the question is genius, and if in, the quality of the education. In fact, Leacock regarded staying ignorant to protect one's authenticity as only an American folly, which protected nothing but an erroneous pride based on ignorance. Leacock takes Twain to task for the false overestimation of America that lies behind his denunciation of tyrannical errors in Europe and Britain. Coming from the United States, with its new and improved brands of oppressive conformity, he comments, these criticisms are the pot calling the kettle black, and he concludes sourly: "But the delusion of American freedom died hard." Yet

Leacock found the insularity of Mark Twain's views inseparable from, and more than redeemed by, their freshness:

> The form of thought consists in bringing to bear an absolutely open and 'innocent' point of view on things already valued and prejudged and showing them as they are. The form of words consists in making terms and phrases take on a new and sudden meaning, obvious when found, but findable only by the same process of 'innocent' application. For both these things — the power of vision and the innocence of expression — Mark Twain has never been surpassed.[22]

With a clear-sighted irreverence Mark Twain had mocked the false pieties that had overawed and domesticated Samuel Clemens. Underneath the generous tribute of *Mark Twain* can be read Leacock's own self-assessment: if he could not match Twain's power, he could more than match him in a balanced view of tradition that did not keep veering between overcooked anger and disabling servility.

Leacock inspecting an icehouse under construction at Old Brewery Bay, in the first winter of the Great Depression.

Courtesy National Archives of Canada C-31966.

The Saving Grace of Humour

A t first, Depression losses in Canada touched primarily prairie farmers and the fishing, mining and lumber industries in the Maritime provinces; the Canadian banks were complacent because they had avoided the failures that were such a dramatic and painful aspect of the Depression in the United States. By 1933, however, damage had widened. National unemployment reached twenty-three per cent. In that year, Leacock published a pamphlet entitled *Stephen Leacock's Plan to Relieve the Depression in Six Days, to Remove It in Six Months, to Eradicate It in Six Years*. For the first time in his practical economic writing, he offered a solution designed solely for Canadian problems. His proposals were three: a massive government works program, including slum clearance and rebuilding projects, operated on a profit basis; a devaluation of the dollar, lessening its gold backing from twenty-three to seventeen grains, and use of the impetus from these measures to rebuild foreign trade. The devaluation of the dollar would put more money into circulation and give more buying power to working people; this aspect of his proposals can be seen as a response, from his independent position, to Bennett's requests for advice on monetary policy. Leacock lectured on his proposals and sent copies of the plan to Bennett and to President Franklin Delano Roosevelt. The plan was widely discussed in the Canadian press, and to a lesser extent in the United States press and by American politicians. Newspaper accounts were generally favourable or descriptive.

The most common objection to *Stephen Leacock's Plan* was that inflation would result from lessening the gold backing of the dollar. It is interesting that the lingering idea that Leacock was not a good economist descends, in large part, from the arguments against him by supposedly "sounder" or "more advanced" theorists of the day, most of whom believed that the gold standard could not be abandoned or weakened without disaster. People have forgotten the issue but preserved the charge. In fact, gold was a subject on which Leacock wrote, across a span of decades, many well-informed and forward-looking articles. He was of his time in that he was concerned inflation would result from an insufficiently backed dollar, but far less conservative than many in this regard and more prepared to see and admit that, in fact, the gold backing of currency was not being maintained. The Depression had a devastating effect on the gold standard; Great Britain explicitly abandoned it in 1931, while North American governments were still maintaining that it was in effect. Leacock determined to demonstrate the folly of this; neither the view itself, nor the colourful method he chose to express it, would have been possible to an economist who felt himself to be in the employ of the Bennett government. He withdrew $10,000 from his Montreal bank and took it to the assistant receiver general's office in the city, demanding the equivalent in gold. The exchange was made; the gold was given to him in coins of small denominations. Leacock then attempted to ship the gold to the United States, whereupon the Canadian government wrote him a letter requiring that the gold be surrendered. When Leacock handed it over, it was accepted at face value but he was charged for "loss of weight through wear and abrasion."[1] For the small charge he had demonstrated publicly and dramatically that the country was no longer on the gold standard: gold would not be given for paper currency to the bearer on demand — the government could not afford to do so. A second, more interesting objection raised to Leacock's plan was one that he himself had made against socialism's positive programs: it would take saints, not men, to run a massive public works project on a profit basis, without corruption and profiteering, and for the good of the disadvantaged.

In general, the pamphlet was well-received; even the quibbles came in approving reviews. A few newspapers of strongly traditional economic views disagreed entirely, one stating, in a joke that had by now become habitual among Leacock's economic opponents, that the work would find its place amid his humour. The pamphlet strengthened his influence. Although Leacock had twitted the government in public over the supposedly healthy gold standard, Bennett now consulted him on a measure to deal with the financial and currency problems: the formation of the Bank of Canada, which was instituted in 1934. Other leaders who discussed the practical economic questions of the day with Leacock included his close friends Sir Edward Beatty, president of the Canadian Pacific Railway, and General Arthur Currie, principal of McGill University. Currie encouraged Leacock, for example, to develop proposals for reconstruction in the farm industry. When Roosevelt's New Deal programs got under way in 1932 and 1933, one of the measures was a devaluation of the American dollar in a manner very close to that which Leacock had proposed for Canada. Leacock's name and ideas had been mentioned in the American discussions of the subject (Leacock used to say that "Stephen Leacock's plan" was being called "Franklin Roosevelt's plan" now that America was putting it into practice). However, reviewers of the pamphlet had drawn attention to the similarity of Leacock's basic ideas and his proposals to those of Keynes and his followers. Although Leacock was not without influence in the United States (he was known, through a 1932 essay, as a backer of

Roosevelt's principles and the broad outlines of the New Deal), in that country his voice only joined a chorus calling for the same general measures. In Canada, where neither major political party was disposed to consider a mixed economy with significant government intervention, his position was more advanced and isolated. He continued to campaign strongly for a mixed economy in which free enterprise would be balanced by government regulations and a government social service program to support working people, dependent women, and children, to educate all the young, and to find jobs for the unemployed. Although he was well aware that some of his specific proposals went directly against historic Tory principles, he urged the government to intervene with programs of minimum wage, civic improvement work projects, and the like. After Roosevelt's election to the presidency in 1932, Leacock's essay in support of his announced economic ideas had praised the United States political system and electorate for creating a consensus for a mixed economy that would preserve basic individual freedoms but restrain big business and speculators and make the national government explicitly responsible for safeguarding workers and the poor. This was the direction of all future successful economies, as Leacock saw it. Indeed, the United States was then in the vanguard of developing the type of mixed economy that emerged in western countries in response to the Depression, and Leacock was again prophetic; in the fifty years following the height of the Depression most industrial democracies and Commonwealth countries outstripped the United States in adopting socialist economic elements, and in fact went farther in that direction than Leacock would have approved.

The pamphlet, first broached to Leacock by Macmillan of Canada in January, had been completed and published by February, and delivered on 16 February as an address, "The Riddle of the Depression," to the Empire Club of Canada, published in the club's annual proceedings, and broadcast on radio. Leacock's major 1933 initiative in popular writing, *Charles Dickens: His Life and Work*, appeared from Peter Davies Ltd. in England in November, and from Doubleday Doran and Company Inc. in the United States in January 1934. Like *Mark Twain*, the Dickens book was widely and enthusiastically noticed, and it earned Leacock a wider audience by establishing him as a successful nonfiction author in areas he had not previously been known for. The Dickens biography immediately began to increase his royalty income, which was assisted by the popular anthologies that resulted from the two biographies; he edited and introduced *The Greatest Pages of Charles Dickens* in 1934 and in 1935 contributed an introduction to an anthology of Twain's work, both successful efforts, literarily and financially. But *Charles Dickens* was the lead horse in this pull in a new direction. It seems to have originated as far back as 1926, for there exists a memorandum of agreement for such a book dated March of that year between Leacock and Doubleday, Page and Company; a *Life of Charles Dickens* was to have been delivered by Leacock in October 1926 and published in Doubleday's "Benefactors of Mankind" series of short biographies. Whatever befell this project, which was being negotiated in the near aftermath of Beatrix's death, Leacock steadily gathered material on Dickens in the succeeding years and shaped it into lectures. Despite the remote origins of this book in an agreement with Doubleday, it was published in the same Peter Davies Ltd. biography series that had brought out *Mark Twain*, and was contracted to Doubleday Doran by an agreement made with Davies. The book appears to have sold reasonably well in England but its American reception was excellent. After the initial edition had sold about 3,000, the title was chosen in 1936 as a monthly selection by the Doubleday Book Club, resulting in sales of about 47,000 of a special reduced-price book club edition.[2]

The book ran to nearly 300 pages. Beginning with childhood and youth, it contained early chapters on the success of Dickens's first novel ("Mr Pickwick Takes the World by Storm") and on Dickens viewed in terms of his own journalistic fictional character Boz ("'Boz' Conquers England," "'Boz' Visits America"). The book as a whole shows Leacock thinking about Dickens through Leacock's own experience. Certain chapters make this particularly clear: the chapter on the 1850-54 period and *Bleak House* addresses Dickens as a social analyst and reformer, and another chapter focuses on Dickens the platform lecturer. Now that Dickens is generally regarded as a literary master of Shakespeare-like breadth and mastery, it is easy to forget that Leacock was among the first critics and scholars of stature to urge appreciation of the novelist as a great writer. Dickens had steadily lost popularity with the general public in the years after his death; among critics and writers, he carried the stigma of his Victorian preeminence and was dismissed for supposedly old-fashioned attitudes and the creation of grotesque character types. Leacock was not especially interested in Dickens as a creator of complexly structured novels; rather, he treated Dickens, like Twain, for his gifts of humour, emphasizing the novelist's power of style and imagination in presenting human life in an artfully altered, exaggerated fashion that revealed its underlying truths. On the other hand, he was objective and, from the standpoint of subsequent critical discussion, presciently insightful in his identification of salient Dickensian limitations as well as strengths. The contradictory clichés in the man's attitudes towards women are treated in the ninth chapter, "Dickens Separates from His Wife (1858)," and the similar contradictions and clichés in the novelist's attitudes emerge in the discussions of various books. Not a complex delineator of female character himself, Leacock nonetheless perceived the failure in this area not only in Dickens but in popular literature generally; his many satires on the typical literary and dramatic heroine in part emerged from and in turn stoked his awareness of this problem in Dickens. He condensed his views in an address, "Dickens and Women," delivered in Montreal in February 1934, which was neatly summarized by the *Montreal Gazette* headline writer: "Two Female Types Found in Dickens; Women Were Either Angels or Freaks..."

Academic 1933-34 was Leacock's first year as permanent chairman of the Department of Economics and Political Science, for it was in 1933 that the McGill board of governors upgraded Leacock's longstanding temporary designation. The change was little more than a formality. Leacock had been receiving the full chairman's salary since 1908, when he was first asked to take charge of the department temporarily. The department had grown considerably under his charge. In addition to J.C. Hemmeon, the 1933 staff included John Culliton, Eugene Forsey, J.P. Day and Carl Goldenberg. Culliton, a former student of Leacock's who joined the department in the early 1930s after study on a royal fellowship in London, shared Leacock's office and gave him important assistance on some of his books. Leacock continued to make the life of McGill one of his principal concentrations, and was especially active in contributing to the literary life of the university; in the early 1930s he wrote frequently for McGill publications on the themes of his professional work, such as the economic factors of the Depression and the dangers of socialism. With his walking stick and ragged, bulky raccoon coat, he had become a campus landmark, and the regularity of his schedule was something of a local legend. Always out of bed by five o'clock and at work by five-thirty, he wrote for about four morning hours each day, seven days a week. His classes were arranged so that they occupied only three afternoons a week. He would arrive at the Arts Building after his customary stroll on the mountain, and after classes he invariably went to the University Club for a game of billiards with René du Roure. On the other hand, there were decidedly irregular aspects of his conduct. A young reporter who visited his Arts Building office was asked to wait while Leacock finished addressing a letter. She was shocked when he calmly drew together a small pile of the correspondence he had been finishing, walked to the window and threw it out onto the lawn. He explained that it saved him a trip to the mailbox: some passerby seeing a heap of addressed letters would post them. This story smacks of the apocryphal but is not necessarily so: it would not be the first time that Leacock had dreamed up such a stunt, which could have come right out of one of his humorous essays, in order to enhance his legend. He was unfailingly diligent in furthering the careers of students he judged worthy, and many who worked under him became prominent in Canadian government, business, the military or literature. David Legate records the story of one student, Sydney J. Pierce, who felt that Leacock went too far in his case. Leacock nominated Pierce for the chair of political science at Dalhousie University, although the young man doubted his own qualifications. Leacock urged him to do some supplemental reading and to take the post; Pierce resigned after only a few months and felt afterwards that Leacock had not properly judged his real suitability.[3] This is reminiscent of Leacock's well-meant but unsuccessful attempt in the 1920s to make a McGill economics professor out of B.K. Sandwell. On the other hand, Leacock could also demonstrate a strictness in maintaining standards, proof of his dedication to quality in teachers, students, and instruction. Several students without proper credentials who applied to him for recommendations received instead scathing summaries of their lack of preparedness or talent for the positions they sought.

The death of McGill's principal, General Sir Arthur Currie, on 30 November 1933 was an indication that Leacock, his generation and his milieu could not endlessly withstand the effects of age and time. Principal and vice-chancellor since 1920, the former commander of the Canadian Corps had grown to be one of Leacock's closest friends; their weekly meetings had given Currie the opportunity to consult Leacock on campus and economic questions. Leacock regularly told stories about his dealings with Currie, whose adaptation of military discipline to campus situations often impressed the humorist with mingled amusement and admiration. On one occasion, Currie was surprised and pleased to find one of his former soldiers entering his office. He told the young man that they could enjoy a visit as soon as Currie had dealt with a discipline problem — a student Professor Leacock had complained of. The officer replied that he was the discipline problem. On another occasion, Leacock recalled, Currie was trying to help a former sergeant, now a professor, who was experiencing difficulty as a disciplinarian in his classroom, and suggested he should try whatever methods he had used with his soldiers. When the sergeant said he had regularly fought with any private who defied him, Currie said he should simply threaten his students with the same. Leacock reported sadly that, whether or not the former sergeant ever took the advice, he remained permanently unable to keep order in his classes. On the occasion of Currie's funeral, Leacock published a tribute in the Montreal *Herald*:

> It is as a great soldier that the world at large mourns General Currie today. It is right that it should be so. His great achievement was in arms. Those who know tell us that he was one of the great generals of the war; and that if the war had continued, this record, scarcely more than begun, would have placed him among the great captains of the ages.
>
> But there are those of us who were not privileged to know him in this wider horizon. Our memory of him is that of the thirteen years as our principal at McGill. There he sat in his college office room, ready and accessible to all of us. Beside him was his pipe with plenty of strong tobacco and plenty of strong language to keep it burning.
>
> There was a man! I have known many college principals and presidents — a poor lot most of them, with a few brave exceptions here and there. But there was never one to match up to General Currie. College presidents, as a lot, must bow to the rich and fawn for benefactions. Not so General Currie. He thought no more of a plutocrat than of a ninepin. College presidents must be careful what they say and how they say it. Not so General Currie. He said what

he thought and he said it in his own way — which was a forceful one. He knew some of the strongest words in the language. Nor was there ever such honesty as his.

For General Currie owed no responsibility to any man. For that he looked elsewhere. Never was there a man so deeply religious in the real meaning of the word. He lived, in peace as in war, with the consciousness of the imminence of death. For him life was but a pathway to something else, and he walked the path with a sense of its meaning and its end that never left him for a day. Beside him as he walked was the shadowed curtain of the infinite.

General Currie knew nothing of scholarship in the narrower sense of the term. His dusty, shabby professors were always a sort of mystery to him. He never could quite understand whether they were researching or loafing. When he first came to us, he imagined that the professors were always buried in the library, each lecture planned and prepared like Vimy Ridge.

Later on he was a little disillusioned. "Some of these gentlemen," he said, only that was not the name he used for them; he had a simple one, "don't research at all." They were like hens who wouldn't lay. But disillusioned or not he was unfailing in the devotion of his leadership.

We never had the place in his heart that he kept for his generals. Nor had we the right to it. His generals were always there in his mind, all nick-named and labelled, as General Currie loved to name people. Indeed as time went on, we too dropped into our nicknames and labels. No one but

General Currie would think of a professor of seventy as "Bill." But he had to have it so. He could not bear a world of idle dignity and pretenses.

There were those of us who served under him at McGill to whom there came during his principalship those dark hours that at some time must shadow every human life. And there General Currie was beyond words, — a tenderness of sympathy, an affection for those in distress that no language can present and that no gratitude can repay.

Now it is over. We have laid him to rest. Yet we who served with him at McGill can only hope that somewhere in the sound of the martial music and the measured step of his soldiers, his soul might hear the shuffling step of his dusty professors, out of step and out of breath, but following him, — as they had been wont to these thirteen years, — as best they could.[4]

Currie had been a high school pupil of Leacock's at Strathroy in 1888, and Leacock frequently boasted that he, like Aristotle, had taught a great general. His tribute was widely reprinted in Canadian newspapers and was issued as a pamphlet through the efforts of an admirer of the piece, J.E. Macpherson, who had it distributed to former soldiers.[5] Immediately after Currie's funeral, Leacock wrote to his mother that he had been with the principal the day before his last illness, at a luncheon Leacock arranged at the University Club with several of Currie's friends. Leacock and the party had gone with Currie afterward to a McGill football game, the last social function Currie attended and the last time Leacock saw him.

In the same letter, Leacock told his mother that he would bring Stevie to Orillia for Christmas and on Christmas morning would be at her house in Sutton.[6] Agnes then was eighty-nine and would celebrate her ninetieth birthday just after the first of the year. The

Agnes Leacock as she looked in the 1930s.
Courtesy National Archives of Canada C-31958.

Christmas and New Year celebrations of 1933-34 proved to be the last family assembly at which Agnes presided. She died on 19 January 1934 and was buried in the family plot at St. George's Church. She had long remained the centre of her family as it gathered for holidays around Lake Simcoe. After leaving the farm, she had lived with her younger children in a large house on the Sibbald estate, then with her younger daughters in Beaverton, and, starting in the 1910s again on the Sibbald estate in the Grange, a white stucco house: it is the address at which she received the news of Stevie's birth. Finally, Charlie built her an attractive, somewhat eccentric house in the village of Sutton West, about four miles west of the Sibbald estate, and for the summers she had the permanent let of a cottage owned by Jack Sibbald that stood just east of Saint George's Church on the brow of a sand cliff overlooking the lake and screened from the lakeshore road by a cedar hedge. The Sutton home, which Agnes called Bury Lodge after the fondly remembered home of her English childhood, stood on the banks of the Black River, and Charlie, who generally lived with his mother, had built a walk down to a riverside landing stage. Both house and cottage were memorable centres of family activities, filled with souvenirs of Agnes's early life in England and the latest magazines from London, including *Punch* and the *London Illustrated News*.

Of her eleven children, eight were still living; one daughter had died of heart disease in early adulthood, and one son, Dick, of accidental suffocation, according to information Leacock gave on a health record for a life-insurance policy. Leacock had been left the eldest son when in early 1932 the other of his two elder brothers, Jim (Thomas James), had died in Belleville, New Jersey, where he was a principal and owner of the A.M. Leacock Company. Throughout 1932, Stephen and Charlie were engaged in settling Jim's estate, eventually valued at $29,500; in this period they also rearranged the administration and distribution of the Thomas Murdock Leacock Trust, a task necessitated by the death of the trust's principal legatee,

Miss A.C. Leacock, a sister of Leacock's father. Leacock's concern for his family about this time shows in many ways. In 1934, for instance, he was helping the financially hard-pressed Teddy by making sure he received advances on money due to him from Leacock estates. Teddy wrote to Leacock in November 1934:

> I very much appreciate what your cheques have meant to me they have relieved me of any worry as to extra expenses, possibly meant the difference of Peter keeping on at U.C.C. I enclose copy of his last report, he does not stand so well as last term, but whether he stand at the foot or top of his class I am sure the life, discipline and education he is getting will be of great value to him in his later life.

Teddy's son Peter had roomed with Stevie at Upper Canada College in 1933-34, and Teddy indicated that he looked forward to the boys doing so again in 1934-35.[7]

During the summers, the eight surviving children and their families gathered around Agnes at Sutton and Sibbald Point, and to a somewhat lesser extent around Stephen and his Old Brewery Bay establishment. In the 1930s, as Agnes aged, her children's love for her was seconded by an urgency to give their children the experience of knowing their remarkable grandmother. All visited as often as they could, which was regularly or very frequently in the case of Stephen, George, Charlie, Daisy (Mrs. Margaret Burrows of Belleville, Ontario), Carrie (Mrs. Jan Ulrichsen of Beaverton), and Maymee (Mrs. Henry Bergh of Toronto); the motherless Sheppards (five boys and a girl), the children of the deceased Missie (Mrs. Harry Sheppard), were also regular guests. Less frequent visitors were Dot (Dr. Rosamond Leacock), whose practice was then in Calgary, and Teddy, a pharmaceutical salesman in the same city. Leacock's distinctive contribution to the society of the group was a steady stream of interesting characters from the outside world, professors and journalists, writers and publishers, celebrities and agricultural scientists whom he would lure to Old Brewery Bay with the promise of trout and bass fishing; he hooked them with the relaxed, unselfconscious, slightly oddball magic of the Leacock summer land, and many of them returned annually.

Throughout the 1920s and early 1930s, Leacock kept in close contact with his mother through letters when he could not visit her personally. She informed him of her flower gardening, which they apparently advised upon together, and discussed her paintings (such as one of lilacs she had done for Dot, since lilacs did not grow in Calgary), her various housekeepers and companions, the comings and goings and the health of various old friends, and her reading. Often in the late 1920s Agnes commented to her famous son in a way that reveals the varied intellectual life she continued to lead in her later years. Of his books, the one that interested her the most seems to have been *The Unsolved Riddle of Social Justice*. She requested that he procure her such books as the new Anglican prayer book and a life of Cardinal Newman and some of the churchman's works; after receiving them, she commented, in a letter, in some detail on the biography and on Newman's *Apologia Pro Vita Sua*. Another book that called forth some remarks from her on the relationship of men to their times was a biography of Goldwin Smith. During the early 1930s, letters show that Leacock was asking her for as much information as she could recall about her origins and childhood in England. Other letters show that Agnes read a letter in Latin that Stevie sent her and replied in the same language, though she was apologetic about the rustiness of her composition skills. For one winter, she provided board for a grandchild at her Sutton West home so the boy could attend a local high school and she coached him in French while he was living with her.[8]

Agnes was, among many other things, a living connection between Leacock and the England of his birth. At the time of his work on Dickens, he pumped her memory regarding a lecture appearance the novelist made in Plymouth, but she could only reply in a letter of 25 November 1932:

> Charlie & I have hunted all through my diaries to find
> an account of that lecture by Dickens but 1865 is lost
> — all I can remember is — Fanny Bradley & I went
> but the hall was so packed we could not hear half he
> said. We were away near the door. I think we gave
> up trying to get nearer & went home.[9]

Then, too, the religious formation she had given him, despite his seemingly opposite beliefs, was abiding. A frequent visitor to Leacock's home in Montreal, Agnes once furnished Leacock with a frequently told story by making a relentless attack, during a Montreal social function, on fellow guest Sir Ernest Rutherford, the Nobel Prize-winning physicist who had taught at McGill until 1907. She assumed that, because he was a scientist, he was inevitably an atheist, and she was determined to argue him out of his supposed beliefs. This is indeed typical of her. On *The Unsolved Riddle of Social Justice* she remarked, "I enjoy it — I am glad to see by the quotations you have not forgotten your Bible." The daughter of a minister, she had brought her children up in the Anglican Church. Although from childhood Leacock had rebelled against the imposition of organized religion, and in many works satirized aspects and effects of religious practice, such as the hypocritical sacrifice of doctrine to expediency or the separation of lovers by confessional differences, he also warned ("The Devil and the Deep Sea") that society should not abandon its traditional moral guidelines in favour of new psychological lessons for conduct. However, he did not apply this warning to his own abandonment of organized religion, presumably the source, or a source, of those values. His Currie eulogy suggested a key to his attitude. Although he objected to all organized religion, he admired Currie as a man "deeply religious in the real meaning of the word" and there can be little doubt that he thought of himself in the same way, although his suspicion of religion, both thing and word, would not allow him to say it directly.

Agnes's religious and moral influence thus persisted in him; it not only persisted but became more prominent and evident in his work starting from this time, perhaps in response to his mother's aging and his own. In a short book on Abraham Lincoln, *Lincoln Frees the Slaves*, Leacock praised Lincoln in terms similar to those he had used in his eulogy about Currie; Leacock characterized Lincoln as a religious man in the true sense, namely, "a man who lives in the daily consciousness of the transience of life and the imminence of death"; the book was begun in mid-1933 and published in February 1934, just after the 1933-34 Christmas-New Year holiday he had spent with Stevie and the rest of the family at Sutton and Old Brewery Bay. In it, Leacock was speaking for a certain acknowledgment of spiritual values, though he did not find the form he preferred in any church; this is another of his links to the Victorian era — to the Victorian intelligentsia. He evidently felt, as had many of the great Victorian intellectuals, that Christian moral principles are one of humanity's highest and most necessary creations but that superior minds can accept their essence and shuck away their institutional and mythological trappings. The trappings must not be criticized too harshly, however, because ordinary persons still need them in order to apprehend and adhere to a morality they cannot arrive at intellectually.

Lincoln Frees the Slaves is another sign that word of Leacock the author of biographies and other short works for book series had gotten around the publishing world, and that he himself was exploiting opportunities in this line. The 40,000-word book was first published by G.P. Putnam's Sons, New York, and then cut down by about 8,000 words at the insistence of Peter Davies Ltd. so it could fit into that publisher's English series of "Great Occasions," which included such titles as *Marathon and Salamis* by Compton Mackenzie and *Gordon at Khartoum* by John Buchan.[10] Leacock had first contracted for his Lincoln study in July 1933; in the same month he was informed by The Bodley Head that the Methuen publishing house wished to include "a volume of extracts from your humorous books about 30,000 words long" in its "Library of Humour" series; the book, entitled simply *Stephen Leacock* and containing seven pieces judiciously chosen by E.V. Knox, appeared in June 1934; in August, Robert M. McBride & Company of New York issued an American version of the same book under the title of one of the included selections, *The Perfect Salesman*. In July the busy publishing summer of 1934 quickly brought forth another fruit, *The Greatest Pages of Charles Dickens*. In it Leacock used exactly the chapter headings from his Dickens biography, under each of them arranging selections from the relevant period of the novelist's career, prefaced by his own brief remarks. The book was announced by Doubleday Doran as part of a new "Greatest Pages" series, a Leacock idea that Russell Doubleday liked; Leacock himself hoped to do anthologies of Mark Twain and Samuel Pepys, but the Mark Twain book foundered on Harper and Brothers' denial of rights for his work and Doubleday nixed Pepys as already over-anthologized.

The Christmas and New Year celebrations of 1934-35 were the first without Agnes. In early January 1935 her famous son was in St. Louis, lecturing on Mark Twain as he accepted the Mark Twain Medal of Honor of the International Mark Twain Society. In late February, with the reality and meaning of his mother's death just beginning to come home to him, he wrote to some friends:

> Very many thanks for your kind letter about Mother's death. I feel that to you & to all the Hett's her loss comes especially close: We were all so much together long ago. It was a wonderful scene at the church yard when we buried Mother: deep snow & bright, bright sun & very still & quiet in the shelter. ...It did not seem sad at the time; it was like a gath-

ering of the family; but now it seems so strange & sad
all the time to think that she is gone.[11]

He later described Agnes's influence on her children in *The Boy I Left
Behind Me*. His own partnership with her in raising the youngest children after his father's departure made him perhaps the closest to her
among her children, although she often snapped angrily at persons
who praised only Stephen. George, she maintained, was at least as
much a wit as Stephen (an opinion Leacock shared and often
expressed in writing); Charlie was also a special favourite. Stephen's
and Agnes's partnership could be at times uneasy. If Agnes had
special influence, Leacock also had a strong sense of male propri-
etorship over and responsibility for the family, which he perhaps felt
he had particularly earned through his youthful sacrifices on behalf of
his brothers and sisters: according to Elizabeth Kimball, one of the
rare disputes ever witnessed between him and his mother arose when
Agnes added her voice to those who were criticizing him for writing
too much and too quickly,[12] and he would have resented such a
remark for its neglect of the family motive behind much of his furious
effort. Friction was rare, however, and mother and son had cooperated closely in creating the joyful family idyll that repeated itself each
summer at Lake Simcoe. Leacock's success first as a professor and
later as an author had made possible his own home at Old Brewery
Bay and the assistance he gave to his mother, the family's heart. He
oversaw the trust conferred upon her at her marriage, which
continued to be her main source of personal income, and stood ready
to provide any other money she might need. It was he, principally,
who enabled the Leacock family to maintain its joyful centre at Lake
Simcoe, and it is not too much to say that this thriving extended family
with its orbit of friends was the primary motive of his work or at least
of his efforts to wring from it whatever money he could. In a family,
as he wrote not long after Agnes's death, "the money they have represents only a means whereby family love and family happiness can be

achieved." While it was Leacock who had enabled that family centre to exist, Agnes was the centre. The Leacock summer kingdom had survived diminishment in the deaths of Missie, Dick, Jim and Beatrix, but the death of Agnes meant the beginning of its dissolution. Without her presence, there was nowhere for all her children to gather with their own children, no one around whom to gather. They continued to visit Stephen, and some of them continued to rent cottages in the Sutton area, to summer there, to stop in Beaverton or Aurora. But slowly, surely, the circle fell apart. Agnes's children were beginning to age as well. The grandchildren, many of them, were growing too old for summer play and socializing; they were marrying and going their own ways. Another factor was the demoralization caused by Agnes's passing, which seems to have particularly affected one key member of the family group, Charlie, the Leacocks' last representative in Sutton; after his mother's death, he suffered increasing physical and mental difficulties. At the end of the decade, Leacock himself managed to bring the Leacock summer world a late flourishing, but it is clear that, from the time of Agnes's death, the story is one of inexorable decline.

As Leacock's income continued to fall, his worries about his own future intruded on him, especially in the form of concern for the legacy intended for Stevie, through his mother, from the Pellatt fortune. In these years he frequently wrote to Mrs. R.B. Hamilton, Beatrix's mother, who under the inheritance was to have the use of Beatrix's portion to draw its interest; the capital would come to Stevie when he was of age. Leacock tried in vain to get Beatrix's mother to entrust the capital to him and let him pay her the interest. He was afraid that her brother, Sir Henry Pellatt, the builder of Casa Loma, who exercised great influence over her, would obtain the money and sink it into his bankrupt interests and his mismanaged attempts at recovery, such as a plan to turn his cavernous castle-home into a hotel. Although Mrs. Hamilton on occasion seemed ready to turn over the money to Leacock in exchange for his assurances that he would provide her an income for life, she never concluded the agreement. At her death, there was very little left of the inheritance that had been meant for Stevie. Despite the tension over this matter, Beatrix's mother was a frequent guest at Old Brewery Bay.

On his return to campus in early 1935, Leacock remained concerned with the Depression's effects in the world at large and in his own neighbourhood. In January he circulated a tentative proposal for economy measures at McGill to alleviate the university's deficit and begin earning needed income; in February, he published a revised and elaborated version of his proposals as a small pamphlet which he circulated to faculty members and administrators, including the new principal, A.E. Morgan. Among his proposals in the two pamphlets were: to stop subsidizing athletics and cut out the School of Physical Education, to make a five-year bond issue secured by McGill property, to contract the staff by abolishing positions left vacant by deaths or retirements of professors ("Statistics will prove that $5,000 worth of us dies each year; with luck, more"), and to retire senior faculty members: "Where the senior professor is not far off pension anyway, give him one and compensate the juniors." In off-campus lectures during the term, he continued to press for such initiatives as slum clearance, insisting they could be profitable as well as socially beneficial, and to argue that the deepest problems faced by Canada and the world were social, not economic, although the two realms had to be seen in their unity. Social change had to come, but all classes were suffering together and must seek a common solution amicably; communism and the doctrine of class warfare were ruinous but those who refused to accept changes that would spread wealth and alleviate the conditions of poorer citizens were equally at fault. He developed an essay-lecture, "How Soon Can We Start the Next War," which he would deliver frequently in the coming years, and which built on the ideas developed in the war satires collected in Part II of *Afternoons in Utopia*: the lecture satirized contemporary bellicosity and the drift toward hostilities and excoriated the notion that war should still be considered thinkable in the modern world.[13] At the same time, however, he was allowing his literary and philological interests again to occupy him. He wrote and lectured on the need for humour, the social messages of the great humorists, the Norman contribution to the English language, the need to preserve higher universities from a "machine shop" educational approach and other such topics.

It was also in January that Prime Minister Bennett surprised the nation and much of his own Conservative Party with a series of radio broadcasts aimed at outlining and justifying a program of economic recovery measures on which he intended to fight the next election. In the Canada of the early 1930s, many factors inhibited the development of an American-style drive towards a mixed economy. Nevertheless, the desperate economic circumstances and the dissatisfaction of the electorate were prodding the Conservatives to do something; influenced by Franklin Roosevelt's New Deal for the United States, Bennett and his closest advisers developed a number of similar measures and, without having consulted the party as a whole, the Prime Minister took to the airwaves on Wednesday, 2 January, at 9 p.m., speaking for a half hour. By now he seemed to have moved very close indeed to Leacock's positions, not only in espousing New Deal-like plans but especially in justifying them by talk of the abuses of capitalism, maintaining just as Leacock had since the beginning of the century that capitalism was the best economic system and a necessary one, but that its manifold abuses needed to be addressed if it was not going foment a catastrophe that might lead to the worse world of socialism. Perhaps Bennett was incautious in couching the justification for his measures in terms liable to shock when coming from a government leader, although they served well as vivid emphases in the writings of an academic expert. Bennett spoke of the "grave defects and abuses in the capitalist system," of which "[u]nemployment and waste are the proof," requiring "modifications in the capitalist system to enable that system more effectively to serve the people."[14]

Writing to Leacock on 8 January, Bennett thanked him for a "kind message of good-will" his unofficial adviser had sent him, and commented, "I realize that my declaration involves me in much hard work and I am no longer young. Nevertheless I propose to go forward with my proposals to the fullest extent of my abilities." Bennett made five radio addresses giving his ideas in full. In February, the Conservatives were preparing to publish them in five separate pamphlets to be grouped together and sent in the same mailing to 250,000 Canadians; Leacock was approached for a forward, which he provided in late March. On 1 April, J. Earl Lawson of the Conservative Dominion Headquarters wrote him that, due to the excellence of his essay, "we decided to print your preface as the foreword to the first radio speech so that it would have priority over all the others." The printed pamphlet, *The Premier Speaks to the People: The Prime Minister's January Radio Broadcasts issued in book form: The First Address*, bore prominently on its title page the words, "With a Foreword by Stephen Leacock, B.A., Ph.D., Ll.D., Head of the Department of Political Economy of McGill University." On 18 April, Bennett wrote to Leacock:

> I have not had an opportunity before this to thank you for the foreword which you contributed to my radio addresses, published in pamphlet form. Your reference to my personal efforts during the past few years touched me deeply, and I appreciate your remarks greatly.[15]

In power since August 1930, the Conservatives now found their five-year mandate drawing to its term, and Bennett had chosen to stand or fall in the coming election on concepts of economic and social reconstruction close to many of those which Leacock had long recommended. Bennett's "New Deal" for Canada represented the apogee of Leacock's influence.

In April, too, some of his thinking about his art and career found published expression in *Humor: Its Theory and Technique* (1935), a work he had been encouraged to write by the great success of his lectures on the technique of humour and the history of American humour. He had first outlined it in a February 1933 letter to Dodd, Mead and had finished the manuscript in December 1934. The book opens with a chapter that gives Leacock's "analysis of humour" and proceeds to chapters that analyze and illustrate word play, parody, burlesque, comic verse, and the art of humorous story telling. The greatest humorists, Dickens and Mark Twain, receive a joint chapter. As in his early essays on humour, he argued that the art always did and should evolve away from ridicule towards sympathy and at its highest is motivated by an underlying kindness towards those who appear to be simply the victims of mockery or satire. His ideas met with little agreement, although many reviewers and readers enjoyed the book for its stylistic adroitness, its interesting exposition of a wise man's views, and the hilarious examples Leacock found or wrote to illustrate his points. Even favourable reviews, however, usually stopped to argue with the idea of kindliness, to question Leacock's analysis of what made certain things funny, and to uphold against him the delights of unkindness in humour, from the scatological to the primitive and brutal. This reception raises the question, first posed by Peter McArthur in 1923, whether Leacock was limited in his achievement by his determination to remain kindly. For the reader who prefers pure imaginative nonsense, which Leacock practised throughout his career but more concentratedly at its outset, this may be true. However, it is not the manner of Leacock's best and most characteristic humour, such as *Sunshine Sketches, Arcadian Adventures* and a host of essays. Such books along with his theoretical writings should have made his point about kindliness sufficiently clear but it was apparently a hard one to grasp, perhaps because it runs so counter to common and preferred notions of humour: he had not restricted himself to the innocuous to avoid giving hurt, but rather had insisted that humour recognize the essential fragility and poignancy of human life. His characteristic hovering between a freely "religious" faith in life and a thorough agnosticism, and his frequent sense of the tragic brevity and inconsequence of human existence, led him to feel humour and pathos are ultimately the same for even brutal humour reveals the human plight. If this is so, then a humour that is fully aware of and takes account of what it reveals must be a superior humour, and this was the form he found in Dickens and Twain and had sought increasingly, as his career advanced, to practise. He had come to see that a sense of the "tears of things" should soften men's and women's hearts towards each other and lead them to use mockery, when it was called for, not to humiliate and dismiss but in the hope that it would prompt reform. Even if satire fails to change its victim, it can change the reader. In Leacock's view, if humour were merely to add scorn to the world it would be increasing by one the very flaws and failings it pretended to mock and stand above. Though he attempted to avoid, not always with perfect success, personal invective and destructive criticism of individuals, types, or groups, the points of his humour often plunged very deep, questioning whether the most cherished attitudes and institutions were not erroneous, illusory, destructive, and equally questioning whether the boldest "revolutionary" reforms were not exercises in self-deception and self-exculpation. In the winter and spring of 1935, honours and acknowledgments of his status flowed to him. His list of honorary doctorates lengthened with the award of a doctor of laws degree by the University of Michigan. The Methuen Library of Humor had included him among its first selections, and in bestowing the Mark Twain Medal — a distinction previously conferred on Guglielmo Marconi, Oliver Wendell Holmes, Rudyard Kipling, Franklin Delano Roosevelt, and Willa Cather — the International Mark Twain Society had cited him as "The Modern Aristophanes," a specific acknowledgment of the dimension of direct and effective social satire in his work.

The boathouse at Old Brewery Bay; in its upper storey, fitted out as an office, Leacock did much of his writing.

Courtesy National Archives of Canada C-33105.

Mc-Guillotined

Professor Frank Dawson Adams, a world authority on geology, had served as McGill's acting principal while the search for a permanent replacement went on in Canada and other countries. The Depression had brought the university severe financial difficulties, which Leacock had addressed in his pamphlets of January and February, but no new direction had yet emerged because no successor to Currie had been appointed. The first mention Leacock made of the new principal eventually selected came in April 1935, when he wrote to a friend, the novelist J.A.T. Lloyd, that "A.E. Morgan of Hull University College is to succeed General Currie here: he will find it a hard job as the finances are in an almost hopeless state." Morgan was to take up his post in the fall. After finishing the spring term and returning to Orillia, Leacock received a letter, dated 12 June 1935, from the treasurer of McGill, A.P.S. Glassco, stating that he was to be retired due to age at the end of the next academic year. Glassco's announcement was little more than a form letter, which cited a recent decision by the McGill board of governors on retirement policy:

Resolved: That all teachers and officers of the University shall automatically retire on reaching the age of 65 years, the Board, however, to reserve the right to retain the services of any officer or teacher beyond that age if it be considered in the interests of the University to do so.

Pursuant to the above resolution, the Governors have instructed me to notify you that you will be retired from the University on May 31st, 1936.

The evening before this letter was dated, Leacock had lectured at an Orillia Board of Trade dinner on "The Outlook for the World at Large, the Outlook for Canada, and the Outlook for Our Own Town," predicting that there probably would not be war in Europe but that further government controls on industry were likely. After receipt of the letter, he went on as usual with his summer activities; there is no record that he responded to Glassco and no indication that the prospect of enforced retirement was an important issue to him until he returned to campus in the fall. The policy was a new one at McGill and provided for exceptions. His attitude toward Morgan seems at first to have been neutral despite circumstances that he could have interpreted as irritants. A letter he wrote to a third party on 29 June indicates that Morgan was being consulted regarding new appointments to Leacock's department. Leacock evidently had objected to a proposed candidate but acknowledged that the principal must have scope to operate: "My feeling is that if the Principal, with a knowledge of the facts before him, wished Dr. Plaut to come, then I or anyone else ought to give way. This is what we would have done with General Currie."[1]

During that summer, Leacock was occupied with continuing work on an ambitious anthology, *The Greatest Pages of American Humor*, which he had first proposed to Russell Doubleday in November 1934, after Harper and Brothers had refused the permissions he needed to produce a representative selection of Mark

Twain's writings. July 1935 did see the publication of *Mark Twain: Wit and Wisdom*, a collection of anecdotes edited by Cyril Clemens, with Leacock's preface. But he was now intent on a historical presentation of American humour and humorists in the form of a mosaic of selections set into a ground of his own ideas on the subject as he had refined them during several years of lecturing. Already in January through May he had been engaged in creating an outline, writing chapters, and dealing with the issue of permissions, partly by dispatching letters to such as Robert Benchley, George Ade, Irvin Cobb, and the publishers of the late Ring Lardner, using his friendships and reputation to obtain material for no charge or a reduced fee. He sent a supposedly final version of his book to Doubleday, Doran on 29 July, but at the publisher's request added further material and selections on contemporary humorists, a labour that took him the remainder of the summer and into the autumn.

In a letter dated 12 July, Prime Minister Bennett asked Leacock to stand for parliament. As the Conservative mandate drew to its term, Bennett meant to fight the next election on economic ideas and measures that were close to Leacock's and that Leacock had recommended in his preface to Bennett's radio addresses in pamphlet form. Bennett wrote Leacock:

> A number of our friends are extremely anxious that you should permit your name to be placed before the Conservative convention in the constituency in which you make your summer home. I need hardly say that I am thoroughly convinced that you would render very conspicuous service to Canada in the next Parliament. Your wide knowledge, your great reputation, and your disinterested approach to problems affecting the welfare of the country could not but be of the utmost value. Won't you favourably consider this matter, and thereby give great satisfaction not

only to those who know you in the community but to the thousands who have read your books with pleasure, as well as to one who subscribes himself, with high esteem and regard,

R.B. Bennett[2]

But Leacock declined, perhaps another indication that he not only preferred the profession of professor and its intellectual independence but expected to be able to continue in it, despite Glassco's communication.

When the 1935-36 academic year opened in September, Leacock found himself engaged in a two front war, that against the Liberals and that against the retirement policy, while at the same time devoting many of his resources to new writing projects, off campus lectures, and his teaching. On 21 September he addressed the initial Conservative campaign meeting in Midland, Ontario on behalf of John Drinkwater, the candidate from the East Simcoe riding in which Bennett had wanted him to run. As reported by the Toronto *Globe and Mail* and the Montreal *Daily Star*, his address assaulted Liberal leader Mackenzie King for do-nothingism and economic misconceptions and supported Bennett's attempts to create an ameliorated version of capitalism, a system for which there was "no substitute" but which needed modernizing. He made similar remarks on 23 and 24 September in Coldwater and in Orillia, and during early October delivered at least two election speeches in the Montreal area. As against the Conservative promise of a new, more dynamic and massive form of governmental economic intervention, King appealed to the "small c" conservatism of Canadians. He announced no Liberal recovery measures, even avoiding the question of the Liberal opinion about the Conservative ones, and instead attacked Bennett for recklessness in making radical proposals before determining whether or not they would be declared unconstitutional at the first test. The

Liberal leader further played on Conservative consternation that Bennett had spoken directly to the nation before announcing his new direction to his party at large. The days of Leacock's greatest influence as an economist ended when on 23 October 1935 King took office, the Liberals having gained an immense majority of 171 seats to thirty-nine for the Conservatives. Although mass defections from the Conservative Party and the success of smaller parties — the Reconstruction Party, the Social Credit Party (which swept Alberta), the Cooperative Commonwealth Federation — meant that the large Liberal majority represented a minority popular vote, the stage was set for a long return to King's policies of nonintervention in the economy and of political isolation for Canada within North America, which did not suit Leacock in any way. Naturally, he was not often called on by the Liberals as he continued to press for a program of social relief such as he had outlined in *Stephen Leacock's Plan* and for various forms of international participation, especially through the Empire. Leacock understood well the grounds on which his party of choice had been defeated; interviewed in the Montreal *Daily Star* on 21 October, he quipped that he was frequently asked by Americans about the Canadian election and always gave "the same answer: The people voted Liberal to show how Conservative they are."[3]

Seeking to be made an exception to the McGill mandatory retirement policy, Leacock now contacted his friend Sir Edward Beatty, a member of the board of governors; the two exchanged letters on 7 and 12 November, Beatty offering no encouragement. Then, in a letter dated 13 November, Morgan wrote Leacock to adjust a few details of the retirement, including a small salary increase in anticipation of Leacock's pension requirements, and told him that the academic year would be considered to end on 31 August rather than 31 May, as had been stated in Glassco's original letter. The principal began by commenting that he had understood Leacock to be aware of the new mandatory retirement policy, which was intended to be implemented immediately. Morgan wrote, "Although it is true that the resolution of the Governors reserves to them the right in very exceptional cases to extend that period, it is the intention of the University to regard retirement at sixty-five as the normal procedure." Clearly, he meant to close the door on the possibility of making an exception for Leacock. On 21 November, Leacock finally replied to Morgan, who had opened his letter with the salutation, "Dear Leacock":

> Dear Mr. Principal,
>
> I beg to acknowledge the receipt of your letter informing me that I have been retired from the active staff of the university, and to thank you — my dear Morgan — for the personal kindliness with which you write.
>
> S.L.

He let nearly three weeks go by and then, on 11 December, sent again to Beatty.

> I would have written sooner but there seemed no use in it. Since I got your earlier letter I had one from the Principal definitely removing me from McGill: so that what I do or don't do, as a professor, is so nearly over that it is of no consequence. I feel deeply humiliated not at Morgan's letter, but at the thankless and unfair letter which it ratified. I am at least certain you didn't write it.

The last sentence is potentially ambiguous; Leacock felt hurt that Beatty as a governor had been part of making the policy, and he may have felt suspicious that Morgan's letter "definitely removing" him had come so soon after his 7 November letter to Beatty. His expressed certainty that Beatty did not write Glassco's letter, or Morgan's, seems a calculated irony meant to strike Beatty's conscience with the sense that in principle he had written both of them.[4]

Beatty's reply, dated 15 December, determinedly refused to take up Leacock's cause or even to understand sympathetically his complaint.

> I do not think that you need feel the least concern about the tone of a routine letter, when you remember your long years of service to the University and the appreciation of them which you already know to be no less than world-wide.

This photograph, taken in Montreal, shows what Leacock looked like in his oft-described costume: homburg, over-sized collar and loosened tie, suit and vest worn with gold watch chain, bulky topcoat.

Courtesy National Archives of Canada C-7869.

But it was precisely his long service that had led Leacock to think he should not have been addressed on the sensitive question of enforced retirement through a "routine letter." Beatty continued, "For yourself, I am afraid that I have no sympathy. You have had a full life and achieved fame. Beyond that I do not see what reward any man can obtain." He opined that Leacock would "have many years during which your influence will be increased in some way by the fact that you are no longer an active member of the staff." Soon after Beatty's letter, the public announcement was made. Thirteen McGill faculty members were to be retired, including Frank Dawson Adams, who had acted as principal; four department chairmen; Doctor Nevil Norton Evans, then celebrating his fiftieth year at McGill; and Dr. Charles F. Martin, senior dean and head of the medical faculty. Alone among this distinguished company, Leacock spoke out publicly. Queried on the subject by a *Montreal Daily Star* reporter, Leacock led the way to his office, where colleague John Culliton and the reporter watched Leacock hastily write out a reply. Given on 18 December, it appeared the following day not only in Montreal but in prominent articles in the *Toronto Mail and Empire* and *New York Times*, among other newspapers: "I have plenty to say about the Governors of McGill putting me out of the university. But I have all eternity to say it in. I shall shout it down to them." The *Times*, which frequently published Leacock's economic articles in the United States, carried an editorial in which it was urged that the retiring professor be hired by an American university "to smoke at its post-graduate students" in the manner Leacock had described admiringly in "Oxford as I See It." Despite local and international outcry, though, the retirement remained in force.[5]

How did Leacock interpret his retirement? Did he believe the responsibility for it lay with the new principal or with the university's administration? His letters indicate that he understood the original decision had come from the board, not from Morgan. In the months after the retirement became public knowledge, however, he found himself at odds with the new principal over questions relating to the future of his department. The progress of his attitude toward Morgan contrasts with that of his attitude toward Beatty. At first furious at the powerful CPR president and McGill chancellor, a friend with whom he had tangled before, Leacock soon glided back into his posture of amiable respect mingled with staunch intellectual independence. In fact, even in the same 11 December letter in which Leacock protested his retirement, he simultaneously chided Beatty for an attack he had made on Canada's young socialist economists. At the University of Western Ontario in London, Beatty had delivered a widely reported speech against the theorists who had helped plan the Cooperative Commonwealth Federation's political program and had written its platform. This group of socialist intellectuals, called the League for Social Reconstruction, numbered among its leading figures Frank Underhill and McGill's Frank Scott, the poet and law professor Leacock had helped seven years earlier, when Scott was a student, with the *McGill Fortnightly Review*; like Leacock, Scott was a member of the Political Science Association, Canada's national professional organization in the field. Beatty had criticized what he felt were the dangerously erroneous ideas of the CCF (the forerunner of today's New Democratic Party), and had attributed the problem to "something wrong with the whole atmosphere of economic teaching in this country," as he summarized his point in writing to Leacock. Frank Underhill then criticized Beatty's speech in a *Canadian Forum* article. On seeing Underhill's piece, Beatty invited Leacock to side with him publicly. At first, in the November exchange of letters between the two, Leacock said only that the young economists were incapable of writing a book or a paragraph that would engage the public's attention, and that they would have no influence unless it was given to them by the ill-advised remarks of railway presidents and university chancellors. Prodded further, he had this to say:

Yes I read today [11 December 1935] Underhill's paper in the Forum. It is written in a [word illegible] strain which will get him nowhere: I will tell him this when I get a chance. I think, if you don't mind my saying so, that in your London address and perhaps elsewhere you do not clearly enough distinguish between political economy in its real sense, and the mere polemics of Canadian politics. A great many people spend their whole lives in working on such things as economic origins and history, and theories of things that have no connection with Canada. Such great men as Thorold Rogers and William Cunningham gave their lives to the history of work & wages and the evolution of industry. Your condemnation struck a whole lot of people of whom you possibly never heard: and who are hurt but cannot answer back. You said "with exceptions," but that means nothing; if I said "With exceptions, Canadian bankers are crooks," how would Charles Gordon like it.

To the end of his life — as witnessed by one of his last books, *While There Is Time: The Case Against Social Catastrophe* (1944) — Leacock continued to endorse socialism's criticism of capitalism. Now, directly confronted on the subject by Beatty, he did not hesitate to rebuff his powerful friend's desire for an unambiguous rejection of socialist ideas, even though he saw it meant nettling Beatty in the midst of seeking him as an anti-retirement ally. Unwilling to defend the ideas of the League for Social Reconstruction, he stood equally unwilling to declare that the ideas were valueless.

On another important score, too, Leacock opposed Beatty in their November and December exchanges and afterwards. In his address, Beatty had said that professors (both Scott and Underhill were university professors) should not espouse radical ideas because they might mislead students and the public. Leacock stated uncompromisingly to him that a professor had a right to say whatever he pleased so long as he did not use his classroom to advocate his own beliefs. Beatty was not restrained by Leacock's remarks. Leacock's friend B.K. Sandwell, editor of *Saturday Night*, and Eugene Forsey, then a junior faculty member in Leacock's McGill department, joined Underhill in publicly opposing Beatty, using approximately the same arguments that Leacock used to his friend when writing in private. Sandwell wrote in his magazine on 9 November 1935 that "if Sir Edward had confined himself to the general question of university men using their academic prestige to further unacademic ends, he would have made an important and much neglected point." This important and neglected point was exactly the one Leacock was interested in, and he soon had a chance to express it more fully. In December 1935, Leacock received a letter from a correspondent who approved of Beatty's views and apparently expected Leacock to agree. Leacock wrote and carefully preserved an eloquent response, dated 18 December:

> The idea seems to be that if a professor makes a speech outside the college, to people not connected with it, and says, "I am a socialist; capitalism is doomed", then he has shown himself unfit to teach in the college and ought to be disciplined. I don't see this. Socialism is not illegal. Its proposals are not revolutionary. They involve only parliamentary voting. Socialism is a beautiful dream, that can never be realized. But it invites the sympathy of many of the kindest and best minds in the world, (including my own) even when they cannot believe in it. In practice it is bound to fail. It is an error that dies in the sunlight. In the long run truth prevails on earth: and fools should be suffered gladly. Rich men always

reach out for methods of repression and always will. But in the end righteousness wins.

No professor has the right to press the propaganda of socialism on a college class; nor has he the right to press the propaganda of Christianity or of aviation or nudism or tariff protection. If he does so, he breaks his contract. But apart from that a professor ought to be as free as you are. There are and have been socialists in many of His Majesty's Cabinets in the British Empire, including the government at Westminster itself. There is no reason why a professor should not be a socialist just as he might be a ventriloquist or a prohibitionist. But he must not start ventriloquism in his class-room.

But I think the present danger at McGill is all the other way. Many people are losing sight of the fact that a University in its first and foremost meaning is a home of learning, a place of thought, a repository of the wisdom of the past and a workshop of the wisdom of the future. It is made up of its books, its classes, its students and its professors, and the writings and thoughts that it inspires. This is a university. This is, — or should be McGill, — not its finances and its accounts and its investment of money. These things are necessary, but they are only a means not an end. It is the same as in a family: the money they have represents only a means whereby family love and family happiness can be achieved. They eat meat, they don't eat the butcher's bill.

Recently one of the McGill Governors spoke to an audience of McGill students and was reported (in print in the Daily) as having told them that the governors were "responsible for what the professors are,"

— and responsible "for what they teach." Personally, I had always thought the responsibility for what we are rests with God Almighty. I know that responsibility for what we teach rests with the college Senate; if a professor were willing to teach for nothing the governors couldn't stop him. The governors for the most part do not understand the curriculum any more than we understand their business.

I have a son at McGill. I would rather have him hear fifty lectures on Socialism, than one lecture as derogatory to his father's profession as that address.[6]

Beatty remained unwilling or unable to see the distinction Leacock made; he repeated his own opinion, that professors should be held in line on their economic views, in print and again in a 1937 address at Queen's University.

The fact that Leacock's efforts to be retained by McGill were going nowhere may have influenced his increased activity during November in arranging new book projects. On 20 November, Frank Dodd sent him a contract for the book that was to become the following year's *Funny Pieces: A Book of Random Sketches*.[7] Throughout the 1930-35 period, Leacock had published ten to twenty magazine and journal articles per year, but very few of these had been humour, and none had been the series of humorous pieces, presented in a leading magazine or by syndication in several newspapers, which had played so large a part in his career during the 1910s and 1920s. The composition of *Funny Pieces* followed what was now his pattern. It collected such essays appropriate to a humour collection as he had published, many of them largely critical and philosophical in nature but presented in humorous terms, and supplemented these with new pieces. The book implied an avowal that, in tune with his recent work on humour's history and philosophy, his humour was now explicitly devoted to probing ruminations on the truth of things, comedy being a light that could both shine into the depths and alleviate the shadows of tragedy found there. Even the section titles that grouped the book's essays expressed the way in which his writing now more explicitly embraced the decidedly intellectual and high-cultural cast it had always possessed: "The School Section," "The Literary Section," "Brain Stuff in General," "Nation and Nation," "Papers of the Ignoramus Club," "Drama Section." Composition of *Funny Pieces* went on throughout the academic year and into the following summer; it was published in October 1936. Thus, the writing process paralleled his fight to be retained at McGill, his realization that the battle was lost, his increasingly angry resentment at Morgan and the chancellors, and his gradual accommodation to his fate. As the book took shape, he allowed it to reflect these events, especially in a final section, "Personalia," which contains four essays he wrote during 1936 expressing his bitter loss modulated to nostalgia, his anger at the treatment he had received, the staunch championship of academic freedom he had maintained in the controversy with Beatty (including his sense of the necessary intellectual distinctions and subtleties it involved), and finally his affirmation that, despite all, Canada was his permanent and fitting home. As a result, this now neglected book was one of his most personal and represented a further stage in his evolution from pure humour and parody to a form of light philosophical essay that complicated and at times seemed even to erase the distinction between the voice that narrated his works and that of Leacock the man. The essay "I'll Stay in Canada" was inspired by a request, published by London's *Daily Express* in the aftermath of his forced retirement, that Leacock move to his native country. His response, entitled "No, I Shall Not Come 'Home'" when it first appeared on 4 February 1936 in the London *Evening News*, stated that he was already at home in Canada, and made a point of the country's unique position between Britain and the United States. If he moved, he would miss the close association with the United States: "they're educated just as we are and know all about kilowatts, but quit Latin at the fourth declension." His fortunes were bound up with the promise of his country.

> We are "sitting pretty" here in Canada. East and West are two oceans faraway; we are backed up against the ice cap of the Pole; our feet rest on the fender of the American border, warm with a hundred years of friendship. The noise and tumult of Europe we scarcely hear: not for us the angers of the Balkans, the weeping of Vienna and the tumults of Berlin. Our lot lies elsewhere: shovelling up mountains, floating in the sky to look for gold, and finding still the Star of the Empire in the West.[8]

November 1935 saw the genesis of another book project. Leacock set to work on a volume of humorous poetry, a genre that his work on the history of humour had brought increasingly to his mind, especially by renewing his love of W.S. Gilbert's *Bab Ballads*. On 29 November, he wrote to the *New York American* proposing that it run a ten-week series of his verses "to be called Hickonomics or Hiccoughs in Verse, Done in Our Social Planning Mill. The idea is to present a lot of the economic discussions and problems and perplexities of to-day in this form of verse, — half mocking and half serious, at times even pathetic." In December he offered the series to the *New York Herald Tribune*; both newspapers declined, and in early 1936 so did the *New York Post*, the Bell Syndicate, the British American Newspaper Service, and *The New Yorker*. In February, even The Bodley Head turned down a book version, its reader reporting, "This is not Stephen Leacock at his best....Up to a point they are stimulating & amusing, but I found them *all* too long." Although on 17 December Frank Dodd sent Leacock a contract for a book version, *Hellements of Hickonomics*, even he wrote two days later, "Quite frankly, we are not as excited over the possibilities...as you seem to be, but very likely I am wrong, and certainly we would like to publish the book and see what can be done to put it over." The book, which Leacock called his "last say" about economics, appeared in March 1936 and disappointed his admirers. Perhaps the most curious mixture of economics and humour he ever attempted, it presented jibes at economic and social theories in the form of light verse. For instance, in "Oh! Mr. Malthus" he mocked the Malthusian theory that would condemn to death those persons unable to support themselves by the wages their capitalist employers provided. Also in March, Leacock renewed a feeler he had first put out in 1933 by writing simultaneous letters to Henry Holt and Company, New York, and Thornton Butterworth, Ltd., London, asking to be given a contract for a book about humour for the Home University Library series, which was published by both firms and editorially controlled by the British one; this book eventually became, a year and a half later, his second book-length philosophical study of the subject, *Humour and Humanity*.[9]

While Leacock was engaged with these books, he was also increasing the number of his periodical contributions and of his lecture appearances. In January, he was invited by the Toronto newspaper *The Financial Post* to write a twice-weekly column; he did not accept but did begin to publish economic and political articles in the periodical in February, and later in the year brought out an important four-part series, "The Financial Condition of Canada," which appeared in the *London Morning Post* beginning on 6 July, in *The Financial Post* two months later, and in October as a short book, *The Gathering Financial Crisis in Canada*. The work criticized Canadian government policy in administering the Canadian National Railway and in combating the Depression. At the same time, it expressed great confidence in the country's economic potential, particularly in the development of natural resources. H.A. Gwynne of the *Morning Post* wrote him, "I was taken to task by your Finance Minister, Mr. Dunning, who let it be known to me...that he thought that the publication of the articles the day after his arrival was intended almost as a personal affront to himself."[10] Other new serious, humorous and personal essays from Leacock's hand were published during the first half of the year in *Atlantic Monthly*, *World Today* (a periodical publication of the Encyclopedia Britannica), *Maclean's*, *London Evening News*, *New York Herald Tribune*, *Reader's Digest*, *Review of Reviews*, *Rotarian*, *American Mercury*, and others. As for lectures, already in the fall he had made a quick four-day six-talk foray into Iowa and Missouri, and in addition had spoken five times in Massachusetts (including three appearances in Boston), and in New York and Chicago; then in January through April he lectured in Philadelphia, Syracuse, Aurora (New York), Chicago (four times), and Buffalo.

As all this went on, his battle with Morgan became more rankling. The lack of courtesy he had perceived in Morgan's letter about his retirement continued as he attempted to consult with the principal, an activity that was important to him in that, as various evidences suggest, he had begun to conceive for himself a role as an active emeritus, a retired promoter and advisor of McGill, which might partially compensate his loss of the classroom. In February 1936, he sent Morgan a memorandum detailing suggestions, which the principal had suggested that he make, about the future composition of his department. Countering a proposal that the Department of Economics and Political Science be combined with other departments, Leacock wrote that its work was already too broad and that it had,

> suffered greatly from the financial stringency of the past few years. It has had to forgo the services of outside examiners from other universities; it has lost various scholarships which it had from McGill and from private sources for graduate students, and, most of all, it has had to suspend the publication of the monographs on Canadian problems which were a chief feature of its work.

There had also been salary cuts (his own salary, for example, had been decreased in 1931 from its long-time level of $5,500). He argued that, as a Canadian institution, McGill needed a political science and economics program of a distinctive character; a product of British universities, Morgan seems to have begun his first year at McGill by finding fault with many departments because they did not correspond to British forms. Leacock made several specific recommendations. Referring to his proposals of the previous January and February, he suggested that his own position not be filled so that the savings of his salary could be used to aid the department, and that one of the existing younger faculty members, J.C. Hemmeon, should succeed him in the role of chairman. He concluded, "I am authorized by my colleagues Dr. Hemmeon and Dr. Day and Professor Culliton to say that they entirely concur in the views as to the department expressed in this letter. Mr. Forsey is ill but I have every reason to presume his acquiescence."[11]

The care and thoroughness of his presentation, in which there was no allusion to his personal disappointment, met with a response that infuriated him. Morgan replied that Leacock had had "no right to ask the opinion of junior men whose opinions were not wanted" and "no right to make a representation in writing" on a subject Morgan had wished to discuss verbally. Leacock then sent a copy of the memorandum to another of the forced retirees, Dean Charles Martin, with a request that it be given by him to the McGill senate. Leacock explained to Martin that Morgan's "manner and language were overbearing and quite unsuited to the dignity of his position or the privilege of mine."[12] Morgan also refused to consider Hemmeon as chairman, although he later relented and informed Leacock that he had invited Hemmeon to act as temporary chairman (eventually Hemmeon did receive the post, which he held until 1945). However much Leacock's original dislike of Morgan was related to the retirement, the new principal had now impressed him as managerially incompetent, educationally mistaken, and morally offensive on issues of tradition and respect. As the academic year drew to a close, the sparring between the two continued; after the dispute about the department's future, they began to exchange public insults. When someone told Leacock that the board of governors had searched for Currie's successor with a fine-tooth comb, he replied, "You know what you get when you resort to a fine-tooth comb." During a speaking tour, Morgan told audiences that his reforms had rid McGill of "university professors who prided themselves on wearing torn gowns." A story circulated that Morgan had greeted Leacock with the words, "Professor Leacock, I am credibly informed that, of all the bad departments at this university, yours is one of the worst." Leacock told friends that Morgan was running McGill "like a boys' school." His bitterness came out in repeated statements that he would speak no more in Montreal, although he expressed it as an avuncular decision to "remain on the shelf" and reflect. On 12 February, he claimed he was making his Montreal farewell in delivering one of his favourite lectures of this period, "The Art and Mystery of Language," at the Windsor Hotel to the Alumni and Alumnae of the University of Toronto. However, on 26 March he gave an address to the Political Economy Club of McGill at a dinner it held in his honour at the Berkeley Hotel; here he hit out explicitly at his forced retirement, claiming that the university administration and board of governors had "executed" the "Senility Gang," remarks that were crafted into "The End of the Senility Gang: An Episode at McGill University" published in *Funny Pieces*.[13]

What Leacock called his "last lecture" as a McGill professor was delivered to an audience of 200 students, alumni and faculty members at a dinner at the Ritz-Carleton Hotel on 4 May 1936. There ended the teaching career begun almost fifty years before at Uxbridge. Leacock's notes for his speech, entitled "Paradise Lost," are on a sheet of Mount Royal Hotel stationery and consist of a list of topics: "My last lecture...old pupils / Subject...Paradise lost / All retrospect...honour college / Tired but...Evening light...Superself / Your gift / Paradise regained / All for to-day." He elaborated on this basic structure in two revisions. The speech made little reference to the retirement controversy. "The time came when the college said it had heard our lectures so often that it would pay us not to give any more," he said, and so he had saved his final appearance for his old pupils because one more talk from him could not hurt them. The paradise he was losing was the university, and he praised "the ideal professor" as careless in his dress and gullible before the wiles of idle students but embodying "that higher idealism lifted above life." He was presented with a charcoal portrait by artist Richard Jack and two leather-bound sets of his works; there were forty volumes in each set. One was given to the university library, the other to "Stevie," that is, to him. In accepting them, he said,

> I am told you were in some doubt whether to let it be Shakespeare's works or my own. You have chosen wisely. I have not only written more than Shakespeare, but what I have written is worth more. Shakespeare's books can be had anywhere at fifteen cents each, while mine run from a dollar up.[14]

Morgan did not attend the Ritz-Carleton dinner, but Beatty, who had been characterized as "the Chief Justice who passed sentence on the Senility Gang" in Leacock's sarcastic account, was a prominent figure in the spring 1936 ceremonies of honour. He sat next to Leacock at the Ritz-Carleton and commented, "We are all sorry to see him leave the halls of McGill." Three weeks later he presented Leacock an honorary doctor-of-laws degree at the university convocation ceremonies. Leacock's notes for his response to this are, "My thanks for LL.D." Now Leacock intended to relinquish lecturing altogether; early in 1936 he sent a printed notice to lecture bureaus and publishing services throughout North America that said, "I am giving up lecturing and planning to preserve the silence which is golden" and added, pointedly, "I hope never to speak publicly in Montreal again." When he returned to McGill at the end of May to receive his honorary degree, he stayed at the home of his friend Sir Andrew Macphail, who had written to invite him with the words, "For the time of your apotheosis would you think it *dignus ut intreo sub suo tecto*. There will be a chamber, a table, a stool, and a candlestick, such as was provided in Shurem for another holy man of God." At the ceremony, accepting his degree from Beatty, he waved to the crowd but declined to offer any word.[15]

His resolution soon gave way, however, in part because of Sir Edward Beatty's encouragement. Although Beatty had not been able, the year before, to convince Leacock to support him in his criticisms of the nation's young socialist economists, he continued to prod Leacock to remain active and provide a contrast to their views. "I still believe your powerful voice and equally powerful pen should be used to combat the inaccurate and loose thinking which the more vocal members of your profession are indulging in." Beatty's prompting was one reason why, in the fall of 1936, Leacock undertook a tour of western Canada, which took him to five provinces in two months for thirty separate speaking engagements; this became his true swan song as a public speaker, for after it he appears to have given only six further talks in the remainder of his life, five of them occurring in early 1937 and representing previous commitments.[16] There were several reasons for him to make the western tour. He had received many requests for lectures since his announcement he would discontinue them. He was partly in sympathy with Beatty's desire to counter both the upthrust of socialist economics in the country and new political movements with decentralizing and even separatist implications in the Canadian west: the Cooperative Commonwealth Federation, which had gained currency especially in Saskatchewan, and Social Credit, which had come to dominate the electoral scene in Alberta. The defeat of Bennett had helped confirm the multi-party nature of Canadian federal politics and in the process had emphasized the sectional divisions within the country. Leacock wished to oppose sectionalism and also to sound a note of optimism. He preached a new empire, this time a Canadian one, whose goals and sources of future wealth would be the development of natural resources and the settlement of a new immigrant population in uncultivated areas. He also hoped that his appearances could benefit McGill financially: former students living in the west might be made interested in the university's financial crisis.

Then, too, Leacock himself needed fresh sources of revenue. His McGill pension provided him with only $2,750; his income for 1935, during the whole of which he had still been on the faculty, had been approximately $14,000, substantially below what he had been earning in the 1920s. His choice of topics for the tour — serious discussions of current political and economic issues in Canada — was perhaps determined, in part, by the changing nature of his enduring popularity. Formerly, his humour books had represented the most substantial share of his annual writing income. In July 1936, however, royalty statements from his publishers in New York showed that he was earning much more from his critical writing than from his recent humour. Dodd, Mead sent him only $453.30 before taxes for six months and reported that $374.95 of the *Afternoons in Utopia* advance was still unearned. By contrast, Doubleday Doran, the publishers of *Charles Dickens: His Life and Works* and *The Greatest Pages of American Humor*, sent him $2,886.53, including $2,353.38 for the Dollar Book Club issue of the Dickens book. Leacock might have hoped for a good return from a tour of lectures on economic subjects, especially with the prospect of being able to sell his speeches as articles and again in book form afterward. In addition, the disappointment of being retired might have suggested that he would gain most satisfaction by proving himself still useful in his academic discipline. But the desire for increased income must have been a prime motive, and the western tour became the first time he charged a fee for speaking in Canada. The organizing agency, Cockfield Brown & Co., paid him $10,000 plus expenses of about $3,000. The tour was publicly sponsored by the Canadian Bankers Association, but Leacock did not know, and never knew, that ten of the organization's member banks had contributed $15,000 to the agency to enable his payment and underwrite other expenses.[17]

Before heading west, Leacock went to the United States at the end of October, speaking in Memphis, Tennessee; Amherst and Springfield, Massachusetts; and Middletown, New York. He started the western trip from Montreal on 25 November, accompanied by Stevie, then a McGill freshman, who had obtained permission to miss classes for the two months required. Just before leaving, Leacock sent Dodd, Mead a proposal for a book based on the trip. He acknowledged that his subject was not commercial, promised that his manner of presentation would make it so, announced he was forgoing an advance, and offered to reduce his royalty to ten percent. The company's rejection, despite these sweeteners, came to him during the tour. Then, however, Miller Services Limited of Toronto wrote asking to syndicate articles based on the trip and offering to produce a book of them. Miller eventually sold the series — "My Discovery of the West" — to the *Toronto Globe and Mail* for $480, or $40 per article, $15 more than Leacock had suggested: "I think the sale establishes," Andrew Miller wrote, "a record in its total amount of any series of articles sold to an individual newspaper in Canada."[18] The *Montreal Star* had earlier contracted for twelve articles, and ran its series approximately weekly over the period of the tour, during which time the more frequent, twenty-seven-part *Globe and Mail* version was appearing in that newspaper and through syndication in eight others coast to coast.

Writing in a hardbound notebook from back to front, Leacock kept a journal record; he noted his and Stevie's departure from Montreal on 25 November and the first lectures, on 27 and 28 November, at Fort William, Ontario; there he addressed a dinner for McGill alumni and lectured on Canadian-United States relations to the Men and Women's Canadian Club. The first of these events, his appearance before the McGill alumni, keynoted his tour. He entitled it "Our Colleges and What They Stand For," but his remarks included a thoroughgoing attack on sectionalism and separatist feeling and a call for "re-union and re-confederation." In Winnipeg, where he had scheduled five events, he turned down several additional offers, including one from the famous Women's Press Club, which had spearheaded the campaign to win the vote for women in the days of the First World War. He spoke at the University Women's Club, the Winnipeg Press Club Dinner, the Women's Canadian Club, the Men's Canadian Club, and the University of Manitoba. He wrote home:

> It is just like a come-to-Jesus parade. I talked at the Fort Gary Hotel and a little while before the meeting they said, "This is the record for seats except for the Queen of Rumania," and a little later, "This beats the Queen of Rumania," and later, "The Queen is nowhere."[19]

As he continued the tour to Saskatchewan, Alberta and British Columbia, he delivered his body blows against sectionalism and his call for a re-invigorated confederation but did not neglect humour, philosophy, education, or the international scene; many of his lectures were on such topics as "Education by the Yard," "College As It Was and Is," "The Theory of Comic Verse," "An Analysis of Humor," "Frenzied Fiction: Murder at $2.50 a volume and Love at $1.25," "When Can We Start the Next War?," and "Brotherly Love among the Nations," the latter two containing mockeries of war, pleas for peace, and a hopeful prognosis that there would not be war in Europe. His schedule was hectic — in Edmonton, for instance, he gave five lectures, three in one day — and it included at least one family event besides the company of his son: in Calgary, he visited his brother Teddy. All three of his final lectures, on 7, 8 and 13 January in Victoria, were given to educational bodies and concerned education. From Victoria, Leacock wrote home to Barbara Ulrichson that she should refuse all invitations for a time because the trip had left him tired.

Still, he was triumphant on his return to Montreal in mid-January. Contracts were in place for the new book, and the success of the tour seemed a guarantee that it would have a wide audience. Only five days after his last date in Victoria, he wrote to Frank Dodd suggesting a new book of humour that would give him a publication based on his career as a lecturer and wrap it up: "I have no[w] finished & done with lecturing forever (except that I have 3 engagements to fill in the next six weeks....so I propose to publish lectures under a fair title....*Here Are My Lectures* or *Lectures They Laughed At*."[20] Then in March, as the "My Discovery of the West" articles were still appearing and Leacock was preparing the book version, he received the offer of a commission to write an article on behalf of the Ontario nickel industry. Acting for the Ontario Nickel Corporation and Johnson, Ring & Co. of Toronto, the law firm McCarthy & McCarthy relayed a proposal that he write "an article on the subject of Base Metals, their value, and use, devoting particular attention to nickel"; the purpose envisioned was "to furnish information to those members of the public who may become interested in nickel and through a more complete understanding of the uses and future of nickel in the purchase of stock in a nickel company." Leacock accepted the job for $500 provided by Johnson, Ring & Co.; he set to work immediately upon receiving statistical information supplied by the company, and by April had produced a twenty-eight-page pamphlet, *What Nickel Means to the World*. Long a champion of Canada's further exploitation of its metal resources, Leacock argued in his monograph for the development of the industry and the future use of nickel coinage. This was the first of a number of writing projects in the years after his retirement that belonged to the realm of public relations; these remained, however, expressive of his own views, since he would only write on subjects of importance to him and would only argue for his own already established opinions. The monograph on nickel was in tune with the articles he had recently been producing on the need to develop Canadian resources. Leacock regarded such commissions as legitimate opportunities to exercise influence as a practical economist.

In *My Discovery of the West*, he wrote as a historian and a political economist, who at once sharpened and softened his points with humour. The book appeared in June, arrangements having been made by Leacock and Andrew Miller for the Toronto firm of Thomas Allen to bring it out and seek an American publisher; one was found in Hale, Cushman & Flint of New York and Boston.[21] The first thirteen of the book's seventeen chapters were composed of the articles he had written for syndication, and the remaining chapters drew on other articles he had recently published and on *The Gathering Financial Crisis in Canada*. He combined analysis of contemporary economic movements, as in "The Pure Theory of Social Credit," with historical surveys of all the western provinces. His basic message was that the west would provide a source of wealth for the country as long as its resources were managed in the national interest. Although he still stressed the potential, for Canada, of the imperial relationship with Great Britain and her former colonies, he began to speak of "the empire of Canada." Exploring the potential of each western province, he also proposed measures that would strengthen the country by placing more power in the hands of the federal government. These included transfer to Canada of the right to amend the British North America Act, consolidation of provincial debts into a national debt, and development of a unified policy for the national railways (they should be either government-owned or privately owned). Reviews of the book were generally positive. They praised Leacock's popular style, calculated to ease the way for audiences disinclined to venture into the serious and difficult subjects he explored. Reviewers did not always agree with his thinking and some of them criticized his efforts to leaven arguments with humour, but his ability to interest people in his viewpoint was unquestioned. "The book as a whole will not end arguments, but start them. And that, no doubt, was what Professor Leacock intended," one critic said. Perhaps because its chapters had circulated widely in newspaper syndication, *My Discovery of the West* did not do particularly well at the book stores, selling about 1,400 copies in Canada and 1,200 in the United States and being remaindered in both countries within a year.[22]

As the first academic year after his retirement, 1936-37, came to a hectic close and 1937 progressed into the late spring and summer, offers and honours flowed to Leacock. He was invited to join the faculty of the University of British Columbia. Lawrence Lowell, president of Harvard University, asked him to deliver the Lowell Institute Foundation Lectures, a series of six to eight speeches on a subject of his choice. Tours were proposed in Russia, Australia and New Zealand. All proposals were turned down, though for a time he considered the Australia offer as a possible way to finance a trip around the world; negotiations continued for some time, but eventually were abandoned. *My Discovery of the West* won the 1937 Governor General's Literary Award in the category of nonfiction. He was awarded the Lorne Pierce Medal by the Royal Society of Canada, the resolution noting his many honorary degrees, his stature as teacher, economist and author, and his contribution "to the growing reputation of Canadian letters." In a letter dated 1 June 1937, Leacock mentioned the Lorne Pierce Medal to a friend in England and made light of the flood of awards he had been receiving.

> Ask them to raise me to the peerage: I have so many honorary degrees and the other day a gold medal that the peerage is all I need. Tell Eddie Peacock to tell Henry to tell Stanley Baldwin to tell Neville Chamberlain that I would accept any peerage from a Duke Sinister to a Baron Scavenger.[23]

That summer his household was disturbed again, this time by the marriage, after ten years with him, of Barbara Ulrichsen to a son of one of Leacock's friends; the groom, Donald Nimmo, worked as the editor of a Detroit magazine. The wedding was held at Old Brewery Bay, and Leacock supervised the building of special tables and trellises outdoors for the reception. He mixed drinks inside at the bar, which he said would be closed for twenty minutes to allow the ceremony to take place. Barbara Nimmo moved with her husband to the United States, but remained in close association with her uncle until the end of his life. At this time, too, the brief and ineffective career of Leacock's nemesis, Morgan, ended. He was fired at the end of academic 1936-37, having survived only two years. When word of the dismissal became public, the *McGill Daily* proposed Leacock as a likely candidate for vice-chancellor. The board of governors chose an American educator, Lewis Williams Douglas, but he too left after two years, because of interests in the United States; Leacock later remarked, "McGill has established a new two-year course, leading to the degree of ex principal."[24]

His work during the summer of 1937 consisted largely in preparing the two books he had recently set in motion, *Humour and Humanity*, which he had proposed in March 1936, and the book eventually entitled *Here Are My Lectures and Stories*, which he had proposed in January 1937; by coincidence, both titles appeared on the same publication date, 15 November 1937. In *Humour and Humanity* Leacock attempted, for the most part successfully, to avoid duplication of *Humor: Its Theory and Technique*; gone were the separate chapters on the history of humour, contemporary humour, the methods of Dickens and Mark Twain, and others. Of course, his concepts remained largely the same but the arrangement of material more clearly reflected a philosophical analysis. An introductory chapter on the nature of humour was followed by four chapters on humour as developed through words, ideas, situations, and characters. Two chapters on comic verse analyzed its surface hijinks and its deeper suggestions and implications. Two final chapters related humour to "craftsmanship" and to "sublimity," that is, to the art of writing and to the deepest meanings accessed through that art. Throughout, Leacock's constant flow of examples, both by himself and others, and his use of humour to express his points makes *Humour and Humanity* a book-length example of the type of essay he emphasized during the second half of his career, one that explores a serious point, not merely driving it home through humour but revealing that humour has something to do with its essence.

Frank Dodd thought that *Here Are My Lectures and Stories* was "an unusually bright and amusing book" and though sales records for it are incomplete, Leacock termed it "a success." The book, divided into chapters, reprinted texts of Leacock's popular lectures, including several of the "Frenzied Fiction" ones, recent favourites such as "How Soon Can We Start the Next War," and a variety of others; many of these were paired with new "interleaf stories," as he called them, hence the "stories" of the title. The inclusion of his recent lecture "How Soon Can We Start the Next War?" gave him the chance to bring to a new audience his polemic against armed conflict and his hopeful prediction that the present world situation would not lead to hostilities due to the palpable foolishness of modern war. During 1937 Leacock also published essays and humorous sketches in publications such as the *Mark Twain Quarterly, Reader's Digest, Lilliput* (London U.K.), *New York Times,* and *Atlantic Monthly,* and articles on Canadian economic questions in *Barron's*; in December, *Banking* brought out a short article, "Can Professors Teach Bankers?," perhaps occasioned partly by his own look back at the western tour, which might also have aroused another question, Do bankers use professors?[25]

While There Is Time

I n early March 1938 Leacock began mentioning to his publishers an illness that was slowing up work on his new collection, *Model Memoirs*. That same month he was admitted to Montreal's Royal Victoria Hospital for prostatic surgery, which was performed by the chief of the hospital's urology department, Dr. David W. Mackenzie. Leacock's correspondence shows him depressed by the ordeal. Mackenzie required him to stay in hospital to recuperate for a longer period than might have been strictly necessary, perhaps to make him rest and remain quiet. In one letter, Leacock recasts events in a revealing way:

> David Mackenzie (the best doctor in the world; I wish
> he could operate on all my friends) has removed my
> sense of humour, — he said it was inflated and must
> come out. I said that that might leave me a little senti-
> mental and he said, yes, but it would do me no harm.

That is, he feared the loss of sexual potency would mean the loss of his creative gift. In its place, there could be only sentimentality, which, despite the doctor's assurances, he feared. Uncharacteristically, he continued over several months to refer in letters to his illness and slow recovery. At the end of April he wrote that he was "better — though I am still in hospital";[1] in the first week of May he was finally released and went directly to Old Brewery Bay, where he spent the summer recuperating and finishing *Model Memoirs*, which contains such outstanding pieces as "My Victorian Girlhood," "Overworking the Alphabet," "The Dissolution of Our Dinner Club" and "All Is not Lost." The last of these is a double-barreled satire that struck at the confused politics of central Europe but more particularly at the confusing and alarmist reporting of it in the press, which served only to keep readers in a state of bewilderment and fear. Leacock picked up the pace of his correspondence with Paul Reynolds, who was seeking magazine publication for the new pieces. Some were completed too close to the book's scheduled release date for this to be possible, but "My Victorian Girlhood" caught the fancy of *The Saturday Evening Post*; Dodd, Mead held up the book's publication so the *Post* issue containing the story could appear first.

Some energy was also devoted to the traditional round of activities: gardening, boating, and theatricals. But in all of them Leacock was, for once, more an observer than a participant. For example, the second year of the "Brewery Nights Entertainment" was under the direction of Peggy Shaw, daughter of Fitz Shaw and former playmate of Stevie, with Leacock and Fitz assisting; on 3 August, it was performed to an audience of two hundred local people and summer residents gathered on the Couchiching lakeshore at Fitz Shaw's home, the Old Brewery, which stood just west of Leacock's property and was the site of the vanished brewery after which Leacock had named his own grounds. The program included Leacock's "The Raft: Danger and Love in One Act" and four brief skits by young friends, among them "The Return of Champlain" and "Lady Godiva Rides By." The *Packet and Times* reported that the weather, a combination of brief squalls and interludes of sunshine, came to the players' aid by giving Leacock's comedy just the backdrop it required. In boating, too, Leacock watched and assisted rather than led. One day he observed a new employee, Albanie Pelletier, the youngest of Tina Kelly's brothers, rowing Stevie on the lake. Calling him ashore, Leacock strictly forbade Albanie to take the boat out again, but told him that if he would learn to swim, he could use the punt and have a gold watch as well. Albanie practised strenuously for weeks and then triumphantly demonstrated his new ability to Leacock. True to his word, Leacock gave him the use of the punt and sent him into town with a cheque for $3.95, the price — he ascertained by telephone — of the largest gold pocket watch in an Orillia pharmacist's shop.[2]

Before leaving Orillia, Leacock made permanent the changes he had already set in motion the year before, when he had spent most of his Montreal residence in a hotel rather than in the Côte-des-Neiges house. He planned again to live in a hotel, this time the historic old Windsor on Dominion Square, and not open the house at all. John and Tina Kelly were to stay behind in Old Brewery Bay and live in the lodge as year-round caretakers; they were given a long document that detailed their duties and compensation, and provided for his will to supersede the document if he should die. But in mid-October when he returned to Montreal, Leacock postponed moving into the Windsor for a few months. He was occupied, first, with writing a memorial for Sir Andrew Macphail, who had died on 23 September, just a month and a day short of his seventy-fourth birthday; the article appeared in the November issue of the *Queen's Quarterly*. He stayed on longer because of a new book project. On 23 October and 30 October 1938, the *New York Times* published two new essays, "Is Education Eating Up Life?" and "How to Keep Education from Eating Up Life." Frank Dodd wrote soon after to ask "whether you are going to continue to do more in this vein," because he saw the seed of a book. In fact, Leacock had already discussed the possibility of such a book with Paul Reynolds back in 1933 but had put the work aside because of the Dickens biography and other projects. Now he told Dodd that indeed a book was possible. Dodd responded within six days of his original praising letter: "We would very much like to publish the book and I am counting on you to have it ready for late spring or early autumn of next year." Spring was out of the question. Although Leacock was able to move to the Windsor Hotel, as he reported to Dodd, Mead in February 1939, he still laboured under the effects of his illness. On 19 April, he gave this as his reason for declining an offer of an honorary degree from Boston University. It is possible, of course, that the inconvenience of travelling to Boston, the need to spend money on the trip and the requirement that he speak at the ceremony may also have affected his extremely polite refusal.[3] He now focused on the new book not only because of the theme's importance to him but also because his finances were suffering from a year of comparative inactivity. His tax return for 1938 reports a gross income of only $13,757.08.

Refreshing his income was an important theme of the summer at Old Brewery Bay. Not only was he writing for the new book, he was also involved in negotiations for a film version of "My Financial Career," to star Robert Benchley, with Metro-Goldwyn-Mayer. Paul Reynolds wired him of the prospect in July and was still negotiating in August, but no agreement was ever concluded. Throughout his life Leacock had been frequently approached for film rights to his works but none of the projected films was made. As early as 1916, a British movie company paid more than forty pounds for rights to consider *Sunshine Sketches* for adaptation into a scenario. Dr. Ralph Curry counted, in the archives of the Leacock Memorial Home, more than 150 letters, spanning Leacock's entire career as a humorist, related to dramatic rights, film rights and radio permissions.[4] In addition, there are letters and records reporting on the successes of his dramatized stories, from widely reviewed runs at famous London theatres to private amateur productions for New York society audiences. Leacock was sensitive to the dramatic and filmic potential of his work.

*Leacock and an unidentified man building a studio at
Old Brewery Bay in 1939.*

Courtesy National Archives of Canada C-31969.

He commented to would-be dramatizers that "My Financial Career" needed only to be "illustrated to become a movie" and that his "nonsense" plays could be performed on the stage with virtually no adaptation. Leacock was also attempting to rebuild his finances by investing his savings along lines suggested by his own economic knowledge and prognostications. In May 1939 he directed his brokers to acquire 1,150 shares of East Malarctic Mines, only one of several such purchases in the late 1930s and the 1940s.[4] He sold other stocks, such as utilities, to finance his purchases of northern mining interests. He was putting to practical test his own ideas that much of Canada's economic future lay in its northern mineral resources, a position he had championed at least since the 1910s, when he was one of the earliest authorities to recommend use of Canadian nickel in minting coins. Eventually, the restored performance of his stock portfolio showed that he had judged the general climate of Canadian mining and metals industries, and the particular companies in which he invested, very cannily.

Summer 1939 was in all respects a time of increased activity. He followed with interest the cross-country progress of King George VI and Queen Elizabeth during May and June, and returned to his previous leadership in Old Brewery Bay activities. He became involved in trying to get an Oro Township farmer to use the land on his fishing property as pasture in return for two tons of hay. His correspondence shows that he had planted eight hundred asparagus roots, a considerable crop, and few or none of them had grown. He blamed the failure on the seeds and demanded replacements; he considered it out of the question that planting methods or soil conditions could have had a part in the failure. On 9 July, he and John and Tina Kelly sighted a boy, Percy Bartleman, whose canoe had capsized in Lake Couchiching near Leacock's point. The three put out in one of Leacock's boats with Kelly at the motor, but Tina became ill and they had to return to land. Leacock went out on his own and threw the boy a line. The incident made the front page of the *New York Times* the next day and was reported far and wide. In quizzical exasperation, Leacock commented to the *Toronto Daily Star* four days after the incident: "Why, the first thing you know they'll make a lifeboat station out of me.... You may quote me as saying that in the future I will rescue no one, not even women."[6] For the new book, he wrote an article that testified again to his love of sport, the region he had chosen as home, and the local people. "Bass Fishing with Jake Gaudaur on Lake Simcoe" memorialized his longtime fishing companion who had died two years before. The manuscript of the book was completed in August and sent off to Dodd, Mead. That summer there was a third season of the Brewery Nights Entertainments. But it was the last year for the company; the players and their audience were never reunited.

In late August 1939, the non-aggression pact between Nazi Germany and the Union of Soviet Socialist Republics was made public; a week later, on 1 September, Germany attacked Poland. Great Britain and France declared war on 3 September, and Canada followed suit on 10 September. In the midst of this international crisis, Leacock and his household suffered a crucial loss. On 6 September, his trusted superintendent John Kelly was killed when the Old Brewery Bay farm truck was struck by a Canadian Pacific Railway train at the Eady Crossing, not far from the house. Another hired man, named Hough, saved himself by leaping clear, but apparently Kelly was unable to do so, or had stayed in the vehicle to attempt to get it off the track. Leacock was one of the first at the scene of the accident; he provided nurses and other medical services for the stricken Tina and saw to Kelly's burial in Orillia's Roman Catholic cemetery, Saint Michael's. Much of the remainder of Leacock's Old Brewery Bay season was occupied with the sad details of arranging for compensation for the burial and for the truck, which Leacock had given to Kelly some time earlier, from the railway, which agreed to pay a variety of costs although it was not at fault. In his customary fashion, Leacock drew up an elaborate memorandum outlining the financial help he was offering Tina, including the gift of a piece of his property where he had intended Kelly to build his own family house; he thinly veiled his regret that, in his circumstances at the time, he could not do more. He was no longer occupying his house in Montreal so Tina could not work there; without Kelly she could not oversee Old Brewery Bay. She had worked for him without interruption for many years, but had to seek other housekeeping work that winter in Montreal.[7]

In mid-October, having settled in at the Windsor Hotel and with the galley proofs of *Too Much College* to read, Leacock became involved in the war effort. First, he prepared a booklet for Oxford University Press in Canada, *All Right, Mr. Roosevelt (Canada and the United States)*. It celebrated the peaceful relationship of the two countries as a model for and contribution towards peace in the world, and at the same time sought to encourage both the United States and its individual citizens to help Canada in any way possible, including enlistment in the Canadian Armed Forces. *All Right, Mr. Roosevelt* was widely and approvingly noticed on both sides of the border. Leacock's second literary contribution to war propaganda was *Our British Empire* (entitled *The British Empire* in the United States), which combined a popular history of the Empire with praise of its role in world civilization. It argued that the Empire with its essential partners, especially the United States and France, provided a model of tolerant, co-operative political and social relationship. *Too Much College* was published on 10 November.[8] The first of its four sections comprised nine numbered essays on higher education, including the famous "Education Eating Up Life" and "Has Economics Gone to Seed"; the second section, "Kindred Essays in Education and Humour," collected four essays, including "When Men Retire." The third section, "Little Stories for Good Luck," which had been syndicated by Miller Services to Canadian periodicals during the early months of 1939, was a miscellany of humorous sketches, many with reference to subjects related to Leacock's years as a student and teacher; with the basically fictional approach of most of the pieces, this collection of twenty-three light pieces looked forward in mood and form to his later collection, *Happy Stories*. The book's final section, an "Epilogue," was the single essay of eulogy for Jake Gaudaur, which served as an elegy not only for Leacock's friend but for his own life in the homeland of his childhood and his choice.

In writing about education, Leacock from first to last maintained that higher learning was an essential element in society. His disapproval, over the years, of a changing university system was always grounded in the conviction that the work of professors, as researchers and as teachers, was at the heart of social progress. In *Too Much College*, he criticized new disciplines like psychology and spoke on the virtues of the study of Latin. He questioned the practice of tailoring university programs to appeal to the mass of students; universities should select the brightest minds for special cultivation. He attacked what he regarded as a uniquely modern determination to take the emphasis in universities and colleges away from study and to place it on social and entertainment activities, often discussing such questions in terms that ran far ahead of the thinking of his own time. Programs of study were lengthening to such an extent that a person's best productive years would be spent in the classroom rather than on the job. He doubted that the gradual elaboration of courses and degrees provided any real benefit; in fact, he said, longer courses of study really only served society's desire to slow the entry of young people into the already overcrowded workforce. He allowed that students needed time to master their subjects but suggested that many new disciplines did not require years of schooling. Some topics were best left to mastery through apprenticeship in a profession. He worried that the brightest students suffered in a university geared to the average. He advised that modern languages should be taught to be spoken as well as read and written, again anticipating the educational theory of the later twentieth century. Whereas *Too Much College* favours traditional aspects of university curricula, in early educational essays Leacock had been inclined to dismantle traditional courses of study in his eagerness to protect the essential work of the schools from hidebound practices of decreasing relevance. As early as 1910, however, he had championed the unworldly university professor against the modern "professors" who crowded the popular press. In "Oxford as I See It," he favourably compared traditional European universities with their modern North American counterparts. Many of the features of Oxford that he had praised were the same qualities he defended in *Too Much College*: retention of the classics as a basis for appreciating all modern languages and literature, the identification and fostering of gifted students, an emphasis on cultivating a life of the mind rather than developing an apparatus of regulations, examinations and schedules. Just as he had decided for himself, as a young man, to seek an unconventional field, he was prepared in old age to be unconventional in defending traditionalist educational principles that were threatened by the widespread innovations of the day.

In his early years, Leacock had been a revolutionary, abandoning his brilliant success with the study of languages in favour of one of the new social sciences, economics. He demanded a field through which he could make a definite and immediate contribution to modern society in a realm that defined it and distinguished it from past ages. However, when he became a university professor, he found that society was pressuring the university to conform to its needs in ways he could not approve. He objected to alliances between business and education that threatened to remove the traditions of independent critical thought in favour of impressive facilities, the most up-to-date and fashionable methods and theoreticians, and a basically conformist, service-oriented, training approach to the education of students. The relevance he championed was one supplied by those shuffling, absent-minded, impractical professors he often pictured, and in whose company he wished to be counted. It was a relevance based on the pursuit of knowledge and the criticism of society from a detached and neutral vantage point. When he joked about learning in his early books, he often ridiculed the evaporation of knowledge in average minds and the empty claims of those professing to possess it.

When he mocked such bumblers, he did not always take great care to salvage the object of their pretensions, education itself. This was especially true when he wrote about the classics; though he proudly retained his Greek and Latin throughout life, he always felt some impatience toward the professors of these "useless" subjects on which he had spent so many hours of his youth. Still, his primary purpose was to characterize the folly created by "a little knowledge." What he wanted most of all, as he had long ago expressed in *Winnowed Wisdom*, was for people to go beyond average attainments.

Leacock was approaching his seventieth birthday, and he seemed in many respects restored to his old self. He welcomed to Montreal an old friend, F. Cyril James, who had been at the London School of Economics in 1921 when Leacock urged the students to write letters to the press about one of his speeches. After a distinguished career as an economics professor, latterly at the University of Pennsylvania, James had been appointed the new principal of McGill. Leacock gave him a dinner at the University Club with René du Roure and another favourite Leacock crony, F.A. Greenshields, chief justice of the Province of Quebec. Nevertheless, there were signs about him that, despite his renewed vigour and purpose, he was conscious of a change. For example, after sitting that winter for a portrait by Frederick B. Taylor, an artist who had graduated from McGill and had a studio near the Windsor Hotel, Leacock exclaimed over the finished work: "My God, Taylor, that's exactly how I feel." He was preoccupied with how he was feeling, how he was different from before. On his birthday, 30 December, his essay, "Three Score and Ten," appeared in the *New York Times*; extending the meditation begun in "When Men Retire," it contained his moving portrayal of extreme old age as an obscure no-man's land of decisive but unknown encounters, an image that linked his own struggles and the war his country was fighting. There was defiance: "Give me my stick. I'm going out on to No Man's Land. I'll face it." But there was also testimony that illness changes old men: he spoke of an illness that was "not a tragic one...

but just one good flap of warning" to garrulous old men, making them be quiet and listen more humbly to the world around them.[9]

The new year began with a family controversy. On 23 January 1940, Leacock wrote to advance Charlie money intended to help him with some debts he had accumulated. The letter ended:

> The plain meaning of this letter is that I am advancing money to pay your debt but neither I nor my estate are to draw any profit from this. And if any doubt arises from the interpretation of this arrangement I promise, and you also promise, to accept the decision of George [Leacock] as legally binding.

He wrote also to Charlie's creditors to say a sufficient sum was being transferred to his brother's bank.[10] Leacock's arrangement included a monthly personal allowance for his brother; on 22 February, Charlie returned the first payment, saying he did not need it and "Many thanks for all your trouble." Charlie's assertion that he was once again in control of his affairs belied an unhappy reality, his growing debility. Leacock's readiness to help came at a time when the hoped-for financial benefits of all his work during 1939 were failing to materialized. His gross income for the year was still low, at $11,717.62. However, he soon began on projects that would restore his reputation and his sales. On 30 April, Frank Dodd wrote to propose a new anthology of his previously published humour. This became *The Laugh Parade*, which appeared later in the year; it sold briskly and steadily, and with his last four books collecting fresh humour — *Model Memoirs*, *My Remarkable Uncle*, *Happy Stories* and *Last Leaves* — restored his currency, and his sales figures, as a contemporary humorist. Also that spring, Stevie graduated from McGill, with honours in English, at the age of twenty-five. Leacock's friend Leslie Roberts, author of *Canada's War at Sea* (for which Leacock wrote the preface), stated on second-hand authority that Leacock missed the graduation exercises;

he remained in the University Club because — to give the gist of an improbable quotation attributed to him — he felt irrelevant and out of place.[11]

In July, Charlie was again a cause of concern. His slowness to pay his bills was another sign of decreasing competence. To Leacock's enquiries, Charlie replied testily that his tardiness had been due only to a slow bank transfer of funds; he was proposing to sell one of his properties (he owned his home, West Ridge, in Sutton, and another local house, Bovaire) to repay the $550 his brother had advanced. "I am again doing business & shall make more profits in this war than last, 1914-18," he wrote on 16 July. No one in the family seems to have known to what this referred; it may well have meant nothing. On 9 August, still concerned about Charlie's behaviour but still considering it nothing worse than irresponsibility, Leacock wrote, "My dear Charlie, While there is still time I wish you would try to get better control of yourself, and to make financial arrangements to carry on." A week later came Charlie's bitter reply:

Stephen Leacock, Miserable man!

I know you for what you are!...Leave me to my life & I'll leave you to yours.

Charles Leacock

Such communications caused Leacock, George and their sister Dot (now a pathologist at Toronto's Hospital for Sick Children) to look more closely at Charlie. They found he was physically ill as a result, at least in part, of emotional or mental disturbances that made it increasingly difficult for the aging bachelor, living alone, to look after himself properly. Late in the summer, he was admitted as a mental patient to the Ontario Hospital in Whitby. On 21 September, George reported by letter to Leacock that "Charlie is back at Sutton.... He is in fine shape mentally but looks pretty *old*." George had paid $239 in bills for Charlie, provided him an amount to live on and extended Leacock's invitation that he winter in Old Brewery Bay, where he would have the staff to help him. Charlie turned the invitation down because, he said, the house was too cold; George commented that Charlie wanted to be in his own home. However, George said, he had commanded Charlie to get at least two good meals daily in a local inn, rather than cook for himself, which would result in a bad diet and a mess in his house. George hoped to get to Montreal to discuss Charlie's plight in person with Leacock. On 18 September Charlie again was admitted to the Whitby hospital. In mid-October he addressed Leacock with childlike affection as "Stevie":

> I am leaving the hospital in a day or so — as soon as
> Dot gets the doctor's letter to say it's O.K. for me to
> leave — I shall be glad to get to my farm & get some
> work for the winter as I like that work of fixing up.
>
> Your affec bro
> Charlie

At this point, the family drew up an agreement whereby Teddy, in Calgary, and Leacock would help to oversee Charlie's affairs.[12]

Around the same time, Leacock's father, Walter Peter Leacock, died in Nova Scotia at the age of ninety-two. Correspondence in Leacock's files relating to the estate of his grandfather, Thomas Murdock Leacock, shows that the humorist and his brothers — or at least George and Charlie, who cooperated with him in family business — were aware of their father's whereabouts, for they oversaw the disbursement of the estate's earnings. Although some of his brothers and sisters had visited Peter on business, Leacock never made any attempt to contact his father.[13] But another loss cut deep into his familiar circle. That summer René du Roure died suddenly at the age of sixty, not long after having tried to enlist in the French armed services, as he had done in the First World War; he had not been accepted because of his age. Both Leacock and McGill Principal F. Cyril James stated that du Roure's grief over the collapse of France had contributed to his death. Du Roure would never again occupy the second bedroom to the left of the staircase at Old Brewery Bay, nor would he smoke and play billiards and contribute to the education of Sergeant Jones.

In the midst of these preoccupations, at the very time that Charlie's problems were coming to light, Leacock received another book proposal, this one from John Bassett, president of the *Montreal Gazette* and the Gazette Printing Company. The publisher of the first edition of *Literary Lapses*, the Gazette Printing Company had been entrusted with production of a book for Distillers Corporation-Seagrams Limited: Samuel Bronfman, president of Seagrams, wanted a book about Canada to be distributed free by his company as a contribution to wartime morale and patriotism. Bassett proposed that an American literary agent visit Leacock on Bronfman's behalf, and on 18 July Leacock cabled back, "Very glad to see representative here stop Please tell him to bring fishing rod." When the agent and a member of the printing company arrived, Leacock immediately conducted them out onto the lake; afterwards he gave them dinner and then, according to his custom, retired early, leaving his guests to ponder. No business had been discussed. The exasperated American, feeling that Leacock was showing his age, was prepared to leave and seek another author. The next morning, however, when the two men went to find him at the boathouse to say goodbye, he came down from his study with a sheaf of writing that comprised an outline sketch of the whole project. A typed version of these notes (or possibly a later draft of his outline) in the files of the Leacock Memorial Home contains a précis of the book and a description of its aims. Leacock's fee was $5,000 and he was to complete the book in four months. While working on this book, Leacock lived at least part of the late fall and winter of 1940 and the spring of 1941 in his Côte-des-Neiges house; he did the same in succeeding years as well. He was providing a home for Stevie, who taught English at McGill during the 1940-41 academic year. Leacock finished his manuscript early in the new year and corrected proofs in July. The work was further vetted in September by the poet A.M. Klein, who worked for Bronfman as a speech writer, correspondence secretary and public relations adviser; a number of his suggestions were incorporated, and Klein also provided an introduction. The book was manufactured by the Gazette Printing Company and was ready for distribution by late November. Leacock hoped that, because it was a privately produced limited edition, Bronfman would soon dispose of the copyright either to himself or a commercial publisher for trade publication; in fact, he offered to buy back the copyright for $1,000. Bronfman retained it however and kept the book in print for twenty-six years; it was given away by Seagrams to anyone who requested a copy, and by 1967, its final year, 165,000 copies had been distributed.[14]

Canada, The Foundations of Its Future was a sweeping panorama of the country, vividly imagined and evoked in a prose that has the vigour of an exploratory voyage. Leacock handled facts easily and added a wealth of poetic allusion, suggestion and depth. The book antedated by nearly three years the volume usually named as the first modern presentation of Canadian nationalism, Bruce Hutchison's award-winning *The Unknown Country* (1943). The works are very different in approach. Hutchison directly addressed the subjects of the people and institutions of contemporary Canada and described the landscape. Leacock evoked these things in the course of a history of a developing nation, a history that was taken to the verge of the future and looked into it. Leacock's penetration of his subject was coloured by the prophetic optimism he professed for the people, land, and nation; he celebrated potential and demanded a will to create. At the same time, he avoided easy or comforting assumptions, such as Hutchison's that English and French Canadians were growing closer together. For many years, Leacock had been analyzing, in articles, the separatist tendencies in Canada, including those in the west and north; he dreamed that development of these regions could make Canada a nation comprising one hundred million people. It was, he believed, a dream based on a sober judgment of possibility, not the simplistic expectation of inevitable greatness that had animated some turn-of-the-century Canadians. *Canada* was well-written and beautifully designed; it contained thirty-one illustrations by Canadian artists, such as Group of Seven member Frederick Varley; at Leacock's suggestion some art was commissioned from Charles Jefferys, the historical artist who had done cartoons for some of Leacock's "nonsense" plays, those collected in *Over the Footlights*, when the series had had its Canadian periodical publication in Maclean's.

At the same time he was finishing *Canada*, in early 1941, Leacock was approached again by the film industry, this time to turn into English the film *Etaient Neuf Celibataires* (1939), by the celebrated French writer-director Sacha Guitry; this project, like others for work in film, never proceeded beyond an exchange of letters. Other projects he was championing for film at this time included an adaptation of *The Pickwick Papers*, which he proposed to independent American producer David O. Selznick. It is regrettable that Selznick was not interested; since the silent era, the only film from this Dickens classic was one made by South African playwright-screenwriter-director Noel Langley in 1953. Leacock also asked his agent to approach Disney studios, for which his friend Robert Benchley had done some work. Stevie did not return to Montreal for the 1941-42 academic year. Instead, he moved to Toronto, where he began working at the publicity firm in Toronto that employed Henry Janes, a son of Leacock's friend Charlie Janes of Orillia; Henry, who had known Leacock as a mentor and friend from childhood and later was his student at McGill, was one of many persons who later recorded his memories of the famous author. In the early 1940s, Stevie seemed launched on a writing career of his own. In Toronto, his main occupation became the writing of scripts for documentary films. *Guns for Victory* and *Pasture Lands* were for commercial clients, Atlas Steel and Quaker Oats respectively. *The Romance of a River* described the Hydro Electric Power Company's diversion of the Ogoki River, and *Heirs of Tomorrow* was a film for the Red Cross, portraying Canada's reception of displaced European children.[15]

A suggestion to write an autobiography came in 1941 from Doubleday Doran and Company. Thomas B. Costain, his editor with Doubleday Doran, said that an autobiography would probably be a Book of the Month Club selection and might sell as many as seven hundred thousand copies.[16] Costain, a native of Brantford, Ontario, had begun editing Leacock's work early since joining the editorial staff of *Maclean's* in 1916. In 1920, Costain had gone to New York as an associate editor of the *Saturday Evening Post*; there again he dealt with Leacock's work. Shortly after joining Doubleday Doran and Company as an editor in 1939, he recruited Leacock as an author, and the two became friends. Eventually Costain left Doubleday in 1946 to pursue a successful career as a novelist: his many bestsellers included *The Silver Chalice* (1954), *The Tontine* (1955) and a book not unrelated to Leacock's own style of history, *The White and the Gold: The French Régime in Canada* (1954). Leacock declined this proposal but accepted another. In December Costain asked him to write an entry about Quebec City in a series of books about North American ports that Doubleday Doran was producing. Leacock quickly answered that he would like to contribute to the series but that his entry should be Montreal. The result was *Montreal: Seaport and City* (1942), which he considered one of his best books. It is as he proposed it in his first letter about the idea: "a happy blend of history and geography, romance and commerce, with plenty of present day interest both for the U.S. and Canada."[17] It stands among the best books ever written about a North American city, and is especially notable among such books for its style. Much of it was written in the summer of 1942 in Old Brewery Bay; John Culliton helped Leacock with the research (and Culliton brought the factual matter up to date when the book was reissued in 1963 as *Leacock's Montreal*). Costain, who had become one of the annual Old Brewery Bay visitors, last saw Leacock that summer and gave this account of an auspicious beginning to the holiday:

> Leacock came out of the house with a letter in his hand, and he was roaring with delight. "Tom," he shouted, "you've got to see this. It's a letter from a teacher in Chicago who's compiling an anthology on absent-minded professors. And the damn fool forgot to sign his name!"[18]

During that same summer, Leacock was also busy writing his brief book, *Our Heritage of Liberty*. Like *Our British Empire*, it celebrated Anglo-American civilization, its history and its values, and at the same time attempted to show that the correct — that is, the Leacockian — interpretation of this heritage demanded an ever more strenuous effort to extend its benefits of peace, justice, freedom and a decent material existence to every individual. Though a historical work, it was directly related to his effort to foster pride in Anglo-American institutions as a means of contributing to wartime morale. It traced the history of democracy and argued Leacock's belief that only modern democracy could provide the social improvements the world needed. The war confirmed Leacock's clear sense of humanity's capacity for evil and regression. Characteristically, though, it stirred him to oppose obvious evil with a vision of what ought to prevail. Even *Montreal: Seaport and City* and *Canada, The Foundations of Its Future* are built on his desire to show the historical movement of British and French culture in building a great city and a great nation with the promise of advanced material civilization and the broadening of freedom. They are among his best books because they unite so many of the essential components of the man: his love and knowledge of history; his imagination, which over the years had fully absorbed the pageant of Canada, from Cartier's departure from Saint Malo to the settlement of the northwest; his deep conviction in British values, stirred by a dire and powerful occasion; his long-matured mastery as a prose stylist; and, finally, his need to contribute publicly, as a teacher, to the world's course. In these books, his attitude toward the possibility of human progress is best represented. It has been said that he had a belief in progress, a supposedly Victorian characteristic, one that bespoke a certain complacency and may have dampened the talent for scathingly satirical social criticism that he showed in *Arcadian Adventures of the Idle Rich*. But his attitude towards progress was related to the critical and skeptical thought of the Victorian poets and thinkers, not to the rosy optimism of industrialists, go-getters and popular philosophers. Progress was possible; the historical record showed that it had been made. It was within the grasp of nations and it was crucial to the fulfillment of individuals. But progress could be very easily lost. It would only be achieved by the most strenuous efforts and by constant vigilance. Lacking these, decline became inevitable.

Leacock produced yet another third book that summer, *My Remarkable Uncle*, one of his best miscellanies. As had long been the case, even his books of humour now fought his causes, but his contribution to the war effort in the 1940s is deeper, more measured and more lasting than was his First World War propaganda, and is virtually free of the offensive caricature he had used in such works as *The Hohenzollerns in America*. "The British Soldier" in *My Remarkable Uncle* is an example of a literary and historical essay, excellent in itself, which also manages to promote public respect and responsibility toward soldiers. Leacock recalls the British soldier's tradition of courage and his historical importance to British civilization, and links him to the poor by pointing out his indigence and low social status throughout the nineteenth century and by recalling that his occupation, ill-recompensed as it often is, had long been an escape for some from even greater need. Finally, Leacock manages to insist that it is necessary to have concrete plans, not merely ideals, for social improvement; in analyzing literature's attitudes to the soldier, he criticizes his own master, Charles Dickens, for being sentimentally opposed to poverty but providing no idea how to end it. Most of Leacock's late humour was even less explicitly linked to the issue of the war than is "The British Soldier," but its mingled mood of nostalgia and affirmation of Anglo-American values was in harmony with the effort to draw strength and renewal from tradition he was making in his serious books. A few of the pieces in *My Remarkable Uncle* contained examples of his purely nonsensical imagination at the top of its form, but most were deceptively relaxed and informal essays that conveyed serious thought through a mixture of humour, historical and literary analysis and poetic suggestion; some of the most notable were "The Mathematics of the Lost Chord," "The Passing of the Kitchen," "Migration in English Literature," "Index: There Is No Index," "Why Do We Fish?" and the title piece, with its barely fictionalized portrait of E.P. Leacock, the jovial charlatan who in the 1880s parlayed his "ownership" of nonexistent interests into a short-lived semblance of wealth and a seat in the Manitoba Legislative Assembly. When first published in *Reader's Digest*, "My Remarkable Uncle" drew the attention of Paramount, Warner Brothers and Twentieth Century Fox. Intrigued by the dramatic possibilities of the flamboyant E.P., the film companies asked Dodd, Mead for copies of the galley proofs of Leacock's book; Leacock wrote to a story editor of his fear that the sketch would not be judged suitable because it was "only a piece — not a book. I have always thought the Winnipeg boom of 1880-82 would make a good setting for a book set up with a character like my uncle as a central figure. If you thought of expanding the sketch to a story, I could be of use."[19] It was another film possibility that never bore fruit.

In the midst of all these projects, Leacock also began seriously planning his autobiography. However, it did not form a part of his consultation with Thomas Costain, probably because he was intending it for Dodd, Mead and Company, rather than for Doubleday. On a contract with Dodd, Mead dating from August, he made a marginal jotting about the project: "I should not wish to publish this till the war is over as I think it would attract more attention in a quieter world."[20] Leacock was also drawn further into his brother Charlie's affairs about this same time. In July the Orillia police charged him $10.50 for the service of transporting Charlie to the Whitby hospital, seventy miles distant. Charlie's debts had become unmanageable; because of his creditors, his farm, Bovaire, was in the hands of the Ontario public trustee, who declared that "the patient had no power whatsoever to deal with his estate in any way," and that Leacock's November 1941 agreement with Teddy to answer for Charlie's debts was invalid.[21] Since his original admission to the Whitby hospital, Charlie had been allowed out on probation but never released; the agreement had been made in the knowledge that he was incompetent. His mental state now apparently continued to alternate between affection and anger, docility and self-will, in a way which made it difficult for his brothers and sisters to take care of him.

On 8 September, Leacock accepted the heavy task of directing and helping to write the revisions of all the entries, more than one hundred, about Canadian places in the *Encyclopaedia Britannica*. Some were only six lines long (on the smallest cities); others were substantial (on the provinces). The main article about Canada was more than three thousand lines. He drew up an elaborate organizational plan to guide the work and recruited qualified McGill professors and other academic acquaintances to revise or rewrite material. He kept much of the work for himself. For instance, he did a substantial portion of the article about Canada, and his correspondence is filled with information sent to him from Canadian municipal and provincial governments, who provided recent economic and social statistics. For help with the encyclopedia project and with another book he was writing, *Canada and the Sea*, he turned again to Barbara Ulrichsen

Nimmo. From her home in Birmingham, Michigan and after mid-1943 from Syracuse, New York, she handled much of his correspondence for the encyclopedia and typed manuscripts of articles and the draft of his book. Leacock was also now preparing a book about the art in which he had laboured for so many years, *How to Write*. Published early in 1943, it was described in a February essay-review by Struthers Burt in the *Saturday Review*:

> This is a lovely book because it is both witty and wise....The title is merely a stalking-horse for the ripe philosopher to say what he thinks of his vocation, whether he denies that noun or not — his avocation is teaching political economy, and he can even be funny about that — ; and about literature in general, and life, and literary style, and above all the English language, that major instrument of beauty and common sense and civilization and articulateness.
>
> And yet it's a good text book; an excellent one. Actually a superb one.... He has a mind that cannot resist its own enchantment, and so he enchants other minds.

To his friend Doctor Gerhard Lomer, McGill's head librarian and the man who became his first bibliographer, Leacock wrote, "This book How to Write is like a favourite child to me because I wrote it purely to suit myself with no eye on editors or sales or the public."[22] The Leacock of this book is the Leacock glimpsed by artist Edwin Holgate around this same time as he painted the portrait which is now in the National Gallery of Canada. Leacock went on Saturdays and Sundays to the artist's studio in his home at Morin Heights, northwest of Montreal in Argenteuil County. Holgate commented, "He impressed me as being a philosopher with a great good humour. But first, a philosopher. He plied me with questions as if he were a small boy —

and listened to the answers with an attention they did not deserve."[23] At his death, it seemed to many that *How to Write, Canada* and *Montreal* would be among his most valuable works, and this judgment has merit, even though the three works, like many of his others, have since been eclipsed by the understandable interpretation of his career primarily in terms of his creative, humorous literature.

There are indications that by early 1943 Leacock was hard at work on his autobiography. In addition, other writing projects and details of his life show him deeply embroiled in reminiscences at this time. For instance, he attempted without success to interest *Maclean's* and *Reader's Digest* in an account of a War of 1812-14 naval battle he had studied for the sake of a family souvenir he had carried with him from early childhood. In May, he wrote *Reader's Digest* to describe the project in terms close to those he later used when presenting the incident in the autobiography:

> When I was a boy of six (1876), about to leave England for America, my grandfather took from his desk an oblong piece of hard wood, about 8 inches by three by four. "That's a bit of the old Chesapeake," he said. Written on it in the old man's writing...was, "Piece of the American Frigate Chesapeake captured by the Shannon 1813." This bit of wood..., is on my desk as I write, the legend on it faded beyond recognition.

He also outlined a plan that would bring the *Chesapeake's* surviving timbers, which he had visited in an old mill at Fareham, Hants, near his birthplace, during his 1921 tour of England, to the United States Naval Academy as a gesture of international friendship. The idea went no further, but the story of the battle remained vivid in his mind. One morning in 1943, Henry Janes recalled, Leacock had been unable to work and had taken Janes fishing. But he had stopped at the water's edge and, pretending that Old Brewery Bay was Boston Harbor, had recounted the entire battle in all its details, tracing out of the movements of the great sailing ships with gestures of his walking stick. Perhaps it is this description he gave to Janes that, translated into literature, appears in *The Boy I Left Behind Me*.[24]

By July 1943 Leacock had completed *Canada and the Sea*; he also sent the first part of the manuscript of a new humour collection, *Happy Stories*, to Dodd, Mead. This book, made uneven by the inclusion of hastily written propaganda pieces, nevertheless contains some excellent material, such as "Pawn to King's Four," "Mr. McCoy Sails for Fiji" and "Boom Time," a fictional treatment of Winnipeg during the 1880s real estate boom, built like "My Remarkable Uncle" around the figure of E.P. As soon as he completed this story, he sent it to Dorothy Purdell, the agent who had first approached him on behalf of Twentieth Century Fox, and she proposed it to Ernst Lubitsch and two other filmmakers and companies. Her letters to Leacock indicate that she regarded the story as an inevitable sale, but it never did find a producer. Before the book was published in November, Leacock received one of the intriguing contacts with the world that his work had consistently provoked, this one occasioned it seems by the figure of E.P. as he had already appeared in *My Remarkable Uncle*. In September, a Mr. H. Shave of Winnipeg wrote to him that his, Shave's, father had arrived in the city in April 1882, and that E.P. had been the first man he had worked for. The elder Shave often had recounted how "he used to be posted at the 'Lodge' on Main Street to watch for approaching dignitaries, so that he could notify his employer before their arrival." Shave enclosed a photograph of the "old Leacock home," E.P.'s former residence on the banks of the Red River, which in 1943 was kept in good condition by its owner, the Saint Agnes Priory.[25] Simultaneously with *Happy Stories*, Leacock was working on a project for Doubleday Doran and his friend Costain: *Read It With Me*, an anthology of his favourite readings framed by his commentaries on them. In August 1943 he sent Costain the final list of authors and works to be included in the purely personal collection; among the writers were Lewis Carroll, W.S. Gilbert, Jerome K. Jerome, James M. Barrie, Lady Cynthia Asquith, O. Henry, Ring Lardner, Robert Benchley, Charles Dickens, Mark Twain, Alphonse Daudet and A.A. Milne. Two of the pieces planned for this never-completed book, "Alice Walks in Wonderland" and "Gilbert's 'Bab' Ballads," appeared in a posthumous collection, *Last Leaves*.

Other essays that would eventually appear in *Last Leaves* were making their periodical appearance throughout 1942 and 1943 in such venues as the *Atlantic Monthly, Barron's, Outdoors* and *Canadian Banker*. These essays, of almost uniform excellence, subordinate humour to a mature consideration of life, society, art and, of course, the immediate concerns occasioned by the war. Leacock writes of fishing, of the "progress" of education, and other familiar themes. "What Can Izaak Walton Teach Us?" has wonderful things to say of Walton, fishing, life and literature; it also shows Leacock sublimely unaware of the huge shift in literary opinion, by then twenty-five years old, that had elevated John Donne and made him no longer a dim figure remembered only because Walton had mentioned him. "Common Sense and the Universe," a model of the popular science essay, displayed Leacock's command of the concepts and inclinations of the advanced physics of his day. The book expressed much concern about the direction of the postwar world. "Gold" revealed that he still felt a redeemable currency should be restored when peace had been reestablished. "Can We Beat Inflation?" intelligently addressed a problem that persists today. The essay offered Leacock's customary blend, in economic forecasting, of warnings mixed with optimism: inflation was an extremely dangerous force that could be controlled only through proper effort rigorously applied. During this same period, Maclean's rejected a proposed article about the abolition of poverty,[26] but in McClelland & Stewart, Ltd. of Toronto Leacock found a publisher for a text that treated the same theme more broadly. *While There Is Time: The Case Against Social*

Catastrophe (1944) expanded on the theme of the postwar world. Once more, Leacock interpreted the British and American past at its best as the source of the values and methods that would successfully transform the brutality and economic chaos of unrestrained free enterprise; once more he credited socialism with a valuable criticism of social abuses but refused to allow its proposals and methods any role in positive reform. Instead, he insisted upon the use of traditional institutions and moral insights brought to a new pitch of social relevance by insights in keeping with the changed nature of the contemporary industrial world.

As If His Pencil Were An Iron Point

L eacock's final illness struck him in late 1943 or early 1944, while he was living at his Côte-des-Neiges house and working busily and happily on several projects. It is hard to know how early he began to feel the difficulty with swallowing that was the first indication of throat cancer, but in November and December he appears to have been attempting to make arrangements for everyone and everything near to him. On behalf of Stevie, who was back living with him in Montreal, he wrote to Harry Napier Moore, the influential editor who had taken over *Maclean's* in 1924 and was now editorial director of the Maclean-Hunter Publishing Company. He boasted of Stevie's work for his Toronto publicity firm but stated that he would appreciate it if Moore would give Stevie the security of a steady outlet for his writing. In November and again in January, anxious for "my old mare, whose life & welfare I greatly value," he wrote to Orillia to ensure that the horse was safely stabled and fed and to find a veterinarian to repair her teeth. He was in correspondence with his sister Dot about provisions he was making for Charlie. Early in 1944, Dot assured him, "Yes, I have plenty of money for Charlie — & Carrie still has a lot left of the amount you gave her in the summer — so don't worry about him."[1]

In January 1944 or earlier, Leacock had apparently suffered what he believed to be an attack of influenza. He wrote in late January to R. Gladstone Murray that he was

> getting better & hope soon to be out of the woods — as an aftermath of flu something went wrong with my swallowing — I believe (and please God), it is clearing up now.

On 4 February, however, he wrote to Murray,

> At present I am a very sick man. With good fortune I may pass a present corner and go on for a good time yet, even years. But at present I find it very hard.[2]

Reminiscing about January 1944 some years later, in 1947, Stevie told Nathaniel Benson that his father had said to him, "It seems to be getting terribly hard for me to swallow. There's something terrible in my throat." According to Stevie,

> He knew almost from the first what it was. But he didn't tell me. I remember his slouching through the snow all that January from our home up in Côte-des-Neiges to Dr. Eddie Archibold's. One day the latter brought a specialist to see him. From an upper window he saw them arriving and he turned to me grimly and said: "Stevie, they're coming up here to tell me I'm finished."[3]

Before an operation for throat cancer on 16 March, Stevie reported, Leacock said to him, "I know the death sentence is on me. Oh, if I can only get used to the truth that I am going to die." Leacock's attitude towards this final crisis was a mixture of faith and agnosticism, of trust in the "Spirit" (which in *Last Leaves* brings "Good Will on Earth") and a sense of the finality of death. He clung with love, but perhaps also with hopelessness, to life.

The specialist Eddie Archibold brought to see him was Doctor W.G. Turner, who confirmed Archibold's fears of cancer, made an exact diagnosis and enlisted the aid of other specialists in deciding how to treat Leacock's condition. A letter to Leacock from Dot on 11 February indicates that he was already receiving regular X-ray treatments. He was reluctant to agree to an operation, perhaps fearing it, perhaps fearing to confirm the seriousness of his illness or to exhaust the only remaining measure. George wrote to him, "She [Dot] is very very strongly in favour of the first small operation that Dr. Wookey suggests to do and I think she is right." Apparently there was some real hope that Leacock would survive. On 14 February Dot wrote to him, "You certainly seem to be pulling 'out of it' wonderfully well." She had talked to his doctors and wrote:

> they evidently *don't* feel that they must necessarily
> leave things as they are. I feel that you can be assured
> that at least they are going to try to 'prolong the
> years' with perhaps a chance of altogether getting rid
> of the darned growth.

As comfort against the throat spasms he was suffering, Dot said that their cause might be irritation rather than a worsening of the growth. She stated that she, too, had had spasms of the esophagus and larynx for the last nine years due to "collection of fibrous tissue in those parts following the X-ray treatments I had in 1934 & 1935."[4]

Confined to bed in his house, his speech reduced to a painful whisper, Leacock continued to work. He collected manuscripts for the book that became *Last Leaves* under a cover sheet, on which he wrote, "Barbara's Book." It seems impossible that he did not recall his own description of Ulysses S. Grant in old age, when at Mark Twain's prompting the general had been able to write his famous memoirs, whose royalties after his death saved his family from poverty.

> Grant, stricken as he was, worked stubbornly on. All the best in the man shone on in his stubborn fight against approaching death. When the cancer in his throat reached the point where dictation was impossible, he took a pencil and wrote on, firmly, stubbornly, as if his pencil were an iron point against the paper.[5]

Leacock concludes the passage, majestic in its repeated knells of "stubborn" and their fading overtones of "on," with the words, "He won out." In other words, Grant had completed his book before death came. Of Mark Twain's last days, he had commented, "Each of

The front verandah of Leacock's House in the early 1950's, before his property was purchased by the city of Orillia and restored.
Courtesy National Archives of Canada C-31929.

Leacock's Old Brewery Bay property from the air. The author's boat-house, in the upper storey of which he did much of his writing, stood at the western tip (right foreground) of the wooded point, at the end of the long straight walk that descended from the house's front door. Leacock's farming, poultry raising and orchard activities took place on the land behind the house, at the top of the picture.

Courtesy National Archives of Canada C-31964.

411

us, it seems, lives, apart from accidents, as long as we want to, but the time comes when we don't want to. So it was with Mark Twain."⁶ Leacock found it was not yet so with him. He left two new books of his writings: *Last Leaves*, which Barbara saw through the press in September 1945, providing an appreciative preface; and the four chapters of autobiography Leacock entrusted to his friend Fitz Shaw and published as *The Boy I Left Behind Me* (1946), one of Leacock's most fascinating serious works, giving his fullest attempt to synthesize the conservative and advanced elements in his educational thinking. And he produced still a third work. From December to February, a series of articles expanded from an earlier *Maclean's* piece, "What's Ahead for Canada," was appearing in the *Financial Post*; as usual, the series had been designed so that it could easily be recrafted into a book. Leacock never had the chance to write it. In March, he was taken from Montreal to Toronto's Western Hospital and on 16 March underwent an operation for cancer of the throat. At first it seemed the operation had been successful, and there were reports that he was recovering. He soon weakened again, however. On 28 March, two hours after an exploratory X-ray of his throat, he died. His last recorded words, spoken with a smile to his radiologist, were, "Did I behave pretty well? Was I a good boy?"⁷

Leacock's hopes and provisions for his family were indicated in his will. Amounts were left to his brothers and sisters and to staff members, especially "Sergeant" Bill Jones and Tina Kelly, who had maintained Old Brewery Bay year-round for him. Charlie was well provided for, with Leacock's bequests and other income in his own name supplemented by family aid. Leacock left him his three boats and his fishing equipment, in memory of happy days with the now failing man, whose love of fishing was greater than that of all his brothers. The Côte-des-Neiges house in Montreal was eventually sold, then torn down to make way for an expansion of Montreal General Hospital, but Leacock intended his Orillia property, Old Brewery Bay, for a permanent family legacy. It was left to Stevie, along with the other main elements of his estate, for example, a trust fund of more than $100,000 and approximately $50,000 in widely diversified, cleverly chosen securities, primarily in mining, pulp and paper and oil — the resource industries in which Leacock had seen the foundation of Canada's future. The estate also continued to be augmented by his writings. The records of Dodd, Mead and Company show that his books for that publisher alone had earned more than $11,000 in the three years before he died; a further $1,000 came during the month after his death.[8]

Although in 1944 the war still dominated other concerns, reports of Leacock's death brought eulogies from all over the world. Leacock's body was cremated and his ashes interred on 31 March at Sibbald's Point in Saint George's churchyard, which lies at the edge of a bluff above Lake Simcoe. The funeral was small and quiet and the day blustery; a sharp wind whined in the cedar trees and swirled a few flakes of spring snow. At two-thirty that day the church held the funeral of Martin Sibbald, head of the most prominent local family, a man who had known all the Leacocks and had encouraged Leacock from his childhood; Sibbald was about twenty years the humorist's senior. Leacock's funeral followed at four o'clock. Archbishop Derwyn Owen, Anglican Primate of Canada, and Reverend P.G. Powell, the pastor, officiated at both ceremonies. Among the pall-bearers and mourners were local friends, representatives of Upper Canada College, Stevie, Barbara and her husband, Donald Nimmo, and George, Charlie, Teddy, Dot, Carrie and Daisy.[9] The ashes were buried under a small umbrella elm in the family plot at the east side of the churchyard. Leacock's grave is close to the grey stone church erected on the site where, on 15 August, 1838, twenty-nine settlers had laboured at an all-day bee to erect the first, wooden church, using fifteen thousand feet of timber that had been rafted down Lake Simcoe to the bluff.

Notes

ABBREVIATIONS

AA   Allan Anderson, *Remembering Leacock: An Oral History* (Ottawa: Deneau, 1983)

BIL   *The Boy I Left Behind Me* in Robertson Davies, ed., *The Penguin Stephen Leacock* (Harmondsworth, U.K.: Penguin, 1981)

BSL   Carl Spadoni, *A Bibliography of Stephen Leacock* (Toronto: ECW, 1998)

DML   David M. Legate, *Stephen Leacock: A Biography* (Toronto: Macmillan, Laurentian Library, 1978; first published 1970)

EK   Elizabeth Kimball, *My Uncle, Stephen Leacock* (Toronto: Goodread Biographies, 1983; first published 1970 as *The Man in the Panama Hat*)

EPS   Stephen Leacock, *Elements of Political Science* (Boston and New York: Houghton, Mifflin, 1906)

LL   Stephen Leacock, *Literary Lapses* (Toronto: McClelland and Stewart, New Canadian Library, 1971)

LaL   Stephen Leacock, *Last Leaves* (Toronto: McClelland and Stewart, New Canadian Library, 1970)

MDE   Stephen Leacock, *My Discovery of England* (Toronto: McClelland and Stewart, New Canadian Library, 1961)

ML   Leacock Archives, MacLennan Library, McGill University, Montreal

MRU   Stephen Leacock, *My Remarkable Uncle and Other Sketches* (Toronto: McClelland and Stewart, New Canadian Library, 1965)

RC   Ralph L. Curry, *Stephen Leacock: Humorist and Humanist* (Garden City, New York: Doubleday, 1959)

SCSL   Allan Bowker, ed., *The Social Criticism of Stephen Leacock* (Toronto: University of Toronto Press, 1973)

SL   Stephen Leacock

SLMH   Leacock archives, Stephen Leacock Memorial Home and Museum, Orillia, Ontario

SS   Stephen Leacock, *Sunshine Sketches of a Little Town* (Toronto: McClelland and Stewart, NCL Classic, 1982)

The bibliographical information for books above gives the editions most likely to be accessible to readers. Other books, and articles, are given full citations when they first appear in the notes and short references thereafter.

CHAPTER 1 MY VICTORIAN BOYHOOD

1   *BIL*, 346.
2   Ibid., 348.
3   DML, 3.
4   EK, 136.
5   EK, 16.
6   Agnes Leacock, diary, April 1914, SLMH. DML, 3.
7   Agnes Leacock's diary (SLMH) makes no reference to a premarital liaison with Peter.
8   Agnes Leacock's diary, 10, SLMH.
9   Marriage settlement, SLMH.
10 *BIL*, 351.
11 EK, 16.
12 *BIL*, 352.
13 DML, 5.
14 EK, 16.
15 *BIL*, 346. Robertson Davies, *Penguin Stephen Leacock*, ix.
16 DML, 5. Agnes Leacock's diary, 8, SLMH.
17 "Stephen Leacock," Stephen Leacock Centennial Committee, B.T. Richardson, chairman, n.d., 4-5. *BIL*, 346-7.
18 *BIL*, 353.
19 EK, 16.
20 SL to Peter Leacock, undated, SLMH.
21 SL, preface to first edition of *Sunshine Sketches*, 1.
22 "My Remarkable Uncle," MRU, 16.
23 *BIL*, 351.
24 Ibid., 355.
25 Ibid., 357.
26 Ibid., 348.
27 Ibid., 357.
28 Leacock, *SS*, 1.

CHAPTER 2 THE STRUGGLE TO MAKE US GENTLEMEN

1   *BIL*, 366.
2   EK, 100-11.
3   *BIL*, 370.
4   Ibid., 375.
5   Ibid., 371.
6   SL, *MRU*, 21.
7   *BIL*, 366.
8   *MRU*, 14. *BIL*, 386-88.
9   *BIL*, 386. RC, 33.
10 *MRU*, 15.
11 EK, 16.
12 *BIL*, 375.
13 Ibid., 378-81.
14 Ibid., 376-78.

15   Ibid., 383.
16   SL, "Going for the Doctor," *The McGill News,* Fall 1931.
17   *BIL,* 389.
18   *BIL,* 401. RC, 34.
19   *BIL,* 392-97. Richard B. Howard, *Upper Canada College 1829-1979: Colborne's Legacy* (Toronto, 1979), 12-67.
20   *BIL,* 393-97.
21   *BIL,* 392. SL, "Mathematics Versus Puzzles," *Too Much College: or, Education Eating Up Life, with Kindred Essays in Education and Humor* (New York: Dodd, Mead, 1939), 55.
22   *BIL,* 389-91.
23   RC, 36. *BIL,* 387. EK, 126.
24   SL to Peter Leacock, 28 June 1884, SLMH.
25   *BIL,* 402-03.
26   SL, *The College Times,* 7 April 1887.
27   *BIL,* 375-81.
28   *MRU,* 28-29.
29   *BIL,* 387.
30   Ibid., 409.
31   EK, 112-18. RC, 41. *BIL,* 387-88.
32   *BIL,* 388.

CHAPTER 3 EDUCATION EATING UP LIFE

1   RC, 42-43.
2   *BIL,* 411. Pelham Edgar, "Stephen Leacock," *Queen's Quarterly,* LIII (May 1946), 174.
3   *BIL,* 411.
4   *BIL,* 411-12. Robert S. Harris, *A History of Higher Education in Canada 1663-1960* (Toronto: University of Toronto Press, 1976), 231-33.
5   *BIL,* 412-13. "Boarding House Geometry," *LL,* 11-12.
6   *BIL,* 414.
7   Lady Matilda Edgar to Pelham Edgar, August 1889, SLMH.
8   F.N. Raines to SL, 1 February 1936; SL to Raines, February 1936, SLMH. *BIL,* 372.
9   *BIL,* 425.
10   George Parkin to William Peterson, 19 January 1900, Peterson Papers, file 70, ML. DML, 31.
11   RC, 50.
12   EK, 124.
13   RC, 53-54. Bruce Murphy, "Stephen Leacock—the Greatest Living Humorist," *Ontario Library Review,* XII (February 1928), 68.
14   Legal indenture, 22 November 1899, SLMH. *BIL,* 387-88. EK, 138.
15   Edgar, "Stephen Leacock," 176-77.
16   *BSL,* 434-35.
17   Howard, *Upper Canada College,* 124-30; Edgar, "Stephen Leacock," 174-79.
18   *BIL,* 410-11.
19   *BIL,* 419. SL, "Parlez-Vous Français?", *Too Much College,* 62-65.
20   EK, 14.

21 Robert B. Pattison, unpublished notes, SLMH.
22 Edgar, "Stephen Leacock," 173-81.
23 RC, 66-67.

CHAPTER 4 HAS ECONOMICS GONE TO SEED?

1 Legal indenture, 22 November 1899, SLMH.
2 SL, "Has Economics Gone to Seed?, in *Too Much College*, 109-24. Harris, *A History of Higher Education in Canada 1663-1960*, 217. K.W. Taylor, "Economic Scholarship in Canada," *Canadian Journal of Economics and Political Science*, 26 (1960), 8.
3 *EPS*, 8-10.
4 *SCSL*, xi. John Diggins, *The Bard of Savagery: Thornstein Veblen and Modern Social Theory* (New York, 1978), 216. RC, 66.
5 Harris, *A History of High Education in Canada 1663-1960*, 321.
6 RC, 59-66. *SCSL*, xi.
7 SL, *My Discovery of the West* (Toronto: Allen, 1937), 136-38.
8 Thorstein Veblen, *The Theory of the Leisure Class: An Economic Study of Institutions* (New York: Macmillan, 1899; rpt. New York: New American Library, 1953), 141, 47, and 68.
9 SL, *My Discovery of the West*, 137. C. Wright Mills, introduction to *The Theory of the Leisure Class*, ix.
10 Diggins, *The Bard of Savagery*, 169.
11 RC, 68. DML, 35. SL, *My Recollection of Chicago and The Doctrine of Laissez Faire*, ed. Carl Spadoni (Toronto: University of Toronto Press, 1998).
12 J. Lawrence Laughlin to SL, undated, SLMH. Charles Starrett to SL, 18 January 1915, SLMH. Cf. also SL, *My Recollection of Chicago* and *The Doctrine of Laissez Faire*, ed. Carl Spadoni (Toronto: University of Toronto Press, 1998).
13 DML, 38.
14 Peterson Papers, file 65, ML. DML, 42. University of Chicago Registrar Maxine H. Sullivan to authors, 15 June 1984.
15 *BSL*, 77-78, 563.
16 *BSL*, 79. *Review of Reviews*, 34 (August 1906), 253; *Outlook*, 83 (28 July 1906), 765; *School Review*, 14 (December 1906), 770; *Athenaeum*, 2 (20 October 1906), 476.
17 *EPS*, 371, 374-5.
18 *EPS*, 283-84.

CHAPTER 5 OUR BRITISH EMPIRE

1 *BSL*, 84, 441. RC, 74.
2 DML, 45. Earl Grey to William Peterson, 25 March 1907, Peterson Papers, file 65, ML.
3 Justin Kaplan, *Mr. Clemens and Mark Twain* (New York, 1966), 350.
4 SL, *The British Empire: Its Structure, Its Unity, Its Strength* (New York: Dodd, Mead, 1940), 42-43. Cf. *EPS*, 283-84.
5 SL, "Greater Canada: An Appeal," *University Magazine*, VI (1907), 132.
6 Earl Grey to William Peterson, 30 January 1906, Peterson Papers, file 65, ML. SL, *The Morning Post*, London, May 1907; rpt. in the Orillia *Packet*, 30 May 1907. *SCSL*, xiv.

7   SL to William Peterson, 24 May 1907, Peterson Papers, file 46, ML.
8   SL, "Greater Canada: An Appeal," 135. *BSL*, 84.
9   SL, *The British Empire*, 41, 38.
10   *BSL*, 86.
11   DML, 58.
12   SL, "Literature and Education in America," *University Magazine* VIII (1909), rpt. *SCSL*, 22.
13   *SCSL*, 25.
14   SL, "The Passing of the Poet," *Canadian Magazine* (May 1906), 72. Susan E. Cameron, "The Passing of the Poet: A Reply to Professor Leacock," *Canadian Magazine* (September 1906), 505.
15   SL to Agnes Leacock, 30 May 1907, SLMH.
16   Grace Crooks, "A Taste of Humor," *Canadian Library Journal* (May-June 1969), 224.

CHAPTER 6 LAPSING INTO LITERATURE

1   Lease, 14 April 1909, SLMH.
2   B.K. Sandwell, "Stephen Leacock, Worst-Dressed Writer, Made Fun Respectable," *Saturday Night*, LIX (8 April 1944), 17.
3   *BSL*, 109. SL to Norman H. Friedman, note in autographed copy of LL, 12 December 1934, Friedman Collection, ML.
4   SL, Too *Much College*, 210.
5   RC, 79-82.
6   Robertson Davies, introduction to LL, x. SL to the Gazette Printing Co., 4 April 1910, SLMH.
7   *BSL*, 90.
8   SL to Norman H. Friedman, note in autographed copy of LL, ML.
9   *Spectator* 105 (9 July 1910), 105; *Independent* 70 (30 March 1910), 670. *Dial* 50 (16 February 1911), 132.
10   LL, 5-7, 10.
11   Ibid., 73-75.
12   Ibid., 80-81.
13   *BSL*, 444-48.
14   SL, "Novels in Nutshells," *Saturday Night* (10 December 1910).
15   SL, *Nonsense Novels*, 83.
16   SL, *Nonsense Novels*, 54. DML, 55.
17   SL, *Nonsense Novels*, 49-50.
18   Ibid., 96, 98.
19   Ibid., xiii.
20   *Nation* 93 (24 August 1911), 165. *New York Times*, 1 October 1911.

CHAPTER 7 THE TRAIN TO MARIPOSA

1   SL, SS, 124.
2   DML, 59. E.A. Collard, ed., *The McGill You Knew: An Anthology of Memories* (Toronto: Longmans, 1975), 56-57.
3   DML, 60.
4   Orillia *Packet*, 7 September 1911. Orillia *Times*, 7 September 1911.

5 B.K. Sandwell, "Stephen Leacock, Worst-Dressed Writer, Made Fun Respectable," 17, and "How the 'Sketches' Started," *Saturday Night* (August 1951), 7.
6 SL, photocopy of notes, 7 January 1912, SLMH.
7 DML, 62.
8 Toronto *Globe*, 26 October 1958.
9 This and subsequent information on the originals of Leacock's characters in *SS* are from research of the SLMH staff in the SLMH files and exhibits.
10 SL, *SS*, xviii.
11 Orillia *Times*, 23 March 1905.
12 Arthur Lower, "The Mariposa Belle," *Queen's Quarterly* LVIII (Summer 1951), 220-7. RC, 99.
13 Orillia *Times*, 27 October 1898.
14 SL, *SS*, xviii.
15 DML, 195.
16 *BSL*, 149-50.
17 Ibid., 132-33.
18 Ibid., 143.
19 James L. Ford to SL, 17 November 1913, SLMH. Frank Crowninshield to SL, 24 November 1913, SLMH. Paul Wilstock to SL, 13 December 1913, SLMH. E.V. Lucas to SL, 5 December 1913, SLMH. Frederick Eckstein to SL, 22 January 1914, SLMH. James L. Ford to SL, 2 February 1914, SLMH. William H. Schultz to SL, 12 March 1914, SLMH.
20 Faith Baldwin to SL, 28 December 1913, SLMH. F. Scott Fitzgerald to SL, March 1917, SLMH. Kenneth Roberts to SL, 16 January 1917, SLMH. Claire Hellwig to SL, 22 May 1914, SLMH.
21 RC, 106. "Nominates Professor Mavor," Toronto *Telegram*, 2 December 1913.
22 *BSL*, 143-44.

CHAPTER 8 SOME JUST COMPLAINTS ABOUT THE WAR

1 SL, *The British Empire*, 42. SL, "The Devil and the Deep Sea," *University Magazine*, IX (1910), *SCSL*, 50. Bertrand Russell, *The History of Western Philosophy* (London: George Allen & Unwin, Ltd., 1946), 746.
2 SL, *The Unsolved Riddle of Social Justice* (New York: Lane, 1920), *SCSL*, 83.
3 *MDE*, 156-57.
4 *BSL*, 569, 542. SL, *Further Foolishness* (London: Lane, 1916) New Canadian Library 60, 23.
5 *BSL*, 569.
6 SL to Agnes Leacock, 19 August 1915, SLMH.
7 Agnes Leacock's diary, 7, SLMH.
8 *BSL*, 610. DML, 63, 82.
9 *BSL*, 156-57. SL, *Moonbeams from the Larger Lunacy* (London: Lane, 1915), New Canadian Library 43, ix, 11, 71.
10 SL, *Moonbeams from the Larger Lunacy*, 114, 116, 117.
11 *BSL*, 542-43. SL to Pelham Edgar, 9 February 1916, Victoria College Library, University of Toronto.
12 SL, "The Woman Question," *Essays and Literary Studies* (London: Lane, 1916), 161.

13 SL, *Essays and Literary Studies*, 269, 274, 445.
14 SL, *Further Foolishness*, 156-58.
15 Ibid., 146, 136.
16 SL, *Frenzied Fiction* (London: Lane, 1917), New Canadian Library 48, 151. Trent Frayne, "The Erudite Jester of McGill," *Maclean's* (1 January 1953).
17 RC, 132. Robert Benchley, inscription in *Of All Things*, SLMH.
18 Charles L. Graves, "To Stephen Leacock," *Punch* (14 February 1917). SL, *The Hohenzollerns in America* (London: Lane, 1919), 31, 26.
19 *BSL*, 181-83.

CHAPTER 9 UNSOLVED RIDDLES

1 *BSL*, 186-87.
2 *SCSL*, 135, 142.
3 Ibid., 140.
4 *BSL*, 192.
5 RC, 136-37.
6 Robertson Davies, "Introduction," *Feast of Stephen: An Anthology of Some of the Less Familiar Writings of Stephen Leacock* (Toronto: McClelland & Stewart, 1970), 26. *New York Times*, 19 December 1920. *Times Literary Supplement*, London, 2 December 1920.
7 SL, *Winsome Winnie* (London: Lane, 1920), 179, 227.
8 J.B. Maclean to Frank Munsey, 3 January 1920, SLMH. J.B. Maclean to Frank Munsey, 2 May 1920, SLMH. H.H. Black to J.B. Maclean, n.d., SLMH. SL to Frank Munsey, 17 May 1920, SLMH. *Collier's* to SL, 18 May 1921, SLMH. Paul Reynolds to SL, 30 November 1921, 7 February 1922, SLMH.
9 John Lane to SL, 4 November 1921, SLMH.
10 Paul Reynolds to SL, 9 November 1921, SLMH.
11 SL to John Lane, 15 March 1921 and 22 April 1921, SLMH.
12 SL to Alfred Chapman, 8 July 1921, SLMH. Alfred Chapman to SL, 12 July 1921, SLMH.
13 *BSL*, 469-71.
14 Ibid., 410-11, 515, 573-76.
15 Automobile accident liability policy, 7 May 1922, SLMH. William Caldwell, "Impressions of Ontario, V: A Visit to a Canadian Author," *Canadian Magazine*, 59 (May 1922), 56. Jefferson Jones to SL, 23 August 1921, SLMH.
16 Dr. Alton Goldbloom, *Small Patients: The Autobiography of a Children's Doctor* (Toronto: Longmans, Green & Co., 1959). AA, 5-6.

CHAPTER 10 WE HAVE WITH US TO-NIGHT

1 Windermere, "Leacock Lurking in the Limelight," *Toronto Star*, 29 September 1921. SS, xvii. "Stephen Leacock, Humorist," *London Morning Post*, 29 September 1921.
2 "A Master of Satire," *London Times*, 27 September 1921.
3 SL, "I Am Interviewed," *London Morning Post*, 9 October 1921. Cf. *MDE*, 36-51.
4 "Our Modest Estimators," *Punch* (London, 12 October 1921), 297. Ernest Jenkins, "Mr. Stephen Leacock: An Interview Gone Wrong," *Punch*

(London, 12 October 1921), 294.

5   "Mr. Stephen Leacock's Lectures," *London Daily Telegraph*, 18 October 1921.
    "Mr. Stephen Leacock's Tour Ended," *London Times*, 24 December 1921.

6   SL, "The Great Detective," in *Here Are My Lectures and Stories!* (New York:
    Dodd Mead, 1937), 8. Cf. SL, "The Great Detective," in *Short Circuits* (New
    York: Dodd Mead, 1928), New Canadian Library 57, 203-16.

7   "Mr. Stephen Leacock's Lectures," London *Times*, 14 October 1921.

8   *MDE*, 165.

9   W.E. Gladstone Murray, *Toronto Telegram*, 8 August 1950. SL, "Barrie and 0.
    Henry," *Mark Twain Quarterly* II (Fall 1937), 3.

10 SL, "0. Henry and the Critics," *New Republic* IX (2 December 1916), 120-22.

11 "A Canadian Club in London," *The London Times*, 12 December 1921. DML,
    119.

12 B.W. Willett to SL, 3 November 1921, SLMH. Frank Dodd to SL, 6 February
    1922, SLMH. SL to Dodd, Mead, 24 January 1923, SLMH.
    Doubleday Doran to SL, 18 January 1922, SLMH. Jefferson Jones to SL,
    January 1922, SLMH.

13 "Mr. Stephen Leacock on London," *The London Times*, 10 December 1921. Cf.,
    MDE, 36-49.

14 *BIL*, 349.

15 SL to Christy & Moore, 30 December 1921, the Leacock Memorial Collection,
    Orillia Public Library, Orillia, Ontario. "Mr. Stephen Leacock's Tour Ended," *The
    London Times*, 24 December 1921.

CHAPTER 11 WOMEN AND WHISKEY

1   B.W. Willett to SL, 9 February 1922, SLMH; SL to B.W. Willett, 25 February
    1922, SLMH.

2   *Boston Transcript*, 16 August 1922; *Saturday Review* 133 (24 June 1922), 658.
    New York Tribune, 25 June 1922. *Outlook* 132 (13 September 1922), 80. *Nation*
    115 (16 August 1922), 171.

3   DML, 127.

4   *SCSL*, 51-60.

5   SL, "We Are Teaching Women All Wrong," *Collier's*, 68 (31 December 1921), 15.
    Margaret Gillets, *We Walked Very Warily: A History of Women at McGill* (Montreal,
    1981), 217.

6   Collard, *The McGill You Knew*, 32. J. Laurence Laughlin to SL, n.d., early 1915,
    SLMH.

7   *BSL*, 464, 545.

8   J.B. Maclean to Charles Schwab, 21 October 1922, SLMH.

9   AA, 9.

10 SL, "The Tyranny of Prohibition," *American Living Age*, 302 (2 August 1919),
    301-306.

11 Toronto *World*, 4 April 1921.

12 B.W. Willett to SL, 3 November 1921, SLMH.

13 SL to Mr. Saunders, 31 January 1920, SLMH. Emma McLean to SL, 24
    December 1920, SLMH. Vilhjalmur Stefansson, 22 November 1922, SLMH.

14 Peter McArthur, *Stephen Leacock* (Toronto: Makers of Canadian Literature,
    1923), 129-30, 134, 158.

15 SL, "O. Henry and His Critics," *The New Republic,* 9 (2 December 1916), 20-22. William Trowbridge Larned, "Professor Leacock and the Other Professors," *The New Republic,* 9 (13 January, 1917), 299.
16 Walter Yust, *Literary Review* (2 August 1924), 934.

CHAPTER 12 FAMILY SORROWS

1 *BSL,* 580.
2 DML, 143-44.
3 Ibid., 142.
4 *BSL,* 583-85.
5 SL to Paul Reynolds, 24 November 1924, SLMH.
6 EK, 81. RC, 168. Sir Arthur Currie to SL, December 1925, SLMH. 7 *LaL,* 4.
8 EK, 81.
9 AA, 22.
10 Goldbloom, *Small Patients,* 210. DML, 152. Alton Goldbloom to SL, 14 October 1927, SLMH. Goldbloom, *Small Patients,* 210.
11 Goldbloom, *Small Patients,* 210.
12 Agnes Leacock to SL, 27 April 1927, SLMH. DML, 178.
13 SL to Kenneth Noxon, 1 September 1928, SLMH.
14 Collard, *The McGill You Knew,* 48. EK, 72-75. *Playbill,* 31 December 1929, SLMH.
15 Gillets, *We Walked Very Warily,* 237. AA, 56, 64-65, 42-49.
16 *McGill Daily,* 25 October 1925. Collard, *The McGill You Knew,* 87.
17 P.C. Kennedy, *New Statesman* 27 (31 July 1926), 445. Harry Salpeter, New York *World* (4 July 1926). SL, *Winnowed Wisdom* (New York: Dodd, Mead, 1926), New Canadian Library 74, 9, 49.
18 *BSL,* 611-13.
19 New York *Herald Tribune,* Books (2 September 1928). *Spectator* 140 (23 June 1928), 942. *BSL.,* 229-30.
20 *BSL,* 234-35. Dodd, Mead to SL, 28 August 1929, SLMH. SL to Dodd, Mead, 3 September 1929, SLMH. *BSL,* 234-35.
21 SL, *The Iron Man and the Tin Woman,* 81.
22 SL, *Winnowed Wisdom,* viii.

CHAPTER 13 BACK TO PROSPERITY

1 DML, 141.
2 *BSL,* 237-40.
3 Draft of promotional copy, November 1931, SLMH. SL, *Economic Prosperity in the British Empire* (London: Constable & Co. Ltd, 1930), 243.
4 London *Times Literary Supplement* (1932), 723.
5 Max Aitken to SL, 31 August 1930, SLMH.
6 *BSL,* 244-45.
7 SL, *Laugh with Leacock* (Toronto: McClelland & Stewart Ltd., 1968), v-viii.
8 *BSL,* 249.
9 Collard, *The McGill You Knew,* 48-49.
10 *BSL,* 251-52.
11 SL to North American Newspaper Alliance, 8 April 1932, SLMH.

12   R.B. Bennett to SL, 2 July 1932, SLMH. R.B. Bennett to SL, 22 September 1932, SLMH.
13   Financial files, SLMH. SL to unnamed correspondent, 9 January 1932, SLMH.
14   *BSL*, 252.
15   Ibid., 258.
16   Ibid., 256.
17   SL to Dodd, Mead and Willett, 18 December 1931, SLMH.
18   Richard Marvin to SL, 16 November 1931, SLMH. Ralph Curry, unpublished article on Leacock's work for electronic media, 2-3, SLMH. RC, 231-34.
19   Charles Neider, ed., *The Autobiography of Mark Twain* (New York: HarperCollins, Perennial Classics edition, 1990), xx-xxi.
20   *BSL*, 263-65.
21   SL, *Mark Twain* (London: Peter Davies Ltd., 1932), 8, 9.
22   Ibid., 12, 21, 142.

CHAPTER 14 THE SAVING GRACE OF HUMOUR

1   DML, 183.
2   *BSL*, 269-70.
3   DML, 198.
4   Montreal *Herald*, 1 December 1933.
5   *BSL*, 271.
6   SL to Agnes Leacock, 7 December 1933, ML.
7   Life-insurance policy, SLMH. SL to Charlie Leacock and Charlie Leacock to SL, various 1932, SLMH. Teddy Leacock to SL, 23 November and 29 August 1934, SLMH.
8   Agnes Leacock to SL, 4 October 1927 and 6 November 1928, SLMH.
9   Agnes Leacock to SL, 25 November 1932, SLMH. DML, 43.
10   *BSL*, 274-75.
11   SL to Frank and Alice Hett, 22 February 1935, SLMH.
12   EK, 49.
13   *BSL*, 555-57.
14   Kenneth McNaughton, *The Pelican History of Canada* (Harmondsworth, U.K.: Penguin Books Ltd., 1982), 252.
15   *BSL*, 423.

CHAPTER 15 MC-GUILLOTINED

1   SL to J.A.T. Lloyd, 10 April 1935, SLMH. A.S. Glassco to SL, 12 June 1935, SLMH. SL to William Dudley Woodhead of McGill, 29 June 1935, SLMH.
2   R.B. Bennett to SL, 12 July 1935, SLMH.
3   *BSL*, 607.
4   SL to Sir Edward Beatty, 7 November 1935, SLMH. Sir Edward Beatty to SL, 12 November 1935, SLMH. A.E. Morgan to SL, 13 November 1935, SLMH. SL to A.E. Morgan, 21 November 1935, SLMH. SL to Sir Edward Beatty, 11 December 1935, SLMH.
5   Sir Edward Beatty to SL, 14 December 1935, SLMH. *The Montreal Star*, 18 December 1935. *New York Times*, 21 December 1935.
6   SL to unnamed correspondent, 18 December 1935, SLMH.

7   *BSL*, 298.
8   SL, "No, I Shall Not Come 'Home'," London *Evening News*, 4 February 1936.
9   *BSL*, 293-95, 311-13.
10 H.A. Gwynne to SL, n.d., SLMH.
11 SL to A.E. Morgan, 13 February 1936, SLMH.
12 SL to Dean Charles Martin, 15 February 1936, SLMH.
13 DML, 198-99. AA, 77. DML, 201. RC, 246. *BSL*, 557. SL, *Funny Pieces* (New York: Dodd, Mead, 1936), 260.
14 *BSL*, 558. SL, speech notes, 4 May 1936, SLMH. RC, 258.
15 DML, 210. SL, mimeographed announcement, 1936, ML. Andrew Macphail letter to SL, 1 May 1936, SLMH.
16 Sir Edward Beatty to SL, 12 November 1935, SLMH. *BSL*, 602.
17 *BSL*, 301, 600.
18 Ibid., 301-04.
19 *LaL*, xvii.
20 *BSL*, 308.
21 Ibid., 302-03.
22 Ibid., 303-05.
23 SL to "Frank," 1 June 1937, SLMH.
24 DML, 217.
25 *BSL*, 308-09, 522-24.

CHAPTER 16 WHILE THERE IS TIME

1   DML, 219. SL to Mrs. John Drinkwater, 5 April 1938, ML. SL to unnamed correspondent, 24 April 1938, SLMH. Frank Dodd to SL, 28 April 1938, SLMH.
2   "Brewery Nights Entertainment," program, 3 August 1938, Orillia Public Library. *Orillia Packet and Times*, 10 August 1938. Jay Cody, former curator of SLMH, report to authors of conversation with Albanie Pelletier.
3   SL, "Agreement with John and Tina Kelly," 1 September 1938, SLMH. SL to Dodd, Mead, February 1939, SLMH. Boston University to SL, 14 April 1939, SLMH. SL to Boston University, 19 April 1939, SLMH.
4   Ralph Curry, unpublished notes on SL's interest in film, radio and drama, SLMH.
5   SL to Leggatt, Cassils, May 1939, SLMH.
6   SL to Mr. Scott, 1939, SLMH. William Rennie Seeds Ltd. to SL, 1 June 1939 and 7 June 1939, SLMH. "Leacock Braves Storm," New York *Times*, 10 July 1939. "Leacock Fed Up on 'This Hero Business'," Toronto *Star*, 13 July 1939.
7   SL, "Memorandum to Tina Kelly," September 1939, SLMH.
8   *BSL*, 322-23.
9   DML, 229-32. RC, 308-10. SL, "Three Score and Ten," New York *Times*, 30 December 1939.
10 SL to Charlie Leacock, 23 January 1940, SLMH. SL to bank, 23 January 1940, SLMH.
11 Frank Dodd to SL, 30 April 1940, SLMH. DML, 233.
12 Charlie Leacock to SL, 16 July 1940, SLMH. SL to Charlie Leacock, 9 August 1940, SLMH. Charlie Leacock to SL, 16 August 1940, SLMH. George Leacock to SL, 21 September 1940, SLMH. Charlie Leacock to SL, October 1940, SLMH.
13 Elsie Churchill Tolson, *The Captain, the Colonel and Me: Bedford, N.S. Since 1503* (Sackville, N.B.: Tribune Press, 1979), 211-14.

14 Gazette Printing Co. to SL, 16 July 1940, SLMH. SL to John Bassett, 18 July 1940, SLMH. Tape recording of talk given by Henry R. Mainer, 29 June 1953, at Leacock Memorial Dinner, Orillia Public Library. RC, 310-11. *BSL*, 336.
15 Henry Janes, unpublished notes, SLMH.
16 Thomas Costain to SL, December 1941, SLMH.
17 Thomas Costain to SL, 8 December and 16 December 1941, SLMH.
18 J.A. "Pete" McGarvey, "'Dream' That Became A Legacy," *Canadian Author & Bookman* 56, No. 3 (Spring 1981), 6-8.
19 SL to Richard Mealand, Paramount Studios, 6 February 1943, SLMH.
20 SL, contract, August 1942, SLMH. SL to *Encyclopaedia Britannica*, 8 September 1942, SLMH.
21 Orillia police to SL, 21 July 1942, SLMH. Ontario public trustee to SL, 22 July 1942, SLMH. SL and Teddy Leacock, "Document," November 1941, SLMH.
22 *The Saturday Review*, 6 February 1943. SL to Gerald Lomer, 11 January 1943, ML.
23 DML, 241.
24 SL to *Reader's Digest*, 22 May 1943, SLMH. Henry Janes, unpublished notes, SLMH.
25 H. Shave to SL, 14 September 1943, SLMH.
26 *Maclean's* to SL, 7 August, 20 September and 23 September 1943, Orillia Public Library.

CHAPTER 17 AS IF HIS PENCIL WERE AN IRON POINT

1 Nathaniel Benson, unpublished notes, SLMH. SL to Napier Moore, 25 December 1943, Orillia Public Library. SL to unnamed correspondent, 7 January 1944, SLMH. Dot Leacock to SL, 14 February 1944, SLMH.
2 RC, 330.
3 Nathaniel Benson, unpublished notes, SLMH.
4 Dot Leacock to SL, 11 February 1944, SLMH. George Leacock to SL, 1943 file but likely 1944, SLMH. Dot Leacock to SL, 14 February 1944, SLMH.
5 SL, *Mark Twain*, 102-03.
6 Ibid., 152.
7 "In the Spotlight," Toronto *Telegram*, 11 April 1944.
8 RC, 340-41, 323. Royalty statements, 1944 and 1945, in files of SLMH.
9 "Stephen Leacock buried on Blustery March Day," Toronto *Telegram*, 1 April 1944.

Index

Index